RAWPIPELINE

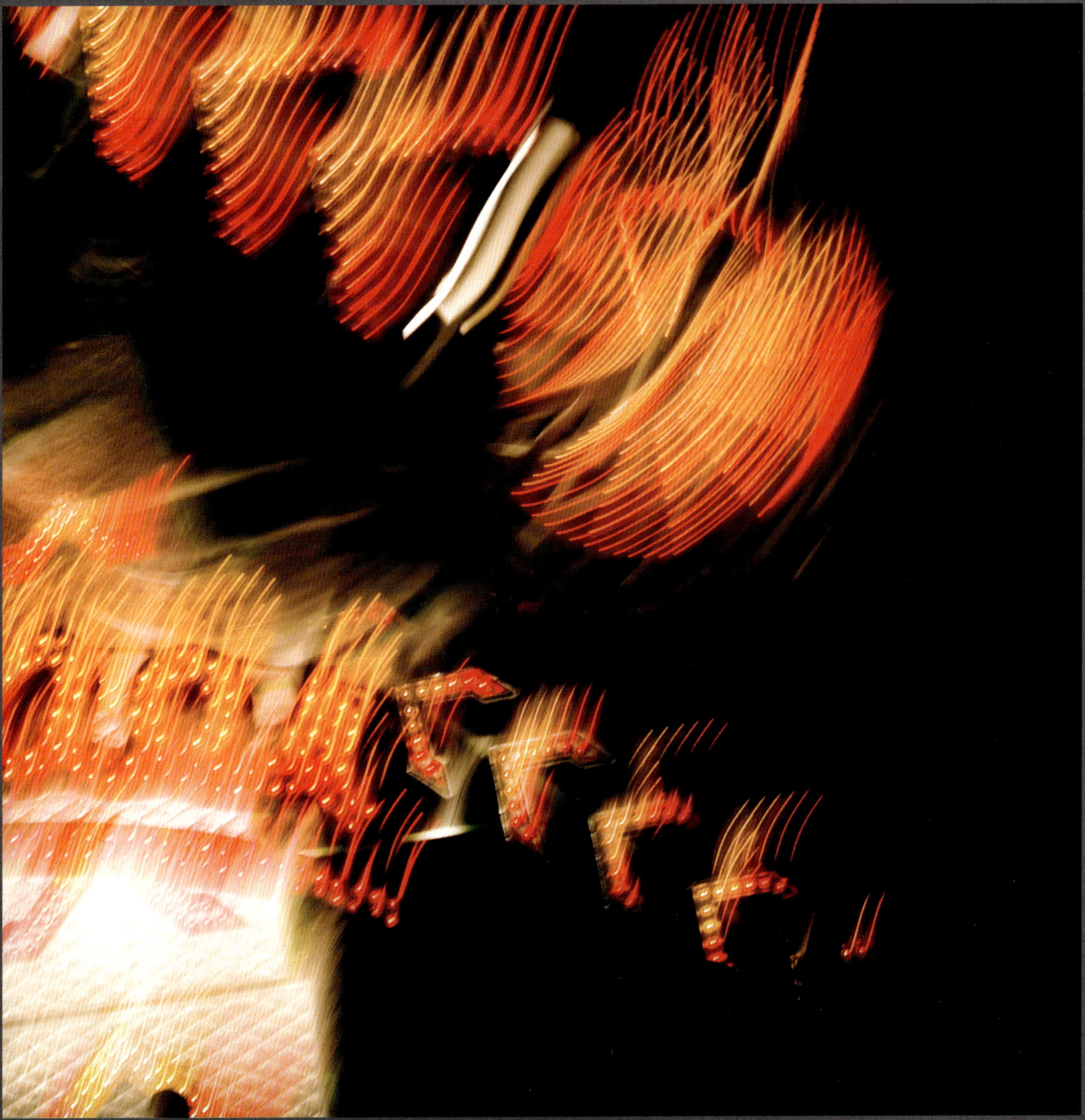

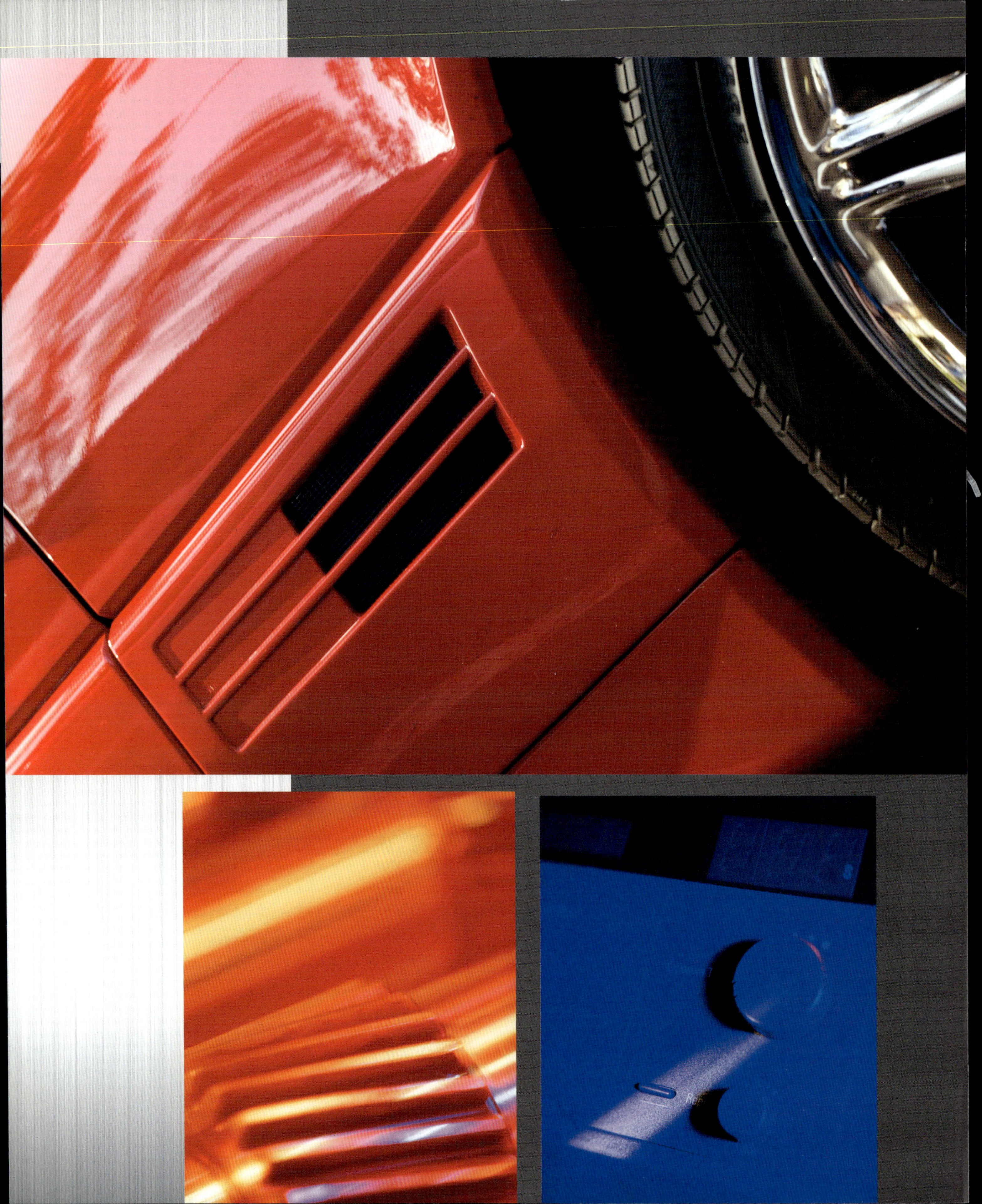

RAW PIPELINE

Revolutionary Techniques to Streamline Digital Photo Workflow

by Ted Dillard

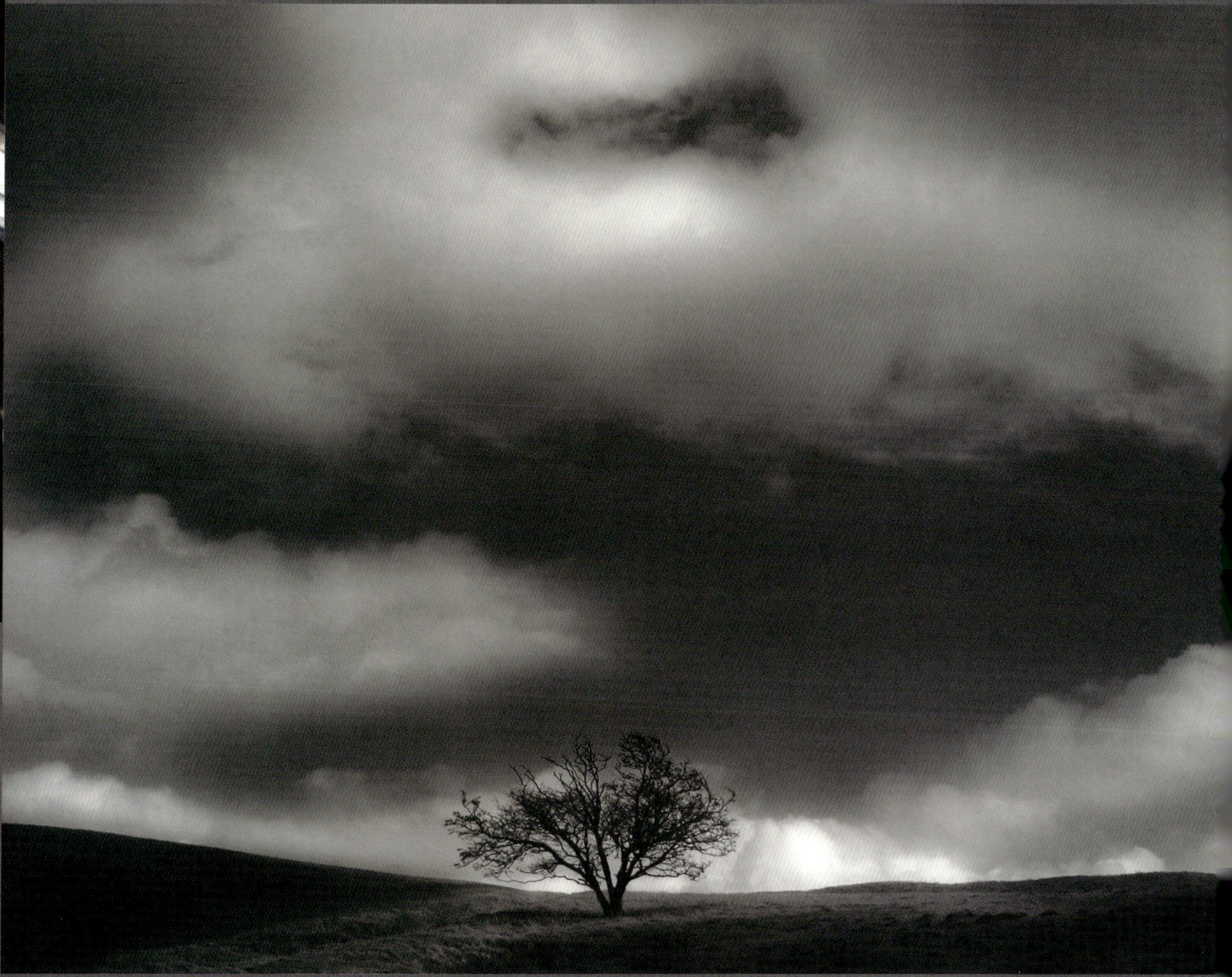

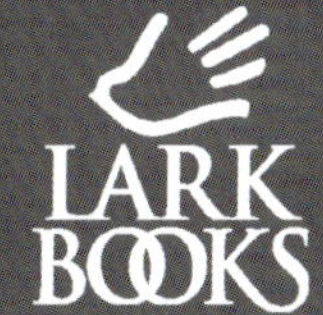

A Division of Sterling Publishing Co., Inc.
New York / London

Editor: Kara Helmkamp
Book and Layout Designer: Ginger Graziano
Cover Designer: Thom Gaines

Library of Congress Cataloging-in-Publication Data

Dillard, Ted, 1956-
Raw pipeline : revolutionary techniques to streamline digital photo workflow / Ted Dillard. -- 1st ed.
p. cm.
Includes bibliographical references and index.
ISBN-13: 978-1-60059-279-9 (pb-trade pbk. : alk. paper)
ISBN-10: 1-60059-279-1 (pb-trade pbk. : alk. paper)
1. Adobe Photoshop. 2. Adobe Camera Raw. 3. Photography--Digital techniques. 4. Raw file formats (Digital photography) I. Title.
TR267.5.A3D56 2008
775--dc22

2007037089

10 9 8 7 6 5 4 3 2 1

First Edition
Published by Lark Books, A Division of Sterling Publishing Co., Inc.
387 Park Avenue South, New York, N.Y. 10016

Distributed in Canada by Sterling Publishing,
c/o Canadian Manda Group, 165 Dufferin Street
Toronto, Ontario, Canada M6K 3H6

Distributed in the United Kingdom by GMC Distribution Services,
Castle Place, 166 High Street, Lewes, East Sussex, England BN7 1XU

Distributed in Australia by Capricorn Link (Australia) Pty Ltd.,
P.O. Box 704, Windsor, NSW 2756 Australia

If you have questions or comments about this book, please contact:
Lark Books
67 Broadway, Asheville, NC 28801
(828) 253-0467

Manufactured in China

ISBN 13: 978-1-60059-279-9
ISBN 10: 1-60059-279-1

For information about custom editions, special sales, premium and corporate purchases,
please contact Sterling Special Sales Department at 800-805-5489 or specialsales@sterlingpub.com.

TABLE OF CONTENTS

Part 2: Photoshop

Part 3: Fine Digital Printing

Part 4: The RAW Pipeline: Streamlining a Workflow

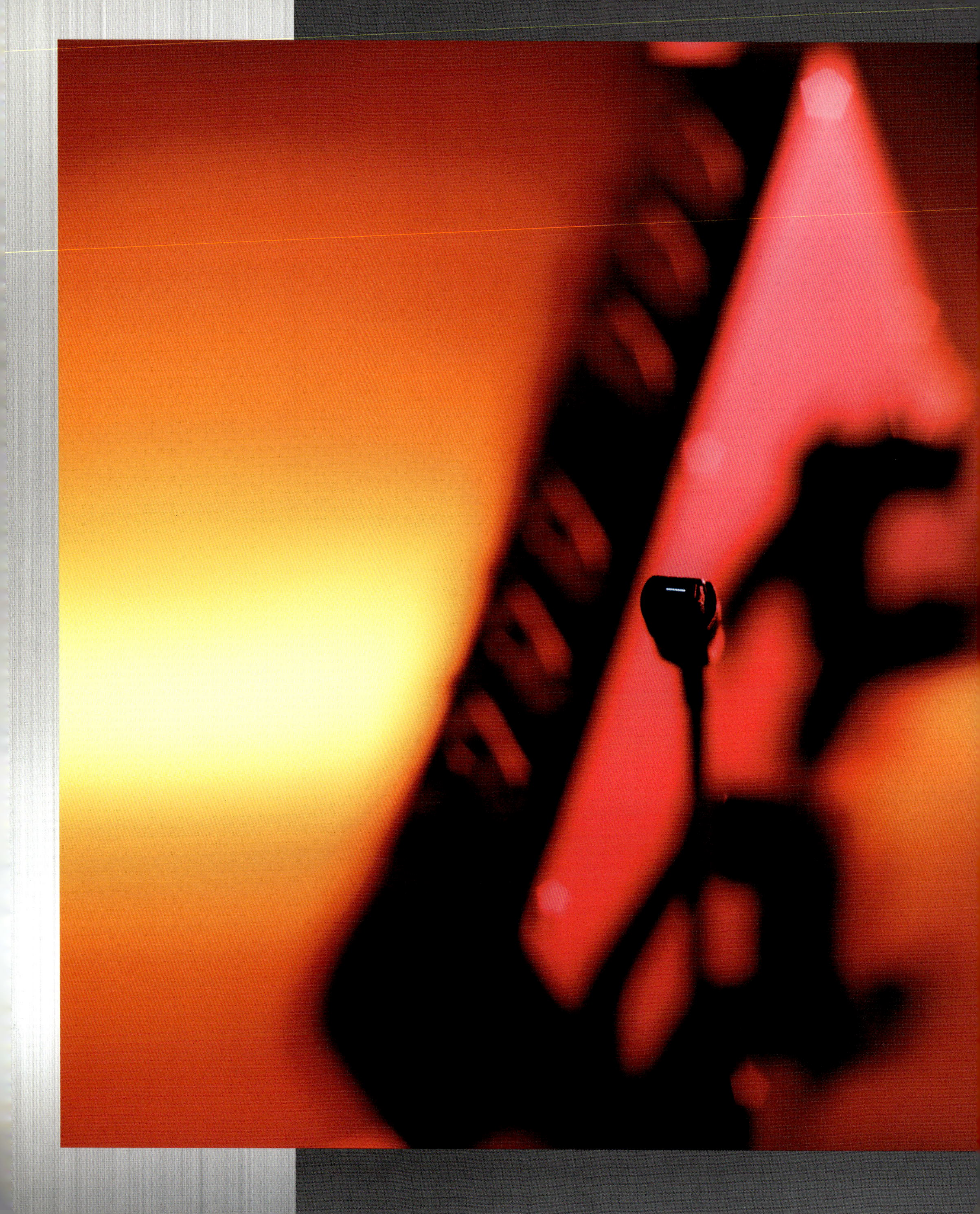

RAW PIPELINE

introduction

**Let's start with the obvious question:
Why do we need another book about Photoshop?**

This book is not a software manual; it is an attempt to get a photographer into the Photoshop driver's seat as quickly as possible, using a skill set that will be a foundation for a solid, professional, and powerful workflow. I haven't found many Photoshop texts that solely address the needs of a photographer, or that get you started quickly on the right foot. This is an attempt to do both.

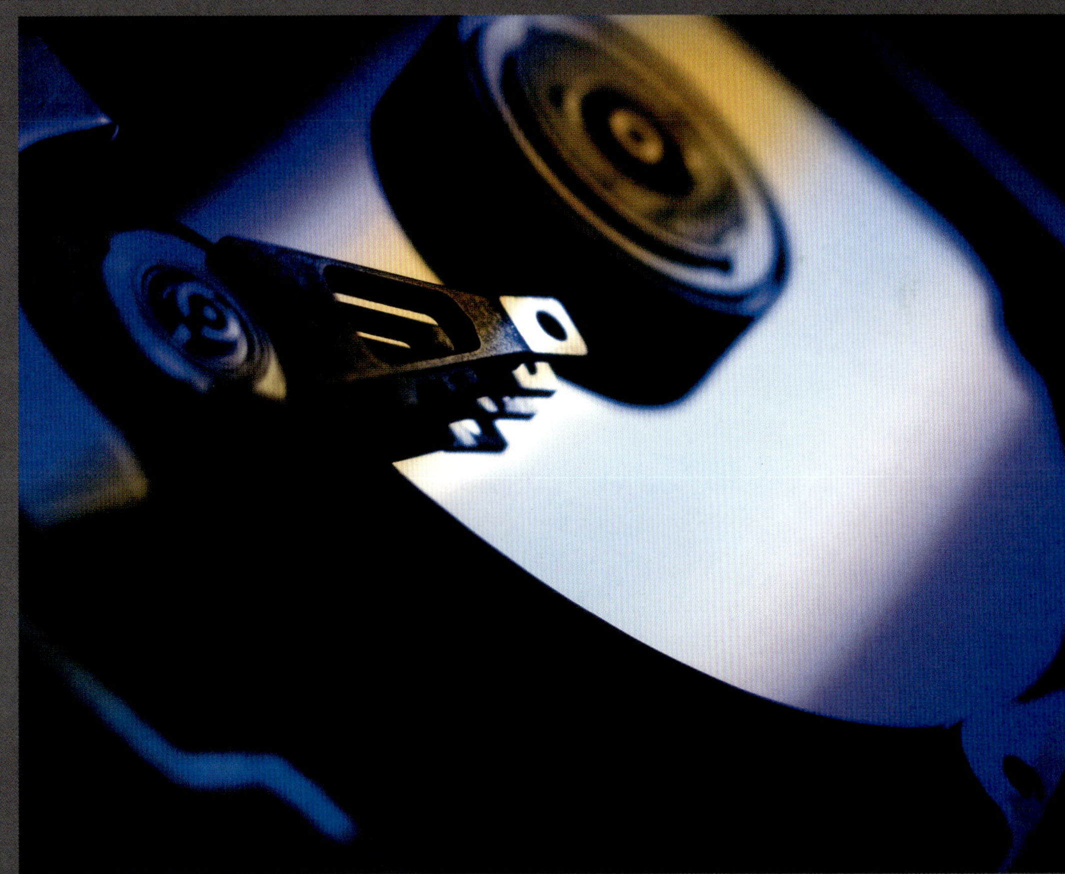

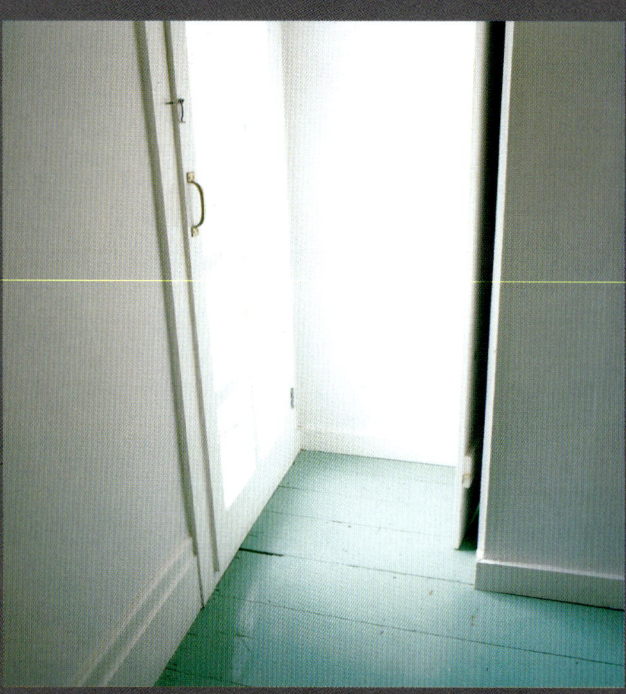

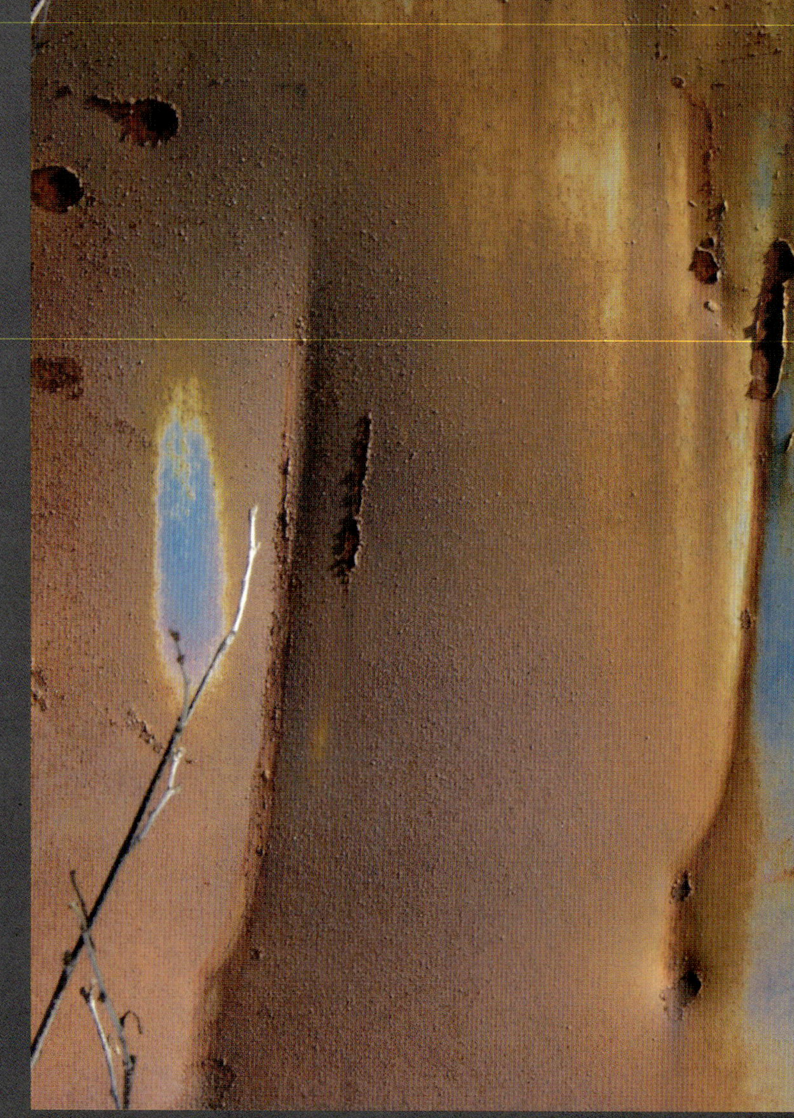

I suggest you have a good Photoshop manual for referencing (like *Real World Adobe Photoshop* by Bruce Fraser and David Blatner). Any of those texts are pretty much the last word in the deep, dark secrets of the program, and I see no need to redo what they have done so well. This book is a roadmap. You may need the others to stop and read the signposts along the way.

A photographer really needs to do three basic things to a photograph: adjust the image size, correct the color and tones, and print the image. The idea is to simplify and streamline the seemingly limitless tools and techniques in Photoshop down to a clean, standard workflow that is powerful, repeatable, and fits with a photographer's skill set. There are at least six ways to do anything in Photoshop, and our goal is to reduce that to the one or two best ways that let you do anything you need to do.

The exercise I always like to do when teaching a class or giving a talk, is to ask you to imagine yourself in your favorite darkroom. Close your eyes. Now, standing in front of your enlarger, reach for the grain magnifier. Reach for the paper safe, the timer, the focus knob on your enlarger, or even your coffee. (You can just imagine what a room full of people with

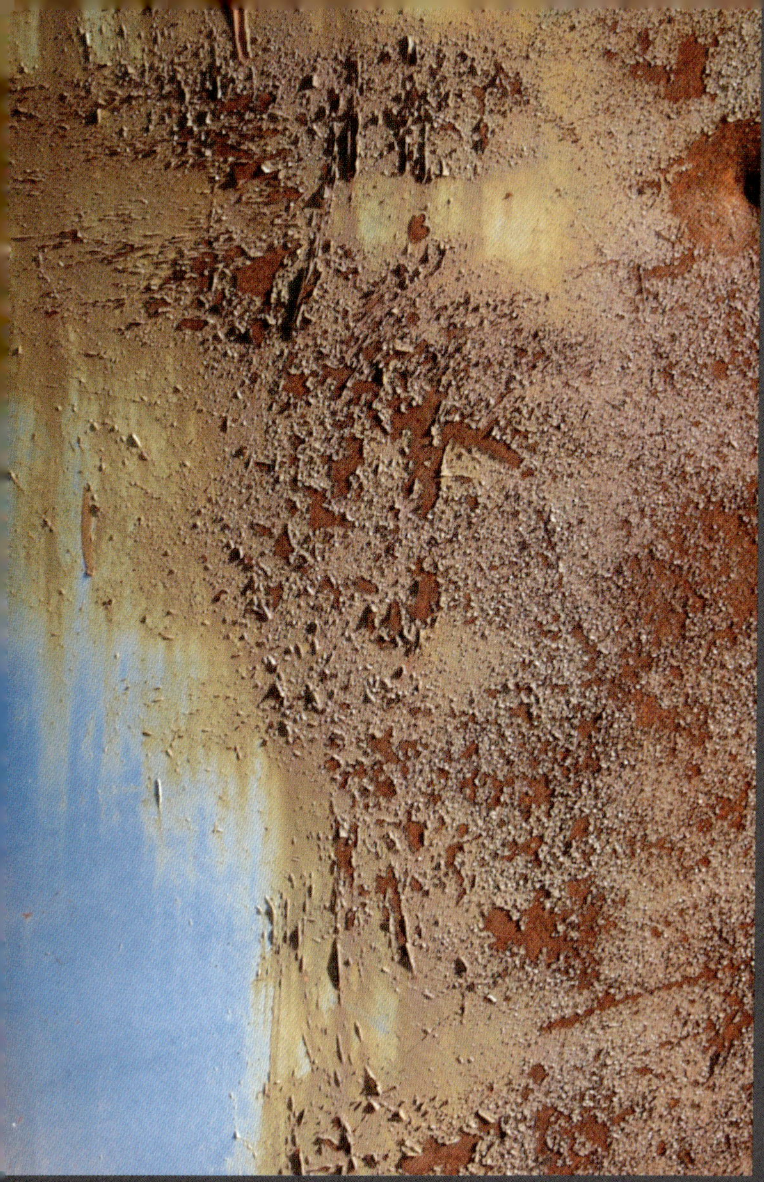

their eyes closed, groping for their coffee, looks like.) If your work area is simple and clean, you can easily find your tools in the dark. If you're working in Photoshop with a simple and clean method, you can find your tools just as quickly and easily.

I like to start by setting up a good working environment: arranging the work area, making sure color policies are correct, and sharing a few tips about how to be fast and efficient. Just like tennis, if you start off with good habits, you'll have fewer bad habits to break later. Once we have that start, I address the fundamental needs of the photographer: sizing, color correction, and preparation for printing.

First, I concentrate on the Image Size window, how to use it, and I walk through various strategies for resizing. Next, I go into how to use Adjustment Layers—specifically Levels and Curves—to learn the basic tools. This leads us into Masks, for fine control of burning and dodging. The Layers discussion culminates with the power of Smart Objects as a part of the RAW workflow. I introduce the Adobe Camera RAW dialog, and start into the basic controls and how they relate to Levels and Curves. Finally, I explore a few of the essential retouching tools, sharpening, and how to send the file to the printer.

One of my goals for all of the books I've worked on is that they are a little more timeless than a typical software manual. I like to think of this book as a way to approach mastering these digital tools, rather than a specific guide to a program, rendered obsolete by the next software update. I'm trying to set the stage for you to bring a working knowledge to any evolution of Photoshop and crack the code, distilling it into a system that works for you. We are at a profound point in the evolution of photography, and I hope this book can be a how-to guide for moving ahead with confidence into this historic journey.

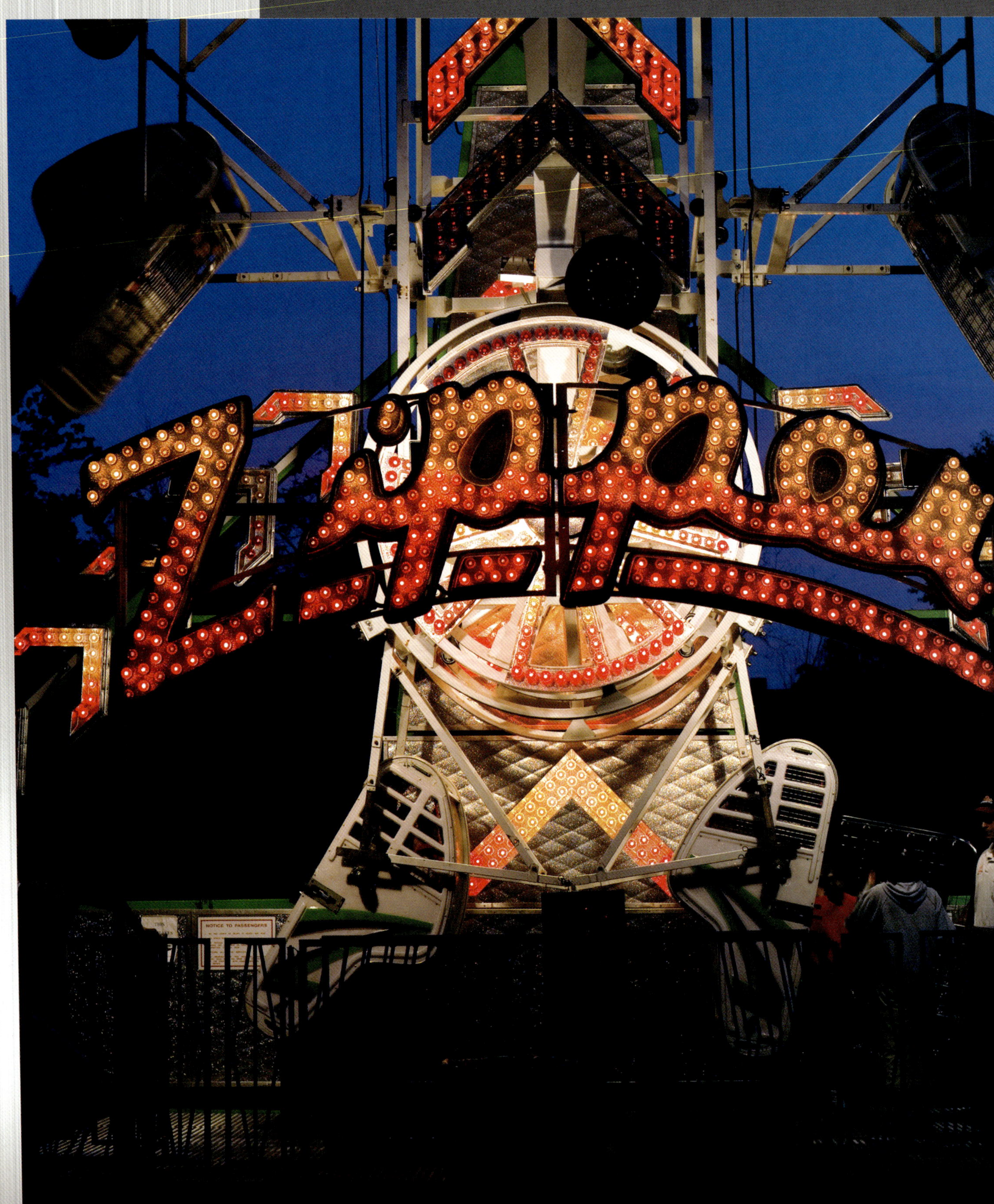
NOTICE TO PASSENGERS

PART 1:
DIGITAL PHOTOGRAPHY

introduction

Recently, I was out shooting with my camera for a few hours. When I came home, I downloaded the files to my computer, backed them up to my hard drives, and then took a look at them. I edited them down to a few shots, did a quick process and adjustment, sized them, and ran out some working prints on nice paper.

I was delighted. I was happy with the images, but moreover I was pleased with the ease of the process and the incredible quality of the prints. It's been a long road, and for a while the tools just weren't working, but now I can think about what I love: making photographs.

If you're just joining the world of digital photography, you've been spared a great deal of struggle. Look at it this way: in the 1940s my grandfather couldn't walk down to the store and buy pre-mixed Kodak D-76 developer. He mixed his own. During the early years of digital technology, photographers were "mixing their own", and trying to get quality out of equipment that just couldn't deliver it.

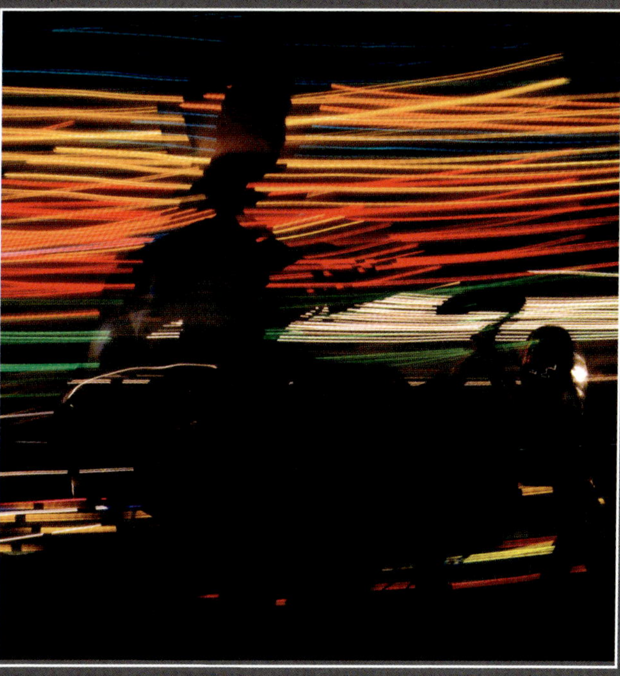

The Digital Revolution to the Digital Evolution

Back when I started doing this "digital stuff" in the mid 90s, digital cameras where incredibly expensive and frankly, not very good. Color management didn't really work, and getting good prints from inkjet "photo" printers was frustrating. Even if you had good prints, you could forget about them lasting more than a few years, even stored properly. There were a few pretty remarkable revolutions that happened within the big "digital revolution," but, as is the case with any developing technology, it was an interesting case of a lot of things happening independently and coming together simultaneously.

The "revolution" became the "evolution." First, color management started to actually work, somewhere around Photoshop 6. Once that happened, we started asking more of the printers, and Epson responded by increasing longevity of inks and papers, hand-in-hand with increasing the color "gamut" of both the inks and papers.

On the camera side, the digital SLR (D-SLR) cameras—targeted at a much larger market than the big, expensive "Pro back" cameras—started to produce profoundly better, bigger, higher-quality files. This turned into an avalanche of technology development. The better the cameras, the more they sold, and the lower prices dropped.

Finally, we saw the introduction of Adobe Camera RAW. This was a plug-in for Photoshop 7, allowing users to process a large number of camera makes and models' RAW files. This was fully incorporated into CS. In CS2, we saw it evolve into a truly elegant workflow with the release of Adobe Bridge. RAW file processing gave us the ability to eek out every bit of information we had in the file. Photographers who were suffering through low quality RAW processing software, or settling for JPEGs, could now work in a fast, efficient method to get remarkably better results from increasingly better cameras.

A good analogy is the development of the modern bicycle. Bikes seem like pretty simple machines, but to build a modern bike you need a number of things we now take for granted: tubular steel, pneumatic tires, and, interestingly the most important, steel roller chains (something not even invented until the early 1900s). Only when you had all these seemingly unrelated pieces to the puzzle, could you envision the modern bicycle. And so it was with digital photography between 2000 and the present. Only when we could bring this all together could we enjoy the ease, efficiency, and quality of today's digital photography workflow.

Now that the process is less time consuming, the issue isn't high-quality images—it's a matter of sorting through all the digital information. This guide builds on solid Photoshop skills and practices to develop fast, efficient, and high-quality methods of working without getting bogged down in extraneous information.

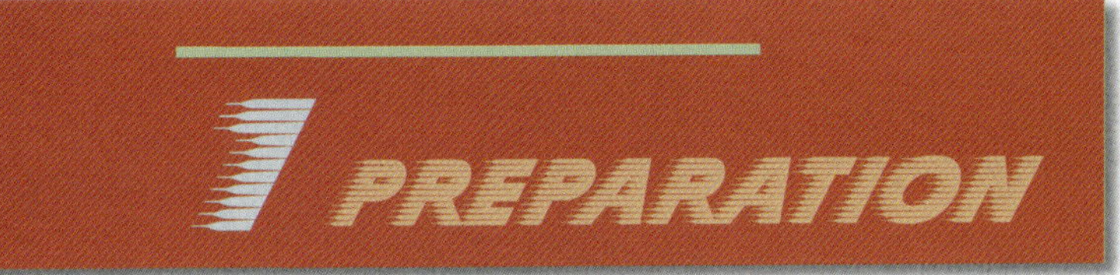

Preparing the Work Area

Before you start any serious project, it's important to set up a work area. You clean off your desk, organize your darkroom, or clear off the dining table. We are working on a computer, so we should do the same for our work area.

I can't emphasize enough the importance of keeping your files neat, clean, and organized. Almost every workstation I've seen has a disorganized pile of files and folders all over the desktop, and worse yet, on the hard drive. I was once working on someone's system, and we needed to download a "patch" from a website. His system was such a mess that we couldn't find the file we downloaded. We downloaded it again, and then had to search to find it, even after we noted exactly where it went. What should have taken five minutes took over one-half hour.

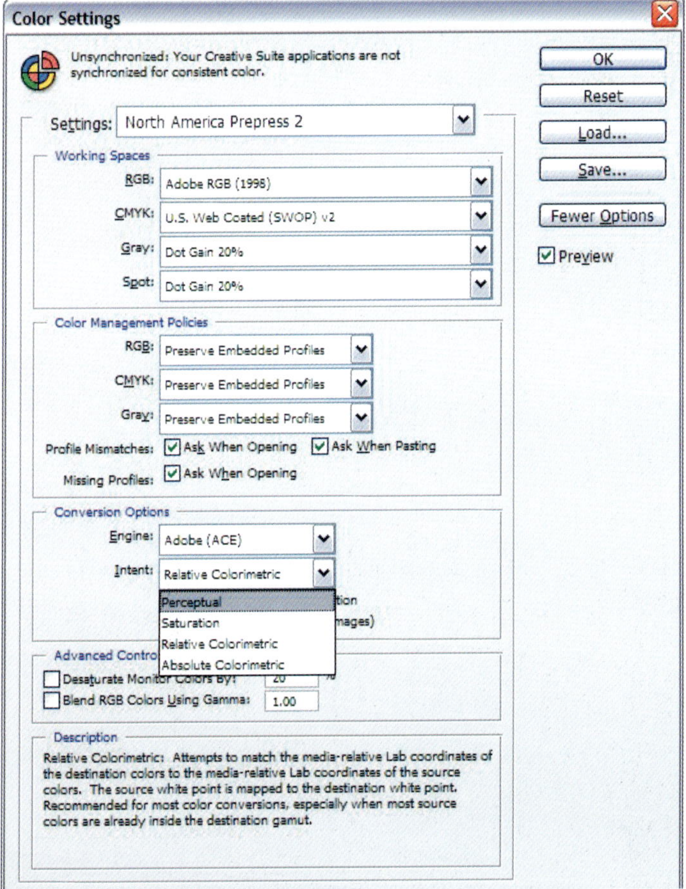

Professional photography studios are almost invariably neat, clean, and organized. On the other hand, the professionals' workstations are almost always a mess (unless they have a good studio manager or production assistant). My advice: prepare your workstation as you would prepare your studio or darkroom.

Color Management

A large part of preparing your working environment is utilizing a good color management strategy. We will be coming back to color management several more times throughout the book, illustrating how vitally important it is to a consistent and high quality RAW workflow.

There are two main parts to good color management: your color settings in Photoshop, and your monitor calibration. If you have an industry standard light box in your studio, you wouldn't hold film up to the cool whites in the ceiling to evaluate the color and exposure. You have to be able to see the film, evaluate it, and have the confidence that you are doing so correctly. Think of your monitor in the same way.

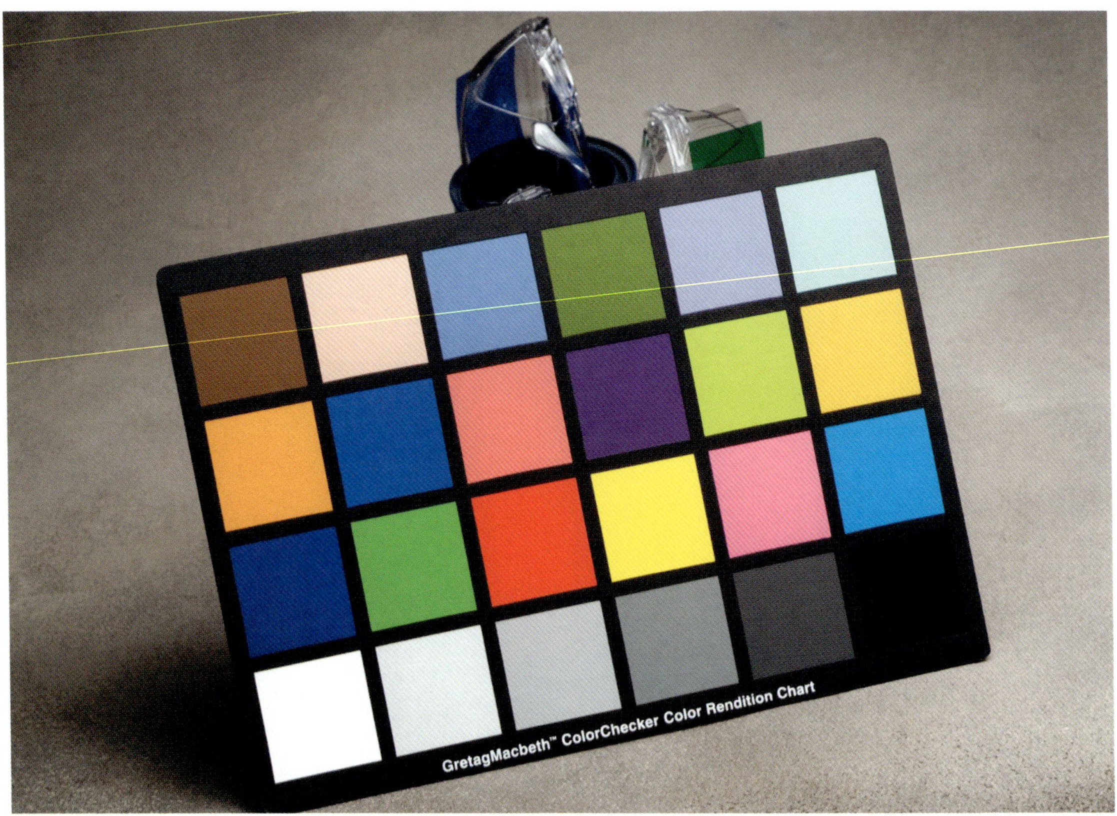

Color targets and other calibration tools are available at www.xrite.com.

Ideally, your monitor should be relatively new, able to display colors accurately, and be calibrated to do so. If you have a monitor that can't recreate the colors, it doesn't matter how well you calibrate it, it simply can't reproduce the wavelength. If you have a great monitor and you don't calibrate it, you're still running blind. Investing in a good, graphics-standard monitor and a calibration system is the first step to having the confidence that you're delivering a quality image. (For more on color management in Photoshop, see page 60.)

Color Management with Your Camera

Along the lines of color management and quality control, I start off almost every project—certainly every job—by shooting an image of the GretagMacbeth ColorChecker chart. I shoot it constantly during an assignment if I'm moving among various types and colors of light. I use this target as a way to batch-adjust files when I open the files in Adobe Camera RAW; to set my camera to a correct neutral balance when shooting in the studio; and as a quality control standard when I deliver files to a client, enclosing it with every group of files I deliver as a file called "target."

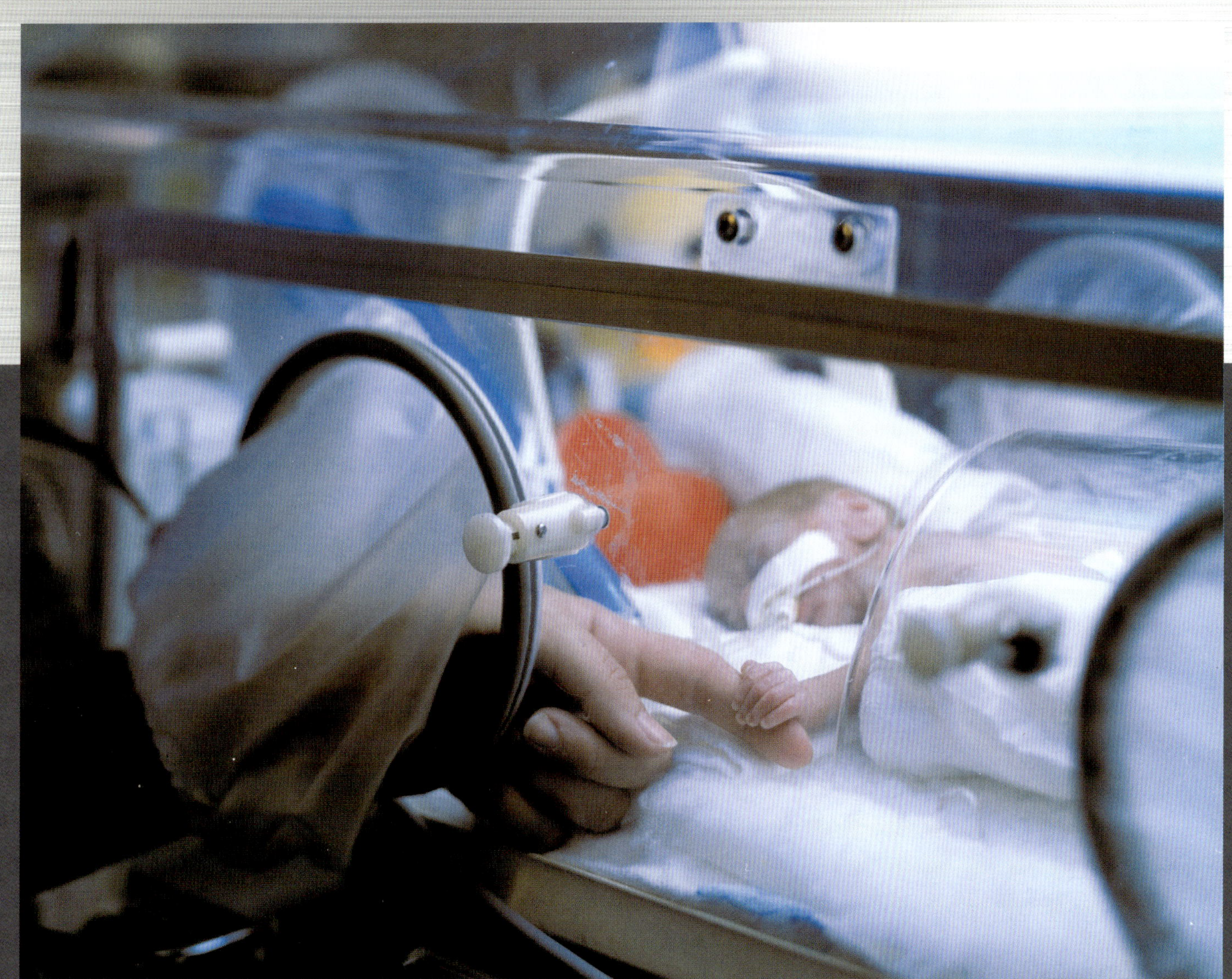

I never used a color target in my entire career as a film photographer, but because the digital medium is so easy and precise, I now use it constantly. When the color target test shot is included in the files I deliver to a client, I can refer to it if a client has color or density issues that may be related to his or her own color management policies.

Treat the target just as you would a light meter: light it evenly and with the same light you're using for the subject.

For the record, I don't use any other target. The ColorChecker is pretty much the industry standard and will be recognized by anyone, from a photographer to a prepress production manager. It gives me detailed color information; I can look at the image in Adobe Camera RAW and use it to fine-tune my hue and saturation of each of the R, G, and B channels to make a very effective global compensation for my particular camera and sensor, as well as to my specific shooting environment.

A

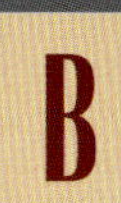

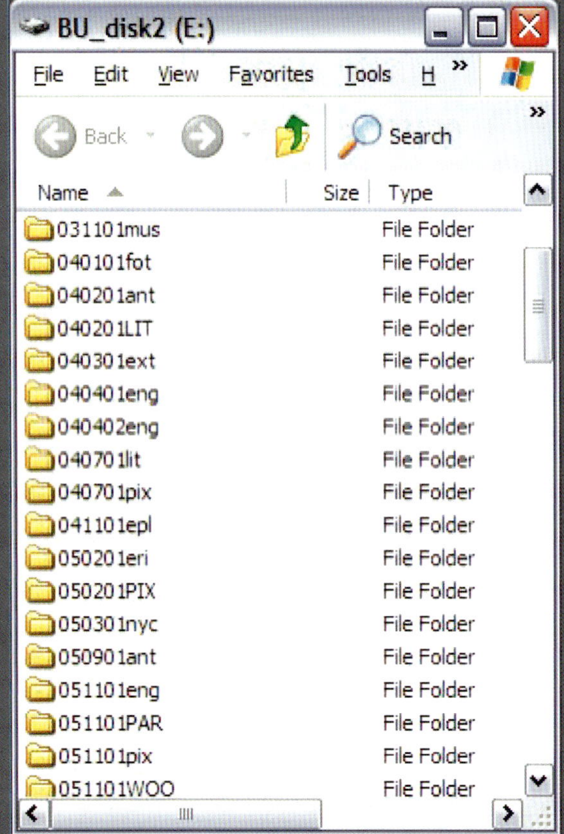

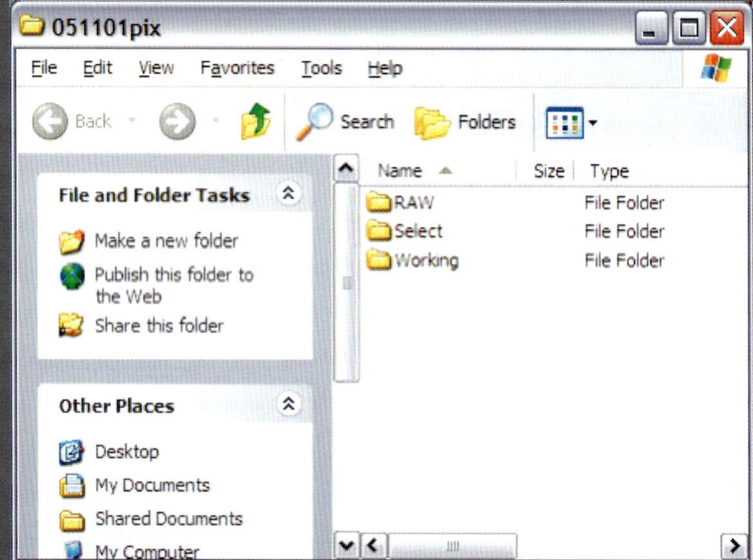

You don't have to copy this filing system—it is an example of how to manage many files. You should create your own management system, one that is simple and repeatable for all of your projects.

Later, in my explanation of the Adobe Camera RAW workflow, I'll show you how to make the best use of this target. Then, in the examples at the end, I'll illustrate how an adjustment on one file—like the target shot—can be applied to a batch of images, saving time and avoiding mistakes in color consistency from shot to shot.

Building an Architecture

The filing system in my studio is based on the date of the shoot and the client's name. Every piece of film went into an envelope marked with a label, for example, "980501JDOE," which translates as "1998, May, job 01, John Doe." Using this system and if I can narrow down the time frame, I can get my hands on any job I've shot within minutes. My system for digital photography is almost exactly the same. The only difference is that the negatives are now computer files, and they sort themselves if I name them properly.

I name the main job folder with the date first, then with the client name: "980501JDOE" (see example A). It sorts itself chronologically in my Finder or Explorer (Mac or Windows). That is, "1998, May, job 01, John Doe." Then I create another folder within the job folder labeled "RAW" (see example B) for the untouched image files, and two more folders, "disk1" and "disk2," for the folders containing the final files that will be burned to a DVD or CD for the client. I modify this organizational system only slightly for my personal or fine art projects.

The essential point here is to set up a system and stick to it. It takes time to figure out the system that works best for you, but too many times I've seen people working without a standard plan. They do things a little differently each time they work, and, as a result, they are completely awash. Without an organized filing strategy, you have no control over backup or archiving, and that is if you can find the files at all.

Another important point is to set up a system before you shoot. Once you have a system, build the folder structure for the project before you even go to shoot it. It is easy to get caught up in all the distractions of a project and build the folders on the fly, as you download, during the shoot, or when you're looking at the images for the first time. You might not be thinking about data management if there are distractions, so you misname things or set up things slightly wrong, and this leads to inconsistencies and confusion later on. Set it up beforehand, when you can concentrate and plan ahead.

Digital Data Management

This is a good place to outline your basic data management strategy. This is a fairly standard procedure for anyone in digital asset management, but because film photographers are not used to being able to make perfect copies of their "assets," it is a process they might be unfamiliar with. Assuming you have the files on a workstation somewhere, the very first thing you should do is back them up to another location. You can back up to a remote hard drive, a separate internal drive, an external drive, or a drive on a network. Typically it's faster to copy to another drive, and burning a CD or DVD is fine, but time consuming. The goal here is to give us something to fall back on if the hardware fails, or if we do something stupid to the files. This is basic data management—make a backup copy before you start processing the files.

The next step is to verify the files, meaning you should make sure your originals and backups are not corrupted. There's no point in backing up and archiving files that you can't read or access. Once you've verified the files, only then should you start working on them.

Archival vs. Backup

It is vital to understand the distinction between creating a backup file and creating an archival file. A backup is a temporary copy to cover you if something horrible happens to your original image file, like if your computer implodes, your hard drive fails, or if you make a silly mistake to a file and want to return to the original. You can backup your work in various stages or you may have six versions of your files, but the backup is what you save until the check clears, so to speak. Then, you have to decide what you want to save, if anything, for the next 25 years, and that is your archive copy.

The backup only needs to last for the next two weeks, the next month, the next six months—whatever timeframe fits into your work method. The archive is the finished image file that you go back to in ten years to reprint or reuse. Your archive is not necessarily the same as your backup, and another fact to consider is that your archives should be maintained. They should be transferred to the latest media (a 3.5-inch floppy disk won't do you any good if there's no system that can read it), and even updated to different file formats in some cases.

Over the years of handling film, photographers built very sophisticated methods for storing and archiving negatives and prints. Many photographers, in spite of the limitations of the medium, even worked out ways of making copies and backups of film and prints. We now have a medium that, in most ways, is very similar to our old familiar materials, yet allows us a higher quality level of duplication and storage. Digital data management is a new skill set for photographers, but is not far removed from what film photographers know and love.

Backup Details

Let's talk specifics here. In my opinion, backing up to a hard drive is the best option. It is the fastest way to get data from one place to another. In addition, hard drives are fairly inexpensive. I can have a hard drive on another computer on my network; I can even have a hard drive sitting on my network by itself. Taking it one step further, many photographers are now backing up to their Internet Service Provider (ISP) server. The low costs of the data transfer, additional storage (such as with an e-commerce website), and the fact that the ISP builds redundancy into their systems (redundancy refers to saving the same files to several different drives at once) make this a very viable option.

The simplest backup strategy is just a couple of external hard drives. Plug them in to your computer, drag the files to the drive, and you're done. I don't particularly like backing up to a CD, because I will back up several versions, writing over the previous version until I reach a final version. Writing a CD every time I make a change just isn't practical for me. I use two hard

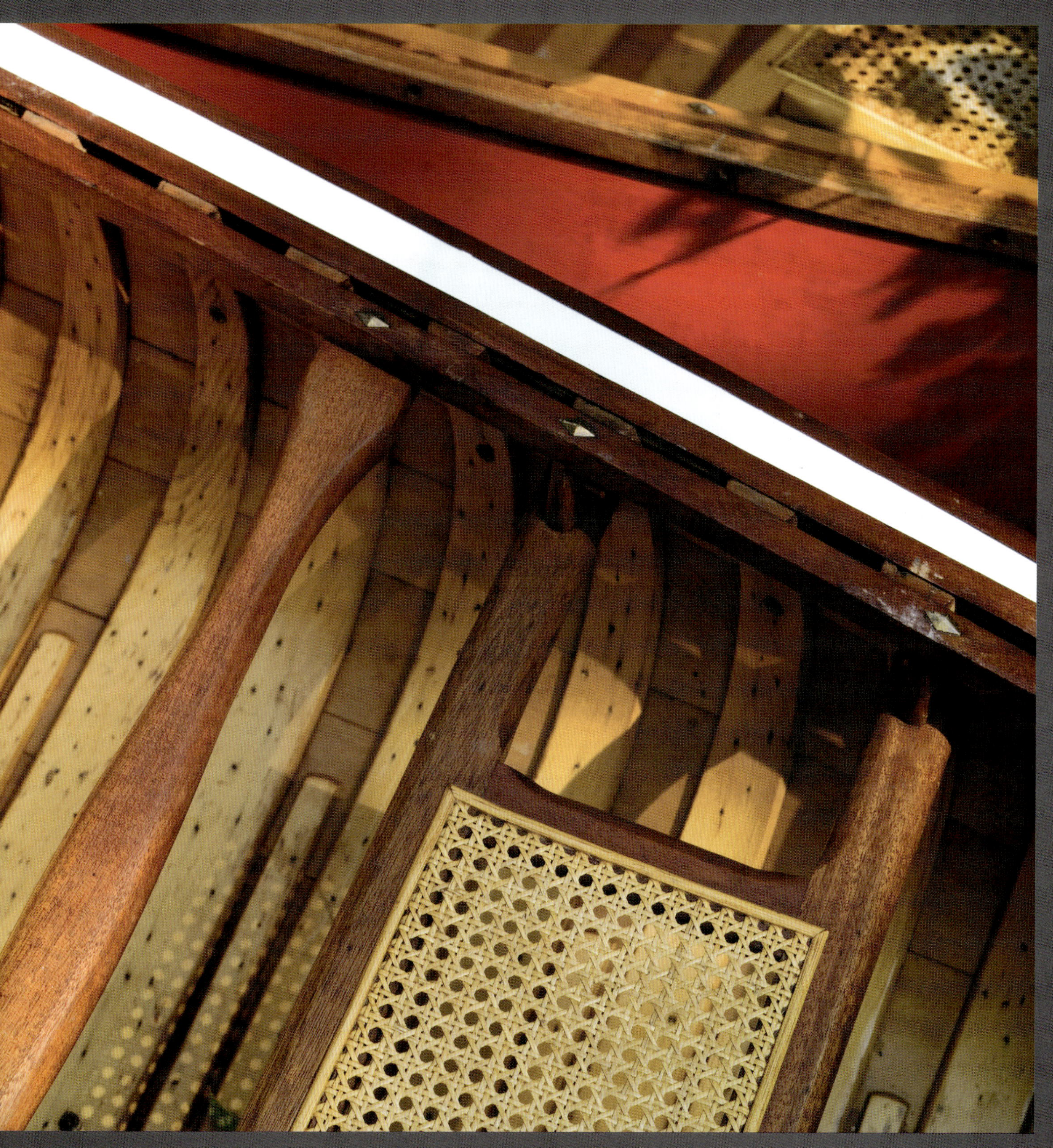

drives, placing the first generation of files on one drive, the second generation on a second drive, then the third generation back on the first drive again, overwriting the first generation. This always gives me my latest version, plus the previous version in case I made a mistake in between generations.

Archival Details

Archival involves a more complicated set of issues. Unlike the old days, when you could squirrel your prints and negatives away in a cool dry place and assume they'd be fine, archiving is now a matter of maintenance as well as storage. The first issue is changes in technology. The second issue is file format and software changes. Not only should you update your media, but you should also remember that some day you're going to need to open these files, and you will need the tools to do so.

Here are some stories, and hopefully you can learn from my missteps. One of the best portrait shots I've done was on a Megavision S3. I can't open any of the RAW files anymore. They're lost. All I have left is the few TIFFs I made for a specific purpose.

I used to have everything archived on 100 megabyte (MB) ZIP disks. Files got bigger, CDs got cheaper, and CD burners got faster. One weekend I copied everything from the ZIPs onto CDs. These were cheap silver CDs

What about DNG files?

The DNG file format developed by Adobe is an attempt to standardize RAW camera files, much like we've standardized on TIFF, JPEG and PSD files, pretty much eliminating other, older high quality image file formats. For every make and model digital camera, you have a very specific file.

If this creates problems within a workflow today, imagine what problems it will create in ten years. Not only will we have a pile of new cameras coming along, but in ten years we will still be trying to open files we are shooting now, today. Adobe, very sensibly, is looking down that road, and trying to address the issue now, by offering a generic RAW file and a method of converting your camera's files to that format (the Adobe DNG Converter).

It sounds like a great idea, and when it first was announced and discussed, I have to say it was a bandwagon I quickly jumped on. There's just one little problem: the DNG format, in reducing the file to a generic set of information, doesn't (at this point), save any of the detailed sensor information. That is, there's a whole raft of stuff you need to know about each individual sensor, on top of each make and model. This information gives you a better idea of where the file is coming from, and results in a better processed file: better color, more dynamic range, better control of noise, sharper images.

For now, I'm ignoring the DNG file. I save my RAW files; I save my processed files. I usually save everything as a 16-bit TIFF in ProPhoto RGB, (more about that later) because that is the largest amount of information I can get, and it's a pretty universal format. I don't convert and save a DNG file.

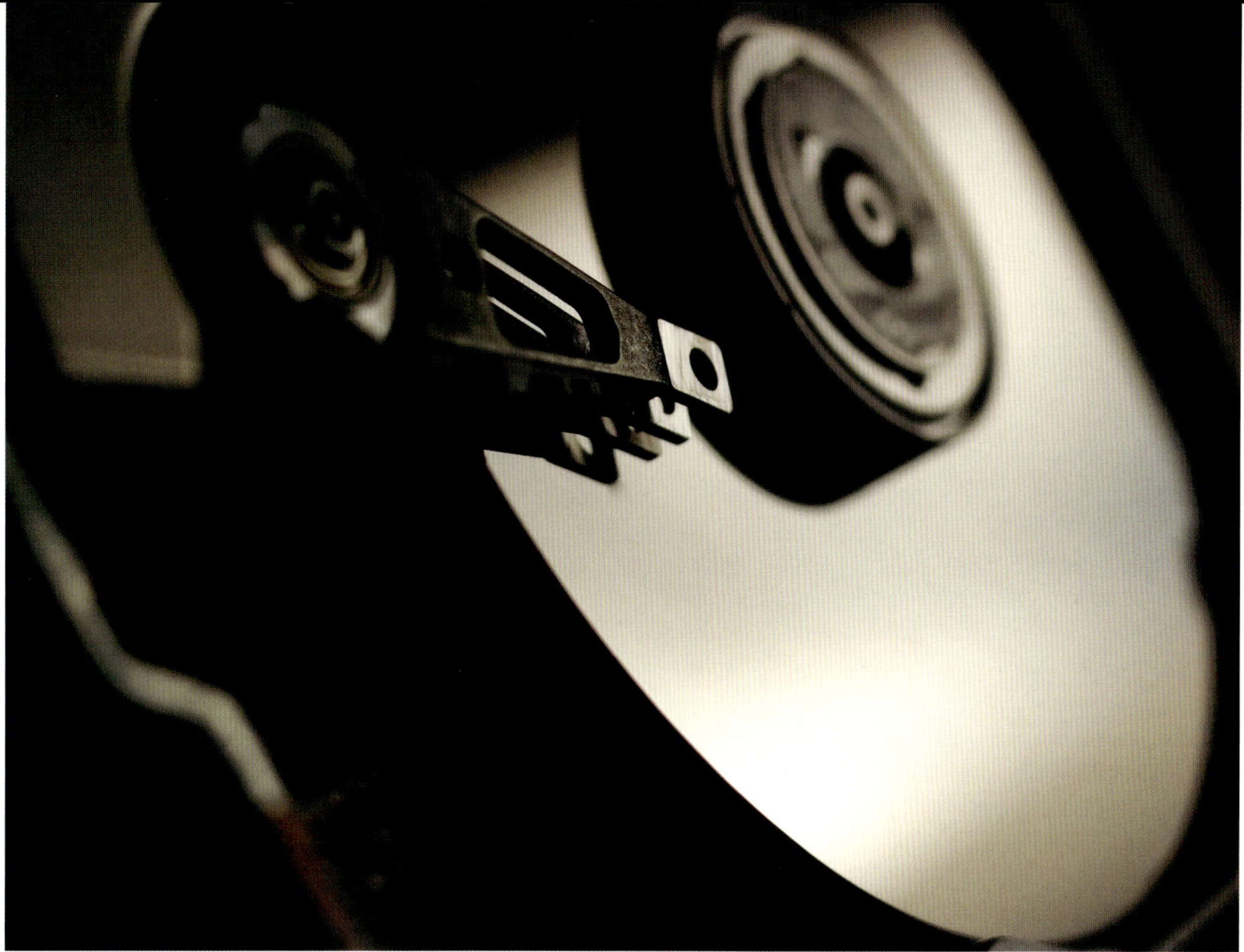

from some office supply store. I then found out that gold CDs are more reliable and more archival-friendly. I copied everything to gold CDs. Along the way, I checked to make sure the files are still viable, and haven't been corrupted. Talk about time-consuming!

Now, hard drives are cheap. A 250 gigabyte (GB) hard drive is cheaper than DVDs when you consider the time it takes to burn a DVD. I've changed my entire strategy to use hard drives for all my backup and archiving. I write the files to both drives. If one fails, I have the other. When they're full, they get labeled and stored, and they're stored in separate locations. It's a beautiful thing.

I have no doubt the next storage media will change my entire strategy again, and there may be a point at which I must update the file formats I have stored because of a software change. For instance, I may very well convert all of my Olympus RAW files (Olympus calls them ORF files) to DNG, because I'm pretty certain that in 20 years no one is going to know what an ORF file is. The point here is maintenance, and it should not be ignored. You have to take the good with the bad, and the increased work to maintain these archives is annoying. The good, however, is that for the first time, I can make perfect duplicates and archives of all of my once-in-a-lifetime images until my heart's content.

Good digital habits are the best way to prevent losing files and jobs. Let's start with some horror stories, to get your attention.

1. Imagine you are on a job. You pull the memory card out of your camera after shooting and put it into your laptop to show the client. You put it back into the camera. After shooting more, you take it to your studio and plug it into a card reader. For some reason, it doesn't show up. You take it out and put it into the camera, and receive a card error message. The card is unreadable, and you've lost all your files.

2. You shoot to the memory card, plug into the card reader, and start looking at all the shots. You sort, rename, and pull a few images off the card that you want to work on. You get distracted, eject the card, and forget that you haven't saved the files anywhere. You shut down Photoshop, and shoot to the card, accidentally overwriting your previous files.

3. You have a large memory card and just keep everything right on it. Really, it's just like a big "jump drive," right? You shoot to it, read from it, work on the files and save them to it, and even "borrow" some iTunes cuts using this card. One day you plug it in, your system says the card is unformatted, and asks "Do you want to format?" Everything on the card is gone.

Don't throw the book down and run out to buy film—all of these issues can be avoided at best, and most of them can be recovered at worst. This is why I call it "digital hygiene." If you take care of yourself and learn good habits now, it will save you from heartache later.

The memory card should be seen as a very temporary method of storing image files until you can get them to safety. Think of it as a nice basket to carry eggs in. If your mom sends you out to get eggs, you go to the chicken house, get the eggs, and bring them to the kitchen. You don't run—you walk. You don't stop and play baseball with your little brother. You don't carry neat rocks back in the basket with the eggs. You

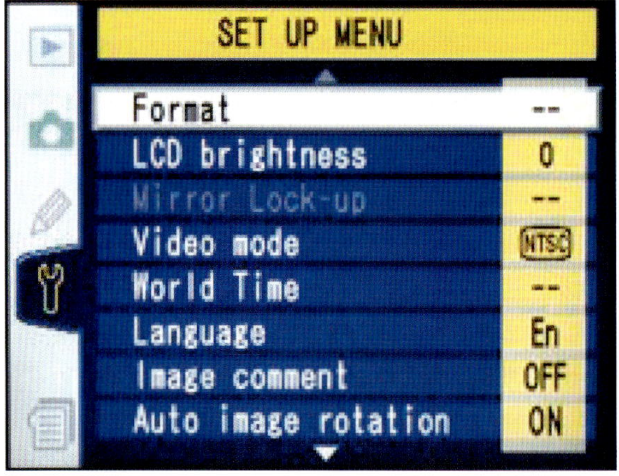

There is a difference between formatting and erasing. Erasing images on your camera not only uses unnecessary battery power, it compromises the remaining images on your memory card. If you want to delete the images from your memory card, format the card in the camera's setup menu.

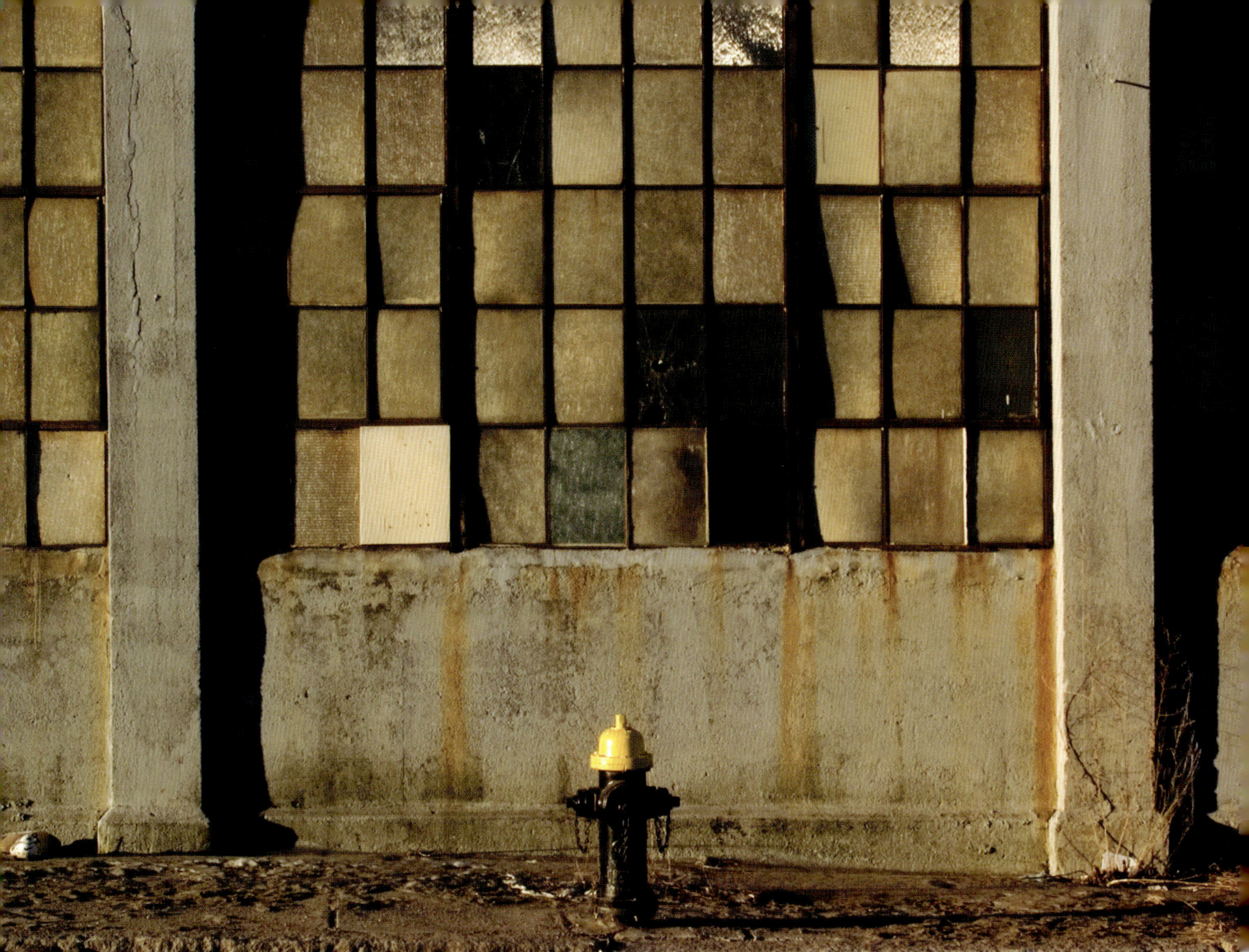

go to the henhouse, carefully collect the eggs, walk directly back to the fridge, and place them gingerly into their storage area, which has been previously prepared for them. Get the idea?

Format the memory card in the camera. Shoot to the card. Download the card to the computer folders you've made, and back it up immediately. Verify that the files are good. Now you can play.

What Not to Do:

- Don't format the card on the computer—instead, format it on the camera. Don't erase images on the camera—instead, download the images to your computer and erase them from your desktop.
- Don't shoot with a low battery or try to squeeze that one last image on the card. Don't shoot to a card with any other camera, especially

the same camera model. Dedicate your cards to specific cameras.

- Don't use programs like iPhoto, Nikon View, or anything else to transfer the files. Simply create your folders, drag the files into the folders, and proceed with your backup and verification process.

- Don't look at your files before transferring and backing up. Don't even peek. Move them first, back them up next, and then you can look when you verify them.

Without going into the rationale behind each one of these statements, the blanket answer to "why not?" is basically that any or all of these things have caused data corruption on memory cards. I've seen it repeatedly. You may have done some of these things and had no problem, but I would say that you've been very lucky. Keep your habits simple and clean, practice good digital hygiene, and you will minimize the risk of losing your work.

Preparing the Camera

Now, let's take a look at the camera. We have all our basic camera settings: aperture, shutter speed, and focus. In addition to those controls, we have a set of new controls on the digital capture side of the process. There are settings that you should check to make sure you're doing what you think you're doing. You have the ISO setting, white balance, file size and type, sharpening, tone controls, and contrast. Shooting in the RAW file format allows you a great deal of opportunity to reassign these settings, but like everything in digital photography, the more you can do up front, the less work you'll have processing your images on the computer. We're going to talk more about the RAW file and how these settings are applied in the next section, but for now, let's discuss how to find them on the camera and set them.

In your preparation checklist, make sure to include extra batteries, a battery charger, extra cables, and extra memory cards. Memory cards and batteries are the cheapest thing in the digital process; it is a shame to lose a shot because you ran out of storage or your battery died. (There's nothing more useless than a $10,000 camera with a dead battery.)

The camera itself should be absolutely clean. Gone are the days that your old Nikon can look like you just spent two months in the wilds of Tangiers. I used to consider it a badge of honor that my camera was filthy, brassy, and dented. Digital technology requires a clean camera, inside and out. The sensor is a dust collector. It builds a charge then dumps it, only to build a charge again—a major dust attractor. If you don't believe me, run your finger over your TV screen to see what you're up against. If you have dust on the back of your lens, as soon as that mirror flips around it's going to stir up the dust, which is going to get sucked right onto the sensor. Dust on the sensor appears as small black spots on the image. Unless you like the Cloning Tool in Photoshop, keep your gear clean. Learn

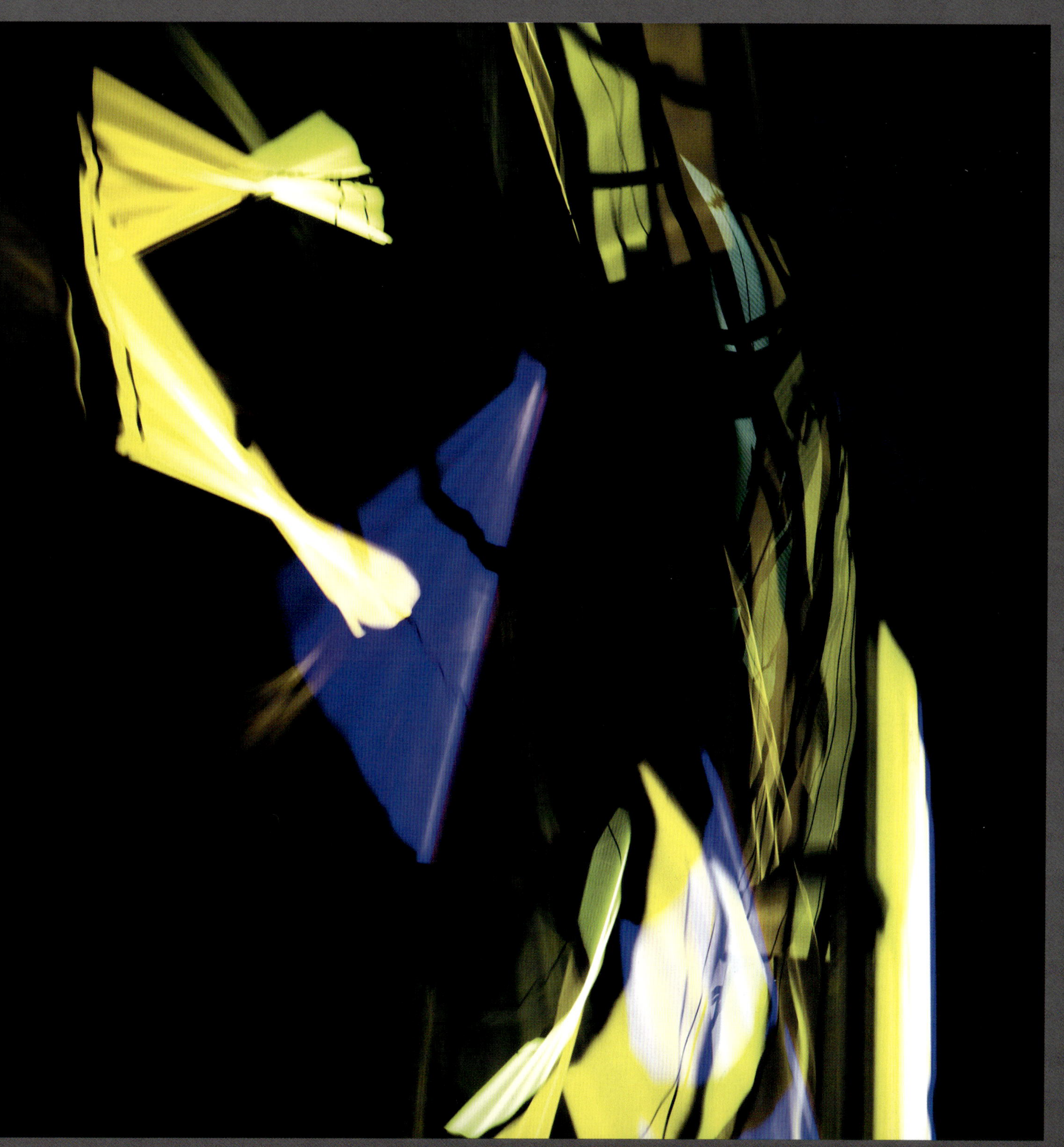

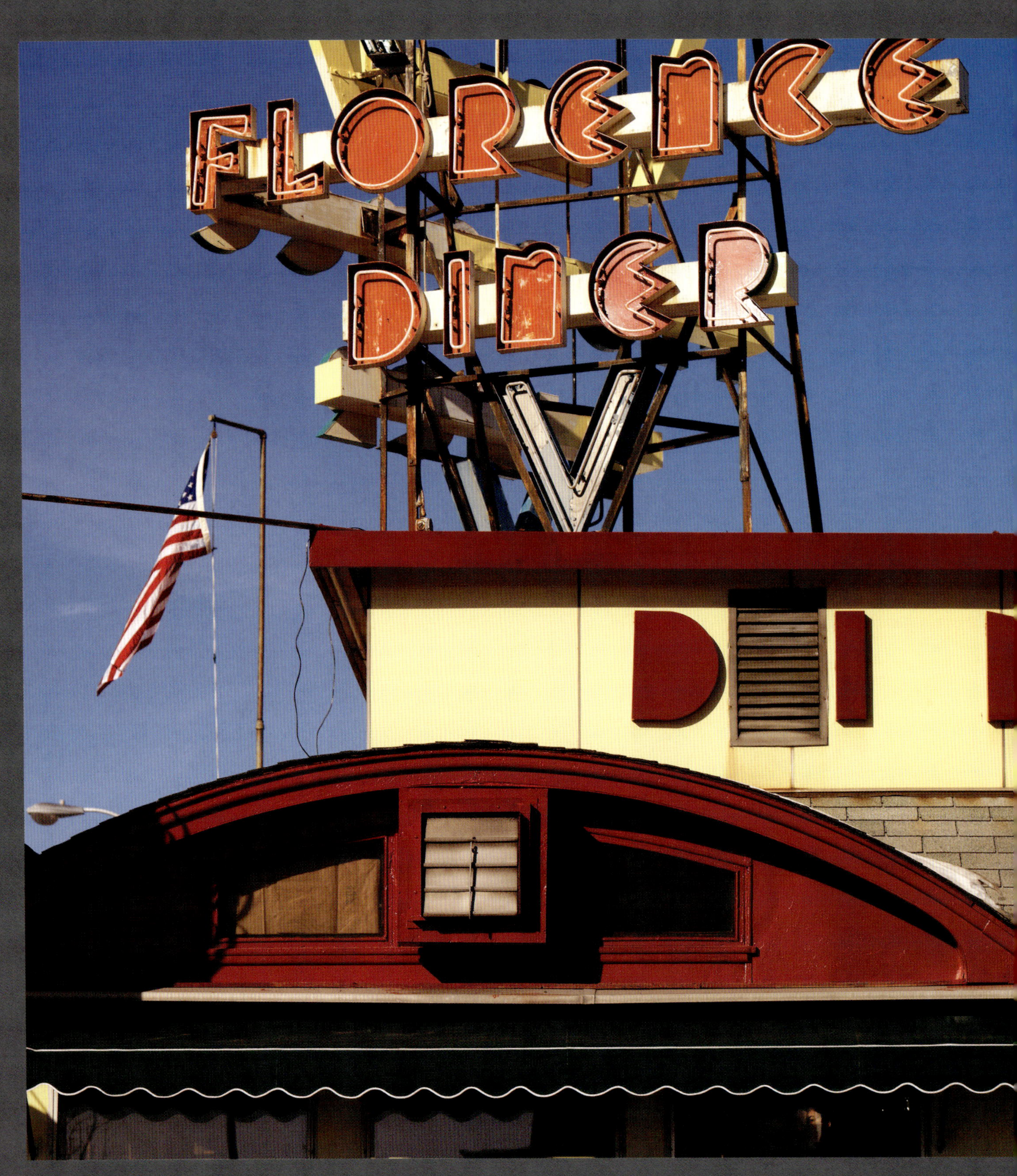
FLORENCE
DINER
DI

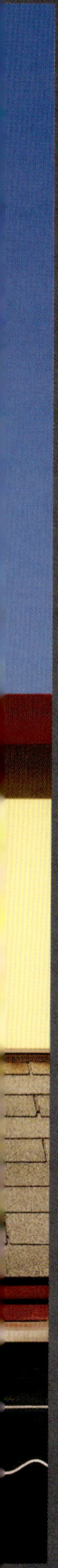

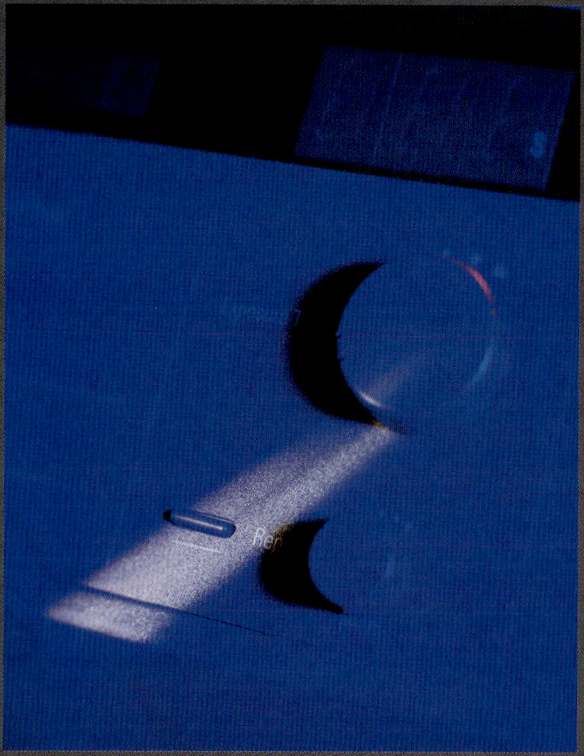

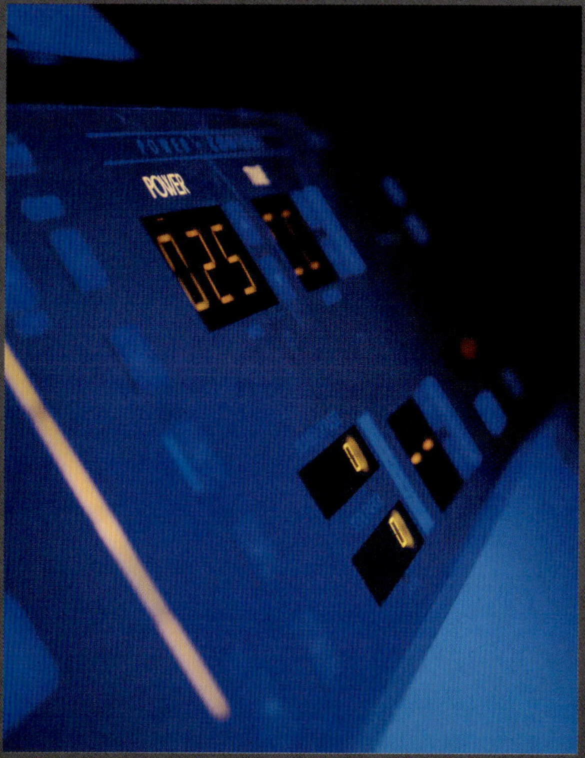

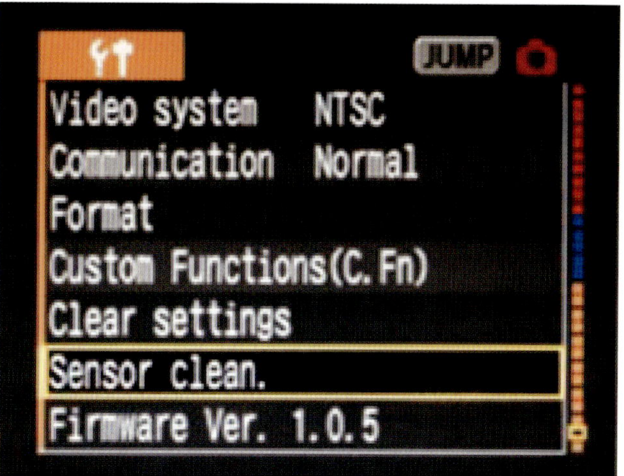

Cleaning your camera's sensor is important, but you should only do it if it is necessary (for example, dust spots appear on your images). Be sure to follow the manufacturer's instructions carefully.

how to carefully clean the sensor, and clean it as needed, but especially before an important shoot.

Cleaning the sensor is not a special, risky, or emergency procedure, as long as you use care and don't touch the sensor. For most D-SLRs you can go into the menu of your camera and find the "Mirror Lockup" command. Follow the directions, and the camera opens the shutter and locks the mirror up without charging the sensor. Blow the sensor off with something safe, such as a rubber bulb blower from a camera store (NOT canned air, because it contains propellants), and you're done. If you do this regularly you should never have to touch the sensor with anything like a wipe or swab. If you have something on the sensor that won't blow off easily, I suggest taking it to a repair facility so it can be cleaned professionally.

Understanding the Pixel

For all the mystery of semiconductors and electronics in digital cameras, the process of getting from the sensor to a photograph is really quite simple. The basic tool the sensor uses is the pixel.

If you are a digital camera user, then most likely you've heard of a pixel. But do you really know what it is? The pixel is simply a very small light meter (from 1.5 to 12 microns in size). It is a photoelectric diode, meaning that the pixel turns the light falling on it into an electric current. The more light a pixel receives, the more voltage it creates. If you have a pixel hooked up to a voltmeter and shine a light on it, you'll get a reading that directly corresponds to the amount of light, and that's what you use to find out exactly how much light is falling on that one spot. Light falls on the pixel, it creates a voltage reading, and you measure the volts.

The pixels on a sensor are placed in a grid, side-by-side, and packed in as tightly as possible. There's a lot of circuitry needed to get the electrical charge off the sensor (among other things).

When you place a sensor in the camera where the film would sit, the image is going to look like this (A). The pixels are simply measuring volts; they cannot see color. (This is an image from a .000384 megapixel camera, at 16 x 24 pixels.) It's easy to see, from this perspective, how you could make a nice image from a sensor full of pixels, except the pixels don't measure any information about the color. If you just have a bunch of pixels measuring light, you're going to get a nice black-and-white image. To get a color photograph, we've got to measure the three basic channels of light: red, green, and blue (R, G, and B). (Remember high school physics class? All colors of light are made up of these three components.)

You can measure the R, G, and B channels simply by putting a colored filter over a pixel (B). A red filter on a pixel will tell you how much red light is falling on that spot. A green filter will give you green values, and likewise with a blue filter. The catch is that you have to do one pixel at a time. That is, every pixel in the sensor goes from being a "luminance" light meter—just measuring the luminance of all the light falling on it—to a "red luminance" light meter, for instance, measuring the red light falling on the sensor. This creates color information from the camera's pixels and effectively measures the intensity of that specific color in the light spectrum.

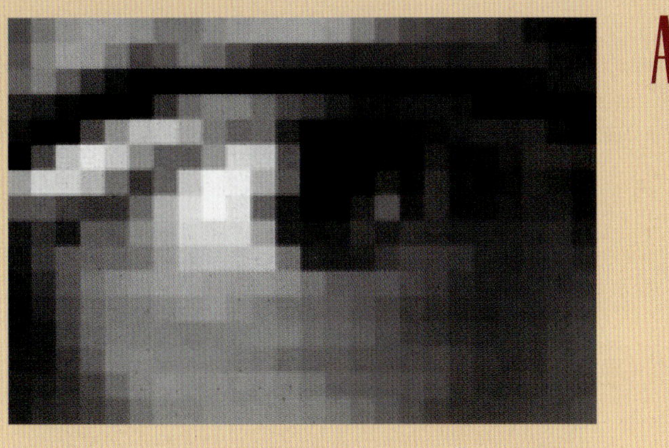
A

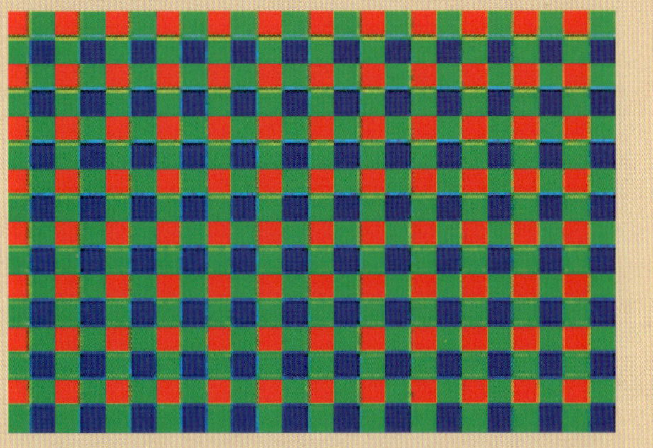
B

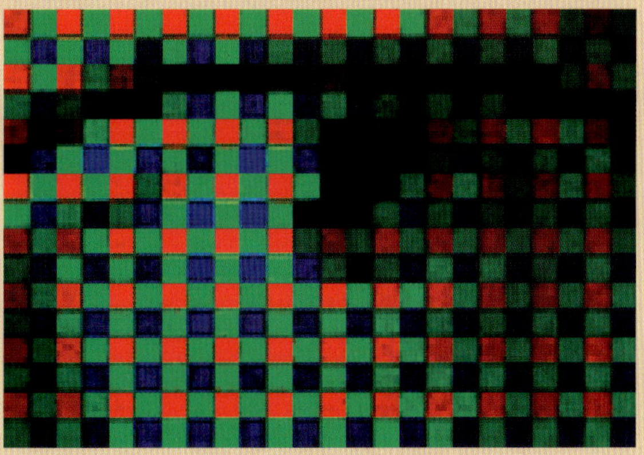
C

The camera's sensor measures the volts generated by light hitting a pixel to determine how intense that light source is. Each pixel is filtered with red, green, or blue, and this measures the color of the light that is reaching the sensor. By decoding this color information through demosaicing, the camera's processors create the RAW image file.

Each pixel gives a value corresponding to that amount of red light, for example, hitting it. The image is going to look like this (C).

This (C), in all its glory, is what the RAW file looks like. It is an image made up of individual pixels with red, green, or blue values. Making this into a real picture is a process of taking this information and translating it into an image made up of individual pixels with combined RGB values, rather than just R, G, or B. You then have to figure out how to get all that color information decoded to make RGB pixels that Photoshop can understand. This RAW file is called the mosaic file, and part of the process of creating a final RAW image is called "demosaicing the file."

Demosaicing

Demosaicing is the process of decoding this "mosaic" of R, G, and B information. Most sensors are designed with a very specific RGB filter pattern, called the "Bayer Array," which provides you groups of four neighboring pixels in the densest pattern possible. We start with a basic sensor that makes a file comprised of black, gray, and white pixels, right? We then add color filters, in a specific pattern, and get a similar image, except now it is made up of separate red, green, and blue pixels. We have to build a file from this red, green, and blue information so every pixel becomes an RGB pixel.

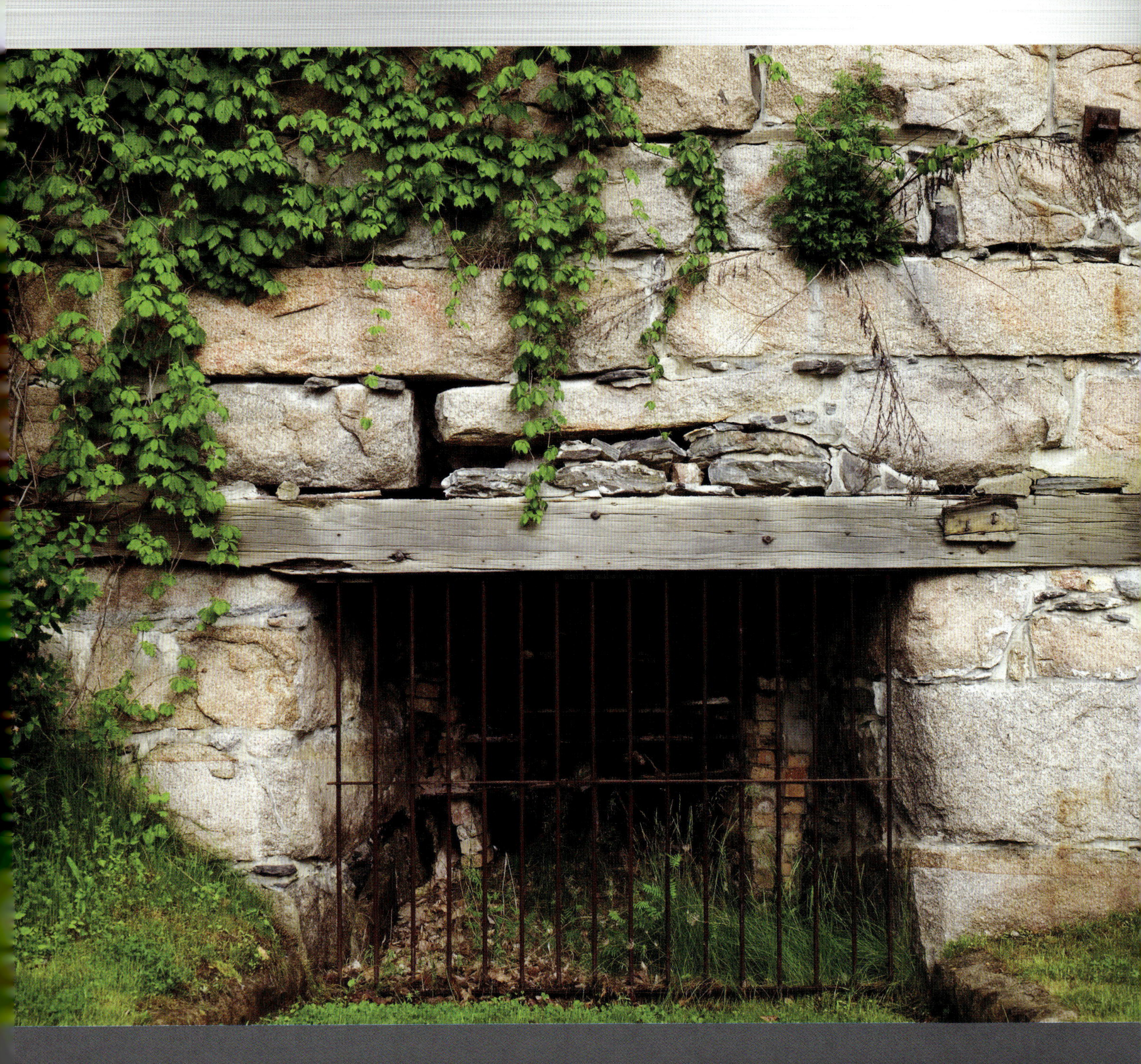

Let's put it this way: demosaicing the file is a matter of taking each picture made up of pixels that are one color (red, green, or blue), and making a file made up of pixels that have all three channels—red, green, *and* blue. It translates the data taken from each individual red, green, or blue pixel to create the complete RAW file (comprised of combinations of red, green, and blue pixels) that you import from your camera or memory card and onto your computer.

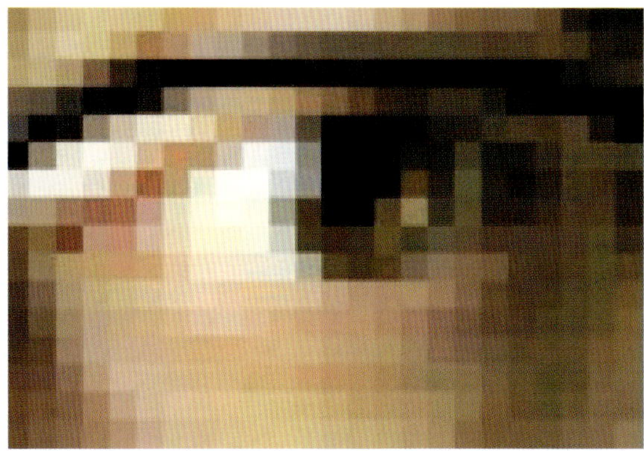

The camera processes the color information from the red, green, and blue pixel readings to create a full color image file, like the one shown here.

Going Digital

Now that we have the luminance and color information from the sensor's filtered pixels, the next thing to happen is to get that information into a form that we can work with: the digital image file.

The first step is going from a mere measure of voltage that comes from the camera's sensor, to a number that means something in Photoshop. This step is digitizing the values: translating them from a simple voltage value to a value from white to black. Photoshop uses a value of 255 to represent white, and a value of 0 to represent black. In the "analog to digital converter" phase of the in-camera processing, a pixel's measurement is assigned a number on this 0 – 255 scale. In the process of doing this, you are taking a pretty abstract measurement and deciding what exactly is black and what exactly is white. What you get is an image with red, green, and blue pixels where each pixel has a number value from 0 to 255.

Once you have this digital information, you can combine values from neighboring pixels to get a "virtual" pixel with all three numeric values. You have a group of R, G, and B pixels with values like this: red=150, green=100, blue=50. You can combine those to create one pixel that has an RGB value of 150, 100, 50.

Next, making sense of the colors once you have them.

Linear Response and the RAW File

Explained simply, the sensor records the amount of light hitting it. If it gets twice the light, it makes twice the voltage and this is called linear response.

The problem is that our eyes and brain do not respond in a linear way to light. We actually compress the data. If you see a subject with twice the light, we perceive it as being only slightly brighter. To better understand this, think back to how film exposure works: to make something a little brighter, we increase it one f/stop, or slow the shutter speed from 1/60th to 1/30th. Remember back to your basics: this doubles the amount of actual light, but the image only gets slightly brighter. This is because film, like the brain, compresses these huge increases in light. This compression is called a response curve.

Film has a nice, human-like tonal response curve that can be manipulated using exposure and processing. Your digital camera also uses a tone response curve, but this is built into the camera's processor.

Here's another way to look at it: remember the Zone System? Each zone represents one stop, from Zone 0 all the way up to Zone X. The tones of the Zone scale are a nice, gradual transition from black to white, and each Zone represents twice as much light as the Zone before it.

The values at the bottom of the graph are the 11 Zones, from black to white, of the Zone System, and they are one stop apart. This means that, although they look like a nice gentle tonal transition, they represent, for each step, twice the amount of light. The RGB values, shown just above the Zones, are the numbers from 0 – 255, which also represent the black-to-white scale in Photoshop. They are about 25.5 points apart, give or take. This is called a mathematical progression, and shows up as a straight line on the graph. The measured light, in the next row, shows each step as double the previous,

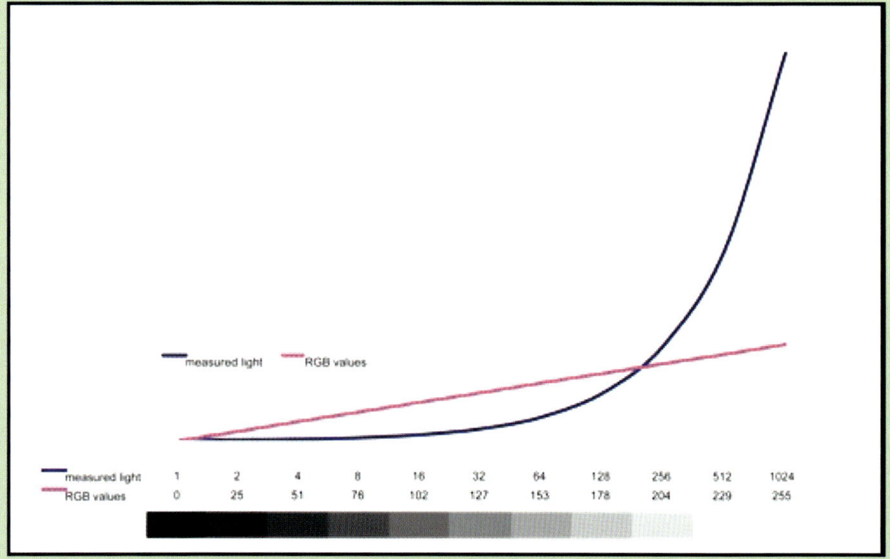

and I just made up a unit, starting with 1. This, graphed as a curve going dramatically up, is a geometric progression.

The point here is that the real, measured values must be compressed to replicate how the human eye sees light. This means there's actually more information at the higher scale values than at the lower. Therefore, we can assume that it is better to place your exposure at the higher end of the curve than the lower end, if you have the choice.

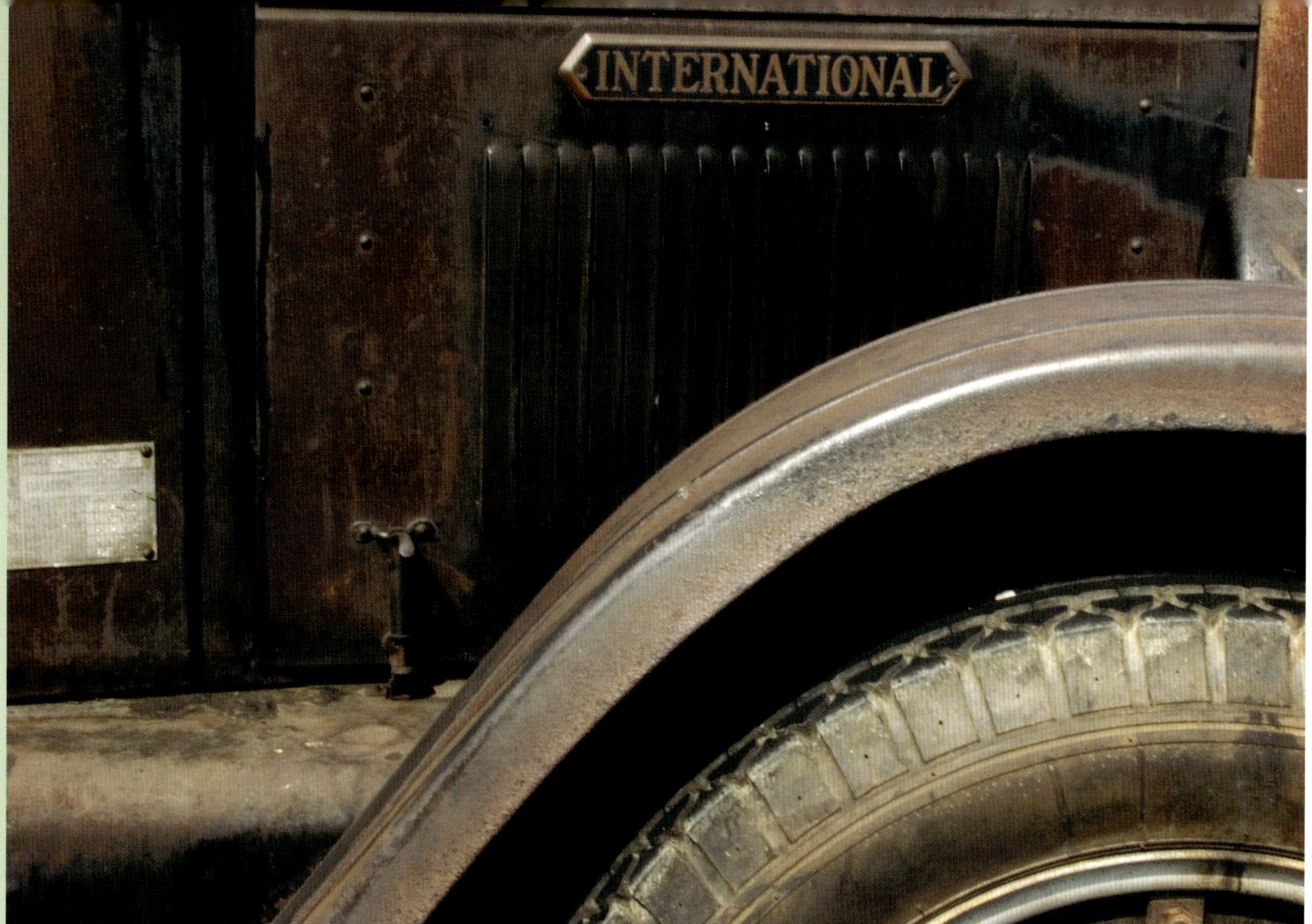

Color Foundation

The next problem is that these colors really have no "grounding," no foundation. We've got to massage them a bit to make them respond the way our eyes respond, and we do that in two steps. First, you have to assign a starting point, a basis to work from, and we use the "neutral gray" to do that. Decide what value in your image is going to be totally neutral (that is, where all three channels will be equal), and you use that to start on the second step: mapping the colors around that point.

Think of it like this: if you want to build a house, you start with a good, level foundation. It doesn't matter what the landscape looks like, you take what you have, level it off, and start the base of the structure. If you're taking photos outside, start by building on the idea that daylight has a certain neutral point (gray), and build your colors around that.

To take the analogy further, the "house" you build depends on many things like taste, individual needs, zoning restrictions, right? The way you map color for the sensor and camera is just as subjective—it depends on how your camera collects the colors, what you like, and how you intend to use the files.

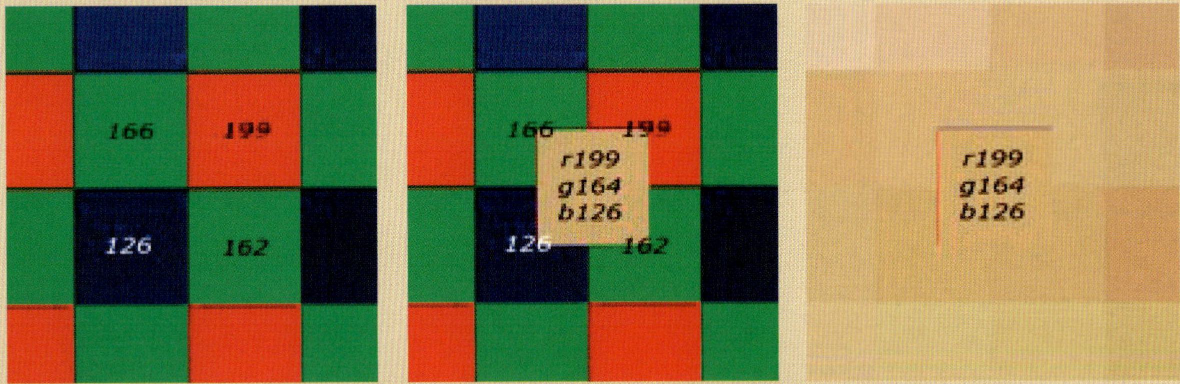

These three images show a simplified version of how the sensor captures color information. The red, green, and blue filters on the pixels measure the light coming in and assign it a neutral value, the grouped pixels are combined to create an average reading from those neutral values, and the sensor processes that average to create a the final color tone.

Digital Image Basics: Color, Contrast, and Scale

So we now have a nice color image. Let's look at how we got there. We started by assigning a black point (0) and a white point (255) when we changed the file from an analog voltage reading into a digital value. This defined the contrast.

Next, we determined a neutral value and mapped color from there. This defined the color.

Finally, remember we are actually creating "virtual" pixels from our real R, G, and B pixels. That gives us the chance to decide exactly how many pixels we want and how they should look together, otherwise known as scaling.

Going from the light that fell on the sensor to a file you can work with in Photoshop is simply a process of deciding how to handle these three things: contrast, color, and scaling. This is the secret of the RAW file process.

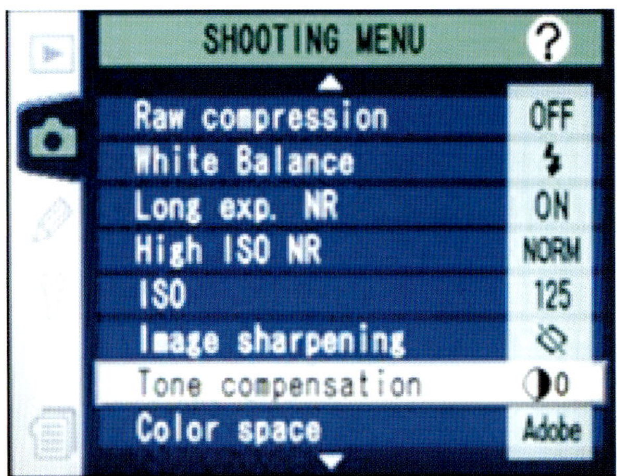

Many advanced cameras give you the option of adjusting how an image file is processed. If you are shooting RAW, then these options are tags added to the RAW image file. If you are shooting JPEG, then these are processing options, which are handled by the camera.

The Digital Camera and the RAW Process: Color, Contrast, and Scale

The process of translating a RAW file to an RGB file like a TIFF or JPEG—whether done in the camera by setting to JPEG or in Adobe's Camera RAW processor—consists of adjusting three basic things: color, contrast, and scale. You're assigning a neutral value (a gray balance), and mapping the color around it. You're setting the black and white values and mapping the contrast curve between them, and you're determining the scaling. RAW processors can do a lot of cool stuff, but at the base, they take the RAW file and process color, assign contrast, and determine scaling.

These three specifications can be set in the camera and applied in the processing. Depending on your camera model, you have a white balance setting, a contrast setting, and a sharpening setting. (The sharpening is part of what gets decided in the scaling process, so I'm clumping them together.) If you are shooting RAW, these are only tags. If you are shooting JPEG, these are processing specifications. Set your preferences before you shoot and you won't have to mess with them later.

The histogram, probably the single most powerful tool on the camera for evaluating the exposure, will display the values in the file data as the camera is set. Set the camera for high contrast and the histogram will display high contrast. This is another argument for setting preferences in the camera according to how you want it to process; do this and the histogram is will display the file as you're intending to process it.

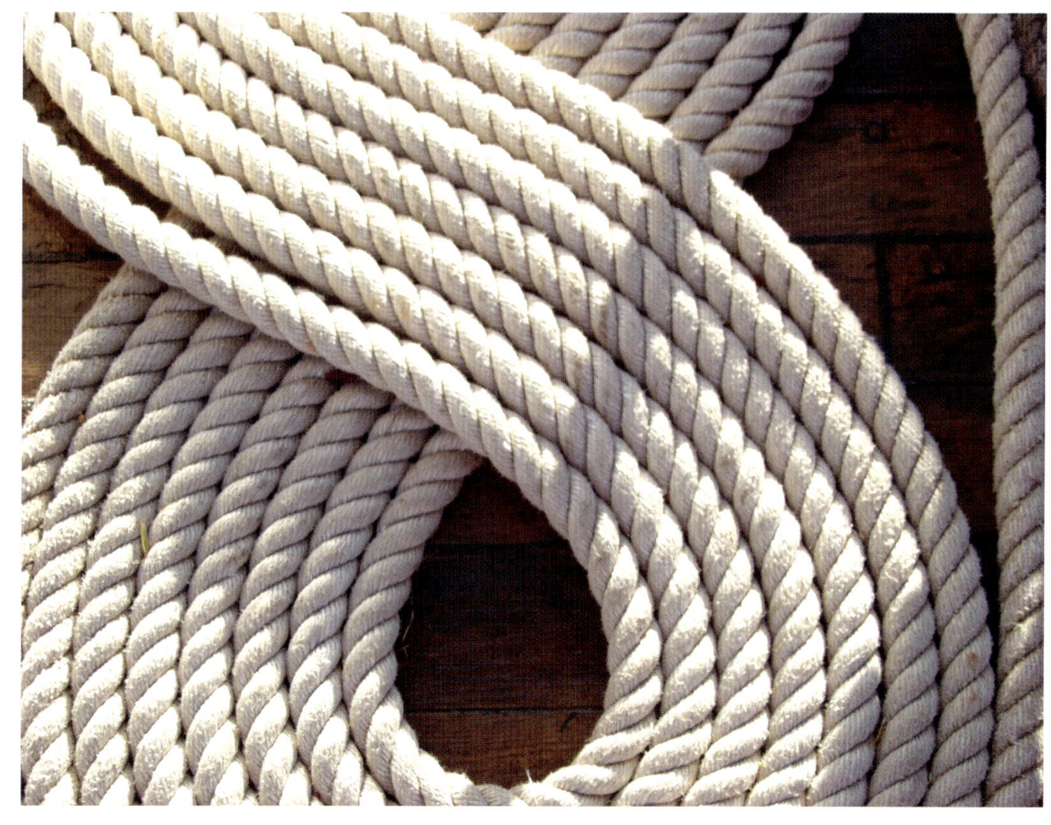

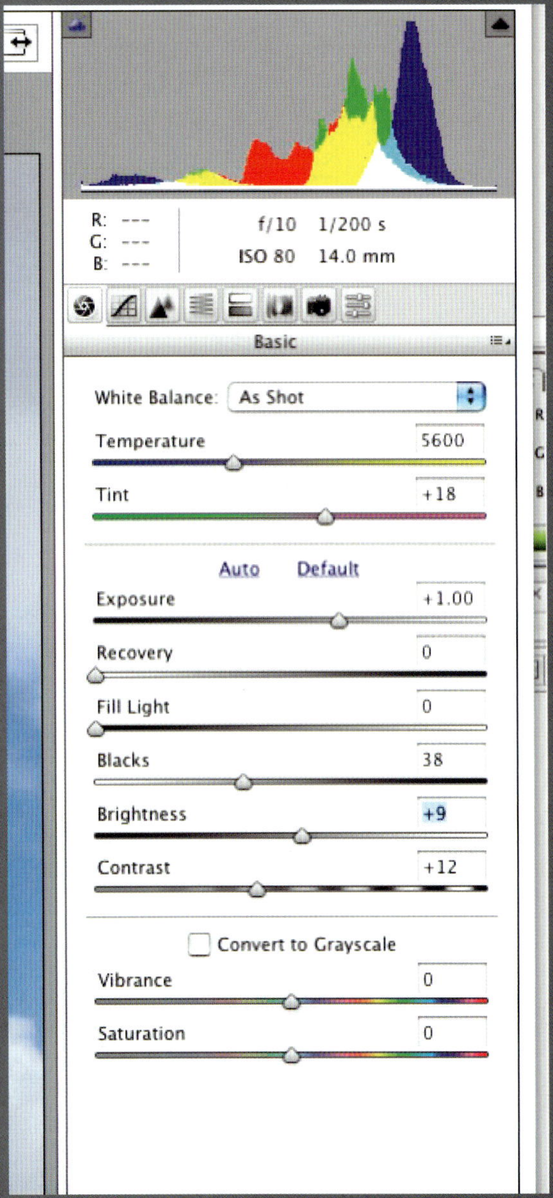

The RAW Process: Adobe Camera RAW

Let's take a look at Adobe's RAW file-processing system. By sitting in the driver's seat, we can put our hands on these basic controls. Here is a quick glance at Adobe Camera RAW and a few of the program's specific controls. In the Basic tab, our color balance (which sets the gray point and maps color around it) is the first thing we see. The "White Balance" control establishes neutral, either with a preset selections (much like in the menu of the camera), a neutral-picker eyedropper, or a manual control. This is where the major decisions are made about how to take the basic R, G, and B measurements from the sensor and make a nice RGB color from it for each pixel. Fine-tuning takes place later on.

Below White Balance is the "Contrast" control. The "Exposure" and "Blacks" controls set white and black points; "Brightness" and "Contrast" set response curve. These adjustments take the measurements from the sensor and, by establishing a low and high range and mapping the tones within that range, create the contrast. You can fine-tune this baseline with the Curves tool in Photoshop, but this is where a starting point is established.

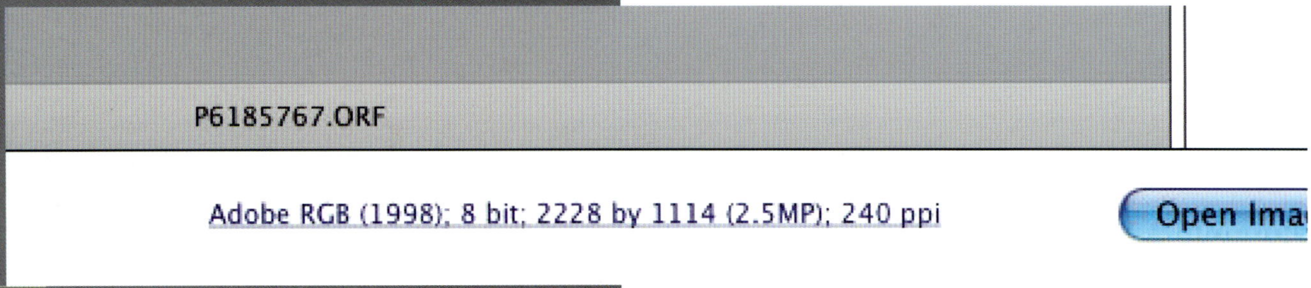

Adobe Camera RAW puts the photographer in control of how a RAW file is processed. Learning the Camera RAW controls is a key to a dynamic and sophisticated RAW workflow.

Finally, there is scaling. At the bottom center of the Camera RAW window, you'll see a line of text that provides the specifics on how the file is being processed. Click on that and you get the "Work-flow" window. The third option down is the size control, and here you can tell Camera RAW how to assemble the basic R, G, and B pixels in the Bayer Array to produce a file of RGB pixels.

In this example I've selected to size up, to 3055 x 1527 pixels. This is not a resample, and it is not strictly "interpolation." It is the basic step in RAW file processing that takes the core information and assembles it into an image.

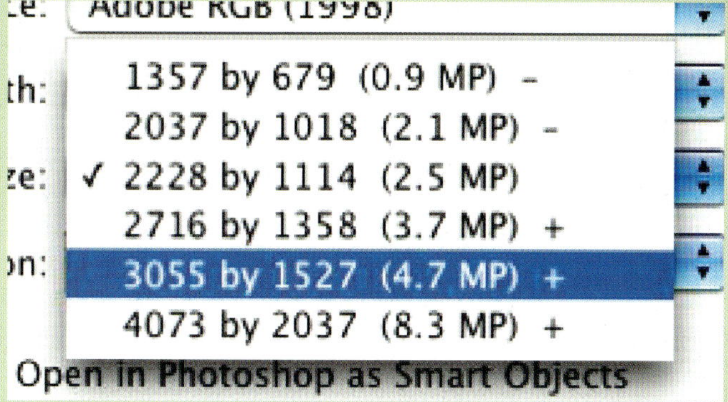

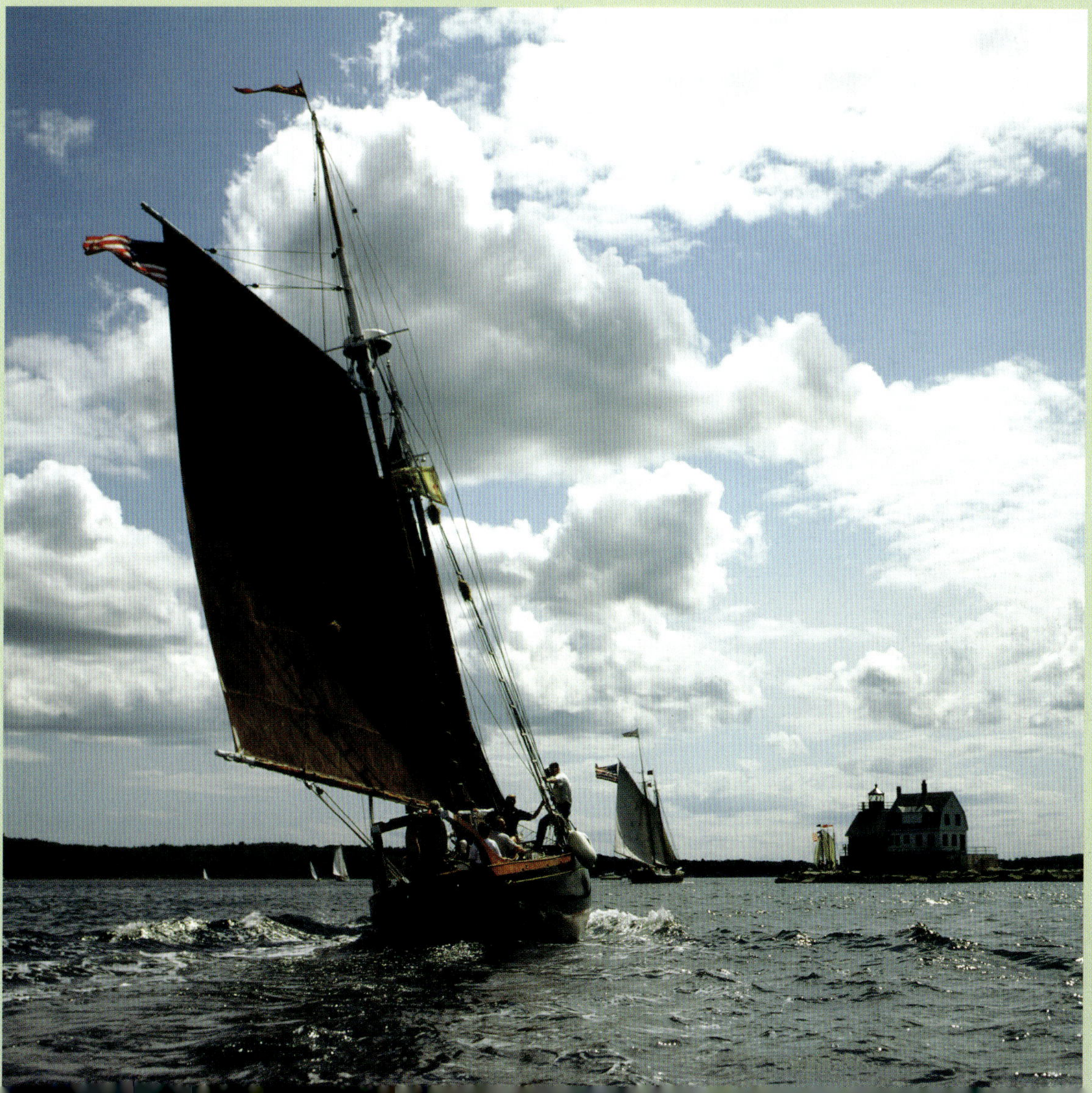

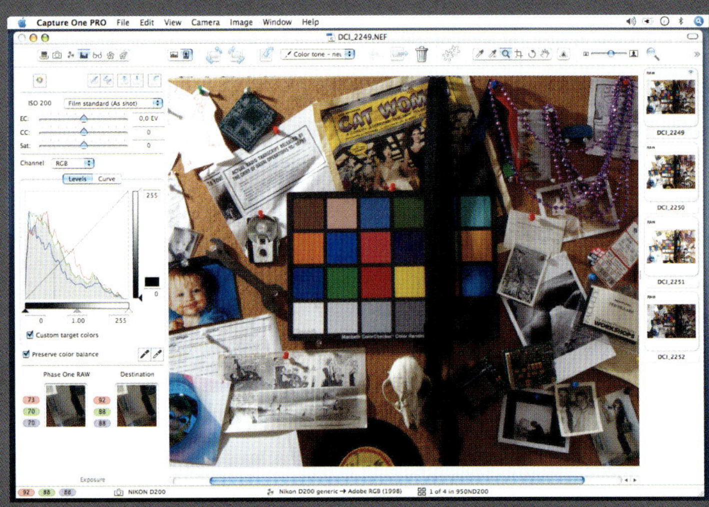
Capture One PRO File Edit View Camera Image Window Help
DCI_2249.NEF

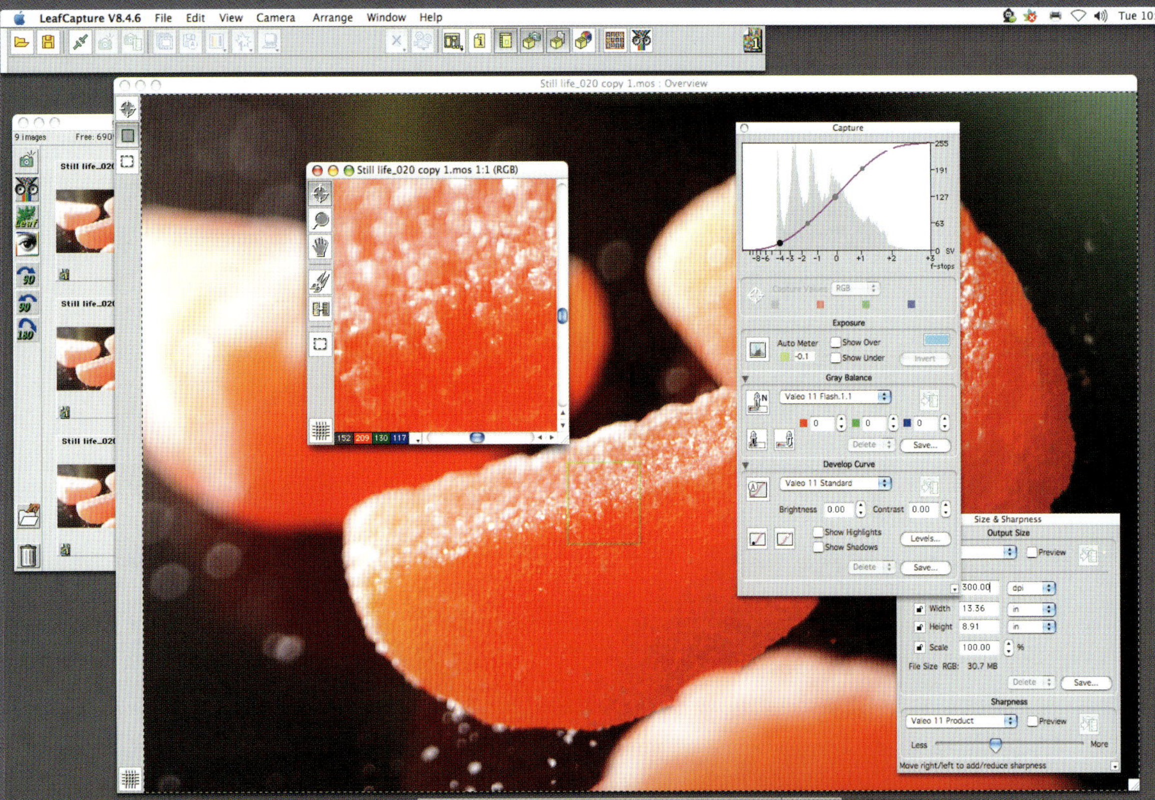
LeafCapture V8.4.6 File Edit View Camera Arrange Window Help
Still life_020 copy 1.mos : Overview
Still life_020 copy 1.mos 1:1 (RGB)
Capture
Exposure
Auto Meter
Show Over
Show Under
Gray Balance
Valeo 11 Flash.1.1
Develop Curve
Valeo 11 Standard
Brightness
Contrast
Show Highlights
Show Shadows
Levels...
Delete
Save...
Size & Sharpness
Output Size
Preview
Width 13.36
Height 8.91
Scale 100.00
Sharpness
Valeo 11 Product
Less
More
Move right/left to add/reduce sharpness

Examples of Other Software

Phase One has adapted their solid, professional software for use with an array of the most popular D-SLR RAW files in an application called Capture One PRO. In this window you'll see a tab array imposing a very straightforward and systematic workflow, and an incorporated file browser. If you look from left to right, you'll see a working folder architecture, image editing tabs, and finally a batching function tab. Phase One has always had a reputation for a good, clean workflow, and Capture One PRO gives us that in a D-SLR format.
www.phaseone.com

Leaf Capture software is unique in that it has a large installed base of users in the digital photography community. Leaf engineers have a unique challenge: they have a lot of loyal users who don't want to lose their favorite features in the latest upgrade, but they want to create a simple, fast interface to attract new users. For this reason, Leaf is probably the most complex package initially, but like most complex systems, will do anything you want it to do, and will do it very well. I really didn't have a true appreciation of the power of the software until I saw it in the hands of a photographer who had been using it since the first Leaf digital back, the legendary "Brick". Out of respect to this legacy, I'm showing Leaf Capture 8, before Leaf made their software look like everybody else's with Leaf Capture 10. You'll see that the browser window is a separate application, where you can specify a batch function, sort and prioritize files, and even send them to Photoshop. The main capture window allows a very simple workflow, but if "Advanced" mode is checked, will give you some of the highest level of quality and efficiency oriented controls in the industry. Much of this logic is counter-intuitive until one processes a couple of hundred images in a day. Then, it starts making perfect sense.

Not to put too fine a point on it, but they all do the same thing. Because Adobe Camera RAW is the only package for which we have detailed manuals from a variety of authors (and a variety of perspectives), many of the other packages demand a good amount of trial and error when trying to understand their subtleties. Start by finding the basic color, contrast, and size controls, and move on from there. Nothing can substitute for controlled testing, even in the well-documented Camera RAW.
www.leafamerica.com

RAW Options: Manufacturer's Software

D-SLR camera software designers have a challenge, much like car designers. They have to make a package that anyone can use easily. They have a large variety of individual brains using these controls, from neophytes to experienced professionals. For this reason, their controls often lapse into the "idiot button" approach, which makes our life a little more difficult. They will often, out of respect to their professional users, embed some very refined controls, but they are often hard to find. Add to that the fact that they don't have people writing incredibly detailed guides on how to use their software, and you have all the elements for a potentially frustrating situation.

Nikon Capture is a case in point. In the illustration you'll see the main window of an old version of Nikon Capture Editor. I have turned off all the "Tool Palette 1" controls, and am only using "Tool Palette 2," with the RAW controls.

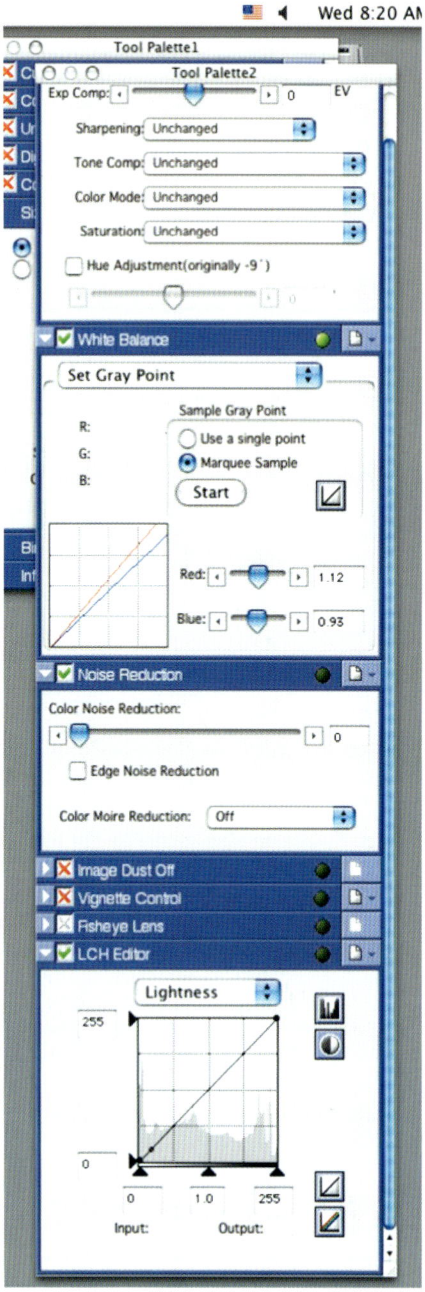

Everything I need is right there. The file browser is integrated, but hidden in a switch called "Multi-Image view." In this case, batching is handled through a third program, "Nikon Capture Control." This is all pretty confusing at first, but once you set up a workflow you can do everything you want. (My rule of thumb with Nikon is to assume whatever I want to do is there somewhere, I just have to find it.)

This software has a couple of sweet extra features. One is a marquee-sample white balance, which averages the white balance from an entire selected area. This is really nice for selecting the gray scale on a Gretag Macbeth ColorChecker, and averaging your neutral tone from white through gray to black. The other is an LCH Editor. LCH stands for "Lightness, Chroma, and Hue," and allows me to control the lightness separately from the color. (You'll notice the color gets funny when you make a strong light or dark correction in Photoshop with the Curves tool. LCH avoids that.)

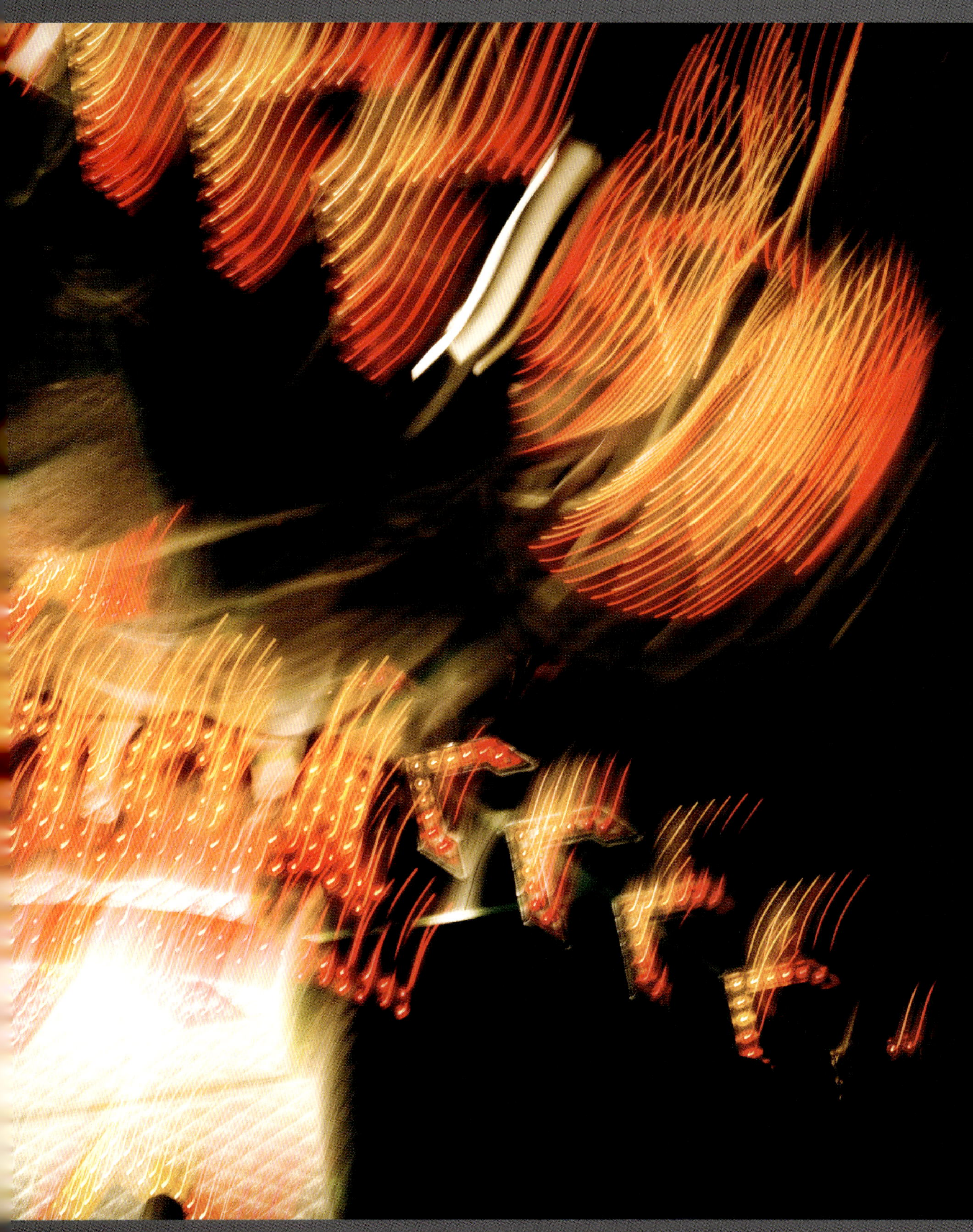

Shooting to the Card

I'm going to show an example where I've shot a bunch of photos for a portrait. I start right off by building a folder on the desktop. I'm calling it "051201tyl," for December 05, Tyler's portrait. I know I'm going to shoot a lot and bring it down to a few, then process the RAW files out to TIFFs, so I build the folders accordingly.

I format the card. I set my camera's ISO, white balance, Low Sharpening, Low Contrast, Manual Exposure, and RAW file quality.

By keeping track of the histogram on the camera, I can make sure my highlights are not blowing out and the exposure is in a decent range. I take the card and plug it into my card slot in the laptop. I click through the folders until I find the files, select them all, and drag them into my "RAW" folder.

Now I back them up to my external hard drive. I pull the card out and set it aside.

Next, I need to verify that the files are OK, so I start up Adobe Bridge. I point it at the folder and give it some time to generate previews. Once the files start showing up I'm pretty confident they're OK, so I start looking through them.

I'm going to go through these and look for six or so of the best. I'll start by giving the ones I like three stars, by hitting "Apple or Cmnd+3" (Mac) or "Ctrl+3" (Windows) when I'm highlighting one I like. After I go through a few times, I have a few files marked. I "filter" down three-star shots.

Next I go through those and give the best a five-star rating. Once again, I filter down to only the five-stars, and I have my final pick. I select all of them and first copy them to the "pick" folder by holding "Alt" and dragging them. I double-click to open them, and they open in Camera RAW.

I generally like to take some red saturation out of this camera model's files, because the reds get rendered a little on the magenta side, so I go into the "Camera Calibration" tab and slide the red hue to more orange, and the red saturation down a bit. I make some small

Be sure to set up your data management filing system on the computer before you download image files from the memory card. This is an important but easy-to-forget step in your RAW workflow.

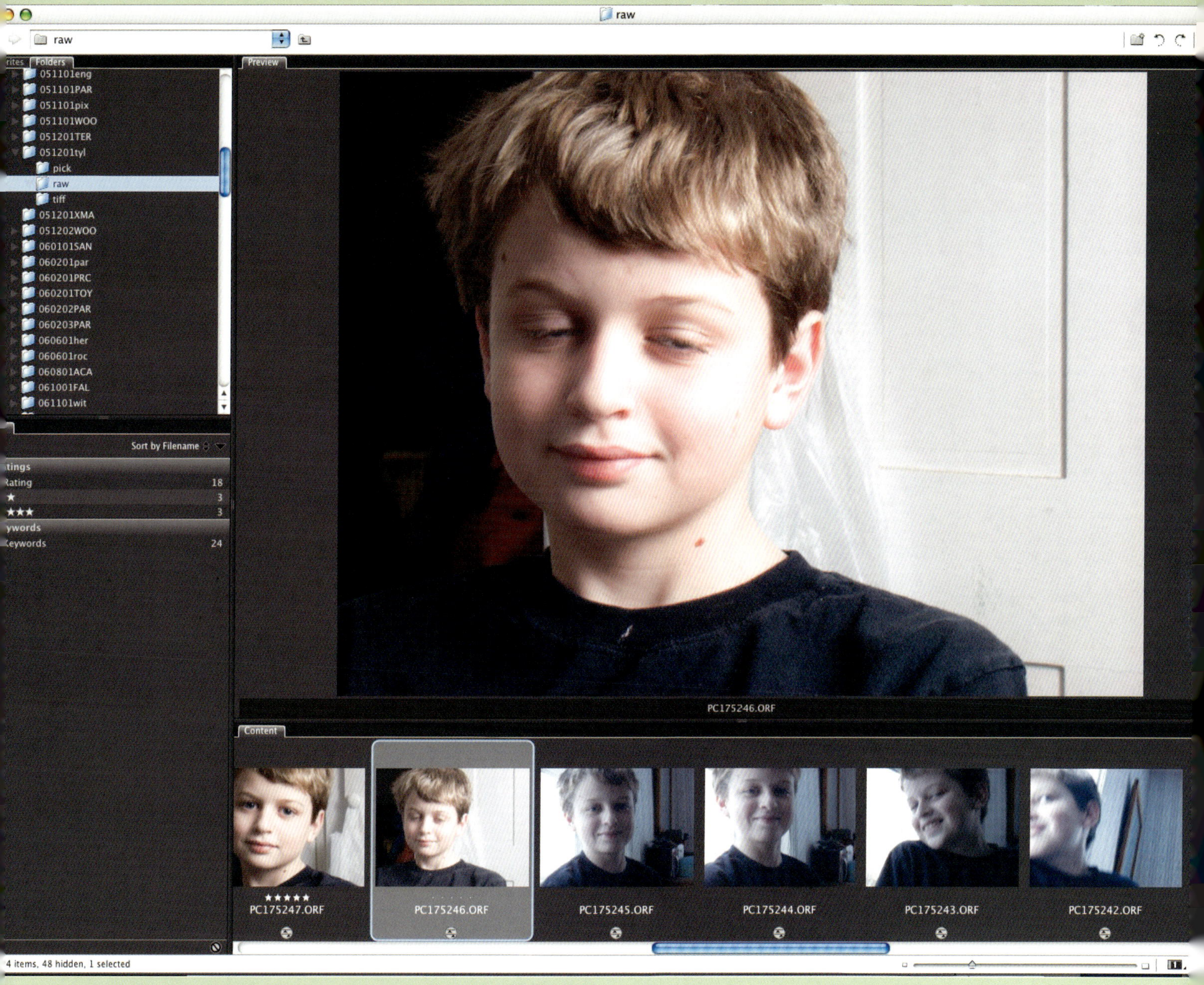

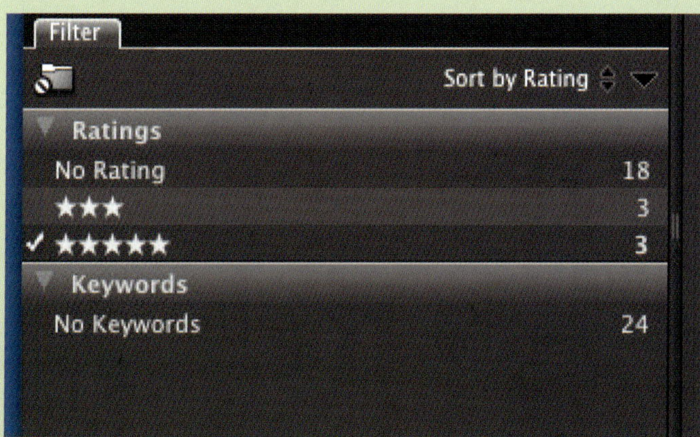

Adobe Bridge makes the image editing process much faster with the one to five-star rating system. Start by rating the images you like with a three-star rating and filter out the rest. From those you can then choose the best shots for your five-star rating.

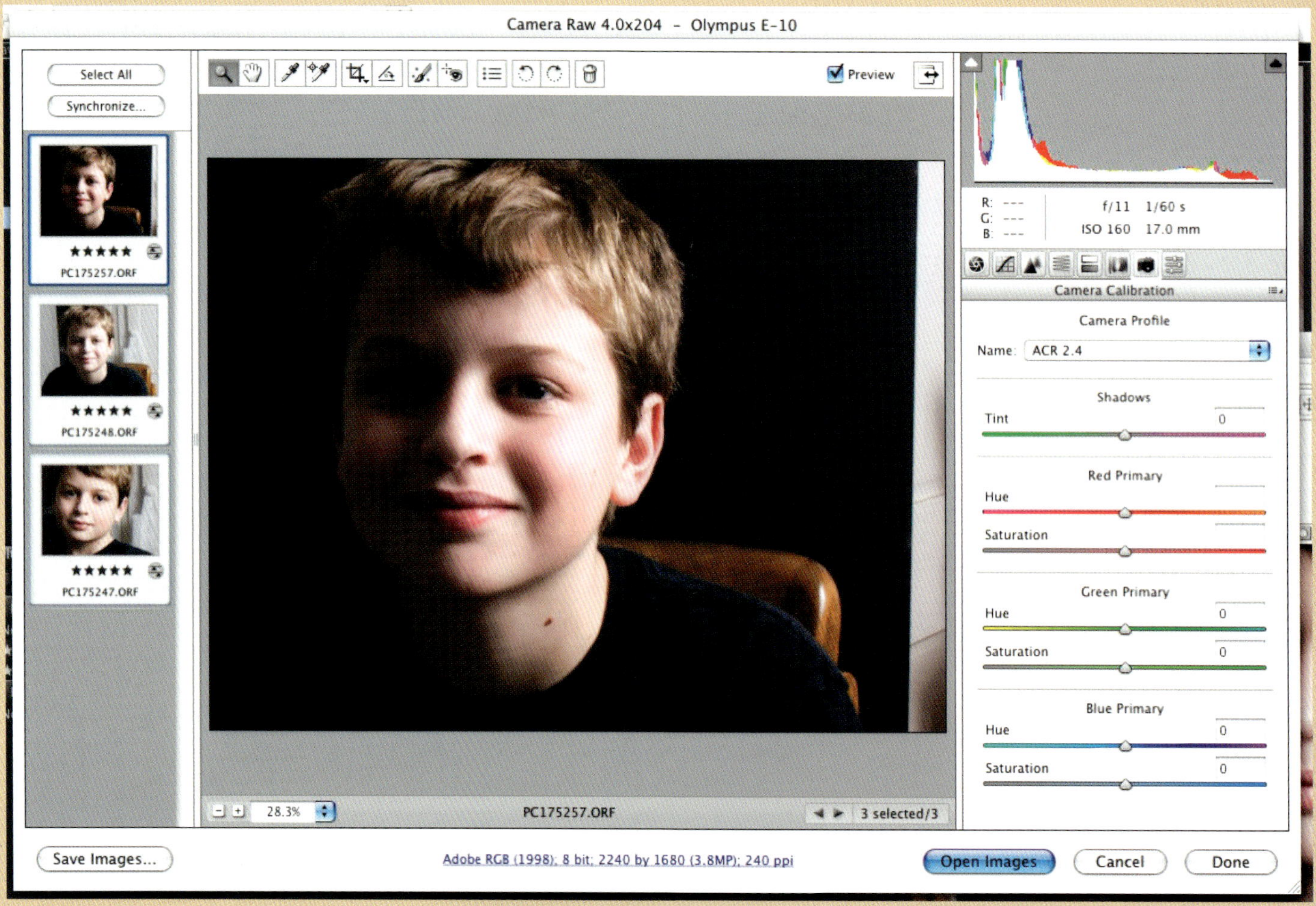

The "Synchronize" button at the top left of the Camera RAW window allows you to make the same adjustment to each image you have selected. For example, if you shoot under a fluorescent light with no white balance and the resulting images take on a green color cast, you can correct one image and apply it to the rest of the affected images. Easy!

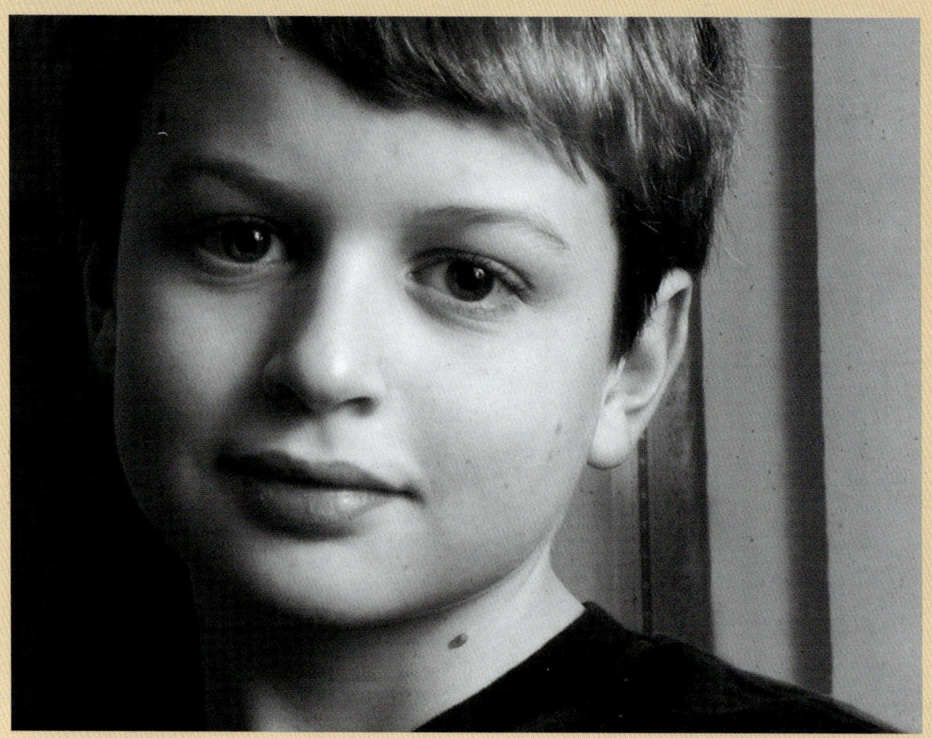

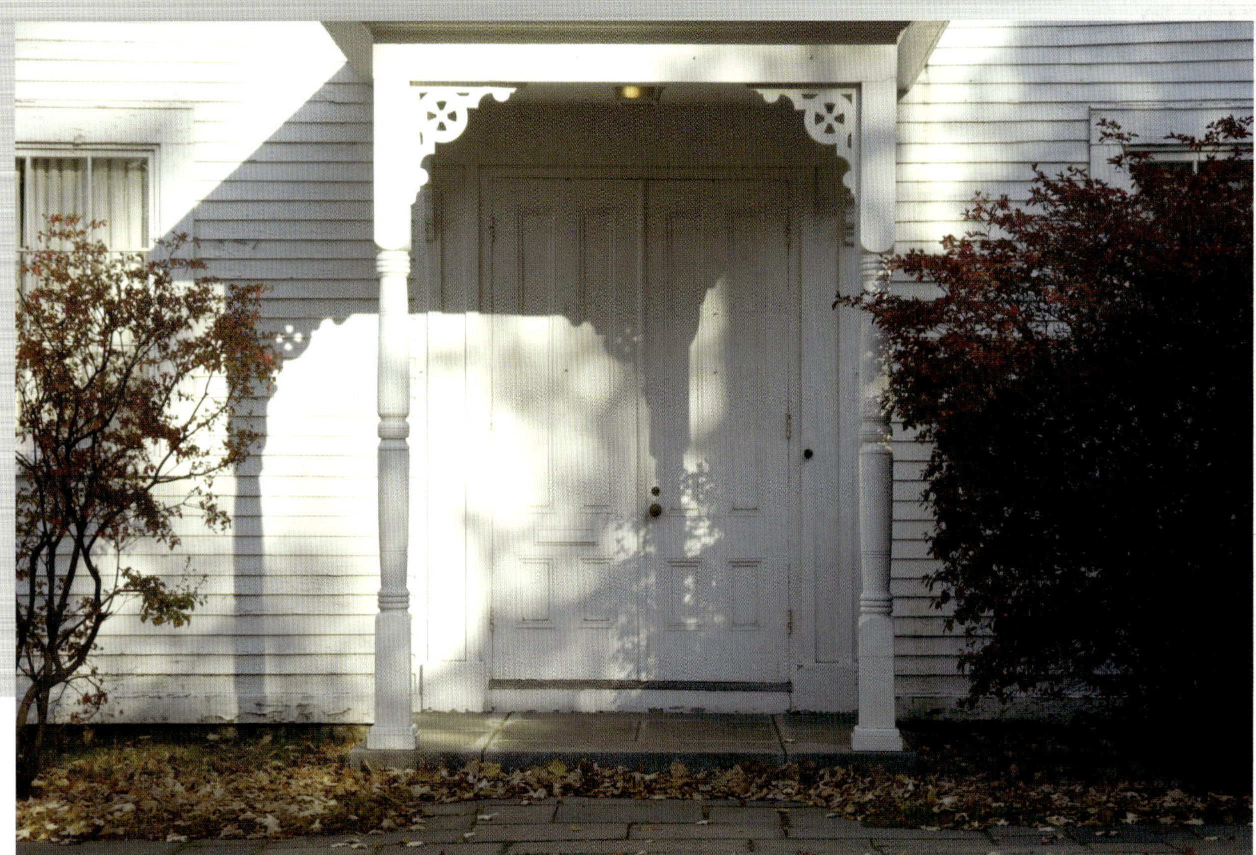

exposure and contrast adjustments, too, and because they are all shot under the same conditions, I can just select all the thumbnails and hit "Synchronize."

Once I get the files looking the way I want, I hit "Save 3 Images," and save them as TIFFs to the TIFF folder I've created.

I'll now make another backup to my second external hard drive. I have two backups now, one first-generation backup on the hard drive, and a second-generation backup on a different drive. If I've screwed anything up, I can go back to the previous generation, in this case the one I made first, the original files.

Now I work on the prints, make some prints, make some adjustments, decide on a single final image, and print it out. I then make a third-generation backup to my first hard drive, overwriting the first backup I did. Again, I have my latest files backed up, and I have the previous version in case I messed something up that I don't know about yet. When I'm done with the project, I delete the folder from my desktop. If it's something I'm going to want to archive, I may burn it to a gold CD just for safe keeping, but because I have the dual hard drives set up I have a workable archive without the CD.

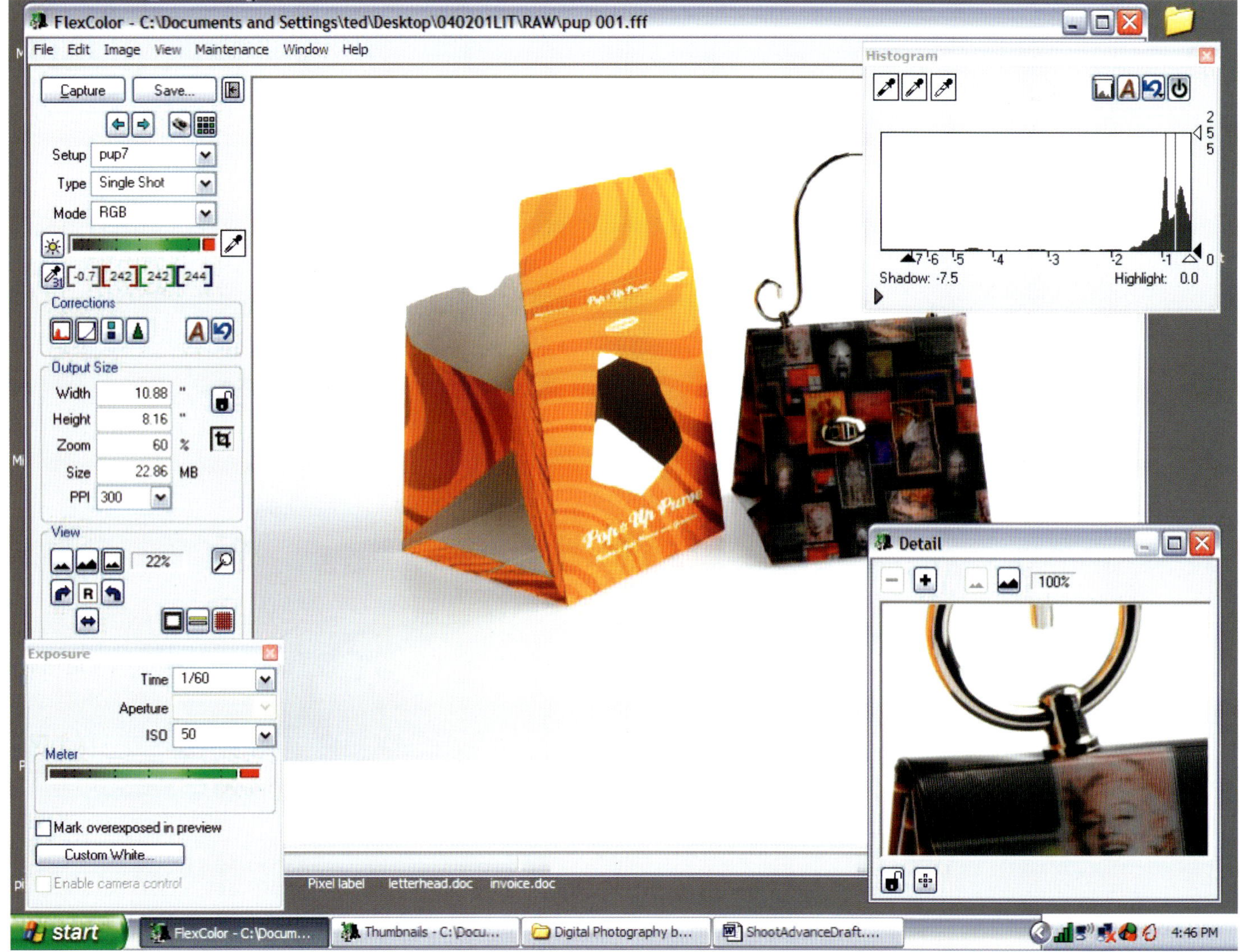

Pro Software: Shooting to the Workstation

Here's an example of a professional-level software package, used for shooting directly to the workstation. One of the big differences in this kind of a program is the speed and efficiency in processing and handling the image files. Think in terms of a long-distance truck. There's a good reason they make the seats comfortable and put a bed in the back; the driver spends a great deal of time at the wheel. This level of software assumes that the operator is going to be processing a large number of files, and wants to do it fast and well.

This example is FlexColor, the software that comes with a Hasselblad digital back system. The first thing you see is the main capture window with the same basic controls that we find in Camera RAW. Two little features, though, are a "Detail" window that allows you to check the focus by zooming in to 100%, and a "Camera

Control" window that lets you adjust and shoot the camera from the workstation.

The file browser component looks, well, like a file browser. But it has some pretty handy little batch-processing features that are specifically engineered for a fast, professional work environment.

Again, I've set up a folder structure based on my naming convention. This job is "040201LIT," which was February 2004 for Little Packrats, and was job #1 for them.

My first shot is of the GretagMacbeth ColorChecker. With this I set my white balance, which gets applied to all the shots for the day. Once the exposure is good and the ColorChecker is neutralized, I'm going to save that file and name it "target," and that file is saved on every disk that goes out from that shoot. This is my safety net. That file is a reference, so that the client can see a file that I know is absolutely neutral, with perfect color mapping. They call and say the files look red, I say check the values on the gray patches of

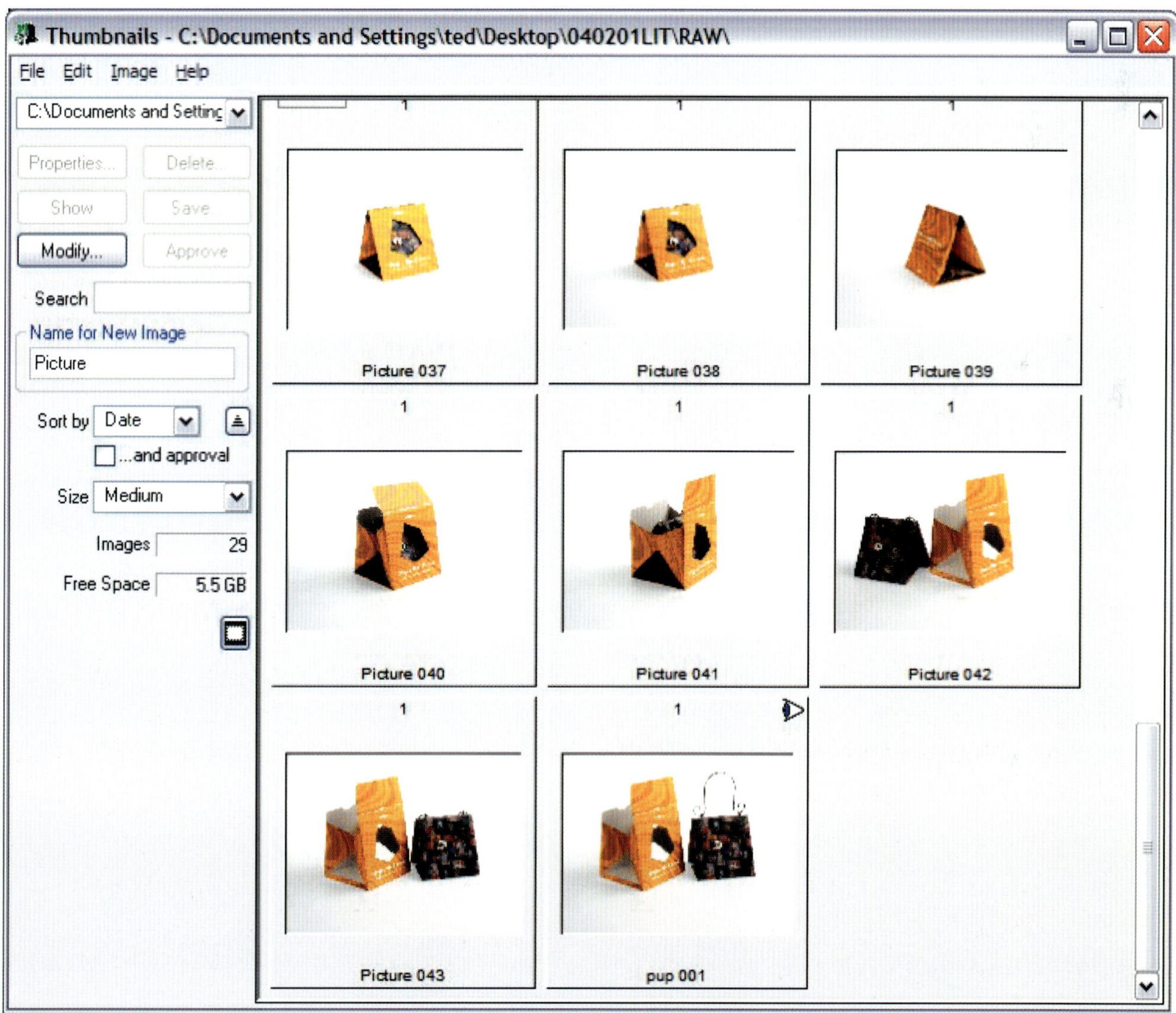

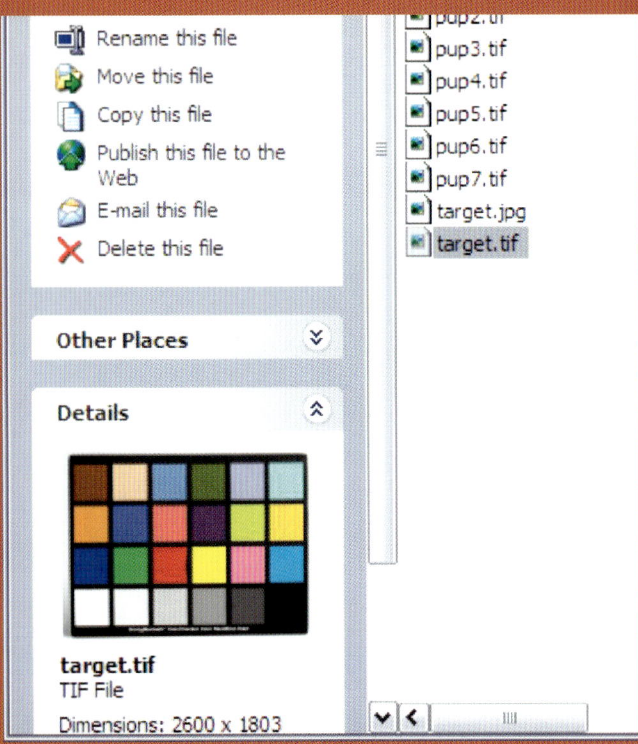

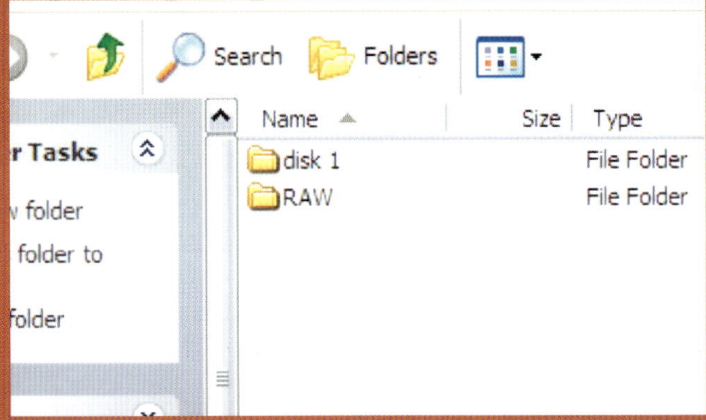

When you are shooting directly to a workstation, regardless of the software you are using, it is imperative to set up a filing system. If you are shooting a color target, such as the one pictured above, make sure it is available on each disc you burn. This covers yours bases with a client, and means less work for you as the photographer in the long run.

the "target" file. I know they're neutral, and once they read the "Info" on it they know it too. If that file looks pink, they have something wrong at their end, such as a calibration error with their computer monitor.

Once we get that behind us, we're ready to shoot. I shoot, shoot, shoot, and finally get a file the client approves. I hit "Save," and save the file as a TIFF to the "Disk1" folder. When the folder reaches 600 megabytes (MB), I start burning the CD, and move to the "Disk2" folder.

Shooting to Adobe Bridge

It's pretty easy to set up Adobe Bridge and Camera RAW to function in much the same way as a professional level software package. First, you have to use the manufacturer's camera control software, which allows you to shoot to the workstation, and control the camera from there, too. Nikon's software, surprisingly enough, is called Nikon Camera Control.

NOTE: By the way, on any camera model, you must turn the camera into a "file-feeder" rather than a card reader. This is done with a setting in the menu, usually called "USB" or something similar. You have two settings, "mass" (which refers to the card as a "mass storage device") or "PTP" (which is "picture transfer protocol"). Select "PTP" and the camera will shoot to the workstation.

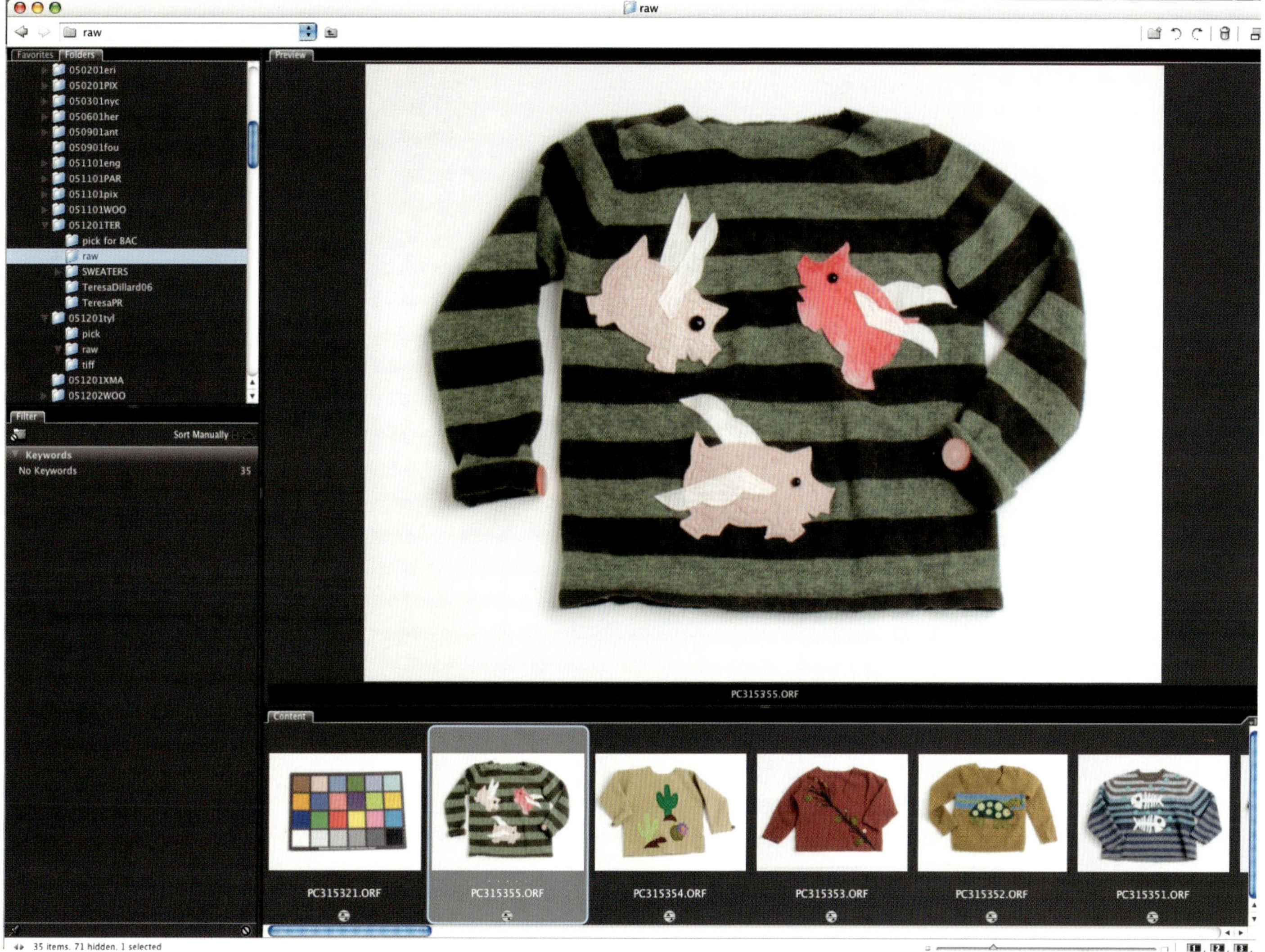

Point Bridge to the folder you've specified in your control software, and it will refresh every time you shoot a new image. You've got your "browser" component of the shooting software. Camera RAW controls how Bridge displays images, so you need to set up Camera RAW to process the images the way you want. You do this by making the adjustments you need, and setting them as the default for Camera RAW.

In the example shown, I've opened up the ColorChecker, set a neutral color balance, and adjusted some "Camera Calibration" settings to fix the reds and the contrast. I select the little button at the top right of the "white balance" slider, and get the menu shown. Select "Save New Camera Raw Defaults," and you have established the settings by which Bridge will display the incoming images. From there, you can shoot, edit, and process your images just like the pros.

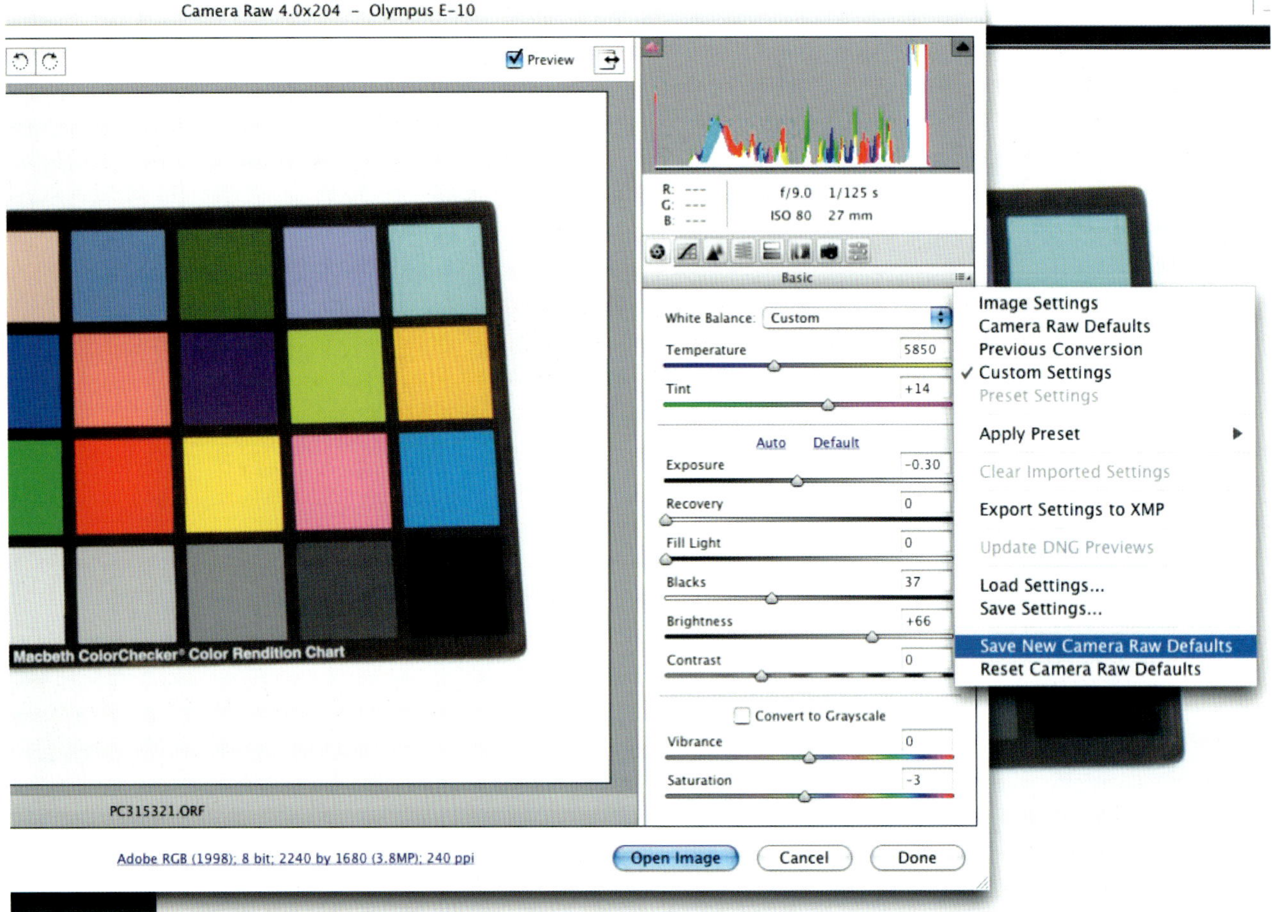

Shooting to the workstation enables you to make corrections, such as color balances, to each shot you take as you make it. This is a great time-saver and a very professional way of working.

Conclusion

At the end of my first talk on color management, just at the point in time when Color Management was actually starting to work, (Photoshop 6), a woman in the back of the room raised her hand and asked a few questions, sort of reviewing the basic procedures and concepts. We discussed a few points, and everyone was on the same page. She said, very pleased with herself for getting her head around this stuff, "I don't see what all the fuss is about; this is the same old stuff we've always done, just with different names."

My point, exactly.

There is indeed a learning curve, and depending on your aptitude and comfort with the tools of the trade, it can be very steep. We are not, however, reinventing the wheel. We're using the same tools, habits, and practices, but with slightly different names.

The products are still moving ahead, but the place we're at now has some very mature products and systems. In 1998, color management didn't really work, and now it does. Now we can get back to work, doing what we do best: taking pictures.

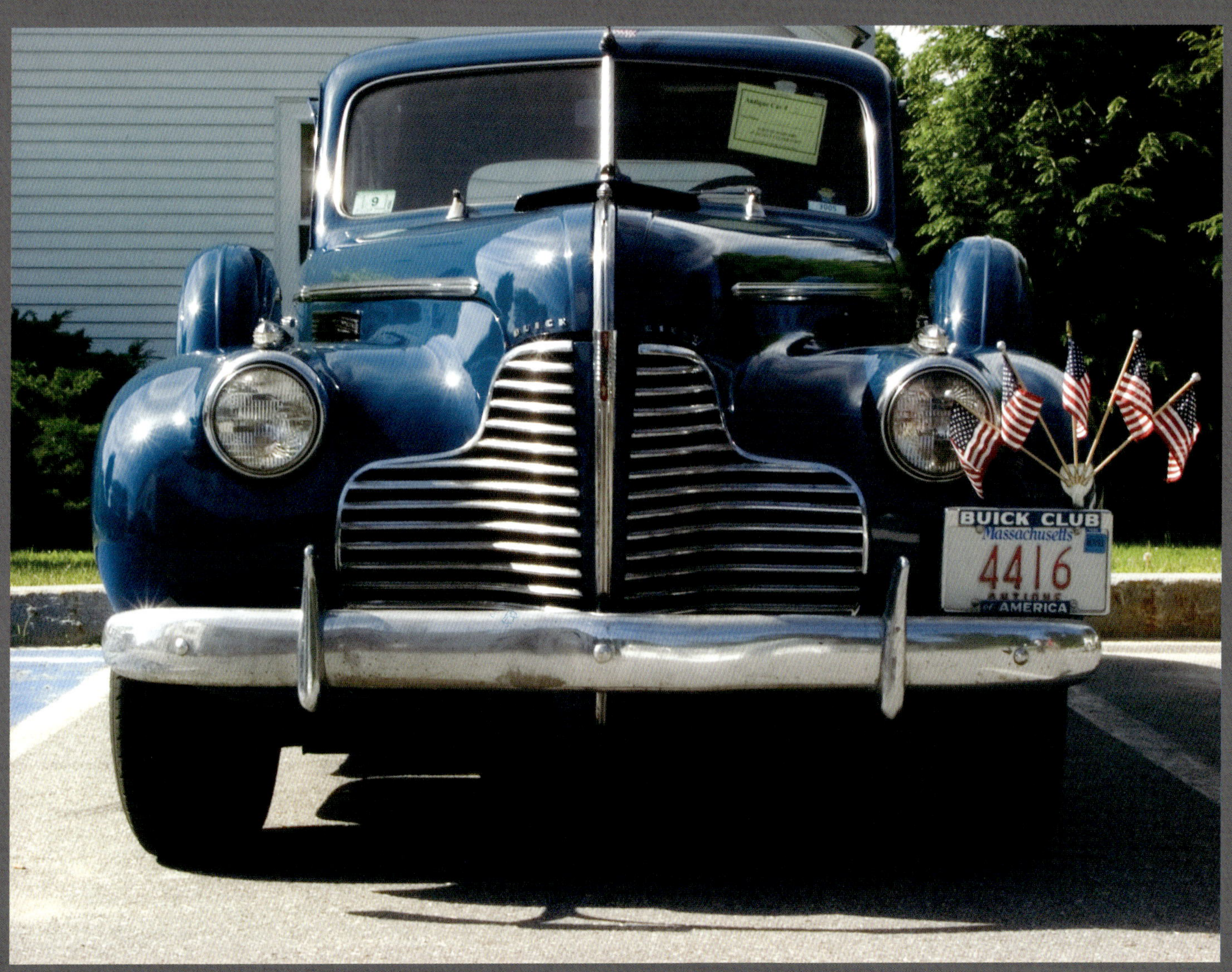

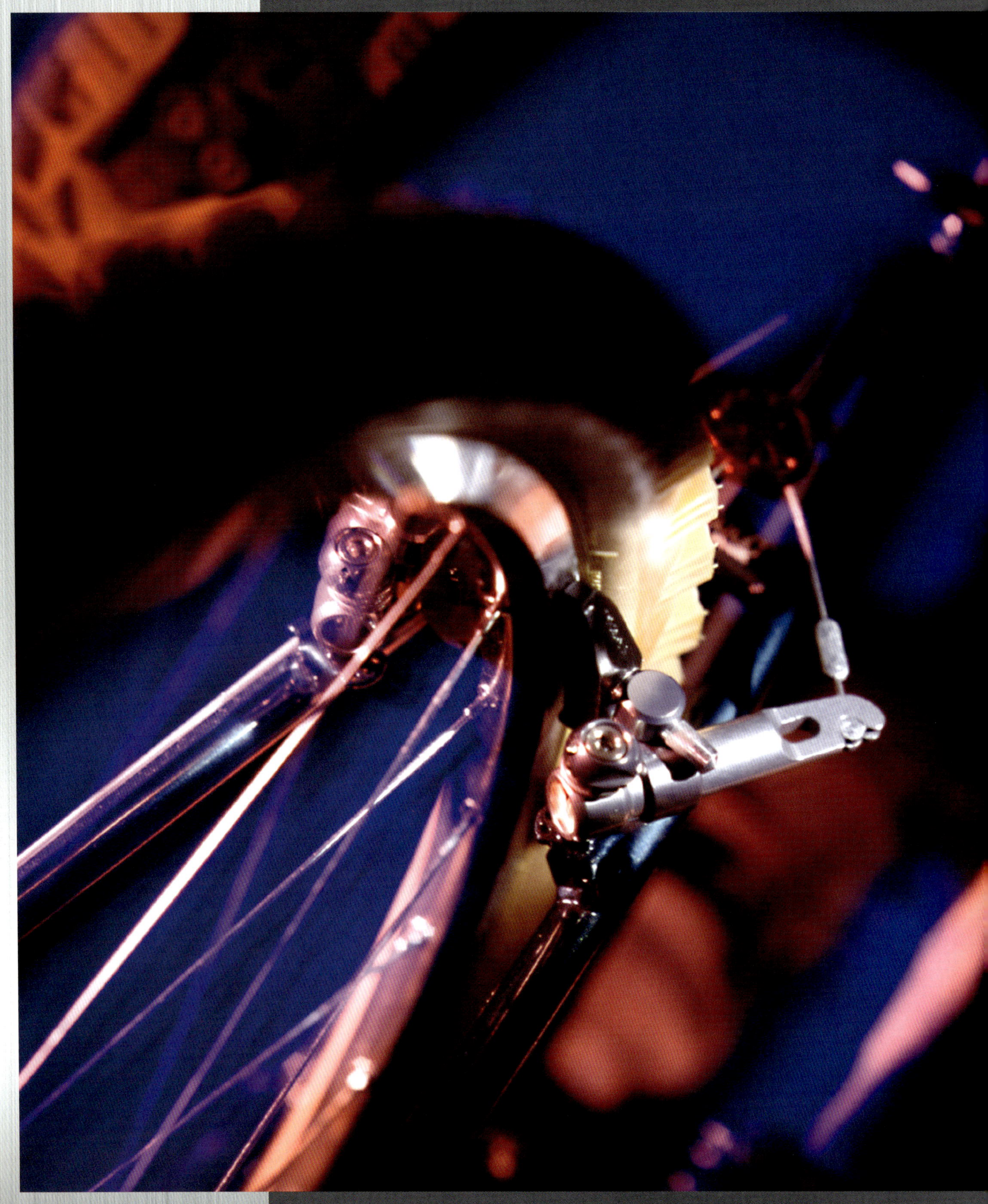

PART 2: PHOTOSHOP

5 SETTING UP PHOTOSHOP

A note about Photoshop, photography, and the process of making a good image:

I worked for a very brief time in the stripping department for a large commercial printer, back in the days before pixels. While there, I made an observation that would be played out time and time again in my career as a commercial photographer. The fact is, in the offset printing process (and in the making of a photograph), you can do almost anything to the image at any time in the process (even pre-Photoshop). However, as you move from the start of a project to the finish, it becomes harder, more time-consuming, and more expensive to make changes while maintaining quality. If you make corrections to the spelling in the galleys, it is faster, cheaper, and looks better than stoning the plate during a press run, but both options are possible.

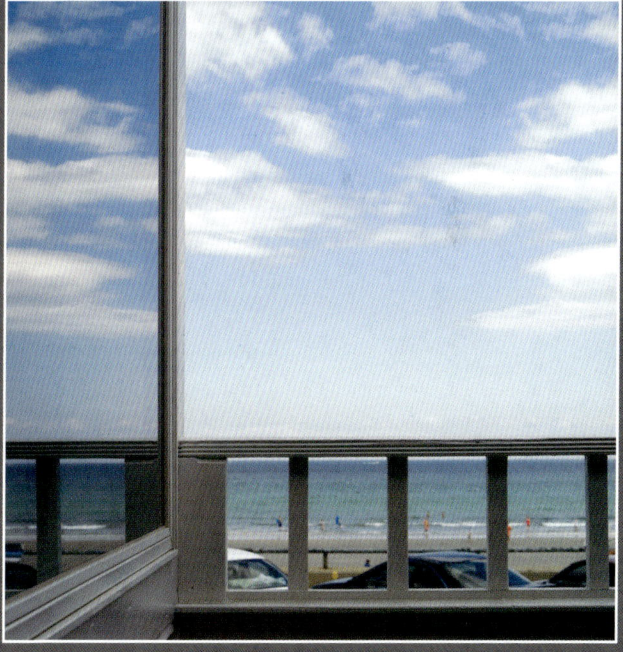

It's just like building a house. If you decide where you want the kitchen at the outset, you can just build it. If the house is built and you decide you want to move the kitchen, you certainly can still move it—it is just harder and more expensive.

In the digital age of photography, we are often tempted to "fix it in Photoshop." The fact is, the same principles apply. The more you can accomplish in the camera, the faster and better you can work. You can fix things down the road in the RAW conversion or in Photoshop, but it's going to take more time and probably not look as good. You can fix problems right before they go to your printer, but that's really opening a can of worms.

When you are shooting digital or film, start with the best you can capture, and move on. In the RAW conversion, get as close as you can to the final print. By the time you get to Photoshop, you should be down to the hair-splitting adjustments so that sending it to the printer is a smooth, predictable process. This habit will make visualizing the final print and "going back to the RAW" that much more powerful.

Tips for Working on a Computer

For most of us who've used our own studio or darkroom, it can be a place devoted solely to work. It can be a haven, a respite from the distractions of the day; it can be a place where you take the phone off the hook, close the door, turn the music on, and concentrate on your work. The darkroom and the studio are a way to shut the world out.

The computer, however, is just the opposite. The machine on your desk is a portal to the entire world. It is anything but a refuge—it is a doorway to endless varieties of distraction.

In a great story by Louis Lesko titled, "Are We Better Off?" *from the magazine* Digital Photo Pro, *(July 8, 2005), Louis talks about working on a print for hours, only to produce nothing usable. He was being constantly distracted by surfing the web, emails, his cell phone, IM, and who knows what else. He then came in to the studio fresh, took virtually everything off the hook, and in about half an hour produced a perfect print.*

So, in the great tradition of Murphy, and with nods to Mr. Lesko, I offer my suggestions for making the worktime in your digital darkroom as productive as it can be.

Teddy's Laws

Law 1: Email is a bottomless pit of time. *As soon as you decide you're going to sit down and do some serious work in Photoshop, a buddy of yours will email you the latest viral clip of the latest pop star doing the latest dumb thing. Next thing you know, you've clicked a link, it's an hour later, and you feel like going out to get coffee.* (Take your email shortcut out of your dock, and off your desktop. Check your email at three specific times

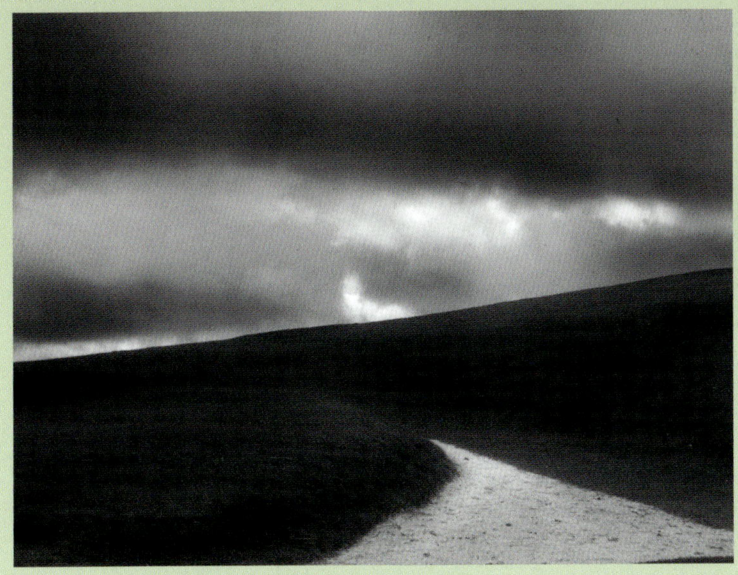

during the day, if you must check it at all. Only respond to emails that cannot wait, during times that you intend to work in Photoshop)

Law 1A: Half of all electronic correspondence is not understood, misunderstood, or ignored. *Any effort to "just take care of this one issue" will spawn an endless trail of misread communication. The confusion will spread exponentially related to the number of people "cc'd" in the email.* (If you email anyone more than three times about the same subject, pick up the phone. If there are more than 3 people "cc'd" on any email, after one response pick up the phone.)

Law 2: IM will always pop up at the most distracting times. *The minute you switch your IM status to "Busy making fabulous photographs, DO NOT BOTHER," everybody on your buddy list figures you don't actually mean THEM, and start to chat you up on the status of the latest viral video clip on the latest pop star doing the latest stupid thing.* (Turn IM OFF during any work sessions. Take your IM shortcut out of our dock and off your desktop.)

Law 3: The Web is, well, a sticky, tangled web. *Just before you roll up your sleeves and start work, you decide to "just check the weather". You notice in the headlines that some pop star has landed in jail from doing something stupid—thus begins a 45 minute surf session that ends in needing a cup of coffee.* (Set specific times for web-surfing. Set a timer if you have to. You guessed it. Remove the shortcuts for our browser from your dock and desktop.)

Law 4: You can never not _answer the phone._ *You've swept all the distractions aside. You're starting to make some progress on that major show that you need to print by next week, and your cell phone rings. You need to pick up pizza, milk, and the latest tabloid.* (Take the phone off the hook. Turn off your cell phone; not the ringer, the phone.)

Law 5: You need to rest your eyes. *You're working hard on an image for hours, doing incredibly brilliant work, and save your work and quit. You go in the next morning and open the file. It's green. Really, really green.* (Your eyes and brain are constantly trying to adapt, to adjust what you see to make it appear neutral. Give your eyes and your head a break by simply looking away occasionally when making color corrections. Think of it like cleansing your palate. Every hour or so, get up and move around. Go outside.)

Law 6: Your available distractions will expand to fill whatever time you have allotted to complete a specific task. *No matter how much time you've set aside to do a job, you can always find something else to do instead that will only "take a minute."* (Stop goofing around. Get to work.)

Get the idea? Make your digital darkroom into your "sanctum santorum." Put up a sign: Do Not Enter When Door is Closed. Darkroom. Keep Out.

Color Settings and Color Management in Photoshop

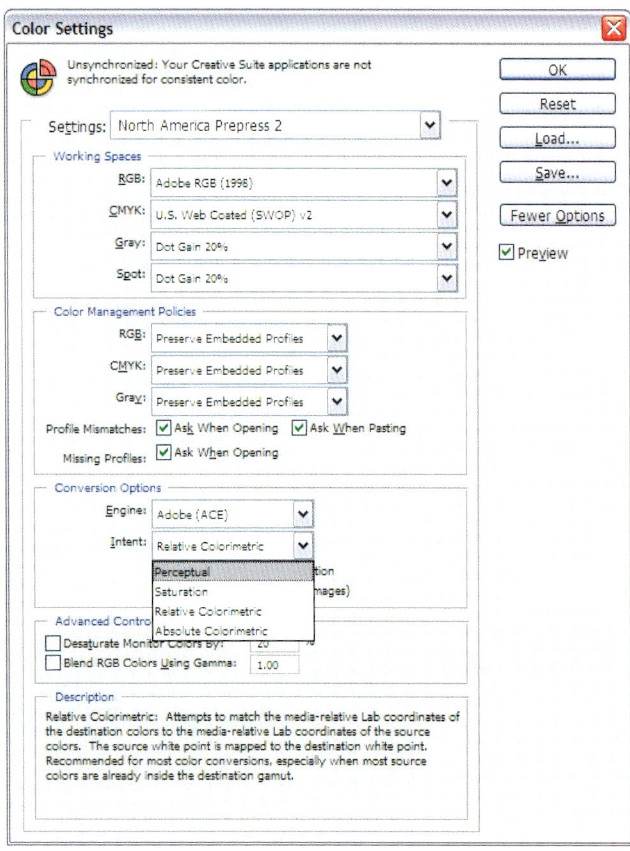

Color management sets up your rules for handling color. As I mentioned earlier, there are two areas we're concerned with—how the computer uses color in controlling the display, and how Photoshop works with color in the computer. Basically, this is all controlled by running a monitor calibration, preferably through using one of the many calibrators, or by running the built-in software that comes with your computer. In my opinion, the calibration device is preferable to the built-in software; it gives you a consistent standard that is not dependent on your personal interpretation of color patches. (Run your system's built-in software once and you'll see what I mean.) Once the computer is playing nice with color, you have to set up Photoshop to display color at an industry standard.

Go to Edit>Color Settings, and click the "More Options" button. The detailed color management policies are there for you to see. From the Settings pull-down menu, select "North America Prepress 2" and you're done.

You'll notice in the diagram to the left I've highlighted "Perceptual" rendering for Intent. This is how we've set things up in the very recent past. Without going into the details of what these policies do, let's just say there's not much practical difference between Relative Colormetric and Perceptual Intent, and in the last year or so I've been flipping between them. Currently, I'm using Perceptual. Close the dialog box and you're done.

Save Button

Before we go any further, let's take a quick look at the Save button in the dialog box. Hitting the Save button saves the settings you have just chosen. If you started with "North America Prepress 2" and changed the Intent to "Perceptual," you'll notice the top pull-down window selection has changed to "Custom." Hit "Save" and you can make a name for the settings you've made and add that to the pull-down menu. If your settings get mysteriously changed, you can simply go into the Settings pull-down menu and select your preferred personal settings. I mention the Save button here, because it appears in almost every dialog in Photoshop, and by getting into the habit of saving your settings for future use, you can develop an incredibly powerful way to work fast and efficiently.

Load Button

You'll also notice the Load button (A). The Load button is a key to working with exact settings consistently. When you use the Save button, you save a small text file on your computer, wherever you've told it to save. (B) In this example I've saved a Levels adjustment in my Documents folder, called project2.alv (the "alv" extension is the Levels identifier; each settings file has it's own extension) (C).

When I hit "Load," I'm taken to a dialog that asks me what I want to load for a Levels file. This gives me

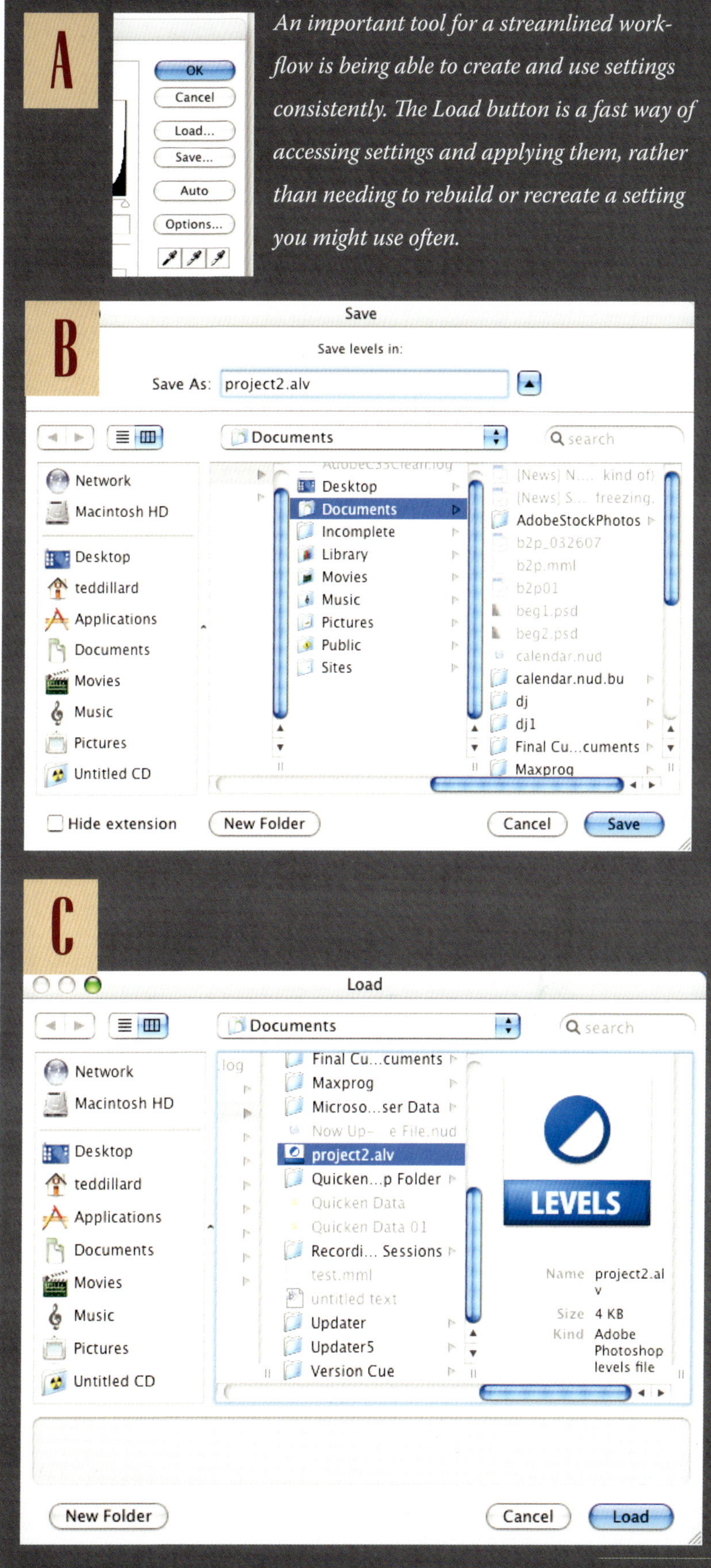

An important tool for a streamlined workflow is being able to create and use settings consistently. The Load button is a fast way of accessing settings and applying them, rather than needing to rebuild or recreate a setting you might use often.

the chance to load my settings file from virtually any location.

For example, if you're just working on one workstation, it's important to organize these settings in a sensible way. In Documents, I like to set up a folder called "work settings." If you are moving between workstations, (in a school environment, at home, or work), you can copy these settings and load them from a jump drive. In a networked environment, you can save standard settings in a central location, (on the server, for example), and everyone on the team can have access to the same settings.

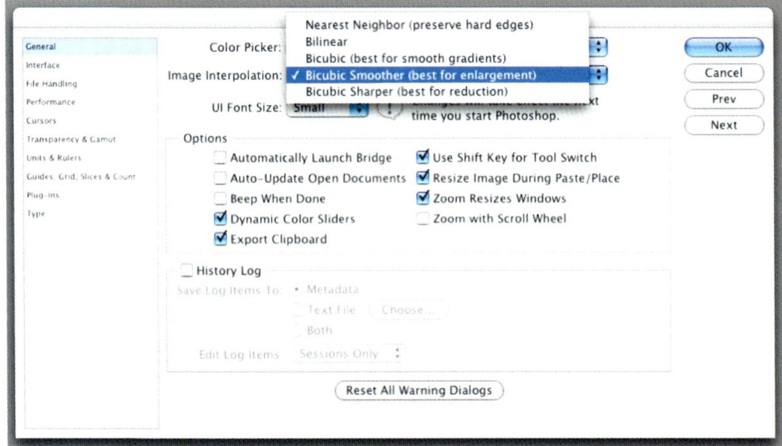

Adobe Photoshop preferences are where you will find most of the options for how Photoshop handles image files. Familiarize yourself with the available options to ensure you are getting the most out of the program, the RAW workflow, and your images.

For example, I have a Curve I like to apply to my Olympus camera file. I "Save" it to my "work settings" folder at home and copy it to my jump drive. When I get to work, I load that curve setting from my jump drive and start working on my file. Also, I can just copy the entire "work settings" folder to my work computer and load it from there, too.

Preferences

Under Photoshop>Preferences (Edit>Preferences in Windows), you'll find all the specifications of how Photoshop will handle things. Start with "General" and scroll through each window using the "Next" button, and you see each personal control setting.

In the General selection, I've chosen the Image Interpolation pull-down, and set it to "Bicubic Smoother," because I frequently size digital images up. (You can read more about this on page 72.)

I mention this because, at some point, you may need to look under the hood and set something up, or reset something to get back to how you like to work. The setting that I change most frequently is the Brush display settings (I add the "Show Crosshair" option), but that's about the extent of my tampering here. Take a look through everything to familiarize yourself with the Preferences options, but my advice is to not mess with it until you need to, unless you are sure of your preferred settings.

Arranging the Photoshop Workspace

This is where you set up your desk. As we talked about in the introduction, setting up your workspace allows you to put everything where you always have it, regardless of where you left it last time, or who's been using it before you. This is a major change in Photoshop CS3. I think it's pretty brave of Adobe to tamper with workspaces.

Remember to keep it simple. There are so many tools and settings in Photoshop, it is easy to get bogged down in an overloaded workspace. If you notice you are consistently using some tools, but not others, customize your workspace.

When you open Photoshop for the first time, you see the Default workspace. Close all of those little windows; most of them you'll never need to see again—remember, we're trying to simplify. Once you've done that, open only the windows that you want. For example, I like to open the Layers window, and set it up on the far right margin. I go to Window>Layers, and the Layers pallet appears on the desktop. I grab it, move it around, and rescale it so it fits where I want it. The default in Photoshop is to open a window with Layers, Channels, and Paths—two of which I don't need. I grab the Layers tab and drag it off to separate it from the other tabs, and I close the Channels and Paths window.

Suppose I use the Info pallet a lot. Again, I go to Window>Info and my Info tab opens, along with the Navigator and Histogram tabs. I can grab the tab for Info and just drag it into my Layers window. Now I have a window with exactly what I want, and no more. I can keep doing this to customize a handy tool-pallet window.

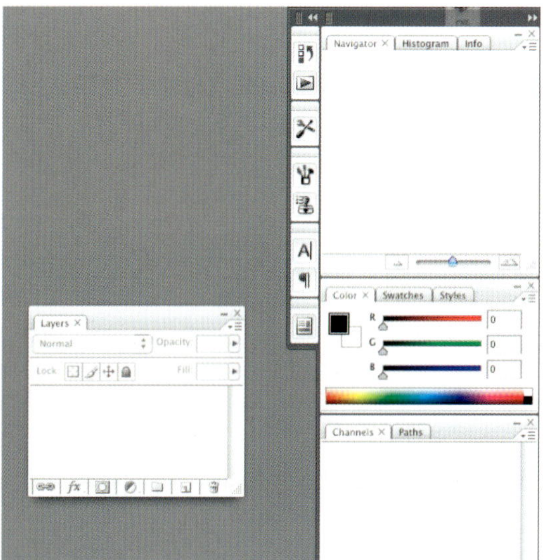

There's another clever little thing here, called the Dock. It sits in the upper right side of the workspace, and shows tabs as well as icons for the tool pallets. The Dock does a drop-down and disappear thing—click on something in the Dock and it drops down; click elsewhere and it disappears. If you want something in the Dock, simply drag the tab of the tool and drop it in the toolbar. Navigator, for example, is a handy thing to have there, because you can quickly refer to it to see where you are, and when you move your cursor it goes away. (To make tabs disappear from the Dock, click and hold the tab, drag it to the main desk, and close the window.)

After I pull out the tabs I want, I resize the window by pulling the corner, moving it to the right side of the desk where I like it, and saving my Workspace. To do this, go to Window>Workspace>Save Workspace and you're done.

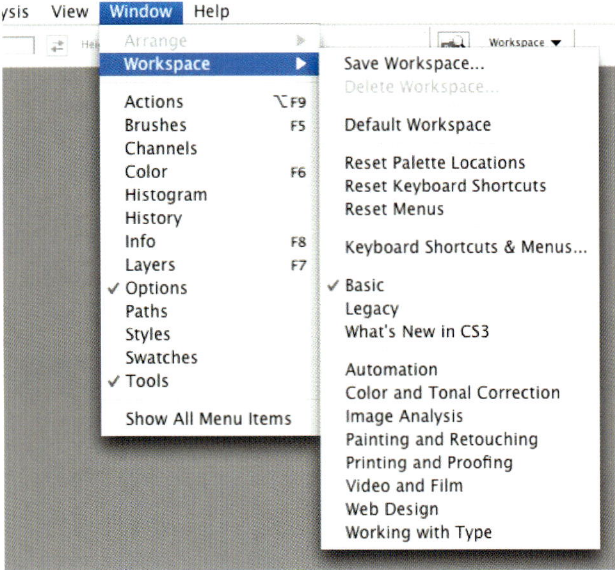

Notice that we are saving settings. By doing this, I can start up Photoshop and immediately reset my tools to exactly where I want them. I can build multiple workspaces, one for editing and adjusting, one for working with Actions, one for my assistant to use, or one for anyone who uses the system. I can get organized and back to my familiar arrangement of tools in a flash. There are some interesting presets here, too. If you're feeling out of sorts with all of this new stuff in CS3, choose the "Legacy" setting, and you'll be right back in what looks like your old digs.

Creating a Data Management Strategy

Now that everything is neat and tidy, you may be tempted to dive in and start working. However, you've got one more thing to do: create a framework for your files. Think of it as putting out the cookie racks before you take the hot cookies out of the oven. If you do this first, you're much more likely to do it correctly and consistently. If you do it while you're working or after you're done, you risk damaging original files, losing your altered files, not making backups, and a whole host of data management-related mistakes.

Once you have created a workspace, save it so you don't have to set it up every time you open Photoshop. You can create multiple workspaces for a variety of things, such as different tasks, users, or workflows.

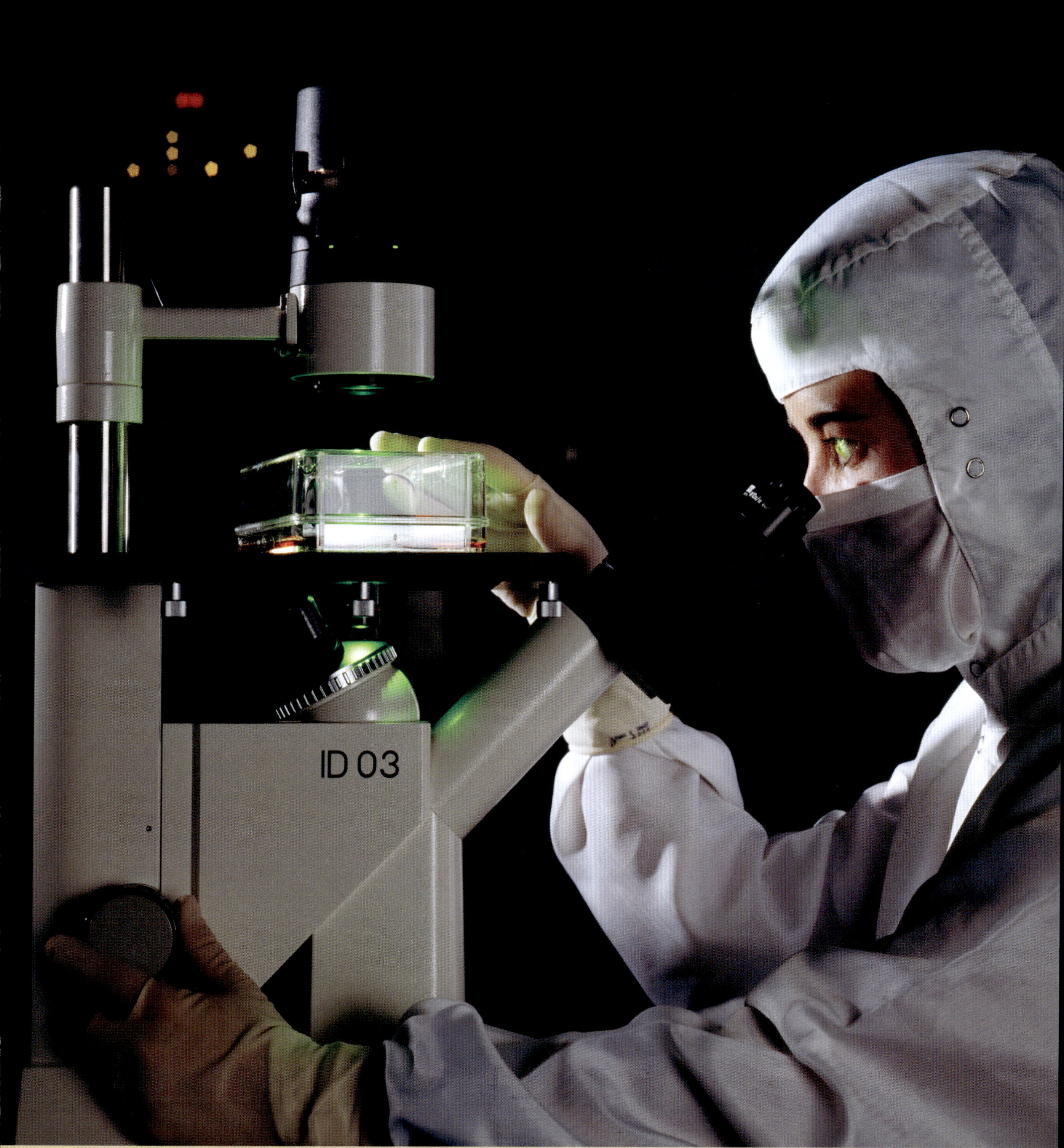
ID 03

RULE 1:

Never work on original files.

This rule is simple enough. Before you even open Photoshop, start by backing up your original files somewhere else. You can burn them to a CD or DVD; drag them to a FireWire hard drive; copy them to another computer on your network; save them to an online FTP site; or whatever you have set up as your strategy to make a backup copy of your data. If you don't have a separate backup option, like a remote hard drive, at the very least copy the files to a different location on your hard drive so you have something to fall back on if you make a mistake.

RULE 2:

Build your work folders first.

To rehash, I typically make a folder on the desktop with the name of the project or job I am working on. I use a simple naming strategy—the same one I created for my film files years ago. The folders are named, for example, 051101pix; "05" is the year, "11" is the month, "01" is the job number, and "pix" is the name of the job, project, or client. So, 051101pix is a project called "Pixel Institute," and it is the first part of that project for November 2005.

Inside that folder, I make several other folders. I usually start with a "RAW" folder, maybe add a "Select" folder, and if it's a project that is going to need work prints and finals, I make a "Working" folder. I copy all my RAW files to the "RAW" folder, and make a backup elsewhere. I use Adobe Bridge to sort and copy files to the "Select" folder, and as I create layered TIFF files I save them to the "Working" folder. Before I shut down, I again make a backup of everything by dragging the whole "051101pix" folder to my remote hard drive. Now my files are set up before I start working in Photoshop. I try to set it up the same way every time.

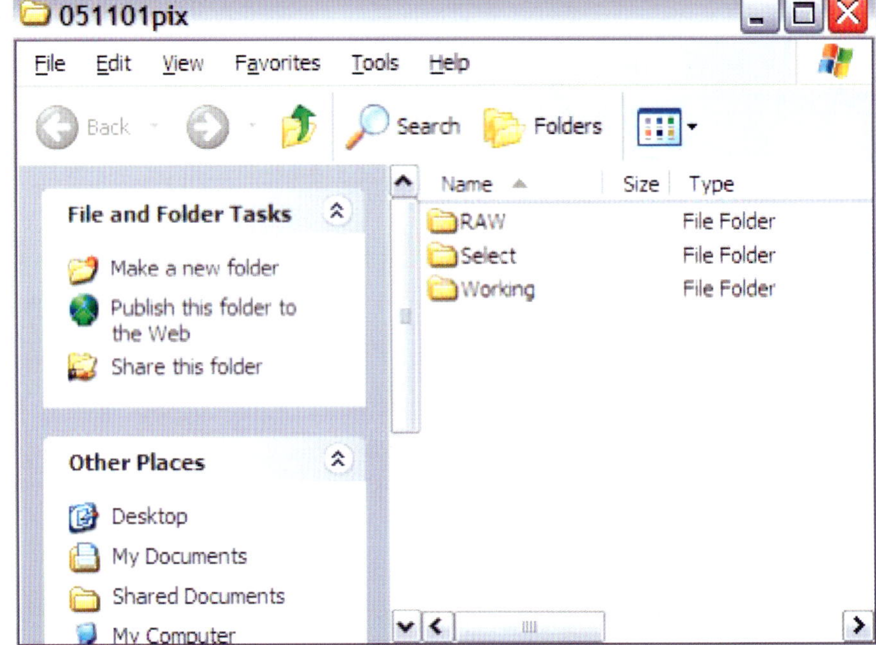

The most important step of a good workflow is building your management strategy. Do this first to save yourself time and to protect your images files.

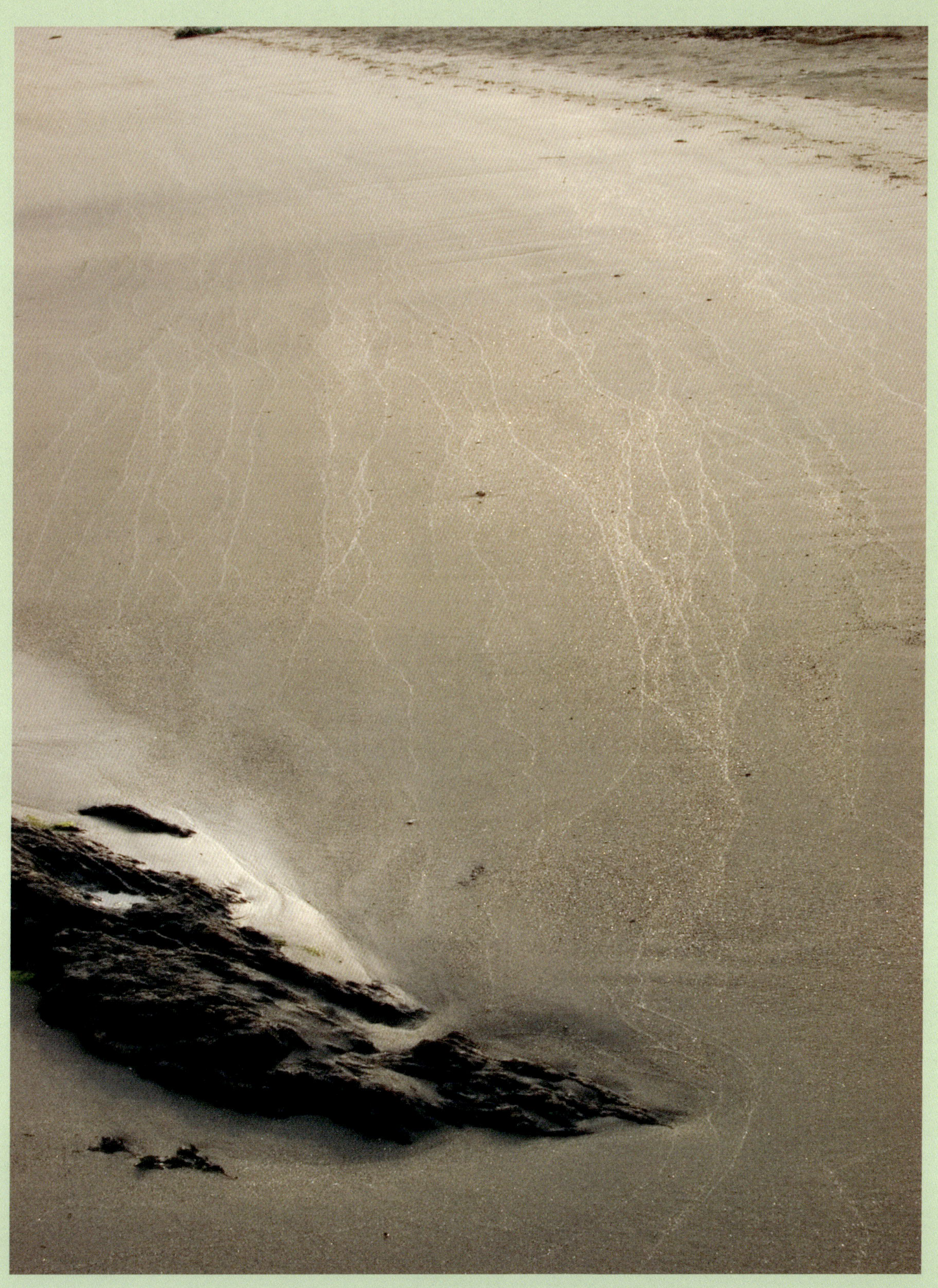

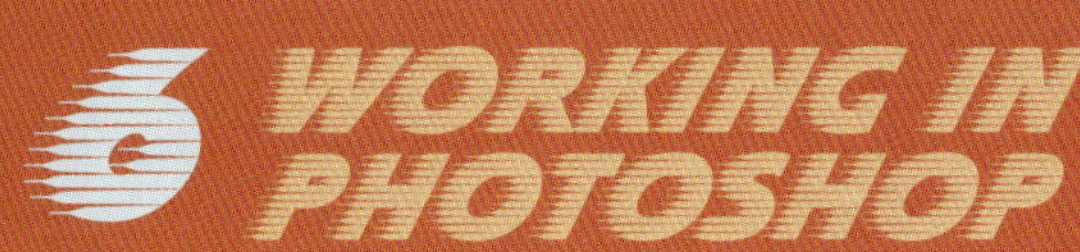

6 Working in Photoshop

Sizing

One of the easiest and most intuitive things a photographer does in the darkroom is to decide on the image size and adjust it. You put the negative in the enlarger, and enlarge it to the size you want to make the print. In Photoshop, there are multiple controls that make the process a bit harder to grasp because, perhaps for the first time, you're looking at each individual mechanism used to make an image larger or smaller.

The first thing to grasp is that the digital image is made up of pixels, and a pixel is nothing more than a square of color. You can make that pixel big or small, depending on the resolution you choose or how you want to display that pixel. That is your pixels per inch (ppi) determination. The image at the right is a sample of the pixels from one of my images (A). Right now, by my estimation, it is being displayed at roughly 7 ppi, because you can see 7 pixels covering one inch. If I take the same group of pixels and shrink it down to half the size, I have the same number of pixels in half the space. Those 7 pixels are now in a half-inch space, so it displays at 14 ppi (B).

The Image Size Dialog

Just so we're clear, you're going to have to get the "dpi" rant. There is no such thing as "dpi." In Photoshop we use ppi, which are pixels per inch. Epson printers claim resolution of up to 2880 dpi, and, if you must use dpi there, at least call it "droplets per inch," not dots. Offset printers use the term "lpi," or "lines per inch," which is ironic because they are, in fact, the only people who are actually making dots per inch. Resolution charts for optics are set up in "line-pairs per mm." But since we're using Photoshop, we use ppi.

I make a point of this because, like all imprecise language, using the wrong term leads to confusion. For example, if you are sizing an image in Photoshop and you think that the ppi is the same as the dpi, you might get all befuddled when you get to the "Quality" selection in the printer and you see you need 1440 dpi for Luster paper. The printer driver is different. It uses different sizes of droplets of ink. In Photoshop,

When you increase or decrease your ppi, you are not adding more or subtracting pixels—you are directing the pixels to show at a certain size.

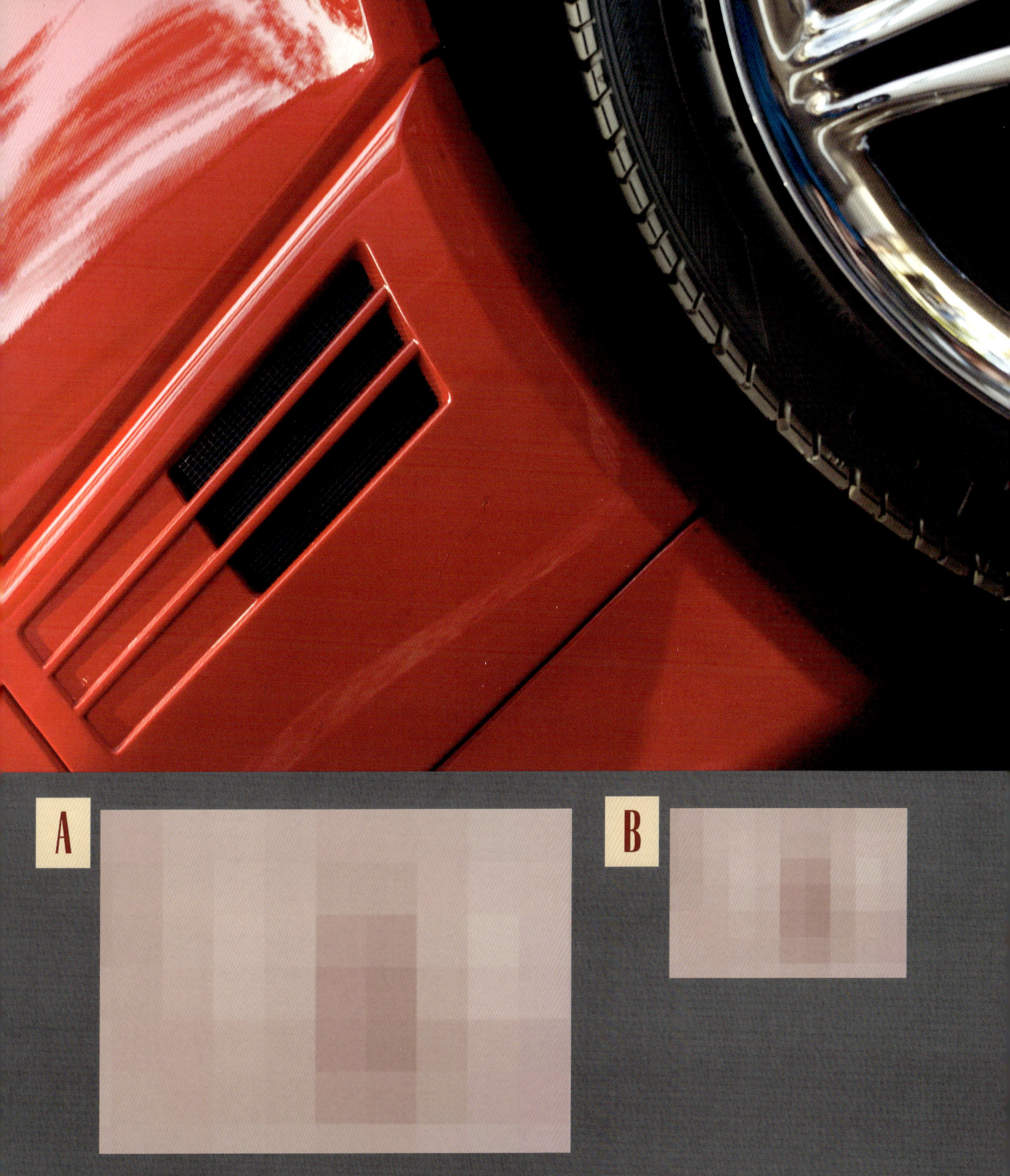
A
B

we use ppi. We'll talk more about what the printer needs from Photoshop to make a good print on page 154.

So let's take a look at the Image Size dialog (A). Go to Image>Image Size, and you'll see that the Image Size dialog is separated into two basic windows: Pixel Dimensions and Document Size. Pixel Dimensions does two things: it shows you what you're starting with, and gives you the absolute number of pixels for the width and height of the image. This is independent of the image resolution. The number of pixels is the number of pixels; the resolution is how you're going to display those pixels. The Document Size section of the Image Size dialog shows you what happens to your image depending upon what you do to those pixels.

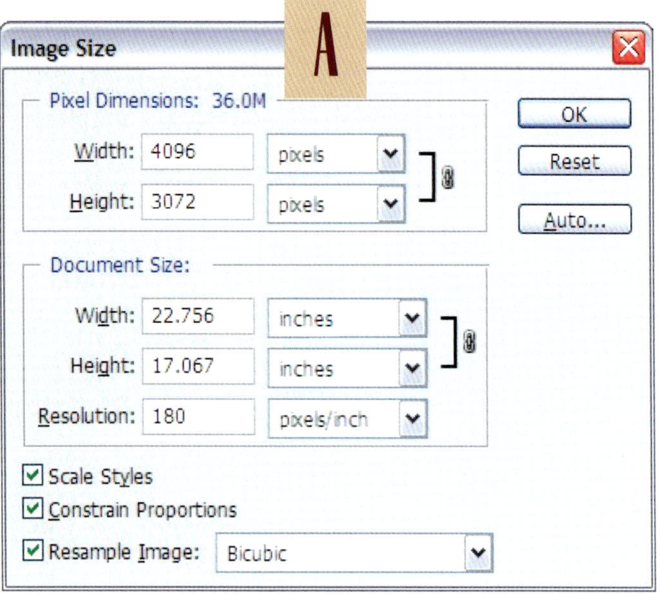

In this example, I'm starting with an image that is 4096 pixels wide and 3072 pixels high (4096 x 3072 pixels). The Document Size tells me how big my picture is going to be at a certain resolution. This example says that if I put 180 of those pixels within one inch (180 ppi), I'll have an image that will print at 22.756 x 17.067 inches (578 x 433.5 mm).

If I deselect "Resample Image" and change the Resolution value, I can see what size the image will display at for different resolutions. If I increase the ppi number, (meaning that I want more of the original pixels to be within one inch), the image is going to display smaller. If I decrease the ppi number (fewer pixels fitting within an inch), my photo is going to display larger.

We'll go into some concrete examples, but before we do that I just want to add that the Resample Image box allows you to change the absolute Pixel Dimensions of the image. You're taking one pixel, for example, and breaking it into multiple pixels (if you're sizing up), or taking multiple pixels and combining them into one pixel (if you're sizing it down). For the record, this is Resampling, not Interpolating. Again, precision in language helps you understand the concepts.

Let's take this image straight from the memory card and make it into an image that is going to print at 8 x 10 inches (203.2 x 254 mm) on my Epson 2400 printer. I know by looking at the dialog that the image is 4096 x 3072 pixels, and

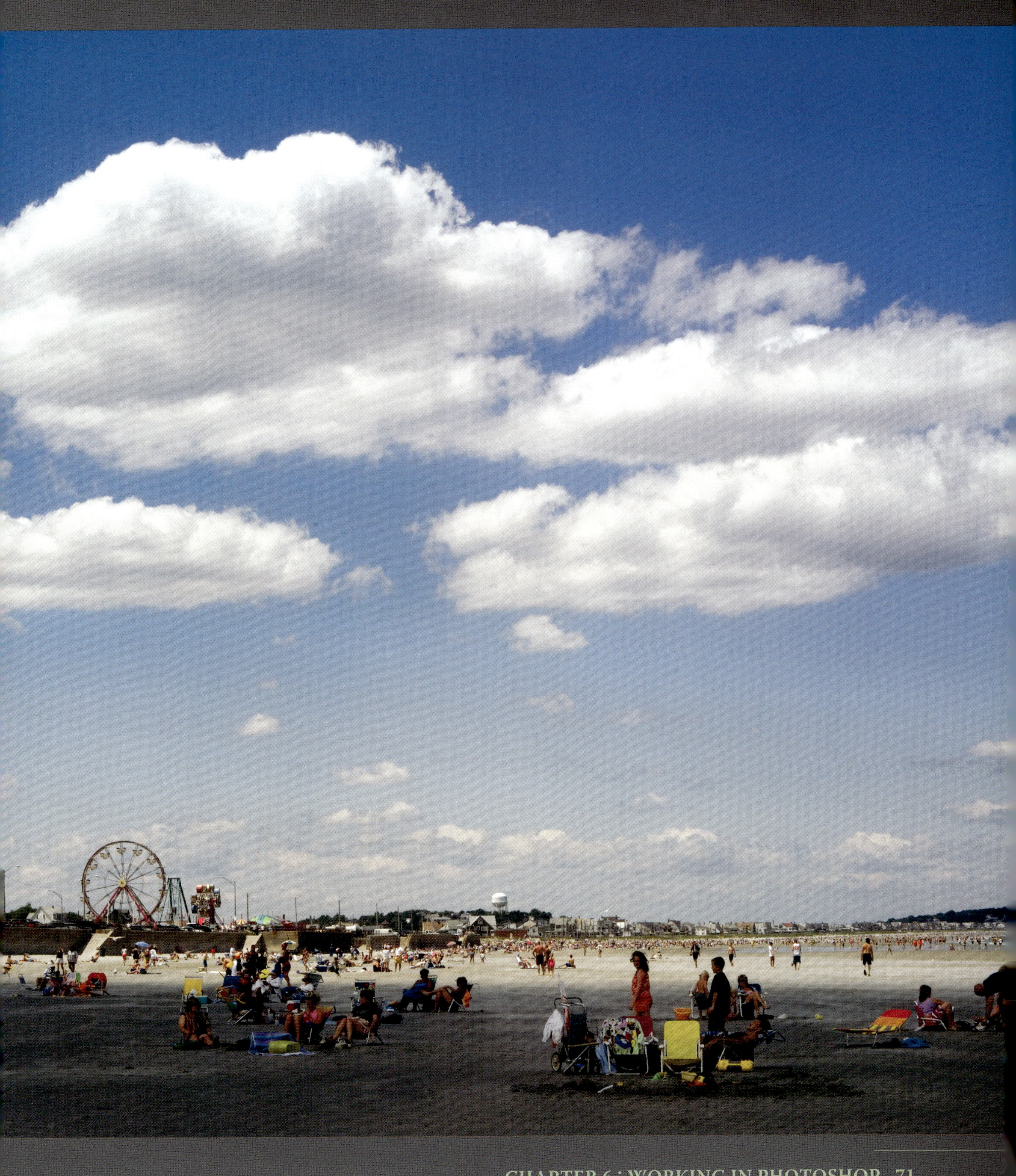

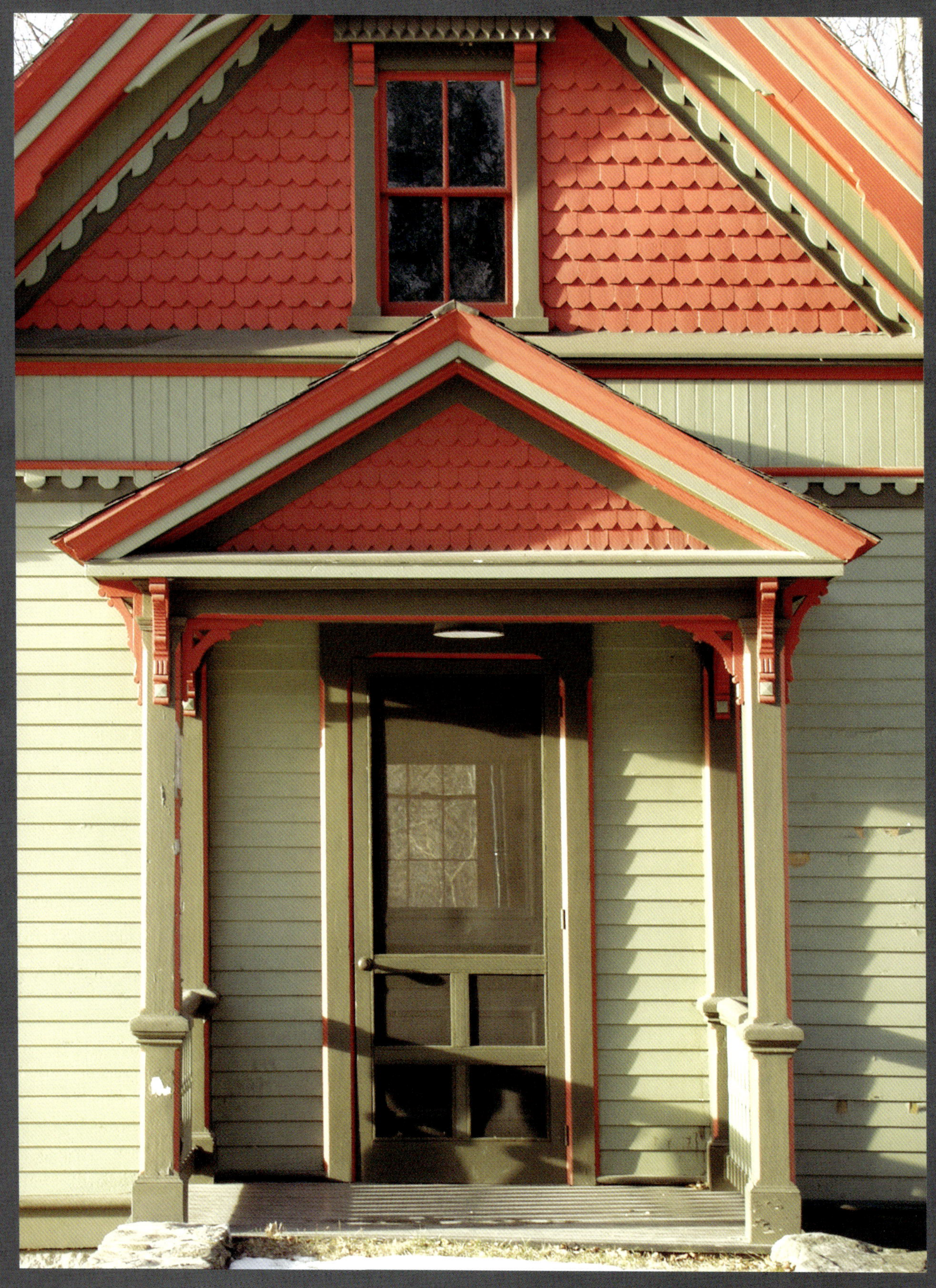

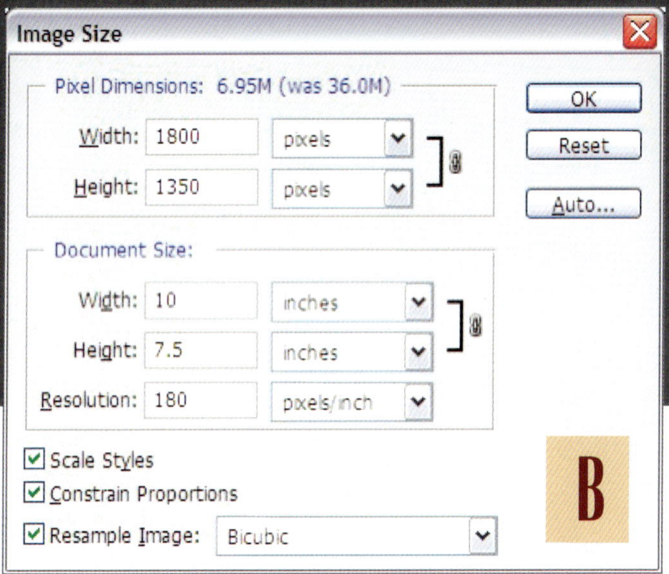

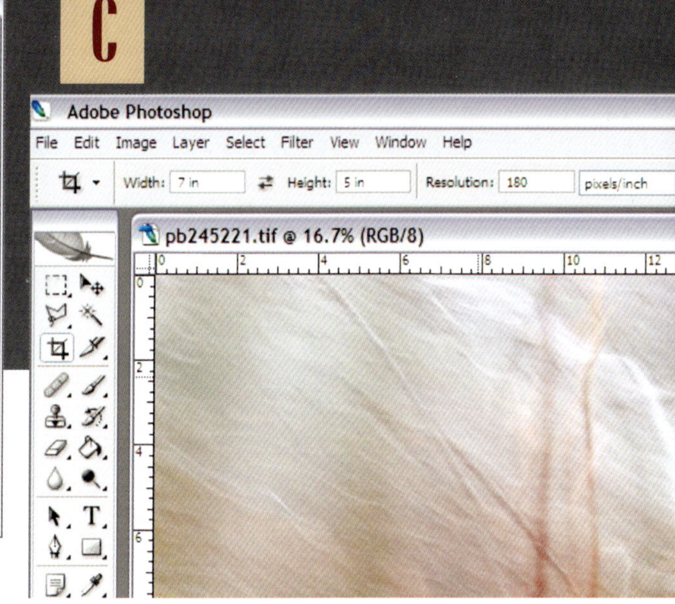

at a resolution of 180 ppi it's going to print too big—22.7 x 17 inches (578 x 433.5 mm), to be specific.

What do I do? I check "Resample Image" and, leaving the Resolution value at 180 ppi, I simply type in the width or height I want, in this case, a width of 10 inches (254 mm). (B) I find that the height goes to 7.5 inches (190.5 mm). This is fine because I've constrained the proportions, and the Pixel Dimensions now show as 1800 x 1350 pixels, or 6.95 megabytes (MB). I've taken 4096 pixels and recalculated them to amount to only 1800 pixels because that is all I need to print this image at 180ppi at 8 x 10 inches (203.2 x 254 mm).

You might be wondering why I chose the Resolution value of 180 ppi. 180 ppi is what I've determined works best on my Epson 2400 to print on Luster paper at the 1440 "dpi" print quality setting. The resolution, in ppi, is a number that is determined by your output device, whether that's a printer, monitor, or something else (such as a film recorder). 180 ppi is the optimum resolution for my printer. We'll talk more about this later on, but for now, find out what you need for your printer, and use that for your Resolution value. The simplest way to determine that is to run a few test prints.

A couple of quick points:

If you want to resize quickly to a very specific size and crop, you can do that with the Crop tool. In the main toolbar, select the Crop Tool and specify the output size and resolution in the bar that appears at the top left of your workspace. Here (C) I've chosen the dimensions 5 x 7 inches (127 x 177.8 mm) at 180 ppi. This constrains my crop to the proportions of my final image, and resamples the image to whatever size I've asked for. A good thing to know is that it uses the Resampling method I have set in the Preferences, which is Bicubic Smoother.

Also, as far as that Resampling method goes, in Photoshop CS3 you probably want to use "Bicubic Smoother" for sizing digital camera files up, and "Bicubic Sharper" for sizing scanned or digital camera files down.

NOTE: Sizing scanned files up, regardless of the sampling method, is bad. Bad, bad, bad.

HINT: Go back and rescan at a higher resolution.

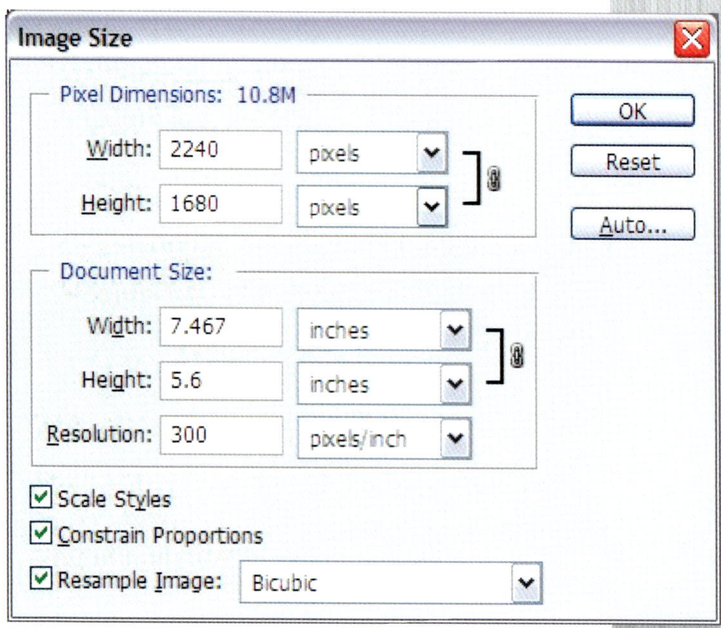

Examples:

Let's recap with some specific jobs.

Job 1: Size photos from a digital camera to a work print, fitting on an 8.5 x 11 inch (A4) sheet of paper.

I import my image from my Olympus E10, and select Image>Image Size to get to the sizing dialog. This shows me the original size of my image in the Pixel Dimension dialog. In this case, for this camera, the dimensions are 2240 x 1680 pixels, which sizes to 7.467 x 5.6 inches (189.66 x 142.24 mm) at a resolution of 300 ppi.

Just to see what I'm doing, I'm going to uncheck the "Resample Image" dialog to see what happens when I change the resolution to something lower. If I put in a resolution value of 224 ppi, I find my width goes right to 10 inches (254 mm), and my height is at 7.5 inches (190.5 mm); this will be just fine for my work prints.

Notice that I have not changed the Pixel Dimensions at all. As soon as I uncheck "Resample Image," I can't alter the pixel count, so my file suffers no destructive edits. This is great, especially for a working file, because I have no idea where I'm going with this. I may print bigger or smaller, and since I've not resampled, I can go from here with original data. Granted, 224 ppi is an odd number.

Job 2: Resize and crop to exactly 4 x 6 inches (101.6 x 152.4 mm) for prints for Grandma.

My first issue here is to make sure my resizing preference is what I want. For general work, I'm going to leave it at "Bicubic" (Photoshop>Preferences>General, under the Image Interpolation selection).

Now I use the Crop tool. At the top toolbar I put in my dimensions: 6 inches (152.4 mm) wide and 4 inches (101.6 mm) tall at 180 ppi. I click and drag the crop, and it constrains the proportion to a 6 x 4 inch (152.4 x 101.6 mm) aspect ratio, resamples, and resizes the image. Bingo! I've got exactly a 4 x 6 inch (A6) print.

Don't worry. The shot in Figure (A) really is blurry. Your vision isn't going bad.

Since I'm not doing a dramatic resize, and it's only a 4 x 6 print (A6), the resampling method is not critical. If I resize an image up from a digital camera file, I'd want to go in and reset my Preferences to "Bicubic Smoother" to get the best performance from the Crop tool.

The Crop tool is fast and easy, but like most easy things it doesn't allow for the specific controls needed to do high quality work. If you're really concerned with exactly how the image is resized, use the Image Size window.

Job 3: Resize for the web.

Here's a trick question. What is the "Document" when you're working on the web? Answer: the "Document" is what gets displayed on your computer's monitor. The "Document Resolution" for a computer monitor, by general consensus, is 72 ppi. If you want to find out how large an image is going to display, simply uncheck "Resample Image" and plug 72 into the resolution value.

A

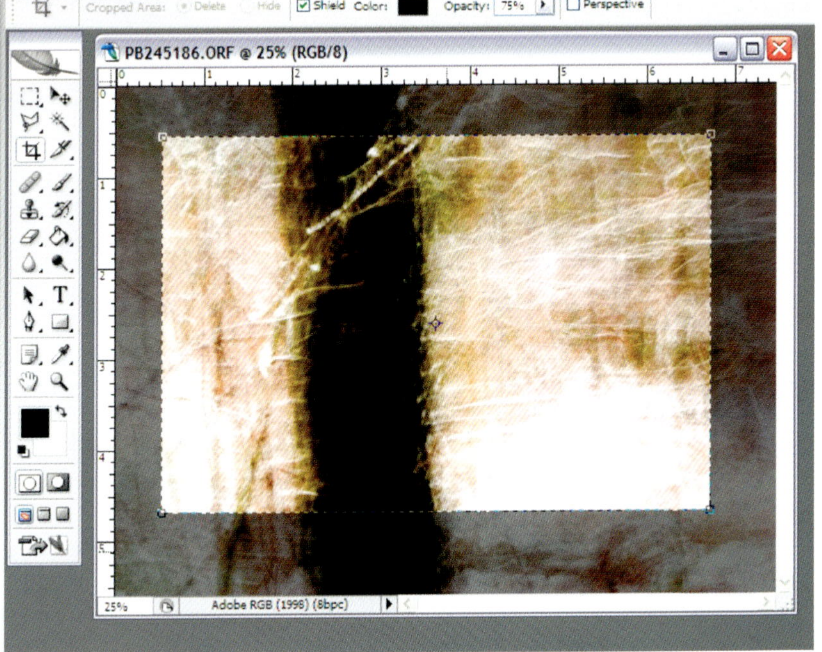

You can resize images a variety of ways; the two most common are in the image size dialog or with the Crop tool.

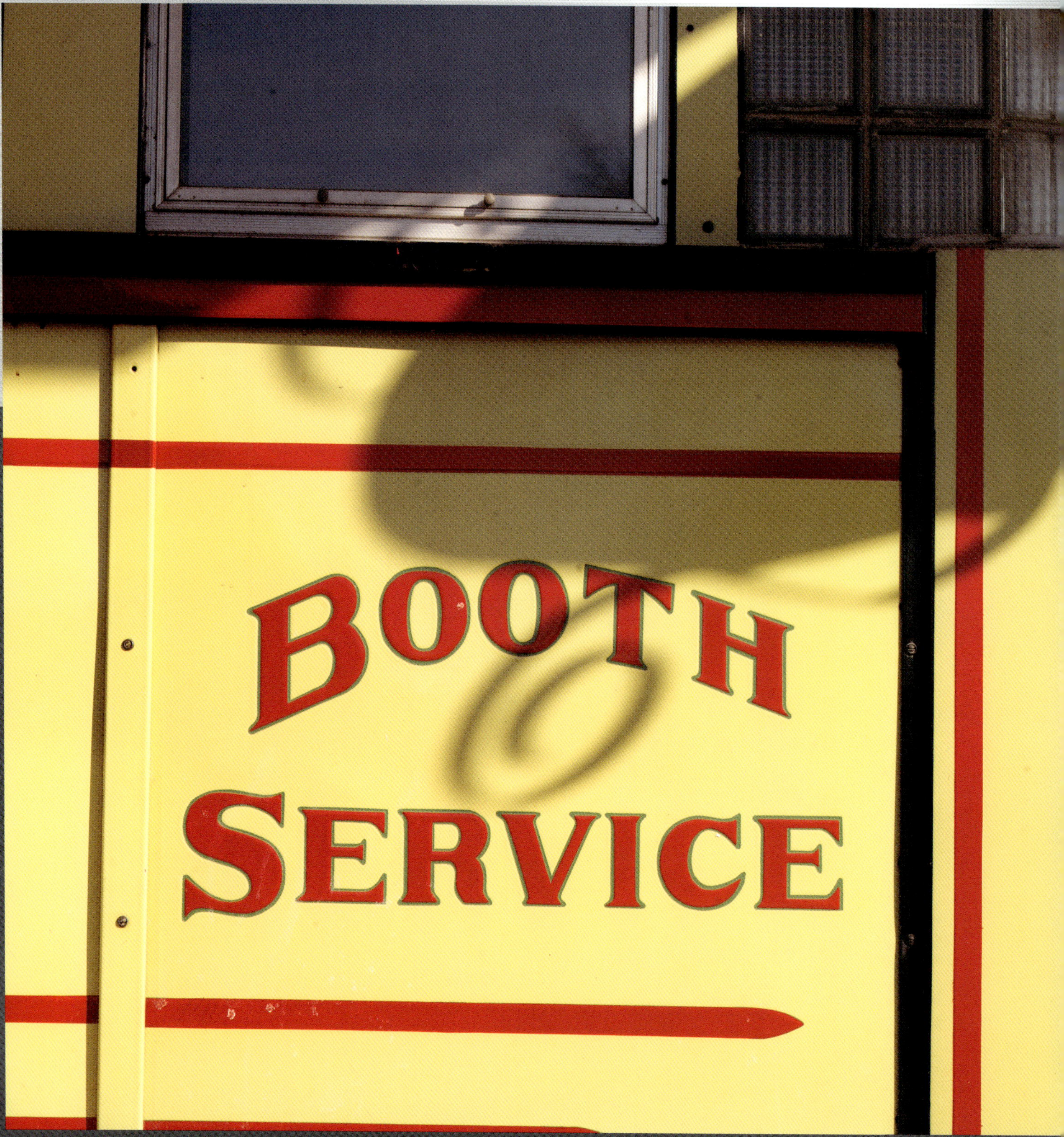

I have an image that I want to appear roughly 4 inches (101.6 mm) wide on my website. I have unchecked "Resample Image," put in 72 ppi, and then rechecked "Resample Image." In the width section under Document Size, I put in 4 inches (101.6 mm). At this point I'm done, but before I hit OK, I want to take a look at my new Pixel Dimensions value.

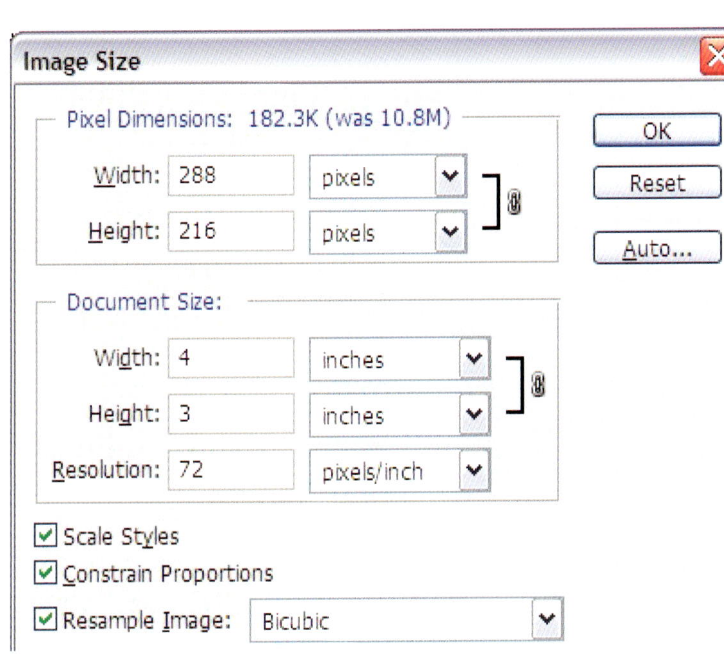

When sizing an image for the web, be sure to set the resolution to 72 ppi. If you are resizing several images, check out the pixel dimension value of the resized image as a guide to how large or small your other images need to be.

If I have more images that I need to optimize for the web at 4 inches (101.6 mm) wide, I now know that all I need to do is Resample the files to 288 pixels wide. I put 288 into the box, and, regardless of what the resolution says, it will display on my viewer's screen as around 4 inches (101.6 mm) wide. How do I know this? The resolution is dependent upon the Document, and the Document is the viewer's display. As long as I send them a file that is 288 pixels wide and I'm pretty sure it's going on a display that is at 72 ppi, then the Document Resolution in the Image Size window is irrelevant.

The Layer Strategy

Adjusting an image can be done any number of ways. In my opinion, however, using Adjustment Layers is the most powerful, the most versatile, and the best foundation with which to start learning the process. It is the process with the most potential for advanced development, and, above all, the most intuitively "photographic" method.

Adjustment Layers

Instead of using the adjustment tools found in Image>Adjust, I have the Layers palette open and I'm using Adjustment Layers through the Layer>New Adjustment Layer command, or through what I call the "oreo cookie-like" icon, a half-black, half-white circle at the bottom of the Layers palette (A).

Even if you are intimidated or confused by Layers at first, try making your adjustments here. You can make all the same adjustments this way, slowly pick up bits and pieces of the Layered working method, and absorb the concepts. Think of it in terms of learning to type. The traditional method teaches you to keep your

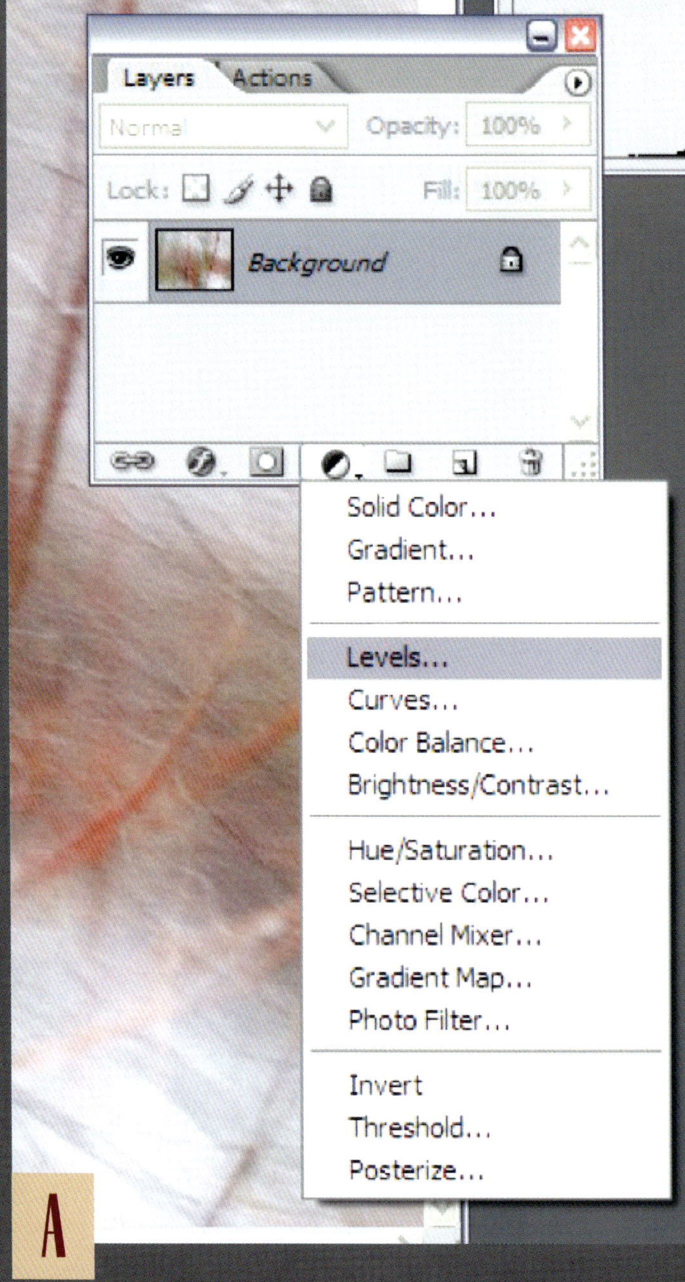

Adjusting an image with an adjustment layer is one of the best ways to create a powerful RAW workflow. This will be your foundation for going to back to the RAW file to make image adjustments, adding information to the image file rather than eroding it, and keeping track of the adjustments that you have made. It is an extremely versatile and effective technique, and is the cornerstone of a streamlined workflow.

fingers in the "home" position, even if you have to look at the keys. That way, you'll learn good habits and a reflex that you can build on to develop your skills. If you get into the habit of adjusting with Adjustment Layers, you're starting on the right foot.

Levels and the Histogram

I want to address the two most basic adjustment tools in Photoshop—Levels and Curves. The reason for this approach is that every adjustment tool is, in some way, manipulating one or both of these two basic tools, Levels or Curves. I don't object to using the "sliders" as long as you do it with a strong understanding of the way that slider is manipulating the curve or the histogram. My experience has been that once you understand the basic tools, the sliders seem useless.

The Levels dialog shows a histogram chart, and the histogram is the single most powerful bit of information you can have as a photographer. Simply put, it is a graph of the black and white tones in an image. The height (which I rarely pay attention to) is the number of pixels in the image at that tonal value. The range from black to white is on the scale of 0 – 255, and is usually a "Master," meaning it is an average of the three RGB channels (red, green, and blue). Using the histogram, I can see exactly what tonal values I have in my image, and more specifically, where they fall in terms of pure black and pure white. The Levels dialog at the right shows that the tonal range in this example is fairly flat. I have nothing that registers as pure black, or 0, and very little that is pure white, or 255.

I usually start my adjustment process with the Levels dialog because it is the most global adjustment—it affects the entire image. I like to work in Layers from the base up. I make the biggest adjustments at the bottom, and then refine as I build up Layers. We'll see more of this as we move forward, but as far as adjustments go, Levels is the most basic.

Let's look at the window. We have the usual OK and Cancel buttons, as well as the handy Load and Save buttons, which we talked about earlier. A quick note—if you hold down the "Alt" key you'll notice that the Cancel button turns into "Reset," which is shown in the figure above. This allows you to go back to your starting point without having to close the dialog and re-open it.) You have the upper section of the dialog, called Input Levels, and the lower part, Output Levels. The Input Levels section allows you to grab the ends of the histogram and stretch it out. You can go into what is a value of 20 and pull it to 0, and grab 240 and pull it up to 255. The Input Levels increases your contrast by selecting tones and forcing them to represent 0 (pure black) and 255 (pure white).

Let's have a demonstration. Start with the Levels window shown (A). In the Input Levels section, grab and drag the far left shadow point from 0 and put it at 40 (B). When I hit OK, it takes those tones at 40 and pulls them down to 0, and everything else follows in suit. Look at the resulting histogram in the next figure (C). It is essentially the same shape, only redistributed over a wider tonal range. We've taken an image that was fairly flat and forced the dark gray tones (at 40) to become black (0). (Granted, there's still only small amount of black, shown as a thin dark line in the histogram.)

You can see the missing tonal values where the histogram shows gaps in the black, showing up because of how you have stretched out the tones (also known as "tonal stretch"). You are not creating anything by stretching the histogram—you are just pulling out the little information you have, like flattening out pizza dough. This demonstrates a fundamental truth about working in Photoshop that you should know. Every edit or adjustment you make is erosive. What I did in the above example was throw out all the information from 40 and below and massage the remaining data to cover it. I'm not adding more information. The more I adjust the file, the more information I erode from the image file. Later we'll go into dealing with high-bit depth files and RAW workflow.

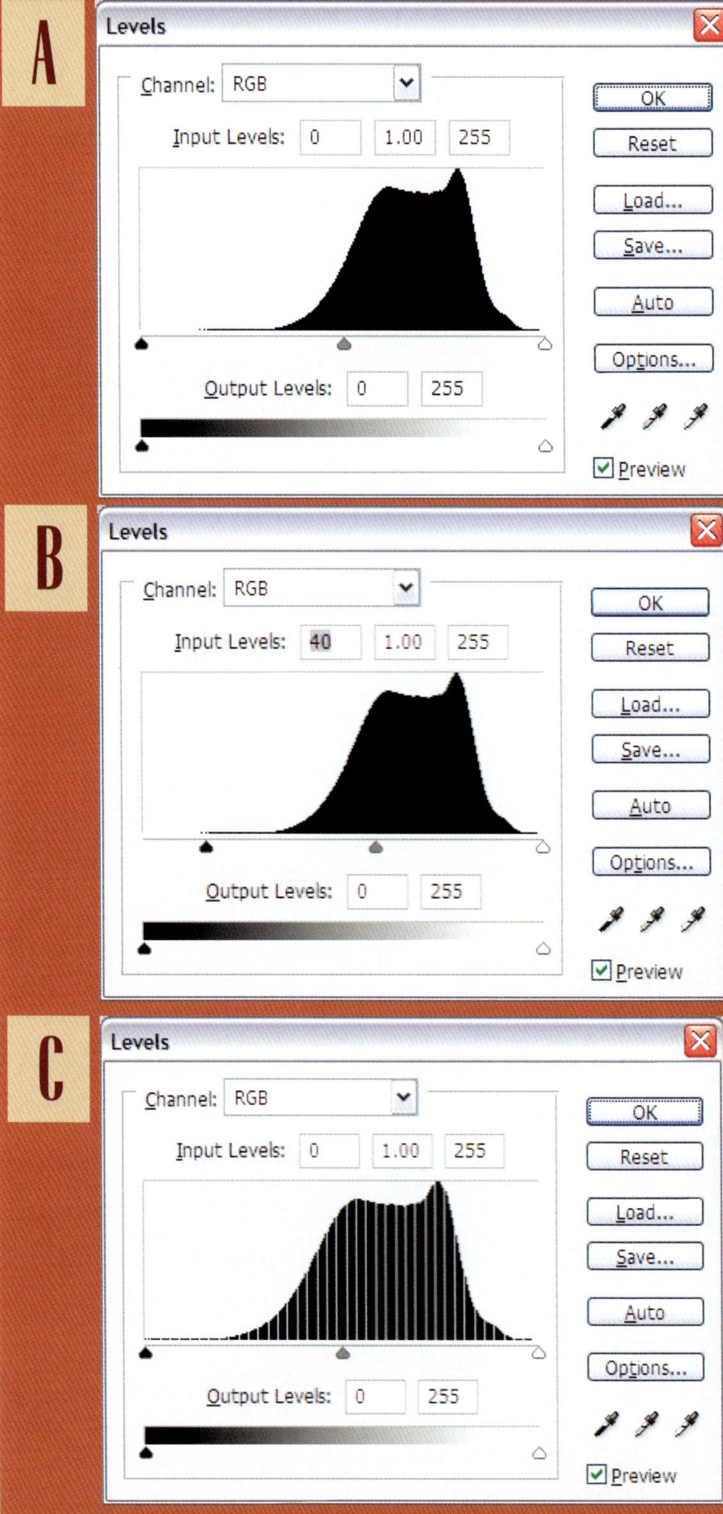

A histogram shows you where your image might be missing tonal information. Every time you make an adjustment on the image file in Photoshop, it will change the histogram—removing image information—because adjusting an image in Photoshop is erosive.

The histogram is no longer a solid black graph. You can now see white lines throughout the black areas of the histogram, and, keeping in mind that the histogram is a graph of the tonal values of the image, you're seeing holes in that tonal range. The white lines represent gaps, or missing information in the image. This shows in a print as banding, or posterization (areas of color with no subtle transitions). You've taken a given amount of information and stretched it out—like pizza dough stretched too thin and getting holes.

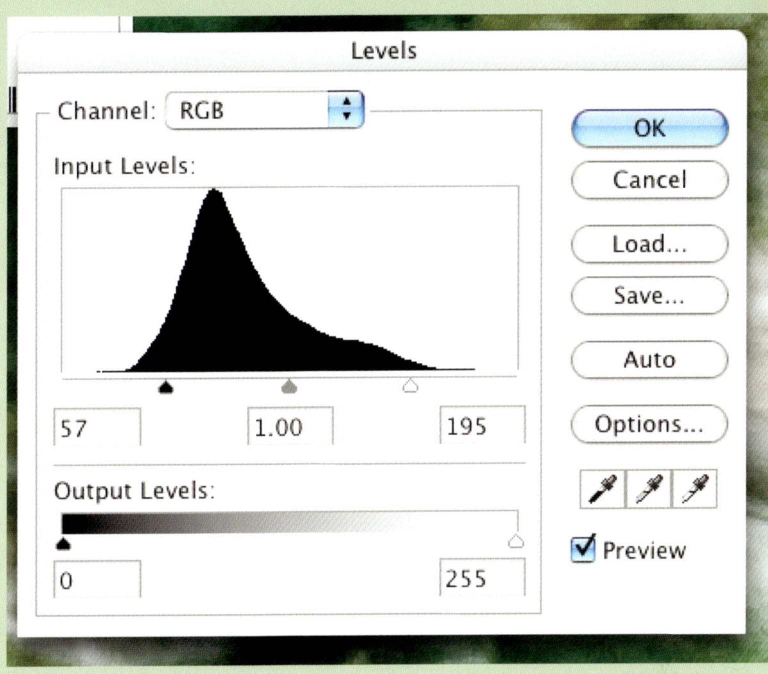

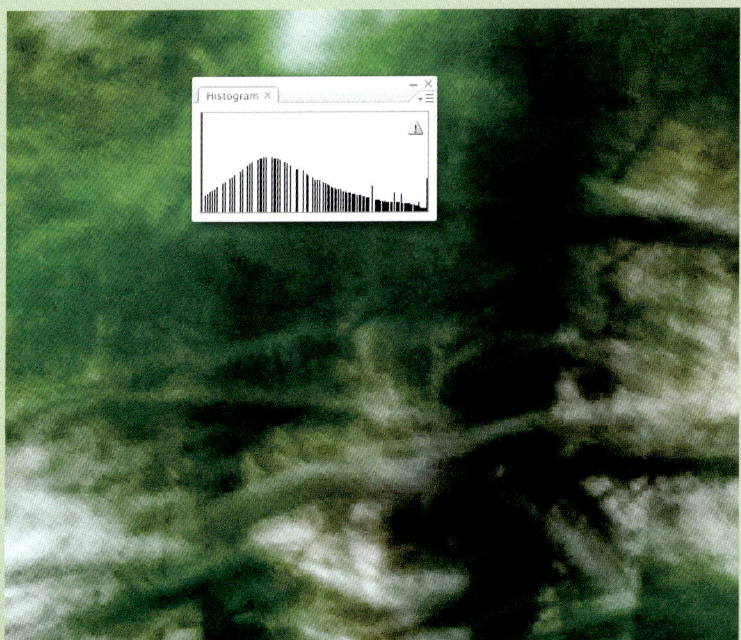

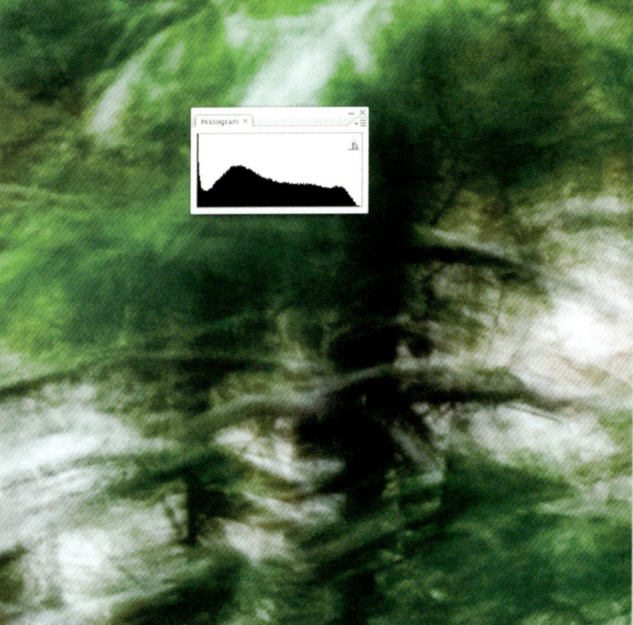

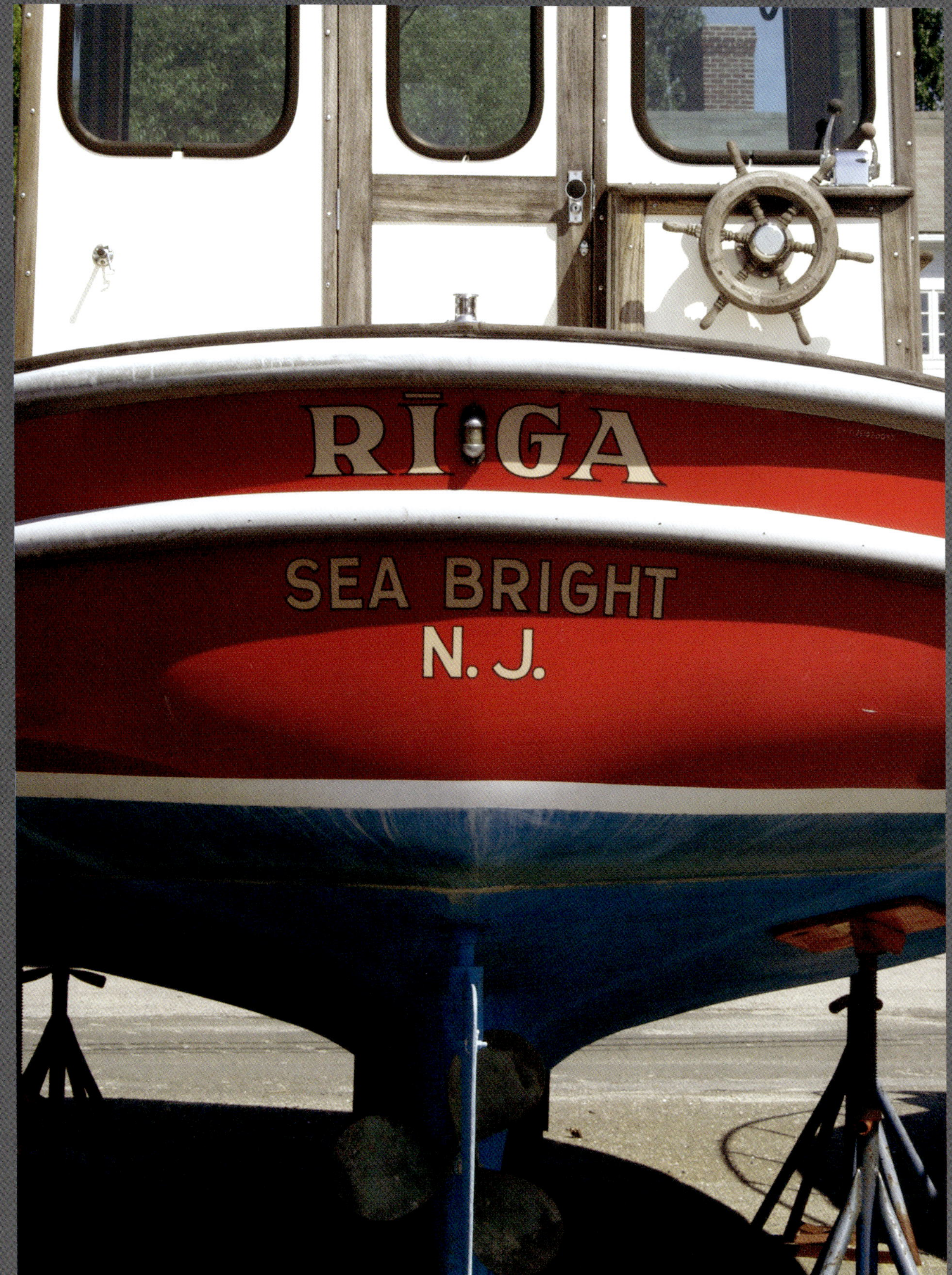
RĪGA
SEA BRIGHT
N. J.

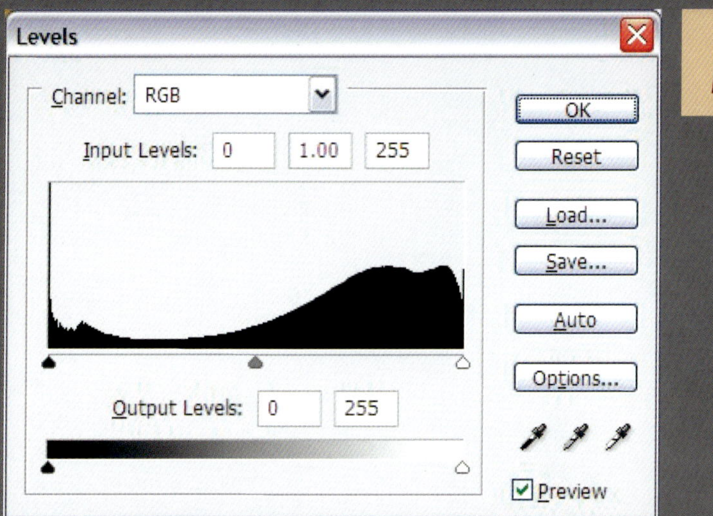

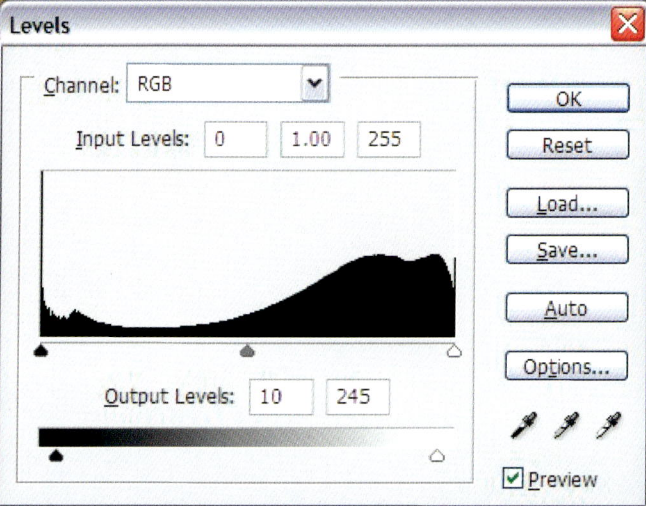

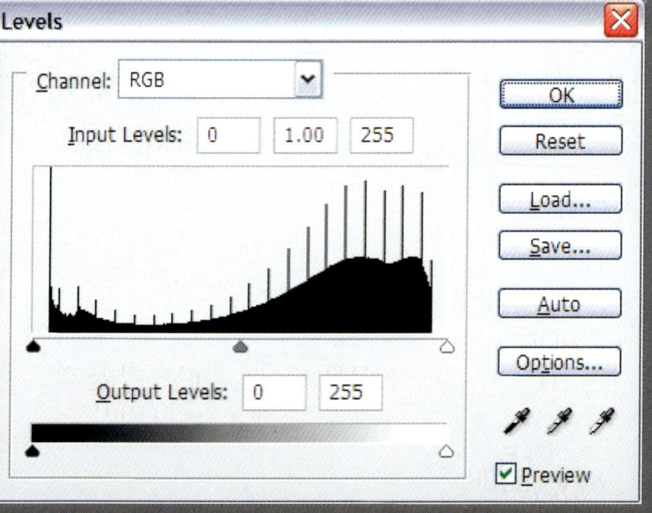

The second part of the Levels dialog is the Output Levels setting section. This setting does just the reverse of the Input Levels, and I just know that's a surprise, considering the name and all. It takes the values in the file and compresses them, rather than stretching them. It decreases contrast (A). Here's a histogram from an image that is very contrasty, with pure blacks and pure whites. If I go into the Output Levels, grab the black point, and move it in to 10, I'm taking the 0 value in the image and moving it up to 10. Likewise, I do the same to the white point, moving it down to 245 (B).

Again, take a look at the resulting histogram (C). The shape remains the same, it's just pushed together a little. Actually, exactly 10 points from both ends. This changes the black tones to a very dark gray, and the white tones move to a very light gray, reducing the overall contrast. This is used to compensate for what's called "dot gain," or the tendency for some printers to build up black faster than they should. An image with detail in the 0 – 20 range may print as pure black if the printer can't render those tones as anything but black. Just move those tones up the scale a little using Output Levels, and you're good.

Now, instead of white gaps in the graph, we have spiked lines. These indicate that the data in the file has been compressed together and now overlaps. Again, we haven't really built anything up, or even stayed even. We've massaged the available data, and have necessarily reduced it.

By finding out how your printer handles shadow and highlight detail, you can use the histogram to fine-tune your files to maximize the quality of your prints. We'll go into greater detail with this discussion later, but know that it all starts with Levels and understanding what the histogram is telling you.

Curves

Now that we've used Levels to set the black and white points, let's look at the Curves tool. More specifically, let's look at using Curves to control the way the tones are shown within those set points, and using Curves to make color corrections.

Open the Curves window using the oreo cookie-like icon, again, in the Layers palette. You'll notice at the bottom and on the left side there's a black-to-white gradient. You can switch the direction with the little arrows in the middle of the bottom gradient. Click, and it goes black-to-white, left-to-right. Click, and it reverses, white-to-black, right-to-left. For the sake of argument, I'm going to set it so black is at the left, just like my histogram in Levels.

We again see the OK and Cancel buttons, (remember that "Alt" changes Cancel to Reset), our happy Load and Save buttons, and the

A

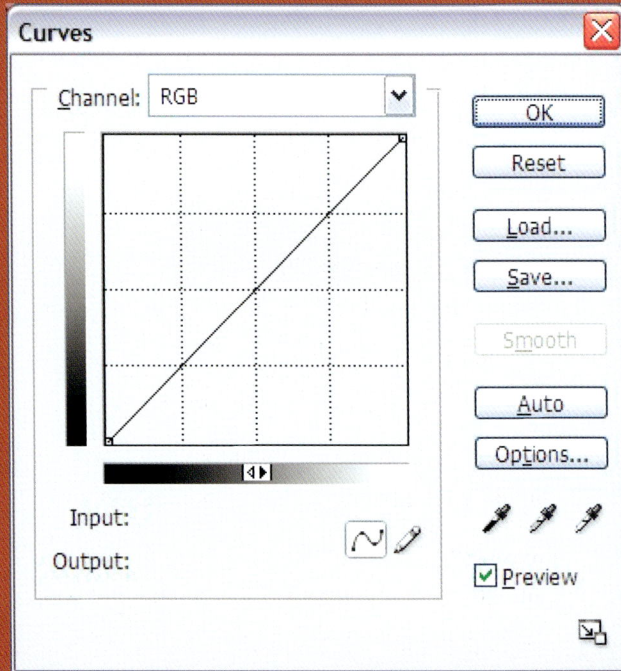

B

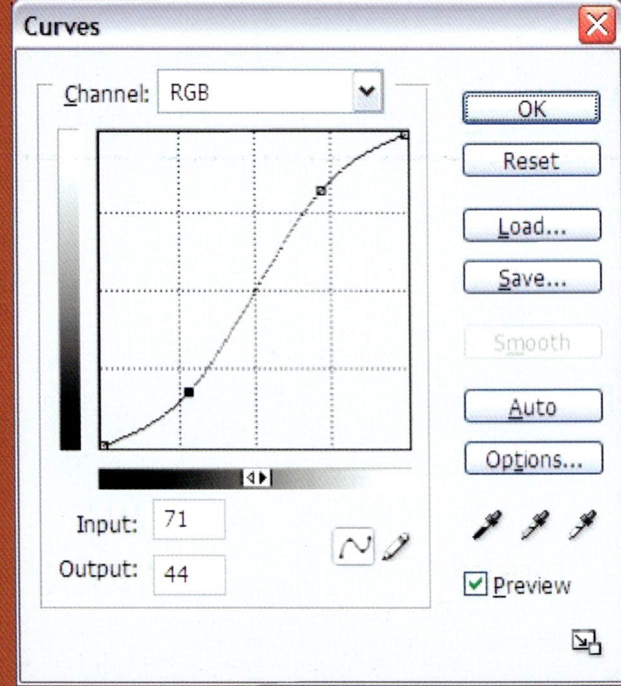

The Curves tool is a powerful image control, especially for fine tonal adjustments. It enables you to hold on to dark areas of the image while bringing up the highlights, or hold on to highlights while adjusting the darker areas.

Auto and Options buttons (A). Go up to the drop-down window that says RGB for a second. This pull-down menu gives you access to each separate channel—red, green, and blue. Store that thought away for now.

Using Curves is really simple. If you feel that it is counter-intuitive, think of it like this: the lower left point on the line is your black point. The upper right point is your highlight. The center of the graph is your middle gray. All you do is grab the line (click and hold with your mouse) and move it up or down. Moving the line down darkens that section of your image; moving it up lightens it. How am I doing?

Let's take it one step further. The bottom point is the black, and the center is middle gray, right? So, the lower part of the graph represents the darker shadow areas of your image. If I want to make those areas even darker, I can grab the curve there and pull it down. How about if I want to make the lighter areas lighter? I simply grab the higher values and push them up. Let's do both at the same time (B).

What we have done here is to control the contrast, or how the tones are distributed between our black point and white point, without changing those points. We're remapping our tonal range. We've taken our shadows and darkened them, our highlights have been lightened, and the result is a higher contrast image within our set contrast range (again, our black and white points).

It's interesting to see who gets this. It is easy for people who were deep into how film works, because it's a standard film-response curve. Engineers love it. For the less mathematically inclined, it seems like it's hard to grasp.

The wonderful thing about the Curves is that it wants to stay fairly organic; it doesn't let you make adjustments that aren't blended into the natural tone distribution of the image. The other thing that's nice is the degree of fine control it allows you to have. For example, I can make the overall image darker while holding a very small area of the highlights at normal or brighter. If I want, I can pull the shadows down, pull the midtones up a little, and pull the highlights down. It can be a very blunt tool, but it can also be a very precise scalpel. It all depends on how you use it.

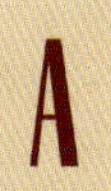

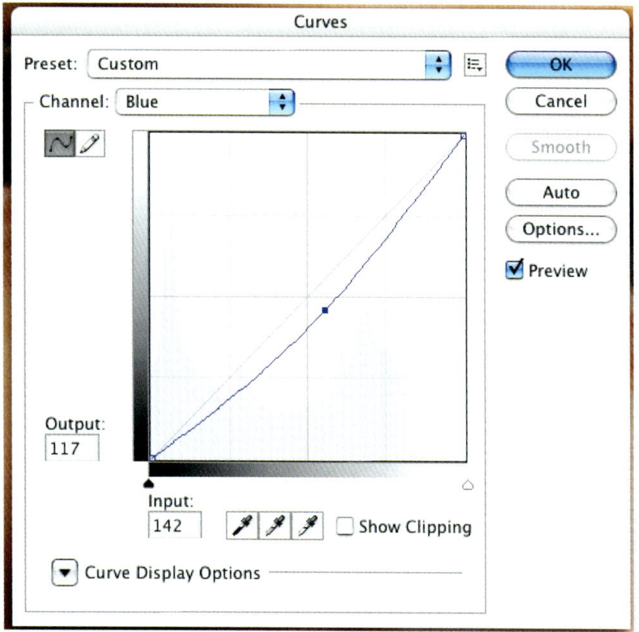

With Curves, you can make general tonal adjustments, or you can choose a specific color channel (red, green or blue) to adjust.

So far, we've just made global tone adjustments with Curves, making our image darker or lighter by using the "master" RGB selection. By going back to the pull-down menu and selecting the individual channels (red, green, or blue), I can make my global color corrections. I can select the red channel and push up the middle. The image gets redder. I pull it down and it gets less red (or more cyan). The same goes for the green channel. Up, more green; down, less green (more magenta). Same for blue: up, more blue; down, less blue (more yellow) (A).

Here we have stumbled on the big secret of color control in Photoshop. We have three basic ranges: red to cyan, green to magenta, and blue to yellow. Think back to basic color theory, and you've unlocked one of the mysteries of the universe: everything that I can do to color in Photoshop, I can do here in the color channels of Curves.

Remember, too, that I can fine-tune the colors in the shadows and highlights because of the degree of control Curves gives me. I can pull blue out of the shadows by pulling the lower values of the blue curve down, and feed more blue into the highlights by pulling the highlight values up. (It's crazy—but crazy like a fox.) For example, I can go into very specific areas of the image and make precise adjustments. If I want more purple in the blue shadows rather than cyan, I select the correct channel—in this case, maybe the red channel—and I add more red, but only to the shadows. I leave the rest alone.

Some Tips and Tricks in Curves:

As a general rule of thumb (and to understand how Curves changes contrast), the more horizontal the slope of the curve, the lower the contrast. This makes sense if you think about it: pull the shadows up and they get grayer, pull the highlights down and they get grayer, and the line in the middle will be more horizontal. The steeper the line, or the more vertical it is, the

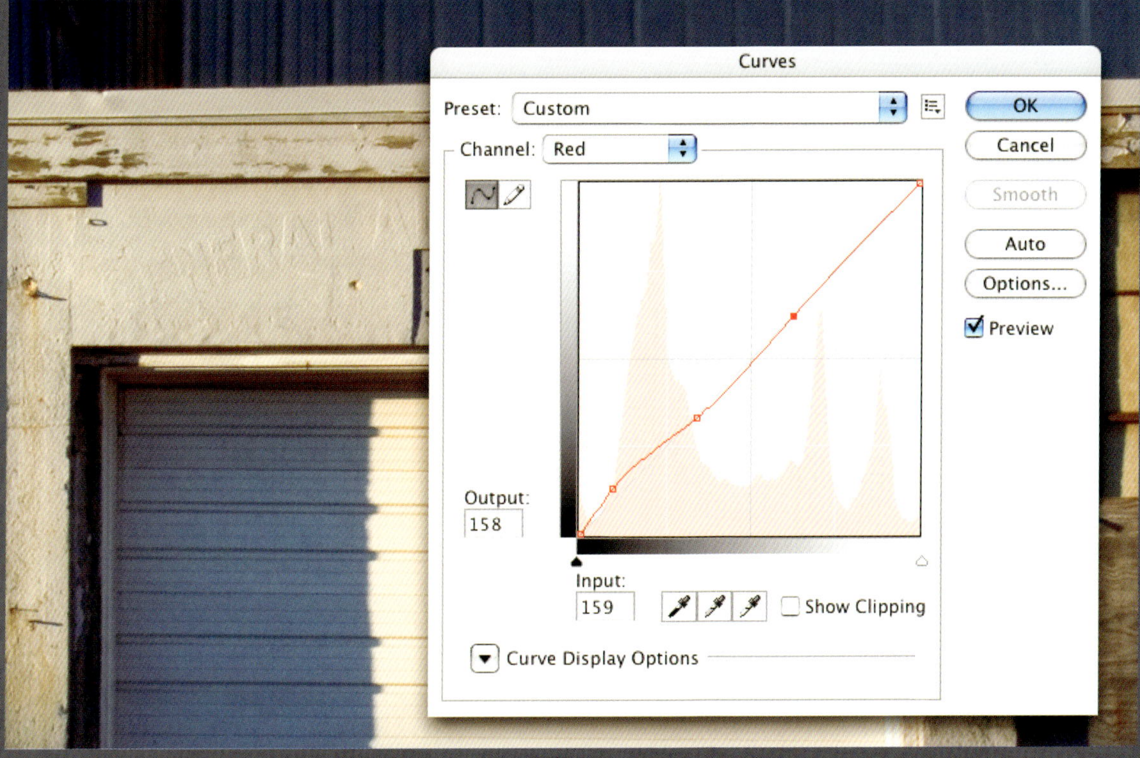

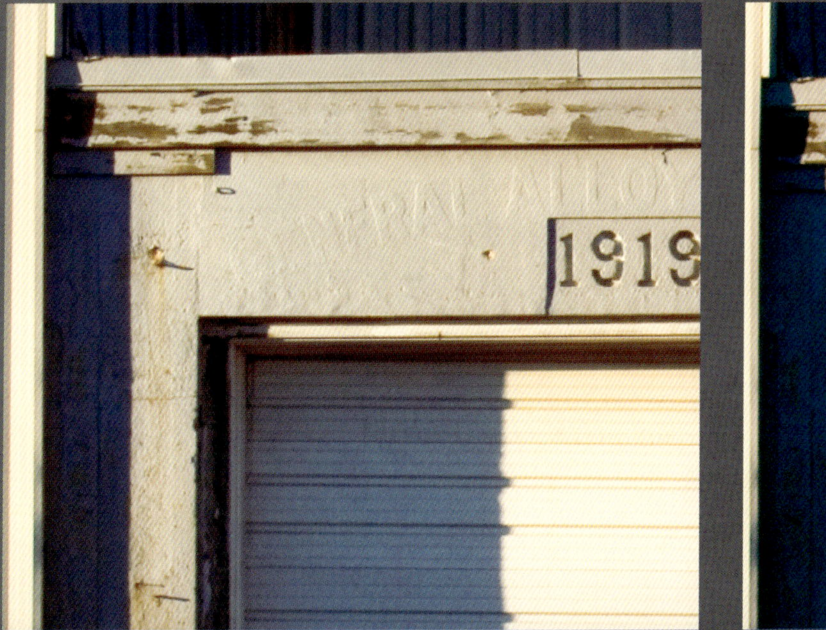

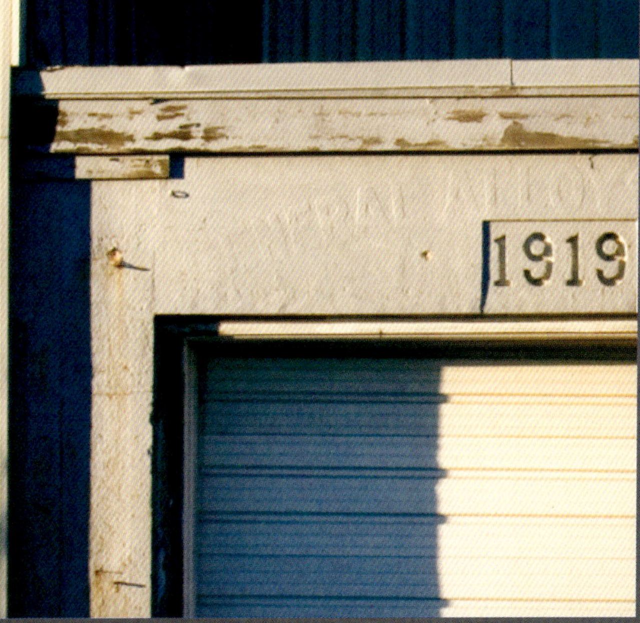

In this example, the Curves tool is being used to increase the red tones in the shadows of the image. Notice the lower left image—the shadows have more of a red hue than the shadows of the lower right image. Also notice that the tonal difference is gradual and natural; there isn't an obvious red tint, simply a more natural warmth. Also notice that the highlights of the image remain unaffected. This is the power of using the Curve tool for fine-tuned tonal adjustments.

more contrast you get. Again, pull the shadows down and the highlights up, and you've separated the midtones and forced them to get darker and lighter, respectively.

To place a specific point on the Curve that corresponds to a value in your image, open the Curves dialog, hit Command ("Apple" on Macs, "Ctrl" in Windows), and click on that spot on your image. You'll set a point exactly representing that value, right where you want it.

You can move that point precisely by using the Arrow keys. Arrow up and the point moves up; arrow to the side and it moves to the side.

Hint: Hold down the Shift key as you Arrow to move faster.

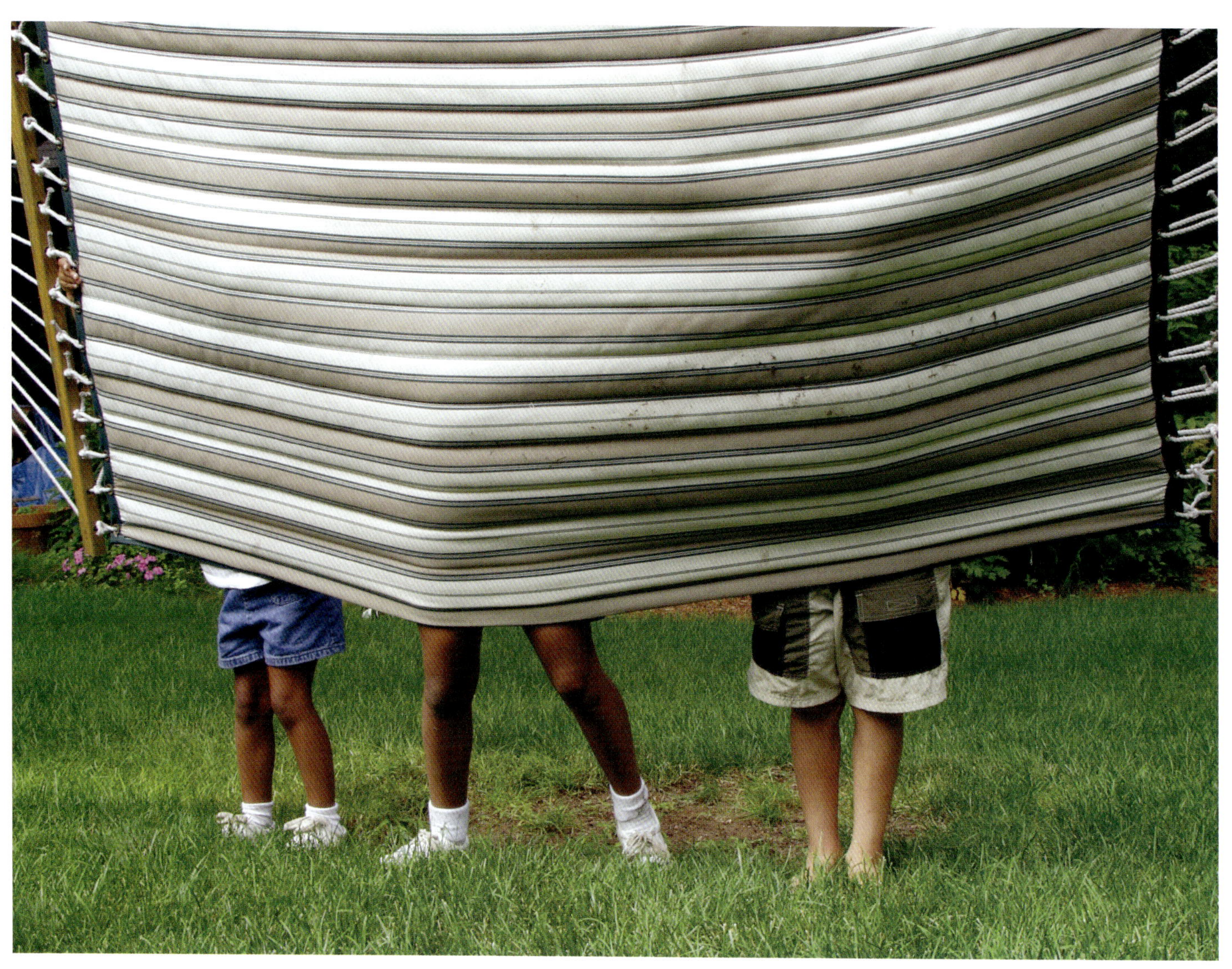

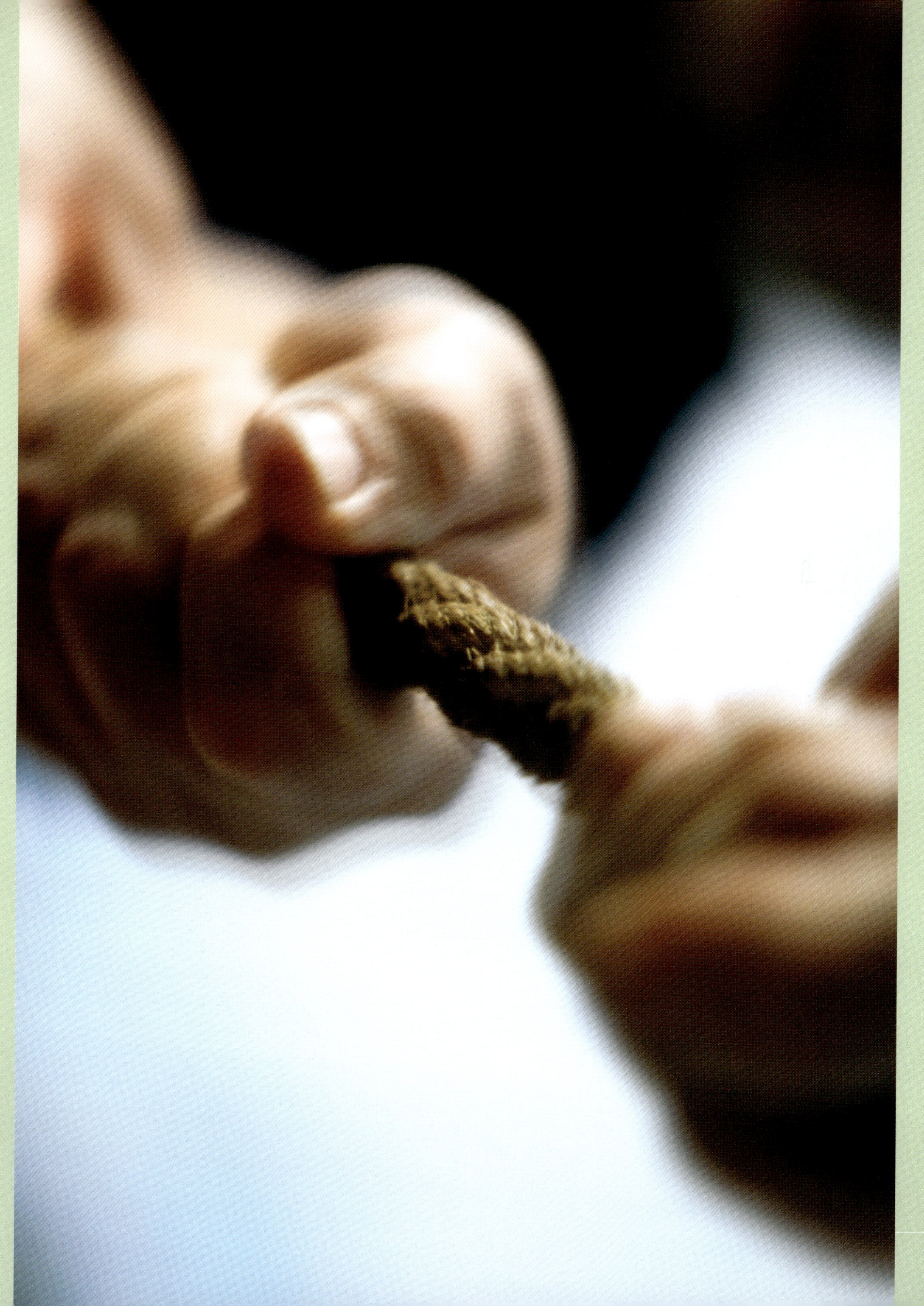

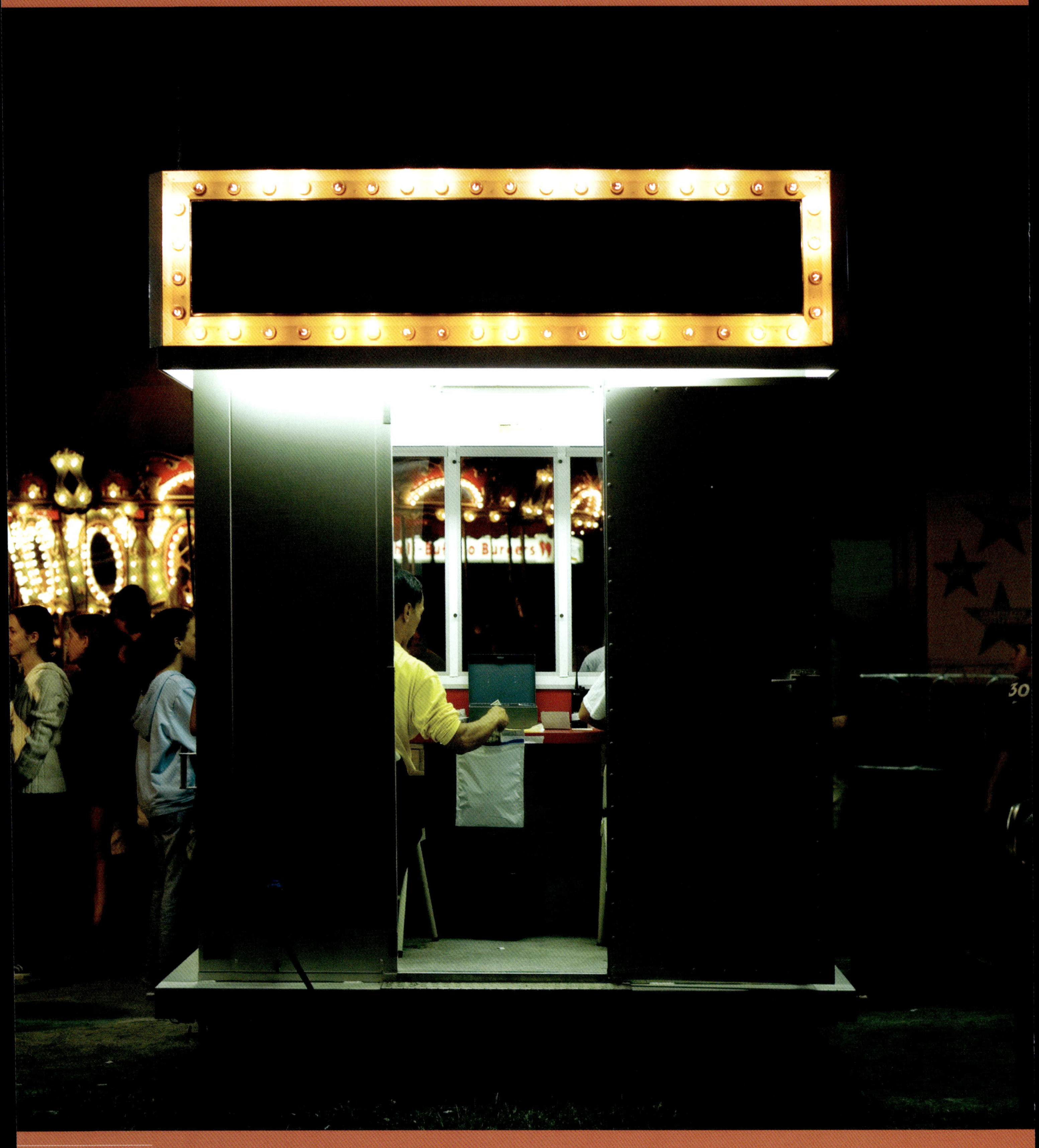
Burgers

Managing Layers

Let's recap with an example. I've opened a file, sized it, and made a few Adjustment Layers. I started with a Levels adjustment to set my black and white points, and then made a Curves adjustment to adjust my contrast. In this case, I pulled down the shadows and boosted the highlights a bit. Then I made another Curves layer to make a color correction (A).

Look a little closer at the Layers window. First, you'll see that for every Adjustment Layer, there is a small icon of the adjustment. Notice the tiny histogram on "Levels 1." If you go to that icon and double-click it, your Levels adjustment re-opens just as you left it. How cool is that? For every adjustment you make, you can go back and change it. If you adjust the Levels, make a print, and decide the black point is too black, you can go to that specific adjustment and back it off a little without altering the other adjustments you have made to the image.

Notice, also, the top layer has a name. By double-clicking on the name, you can edit it. I strongly suggest you name your adjustments to leave yourself a trail of notes.

A

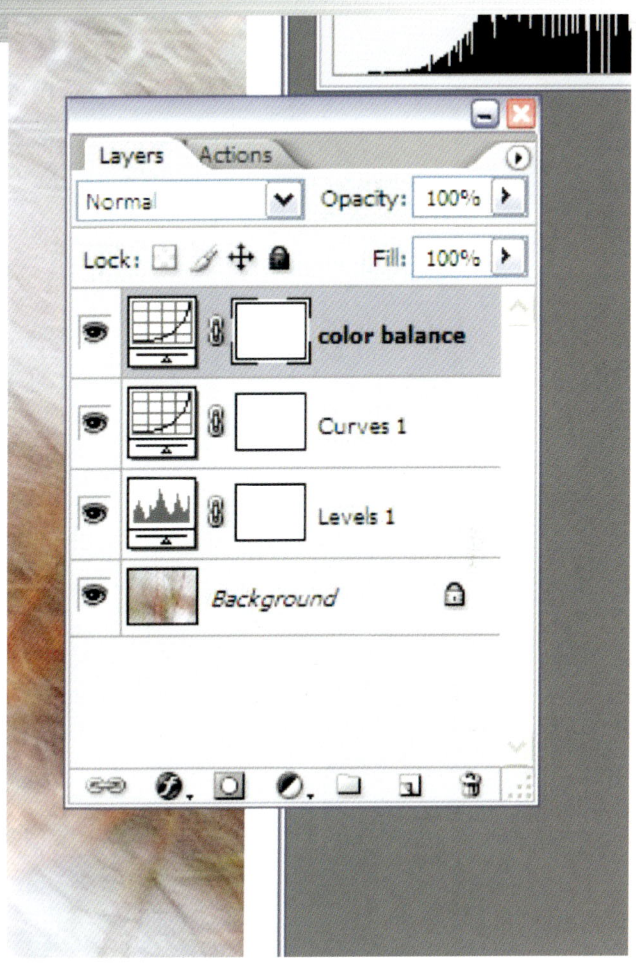

It is important to name each layer with the appropriate image edit. This leaves you a series of notes on what you have already done to your image, and it makes it infinitely easier to access each edit. This becomes even more necessary as we get into adjusting the RAW file in Adobe Camera RAW (more about Camera RAW on page 120).

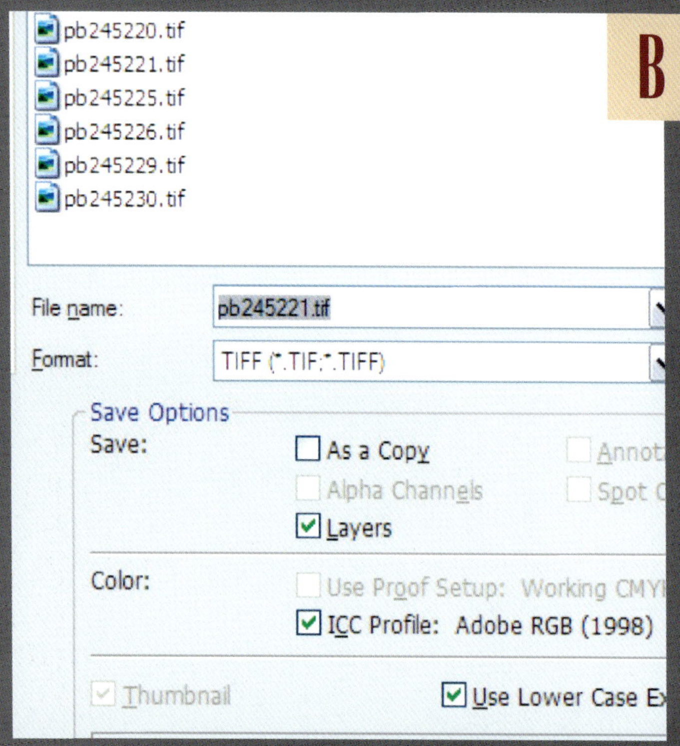

Being able to save the individual layers is incredibly helpful. This means that you can always go back to that image file and readjust it as many times as you want, whenever you want.

Here's where things start getting really powerful. If I want to save this as a TIFF, I can save the image as well as all the Layers (B). When I do a "Save As" there's a little box named "Layers"; if I check the box and then save, I can re-open the file with every Layer I've made.

All your work is right there. You can go in, make adjustments, close and save the file, and go back six months from now and re-adjust the image without having to re-do anything. (All I can think about is how it used to take me hours in the darkroom to get back to the work print that I left off with the day before.) This is also why I don't bother with the History tool. Once you close a file, your History is lost. The Layers, on the other hand, last as long as you want.

Take a look at the figure (C). At the top right of the Layers window is a little box called "Opacity." This is one of the coolest things in Layers, because it allows me to turn the adjustment I've

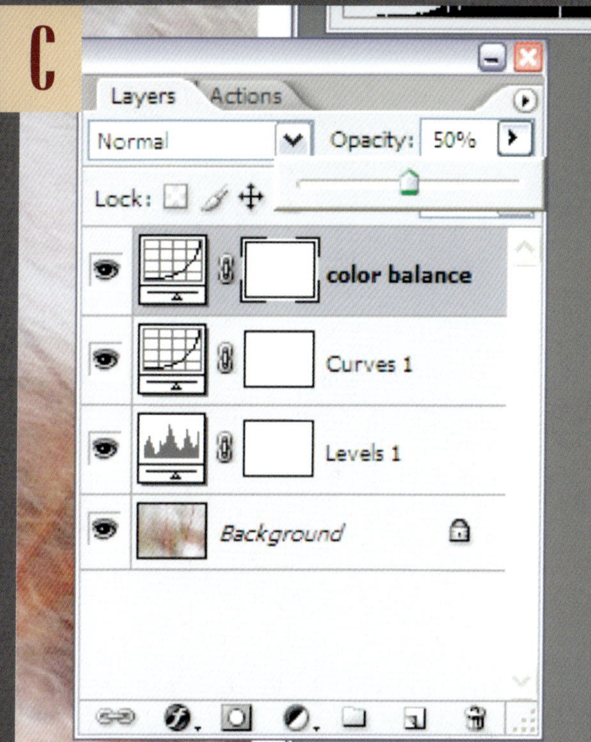

The Opacity control in the Layers palette allows you to control the intensity of each individual layer and it's corresponding adjustment. If, for example, you make a print of an image and the Levels adjustment is too light, you can just slide the Opacity for that adjustment down instead of re-adjusting the Levels adjustment.

made back a few notches. If I select the Layer in question, click the "Opacity" slider, and ramp it back to 50%, I've taken my base adjustment and turned it down.

This is really astounding. It means I can simply go in and turn down an edit without changing the edit itself. Add to that the fact that it all gets saved in the TIFF as a Layer edit, and you start to see what I'm talking about. Working in Layers sets the stage for a workflow that utilizes an incredibly powerful set of tools—tools that we can use from basic adjustments to the highest levels of our digital darkroom techniques.

What is that little white box between the adjustment icon and the layer name, you may well ask? That, my friend, is (drum roll please) a Mask.

A

Layers
Actions
Normal
Opacity: 100%
Lock:
Fill: 100%
Curves 1
Background

B

Adobe Photoshop
File Edit Image Layer Select Filter View Window Help
Brush: 400
Mode: Normal
Opacity: 50%
Flow: 50%
PB245186.ORF @ 25% (Curves 1, Layer Mask/8)
Layers
Actions
Normal
Opacity: 100%
Lock:
Fill: 100%
Curves 1
Background
25%
Adobe RGB (1998) (8bpc)

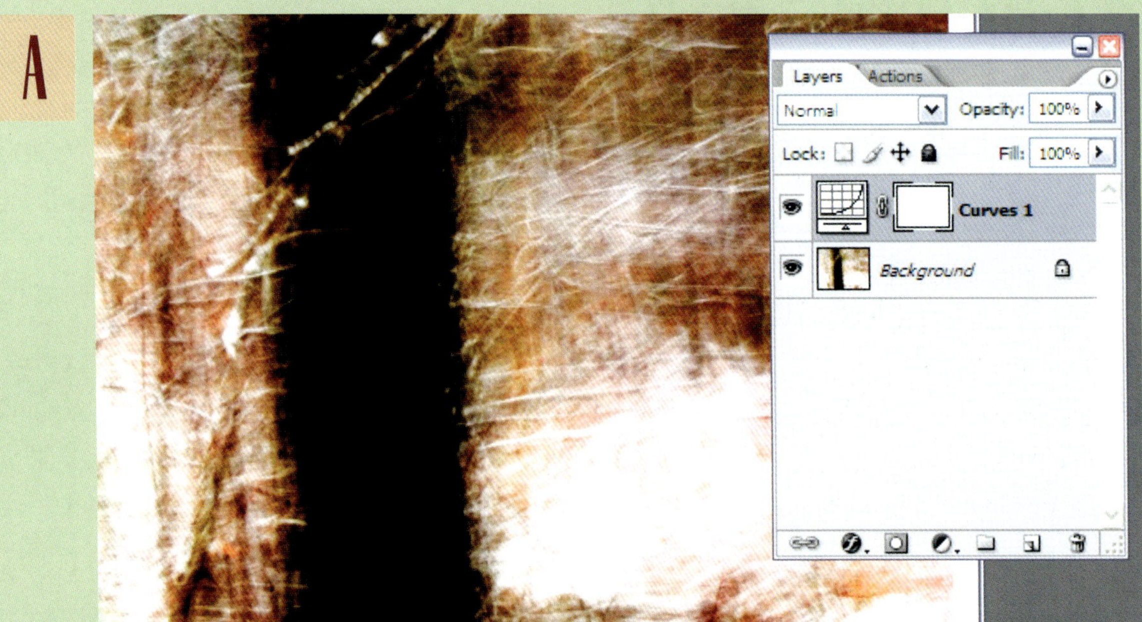

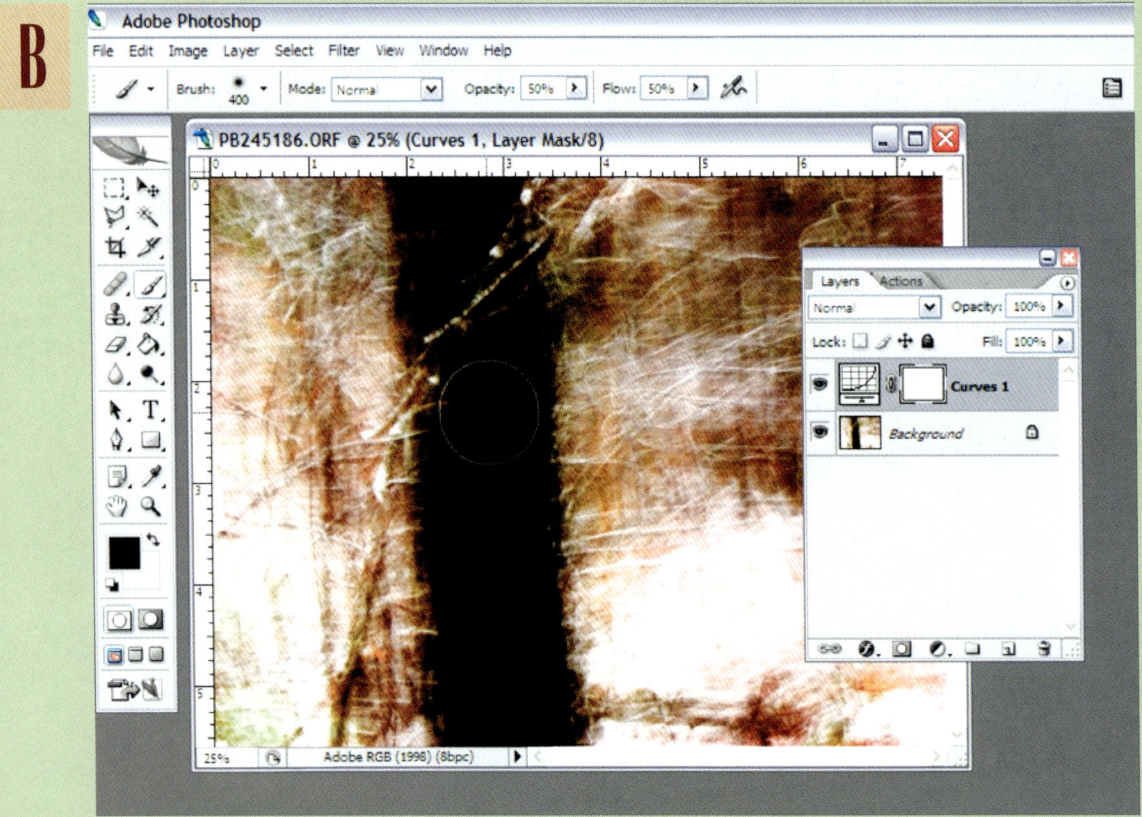

Masking

The Mask is a particularly photographic concept if you think of it in terms of film. The Mask, as you see it on any Adjustment Layer, appears white. Envision it as a "clear" or transparent in a piece of film. If the Mask appears black, then, like film, it's opaque. It can only be black (opaque), white (transparent), or a shade of gray (translucent), just like black-and-white film negatives. When I make a new Adjustment Layer, the adjustment is applied globally because the Mask (created automatically with the new layer) is white, or clear. If I make areas of the Mask black or gray, those areas become translucent or opaque. That means the adjustment on that layer is not applied to those areas—the adjustment affects only where the Mask is white. You are "masking" the image where you want the adjustment applied, allowing you to select specifically the parts of your image that you want to change. This makes a mask an extremely flexible and creative tool.

A mask is just another way of making a selection in your image. We're going to use it as a selection of the adjustment that we made on an Adjustment Layer. Keep this in the back of your mind—a mask is a selection of the adjustment. Let's look at an example.

(A) In this example, I've taken an image of a tree and tried to darken the background by applying a curve. Naturally, it has darkened the entire image because I haven't specified a selection; I'm applying the adjustment globally.

(B) In the next example I have masked out most of the tree. (C) You can see it's lighter. You can also see the mask, which used to be all white, now has a strip of black-gray running down the area corresponding to my tree.

The Mask is now determining the area that will receive my Curve adjustment. It's applying the Adjustment to the areas that are clear, and blocking out the Adjustment on the areas that are black and gray. This is just like burning and dodging in a traditional darkroom, but the best part is that it gets saved in the Layer with the TIFF file as additional pixels, keeping your underlying image as large and full of information as possible.

C

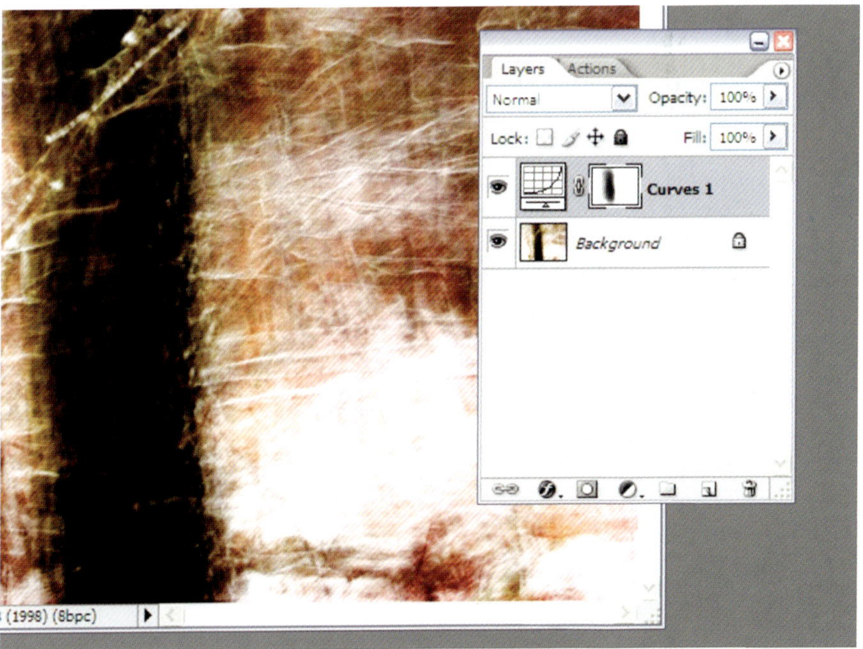

How to Create a Mask

When you make an Adjustment Layer, you get a mask automatically. It's white (transparent) and sits as an icon right next to the little Adjustment icon.

To make parts of it black, paint it black with the Paintbrush tool. Select your Paintbrush tool, make the foreground color black, click on the little white "Mask" icon on the Layer to ensure you are only applying the brush to the mask, and then work your Paintbrush on the image itself. You won't be painting black on your image as you might expect, you'll be painting black on the mask.

Figure (B) on page 94 shows that basic setup. I have my Adjustment Layer, and I've made sure I'm working on that mask by clicking on it. My foreground color is set to black.

I click and drag, painting all over the tree trunk, and the mask slowly fills in black, hiding my Adjustment.

NOTE: My settings for the Brush are Mode: Normal, Opacity: 50%, and Flow: 50%. The Brush is set at "full soft". With this setting, the brush paints shades of progressively darkening gray in a very controllable way, and makes a nice soft path.

NOTE: Because I'm making a major adjustment and selecting small areas that I want to exclude in this example, I'm starting with a white mask and painting in black. If I had a very small area I wanted to adjust, I'd do the reverse—I'd turn the mask to black, and paint in white.

NOTE: It's important to remember we are masking the adjustment, not masking the image. We're making a selection of the adjustment that we want applied to the image.

Masking Shortcuts

- *Hitting the "D" key ("Default") sets the foreground color to white and the background color to black. The "X" key switches the background/foreground colors.*
- *If you want to make a mask all black, select the Mask icon and hit Apple-I ("Command"-I, or Ctrl-I in Windows); this will "Invert" the color and make it black.*
- *The Brackets [ ] make your Brush smaller and larger. Make sure your Preferences are set to "Normal Brush Tip" and you'll get that nice circle.*
- *You can copy a mask from one Layer to another just by holding the "Alt" key and dragging the mask to another Layer.*
- *By changing the Brush size and hardness, you can make incredibly precise selections, down to exactly one pixel.*

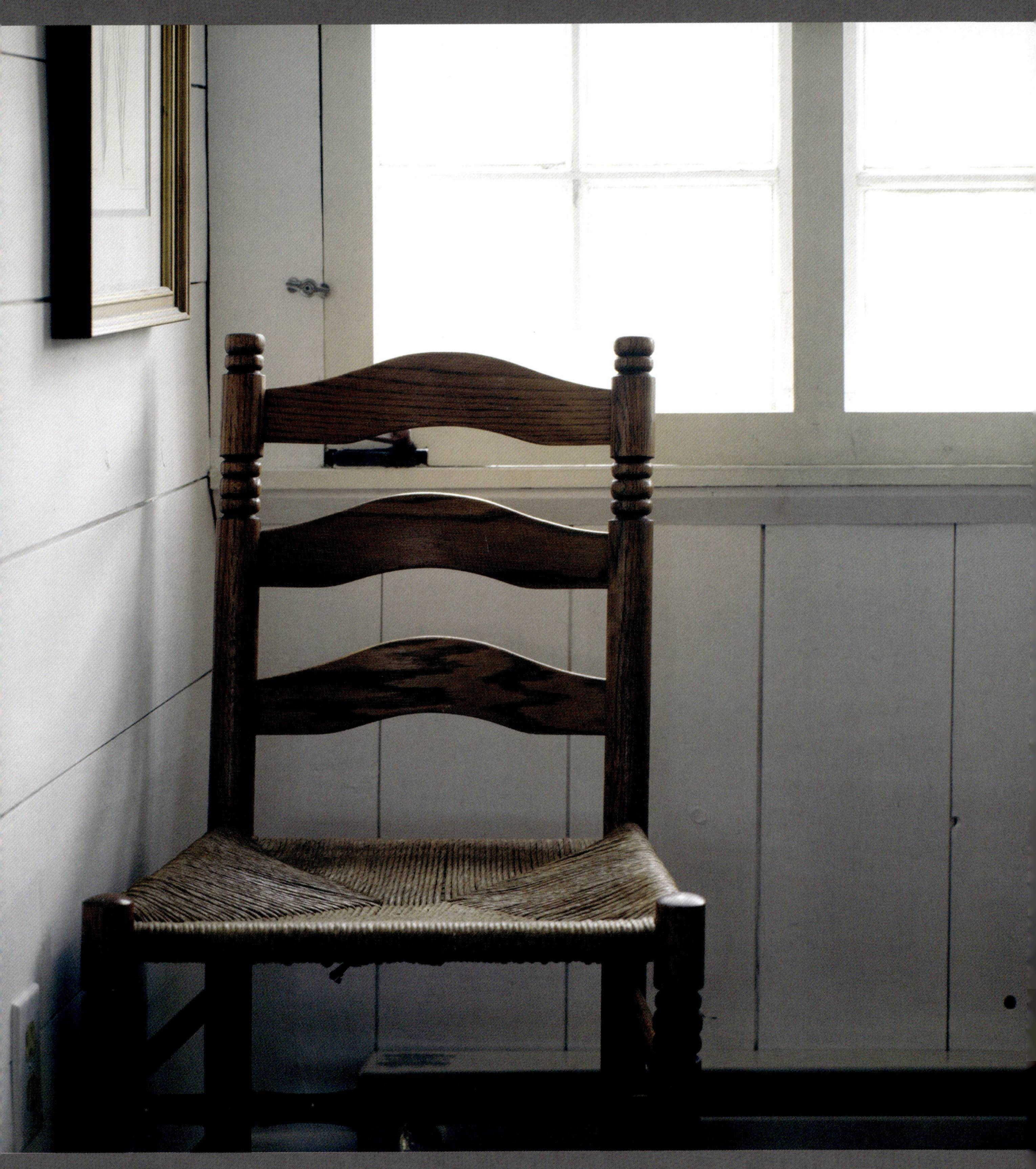

This stuff can get crazy if you let it. There are several books devoted to the intricacies of Masking, but this little method is all I ever use. I make my basic, global adjustments then burn and dodge my image (just like I would in the darkroom) by using the Mask. The Mask is saved in the Layers, and I can go back and change it any time, by painting over it again in white to open it up, or in black to fill it in.

Converting to Grayscale

There's one more thing I do in Adjustment Layers, and that is black-and-white conversions. I always start with a color image if I can. If I'm shooting with a digital camera, I shoot in color mode; if I'm scanning an image for black and white and the film is color, I scan it in color. Why? If I start with the most possible information, I can control the tonal ranges created in the grayscale conversion.

One of the most common ways to convert to grayscale is to simply go to your Mode and change it from RGB to Grayscale. That would be Image>Mode>Grayscale. Another option is to go into Image>Adjustments>Desaturate; or Image>Adjustments>Hue/Saturation and do a "Master" Desaturate. These methods all give you a grayscale image, but the problem is they give you no control over how the grayscale is rendered. They do what's called a "linear desaturation;" this just ramps down the color according to Luminance.

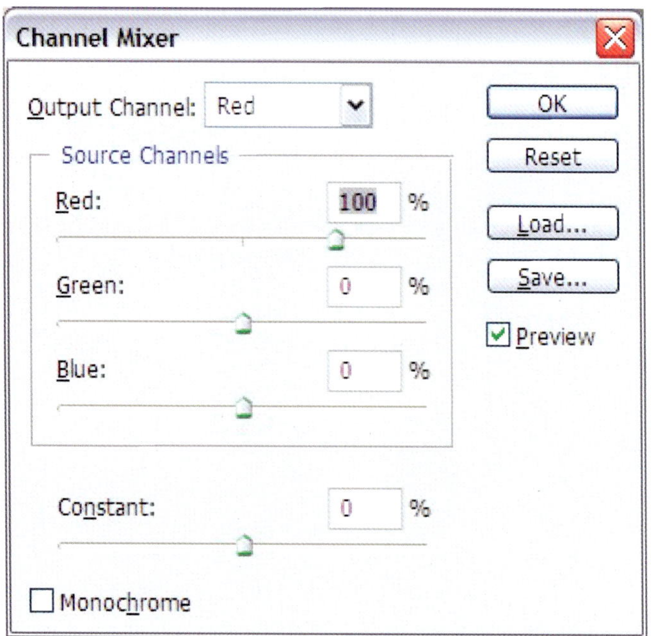

Channel Mixer is a more controlled grayscale conversion tool than the Image>Mode>Grayscale option. It gives you the choice of changing the hues that create the varied gray tones in an image, and changing these hues can result in very interesting grayscale conversions.

I use a device called "Channel Mixer." Go to your Layers palette, click the oreo cookie-like icon, and around the middle of the list you'll see "Channel Mixer." Select that, and you'll see the dialog shown here.

The first step is to check the "Monochrome" box at the bottom, changing your Output Channel to "gray."

Now you can control what parts of each channel you want to use to create that gray channel. Bear with me. As it starts out, you see the red (R) channel at 100% and nothing in the other two. The result is a grayscale rendering that looks interestingly similar to the effect you'd get shooting black-and-white film with a red filter over the lens—dark skies, light skin tones, etc. That is because it's using only the R channel to map the Luminance.

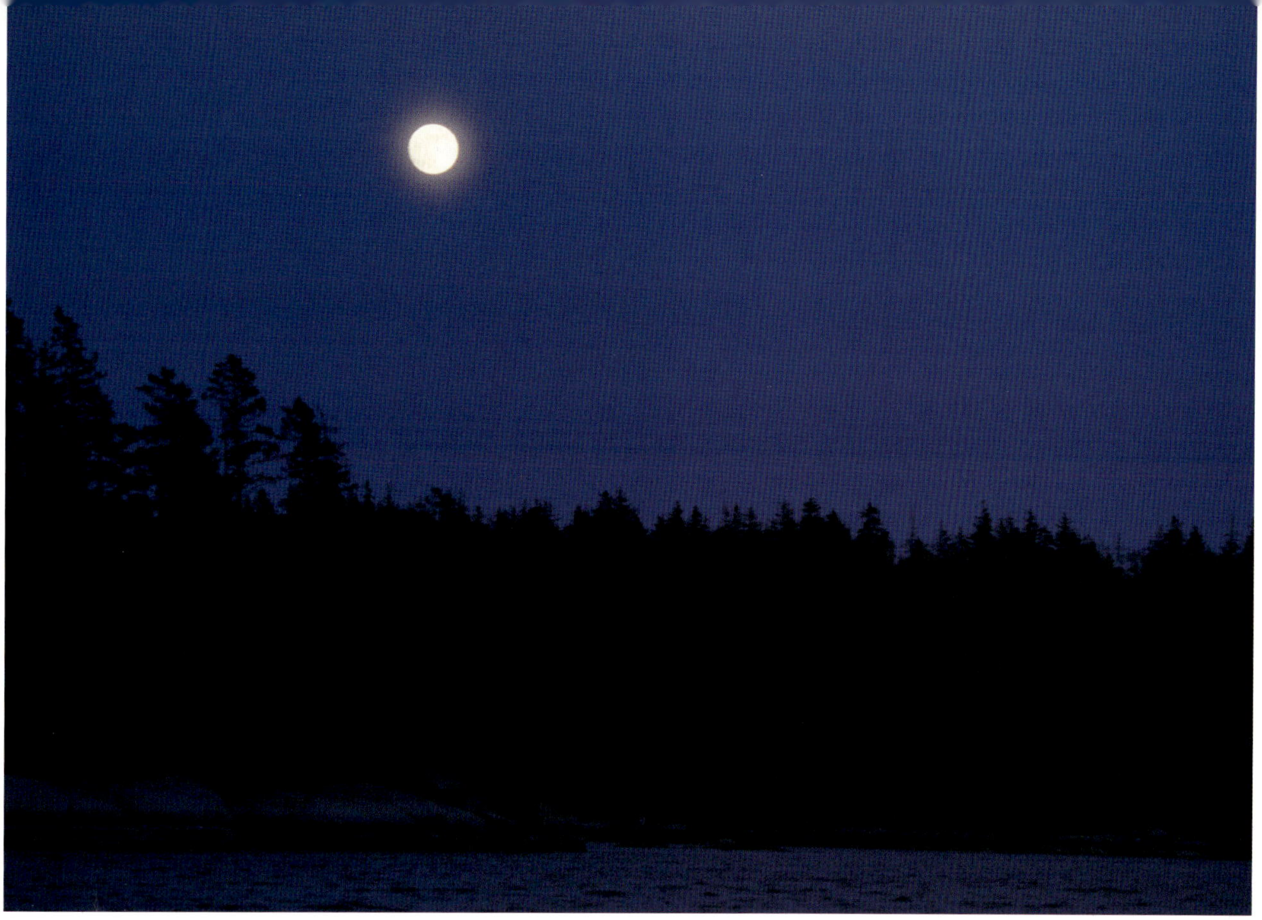

If I put 33.3% into each channel, I'm going to get the exact effect as if I did the Mode Grayscale conversion. It uses all three channels equally to figure the Luminance. I can change the way each channel affects the grayscale tones by changing the percentage I apply from each channel. For example, if I put in numbers like red (R) 60%, green (G) 20%, and blue (B) 20%, I'm going to get a slightly different tonal mapping—one that leans more toward red. This particular setting reminds me of shooting old-school Tri-X film and processing it in D-76 1:1. It

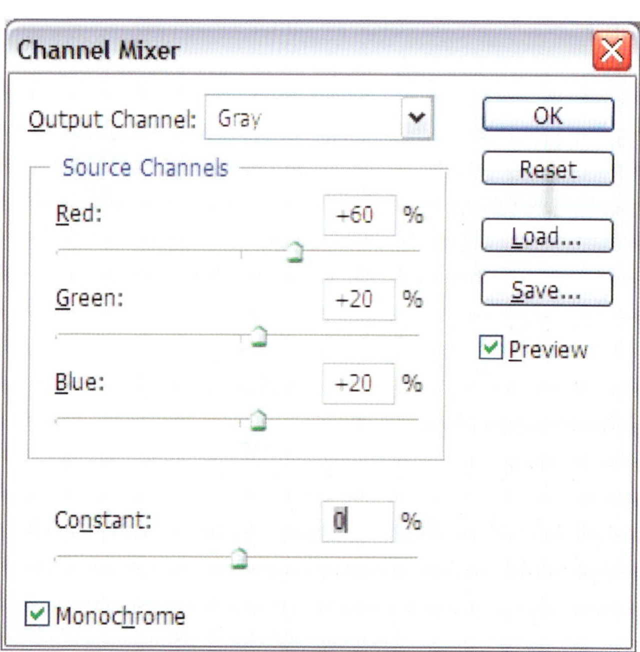

You can mimic various black-and-white photography techniques, such as filters, when you use Channel Mixer to convert an image to grayscale.

gives me lighter skin tones and deeper blue skies.

With Channel Mixer, I can make very specific decisions about how I want my tones to look.

One suggestion for using this tool is to keep the sum of the three channels' percentages to around 100%. For example, R 80%, G 10%, and B 10% looks like Tri-X with a Wratten 25 filter. R 200%, G -100%, B 0% gives you an Infrared effect. And, for the record, I never change the "Constant." I don't really even know what it does.

So, my final standard setting for Channel Mixer is shown here. Once again, you also have your Cancel/Reset, Load, Save, and Preview buttons. I can make some standard renderings and save them, like, Tri-X/Wratten 25, for example. I like to standardize these settings, rather than building new custom conversions for every file, so that the conversion is predictable, and consequently, I can visualize it. Again, I'm limiting my tools so I can learn to see with them.

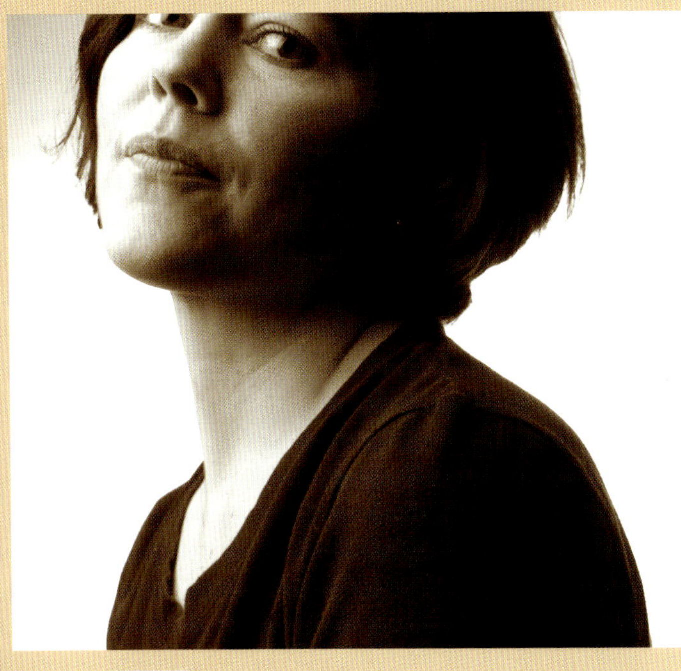

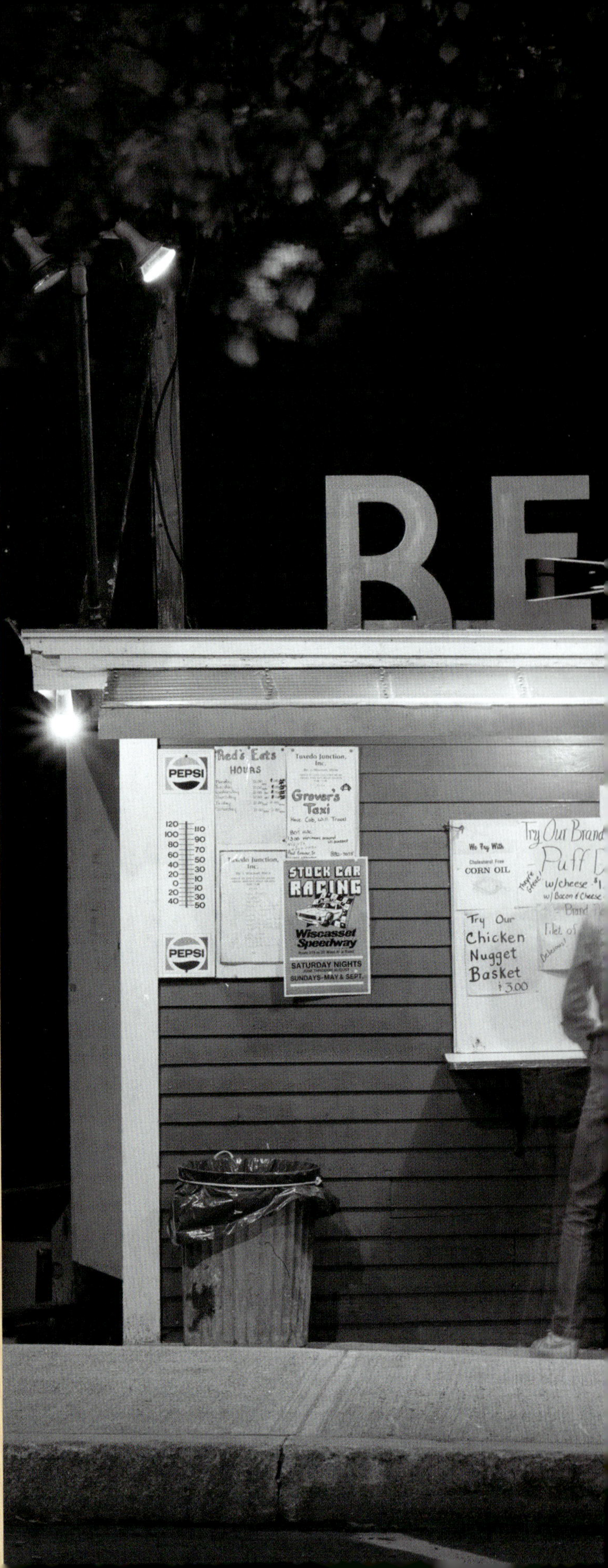

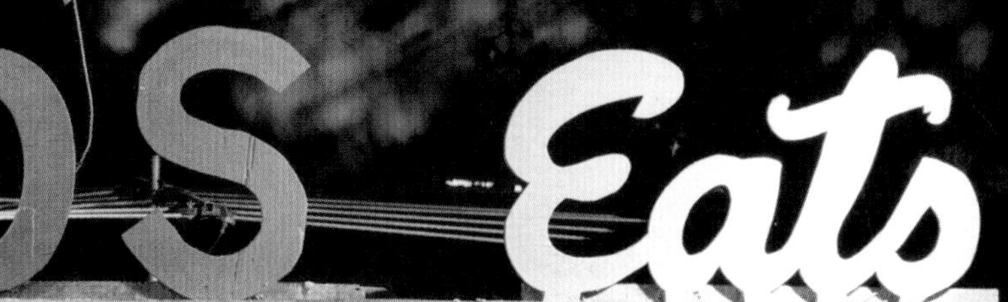

Eats
HAMBURGER 1.25
" ROYAL 1.50
CHEESEBURGER 1.35
" ROYAL 1.60
HOT DOGS .75
" w/ Sauerkraut 1.00
STURDLEYS 1.00
" w/ Sauerkraut 1.25
GRILLED CHEESE 1.00
" w/ Tomato 1.20
CHICKEN ROLL 1.85
ZUCCHINI LARGE 1.25
" SMALL 1.00
CRABMEAT ROLL 3.00
CLAMS PINT 5.60
" 1/2 PINT 3.00
FRENCH FRIES LARGE 1.25
" SMALL 1.00
ONION RINGS LARGE 1.25
" SMALL 1.00
SOFT DRINKS LARGE .80
" SMALL .55
FRUIT DRINKS .65
MILK.45 COFFEE.TEA.HOT COCOA .60
CIGARETTES 1.40
WATER ST.
COASTAL BUSINESS CENTER
OFFSET PRINTERS
Marilyn's Beauty Salon
WISCASSET BAY GALLERY
WISCASSET BAY ANTIQUES

8 RETOUCHING TECHNIQUES

The first step in retouching (and by that I mean spotting and cleaning up the image, not putting my head on Christie Brinkley's body) is to make a duplicate Layer to work on. This insures that you won't make any horrible mistakes to your original image information. Just drag your Layer to the "Create a new Layer" icon at the bottom of the Layers palette (the icon resembles a sticky-note pad) (A).

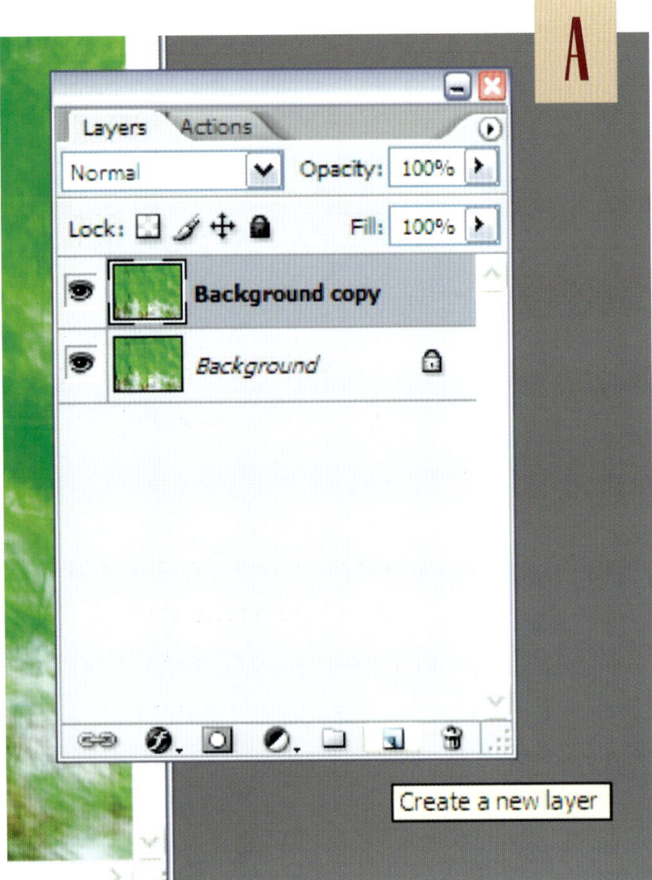

Clone Tool

The Clone tool is a simple concept to grasp. It's really just a "copy and paste" command. Select the area you want to copy by "Alt-click" (your mouse icon will turn into a target) and click on the area you want to copy to.

The first frame (B) is the sample click, and the next one (C) is the paste click.

You generally want the settings on the Clone tool to be really soft so that the retouching is not too visible. One issue with this is if you clone the pixels in the same area repeatedly, the softness blurs any fine texture in the subject. A good case in point is skin tones. It's fine if you're fixing a blemish or two, but if you're retouching a large area, you're going to blur all the nice pores and things that make skin so, well, textural. How do you fix it? Enter the Healing brush.

Healing Brush

In its simplest form, the Healing brush works similarly to the Clone tool, but instead of being a simple copy-paste function, it mimics the texture of the sample and blends the tones of the target around that texture. The simplest

Always create a new layer when you are making an image adjustment, especially for the more image-destructive edits such as Cloning.

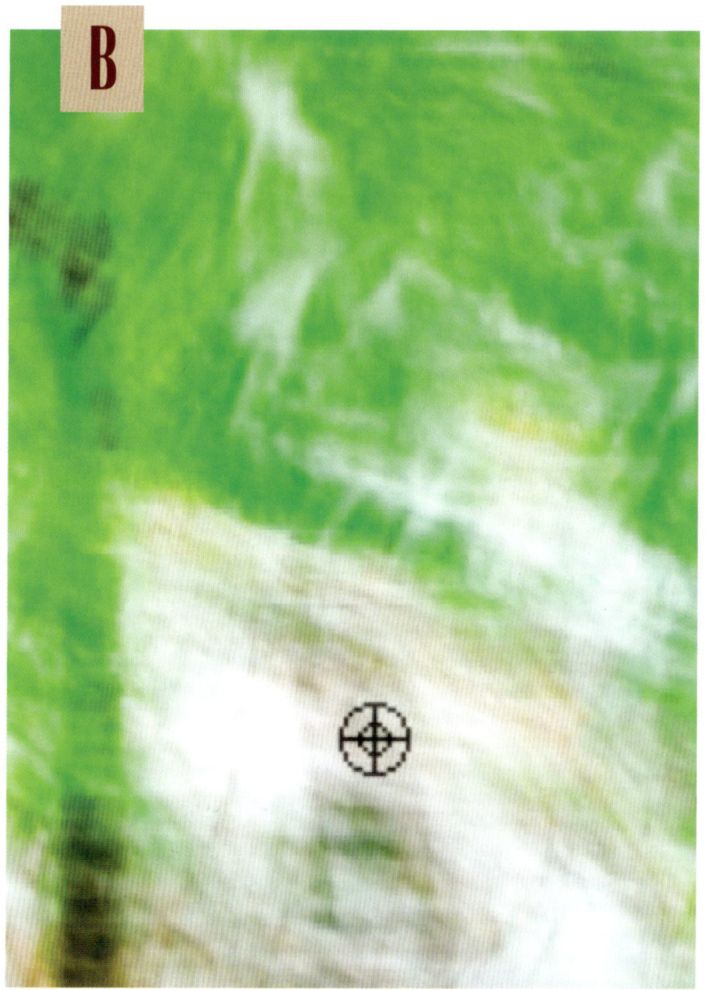

The target click of the Clone tool is the "copy" part of the "copy and paste" function, and determines where the pixels are copied from in the image.

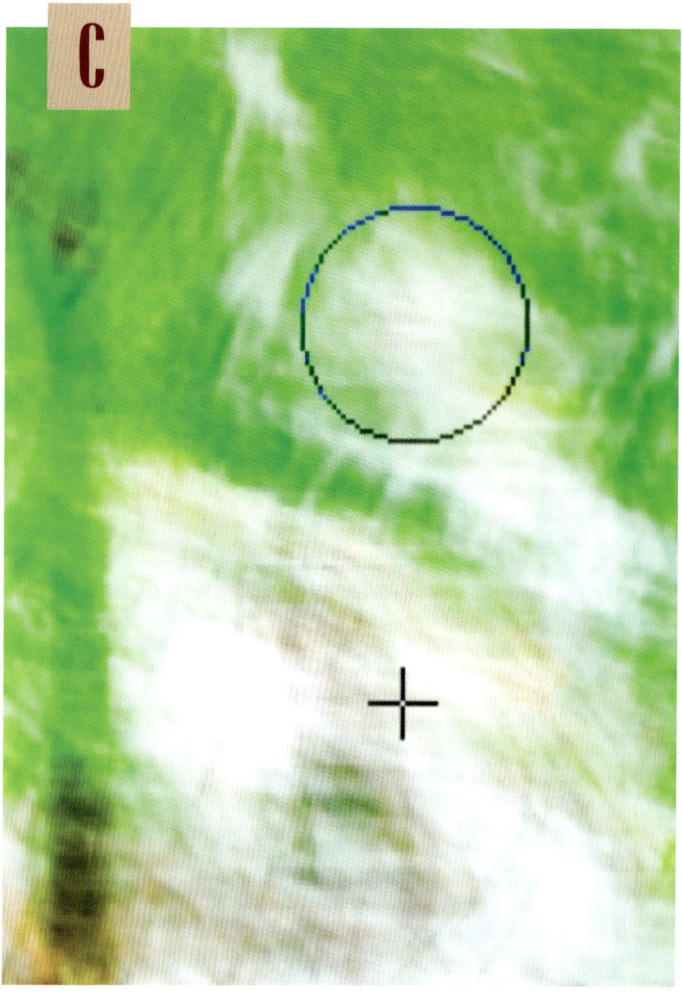

When you paste the pixels from one area over another, you will see both areas of the image that are involved. The circle in the image above is where the pixels are being pasted, and the cross is where the Clone tool is copies those pixels.

thing is to try it out. Find a texture in your image, sample it, and then spot it into a "blemish." It takes the blemish and blends it into the surrounding tones using the same texture as the sampled area.

Just like spotting prints or negatives, this technique takes practice and experimentation. The good news is practicing on a duplicate Layer means you're not causing any permanent damage to your image.

Using Layers and Masks for Retouching

If you retouch on a new Layer, you can use that Layer's mask to select how the retouch is applied. Whether I'm using the Clone tool or the Healing brush, I can go to the mask and select specific parts of the retouching and restrict that spot. I can also go in and adjust the Opacity of the retouch Layer to feather the retouching back. Because this is so flexible and controlled, I go a little overboard with most spotting. I can always go back to blend and soften the work with Opacity. Are you starting to warm up to Layers, yet?

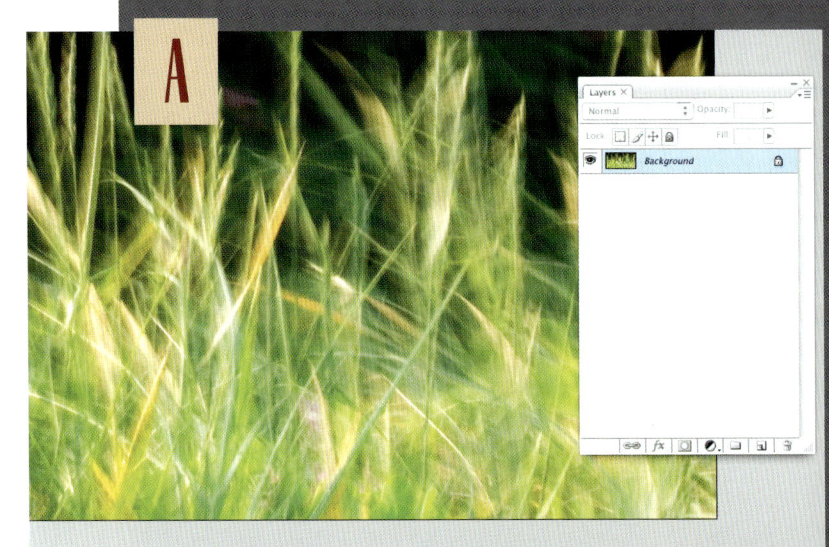

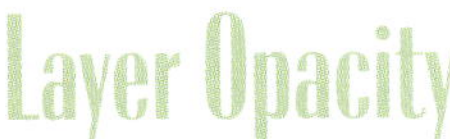

Layer Opacity

Up in the upper right corner of the Layer Pallet, there's a little slider called "Opacity." Opacity controls how transparent the layer appears, and allows you to dial down any effect from a layer, even to zero. Here's a little example.

On a color image (A), I've made a Channel Mixer adjustment layer to convert it to a grayscale image (B). Look at the Opacity window. It defaults to 100%, so it is 100% opaque—not at all transparent.

If I click it, it opens a slider that I can drag to whatever level I want. In this case I'm going to 65% opacity (C), so some of the color image

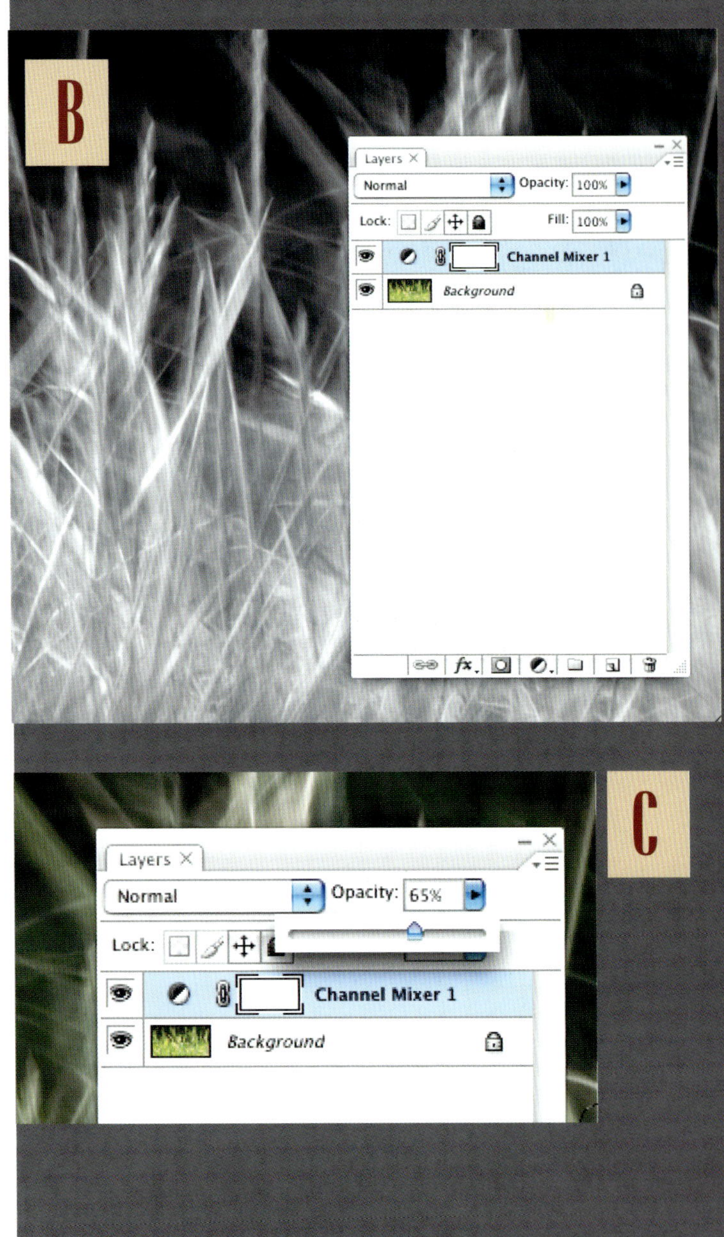

underneath is going to show through. Actually, exactly 35% of it is going to show through (D). Here's what that looks like (E).

This is a powerful tool—it allows you to make fine adjustments to any edit. You can apply it to literally any Layer—an Adjustment Layer, an Image Layer, or even a Smart Object and Smart Filter Layer (which we'll explore later on).

D

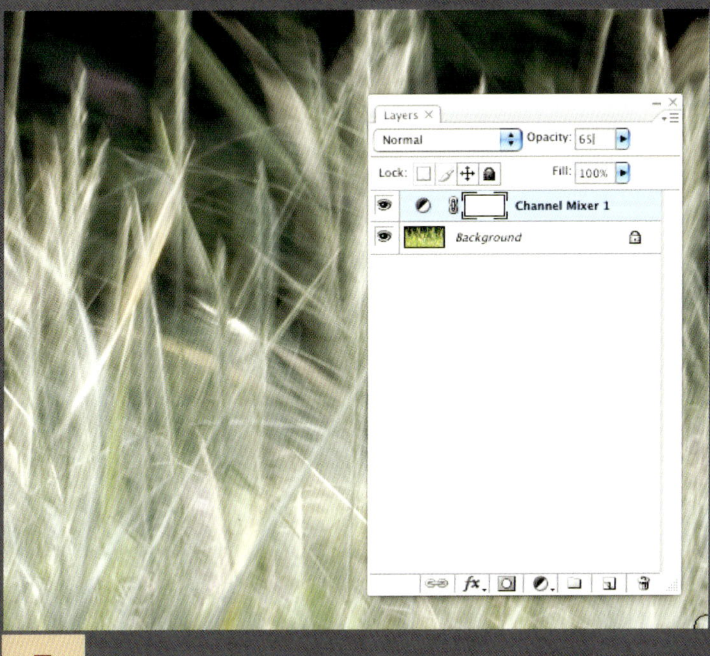

E

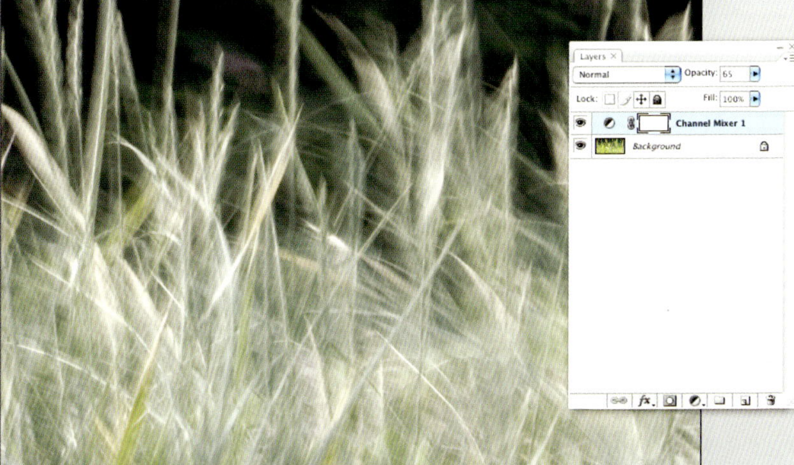

However, it only goes one way. You can only turn the adjustment back; you cannot increase the adjustment. As a result, I tend to go a little overboard on my adjustments so I have room to "feather" them back later.

Note that this is a unique way to feather an adjustment back. I will not get the same result if I go back to my adjustment and try to turn it down, because it is taking the various subtleties of the fixed adjustment and just making it more transparent. Because of this, I use it together with my fine-tuning of the adjustments, not in place of it. Go in, make your Adjustment Layer, go ahead and over-do it a bit, and then turn it back with the Layer Opacity to see what you get.

Sharpening

Sharpening is done using either the "Unsharp Mask" command or the "Smart Sharpen" command (which is just Unsharp Mask with more control). Don't let the "Unsharp" name fool you—it's a relic from the prepress days. It really does sharpen the image. To simplify the discussion, I'm going to concentrate on Unsharp Mask. Smart Sharpen is really cool, but truthfully, I rarely use the enhanced controls it offers.

A couple things to know about Unsharp Masking: it should be done on a duplicate Layer as a very last step—ideally just before you print; and it is done relative to the final image size—a bigger image means more sharpening.

To understand the controls, let's get our heads around what they are actually doing. Unsharp Mask takes neighboring pixels and enhances the differences in their values. Suppose we have six pixels in a row, ranging from black to white (image one). If I take the three on the left and make them all black and the three on the right and make them all white (image two), I've created a distinct border between them. If I take the two on the left and go black, the two in the middle and go gray, and the two on the right and go white (image three), I've made a finer border than before but more distinct than the original.

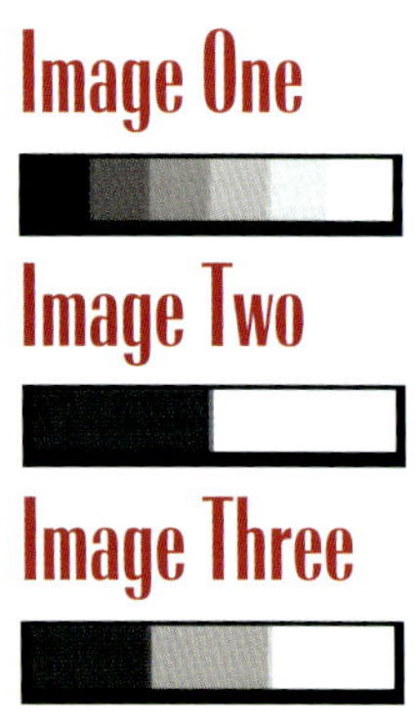

You control all that with the three basic controls of Unsharp Mask: Amount, Radius, and Threshold.

I just want to suggest some settings along with my preferred strategy, but let me add that this turns into a debate very quickly. Experiment a bit and settle on your own method.

I prefer to use a Radius of .5 pixels. That generally keeps any unattractive haloing down to a minimum. To compensate for that, you have to ramp the Amount way, way up—anywhere from 200 – 350%. The Threshold blends the effect, controlling the amount of steps or levels (in pixel value) that you are working with. I usually place that somewhere between 3 and 7.

One more point about my theory of applying this technique. View this adjustment at approximately the size it will print, and maybe a little bigger. Why? You have to evaluate it based on how it is going to be reproduced. If you're viewing the image at 100%, you're not going to even see the effects of the work on the wall. If you're not looking at it big enough, say at "Full Screen" size, you may apply too much. You have to view the image as it will print. This goes for spotting and retouching, too.

This brings us back to the Layer idea. If I apply Unsharp Masking to a Layer, like any other Layer, I can control it with masks and Opacity, too. I'm using the same set of tools and the Layer workflow for all of these jobs.

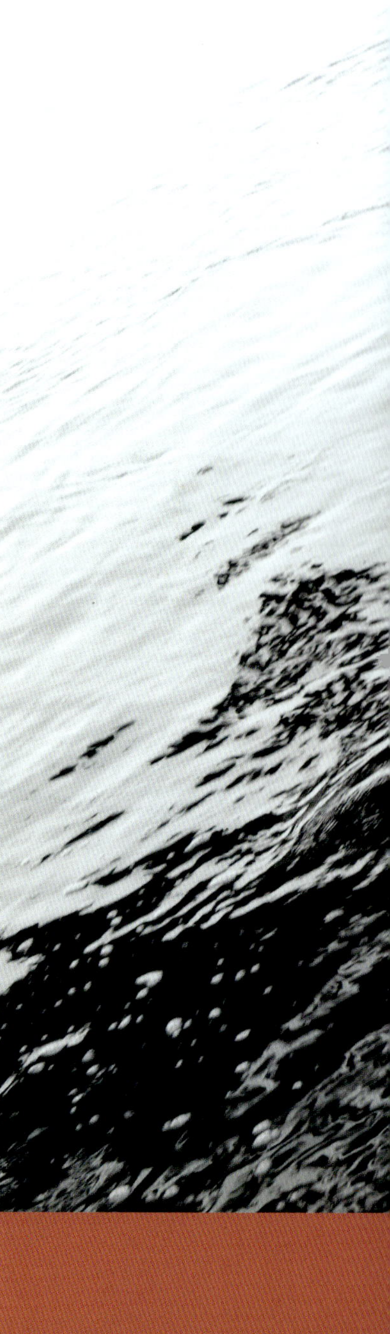

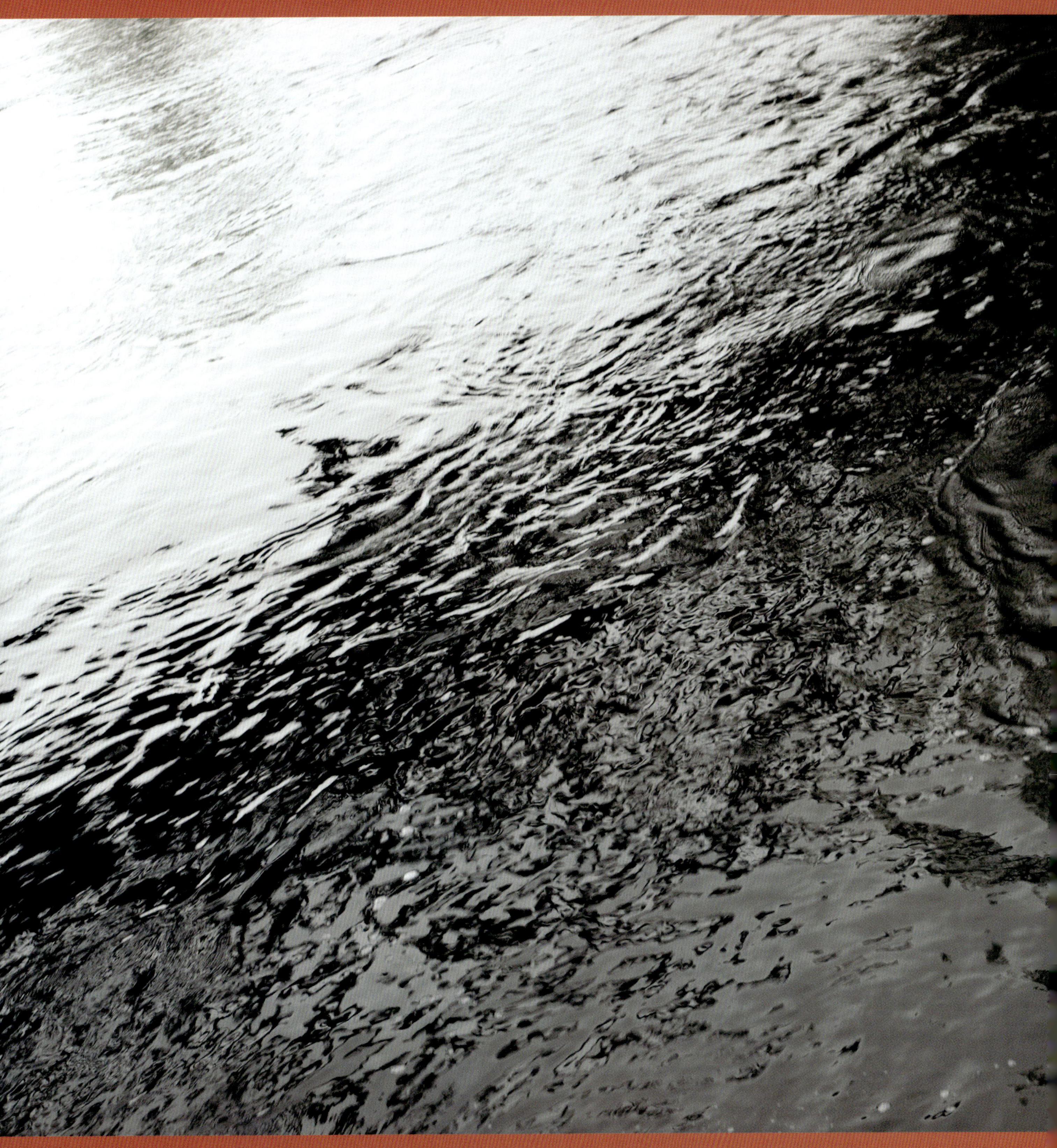

9 BUILDING ON THE FOUNDATION

Up to this point, I've tried to give you some specific information for using tools and techniques in Photoshop to get you started on the right foot. This section is more about signposts pointing the path to show you what you should explore. Working within these paths will allow you to build habits for a good, solid workflow.

Many of the details of Actions, Bridge, and Camera RAW can be found in other texts. Get started here, build the habits, and you can hone your skills with any of the other texts.

Automation

Automation in Photoshop comes in two basic levels—what you get for free with Photoshop in File>Automate, and what you can build yourself in "Actions" and apply in "Batch." There are some sweet little deals in "Automate," like the ability to build a "contact sheet" (File> Automate>Contact Sheet II), and a web-page gallery (File>Automate>Web Photo Gallery).

I'm not going into each feature here, but I encourage you to dive in, play around, and discover how much fun and how powerful these things are. I use Contact Sheet II for printing

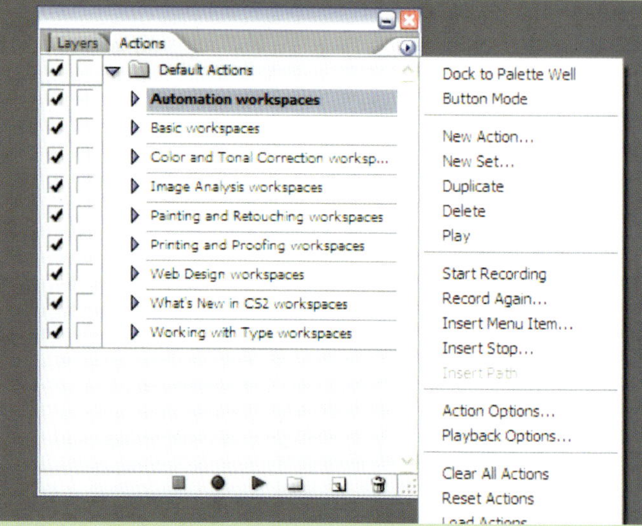

You can use preset Actions created by Adobe, or you can customize your own Actions to better fit your workflow and image editing style.

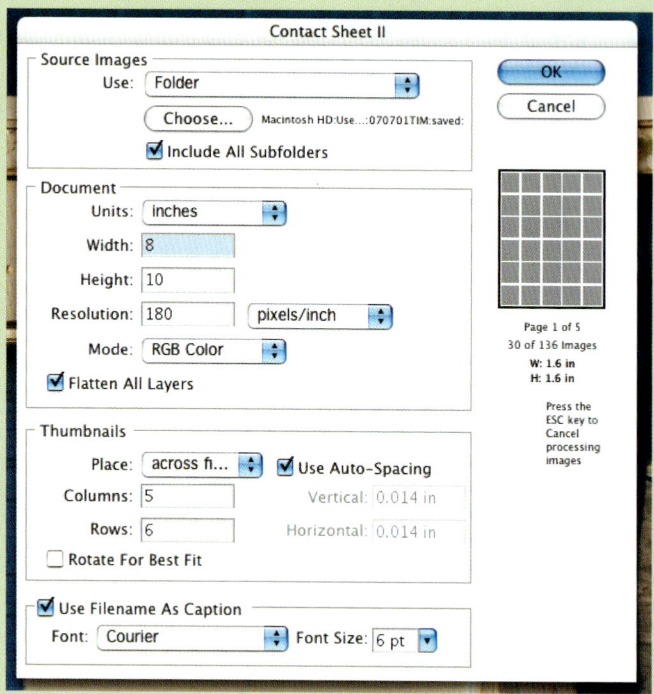

The Contact Sheet option in "Automate" is very handy for professional photographers. You can include this when you deliver image files, or you can use it to quick reference along with your data management system.

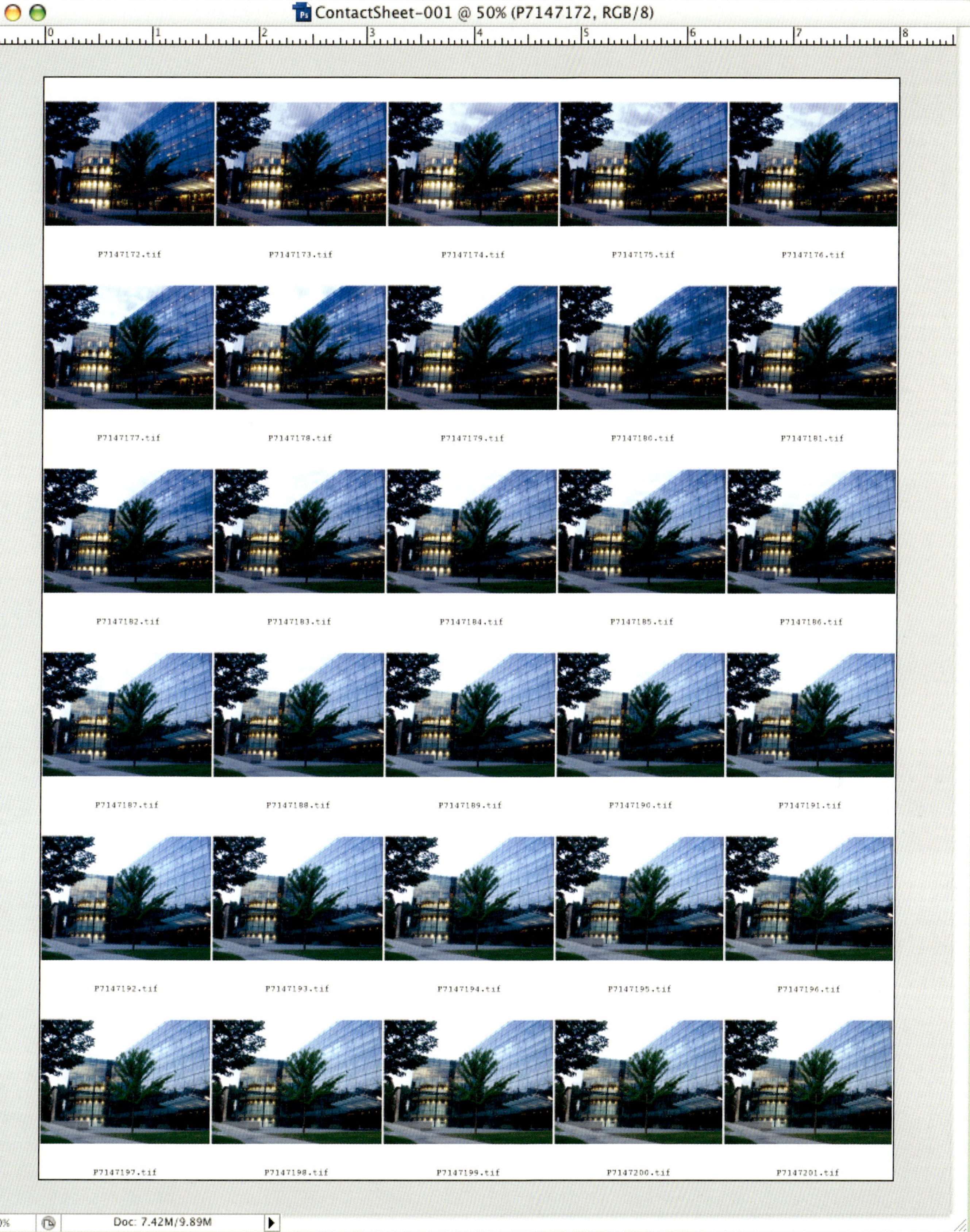
ContactSheet-001 @ 50% (P7147172, RGB/8)
P7147172.tif
P7147173.tif
P7147174.tif
P7147175.tif
P7147176.tif
P7147177.tif
P7147178.tif
P7147179.tif
P7147180.tif
P7147181.tif
P7147182.tif
P7147183.tif
P7147184.tif
P7147185.tif
P7147186.tif
P7147187.tif
P7147188.tif
P7147189.tif
P7147190.tif
P7147191.tif
P7147192.tif
P7147193.tif
P7147194.tif
P7147195.tif
P7147196.tif
P7147197.tif
P7147198.tif
P7147199.tif
P7147200.tif
P7147201.tif
50%
Doc: 7.42M/9.89M

index sheets, with file names, for every project I shoot. I have used the Web Photo Gallery frequently to post large pools of images on my site for general viewing.

Actions

The second level of automation is based on the Action. An action is a way of recording a number of commands in a string. You record the steps, save the action, and then apply it through the "Batch" command, which you can get to a few different ways. Here are a few examples.

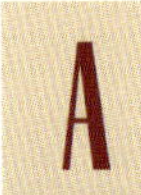

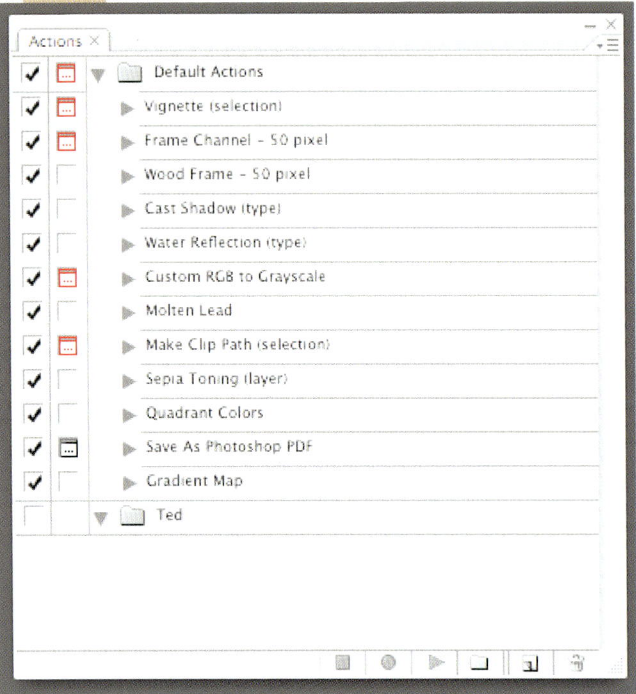

Open the Actions Palette (Window>Actions). You'll see the default "Set" of actions available in Photoshop (A). I want to start off by making my own folder of actions so as not to be confused by all the default selections. I do that by selecting the tiny little triangle in the upper right corner and that opens the options dialog. I scroll down to "New Set," name it "Ted," hit OK, and I have my new folder. (You can also use the folder-like icon at the bottom of the dialog as a shortcut to creating a new set.)

I open an image and plan out my moves. I want to size it to 400 pixels for my website and save it as a JPEG—simple enough. With my file open, I go back to that little options triangle and select "New Action." I name the action and hit "Record," and it will record every command I make, as well as the specific details of each command.

The next example (B) shows my Actions Palette with the "Default Actions" set closed, my custom set ("Ted") open, and the action "ebay" being built. I have two commands so far, "Image Size" and "Save," and you can see exactly what they do under each name. Also notice on the bottom toolbar of the window there is a little red circle, which means we're still in "Record" mode. Hit the little square to the left of the circle, and you're done.

Building your own action may be intimidating at first, but once you try it and understand the steps, it can be a great tool in your RAW workflow.

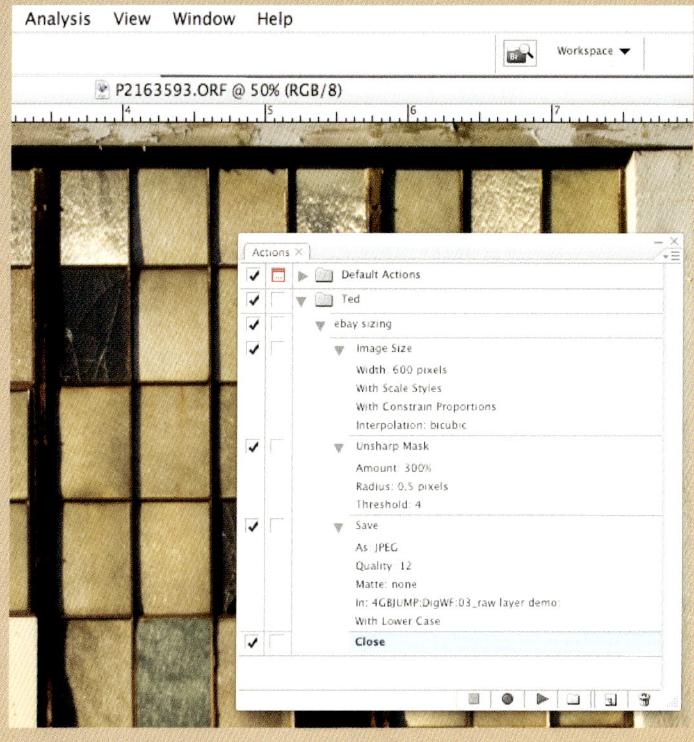

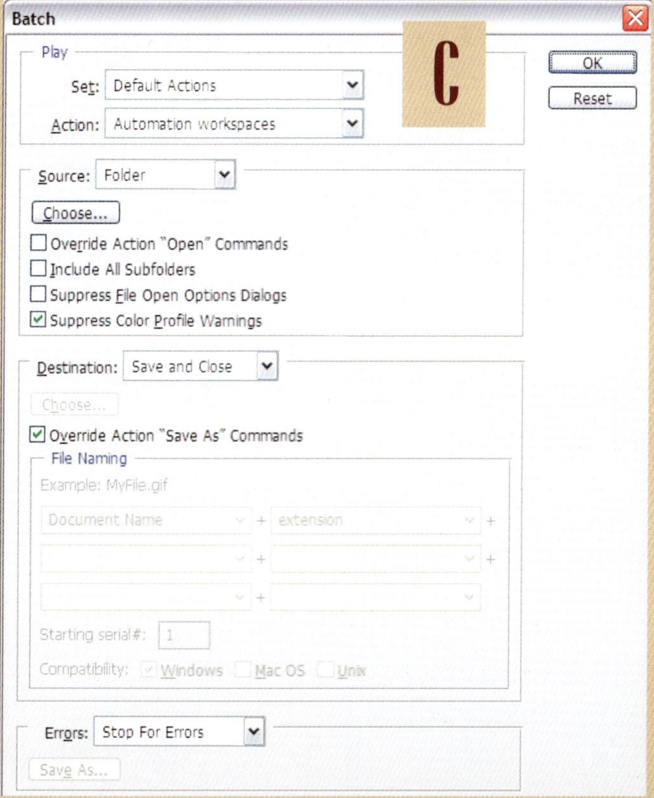

You've built your first Action. Woohoo!

Great, you may be thinking, now how do I actually run this thing of which you speak? That would be the Batch.

Batch

The "Batch" command applies to Actions, so to run it you should have your action built first. You'll see three main windows: "Play" asks you which action you want; "Source" asks you where the files are that you want to work on and how you want to handle file issues like "Open" and folder questions; and "Destination" asks you where you want the files to go, if you want them renamed, etc. (C). Let me introduce you to the Bridge.

This part of automating is where things can go horribly wrong. You can check these features out by researching them or by trial and error, but please do not ever run this on your only copies of a set of files. Always work on backup files. You will make mistakes, even after you think you know this stuff. No need to be afraid; just be careful.

Fine, you say. How do I run these things?

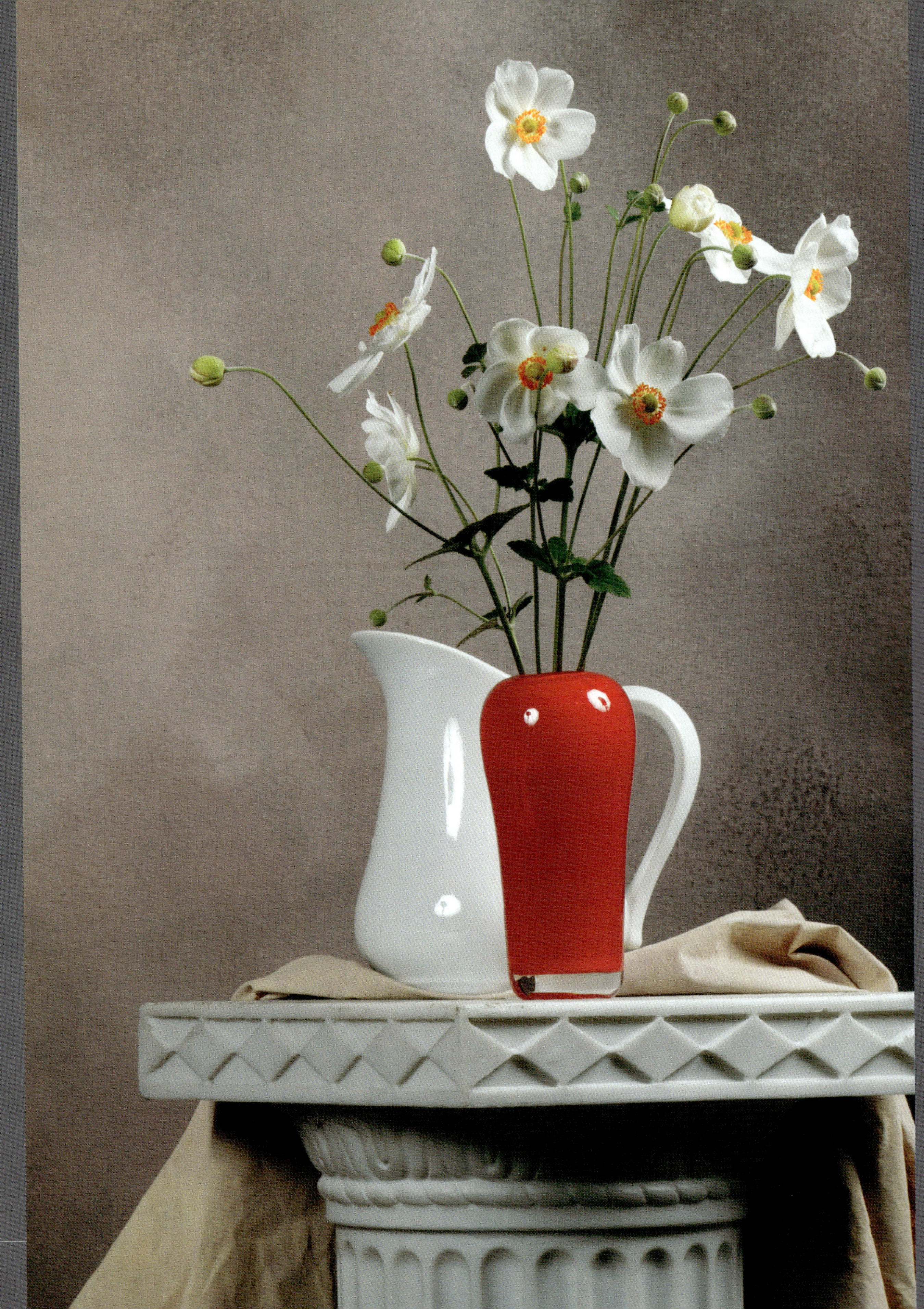

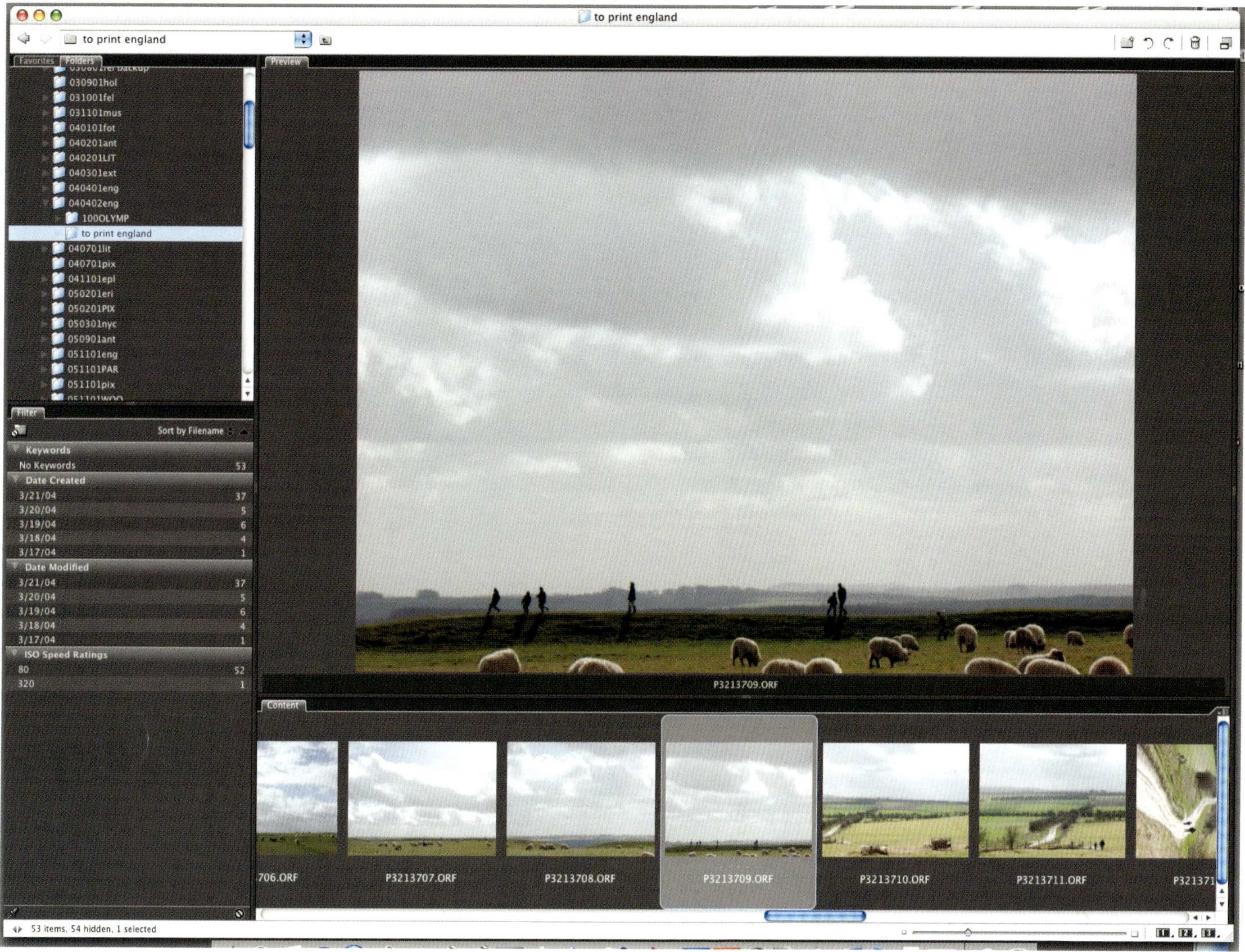

Adobe Bridge

It was first called "File Browser" in Photoshop 7, and didn't work very well. Photoshop CS brought Browser to the point where it became usable, and in CS2 named it "Bridge"—a separate program that allows you to see, sort, tag, move, and process image files, as well as a host of other things in Creative Suite.

The basic function of Bridge is to act as a file browser—a way to see fast, detailed thumbnails of your images. There are many programs out there, including Windows XP and MAC OSX, that make thumbs for you, but I like to use Bridge exclusively. There's a method behind this madness. First, I want to stay simple, and thus stay in one program (and Bridge is basically Photoshop). Second, if I go to Bridge to

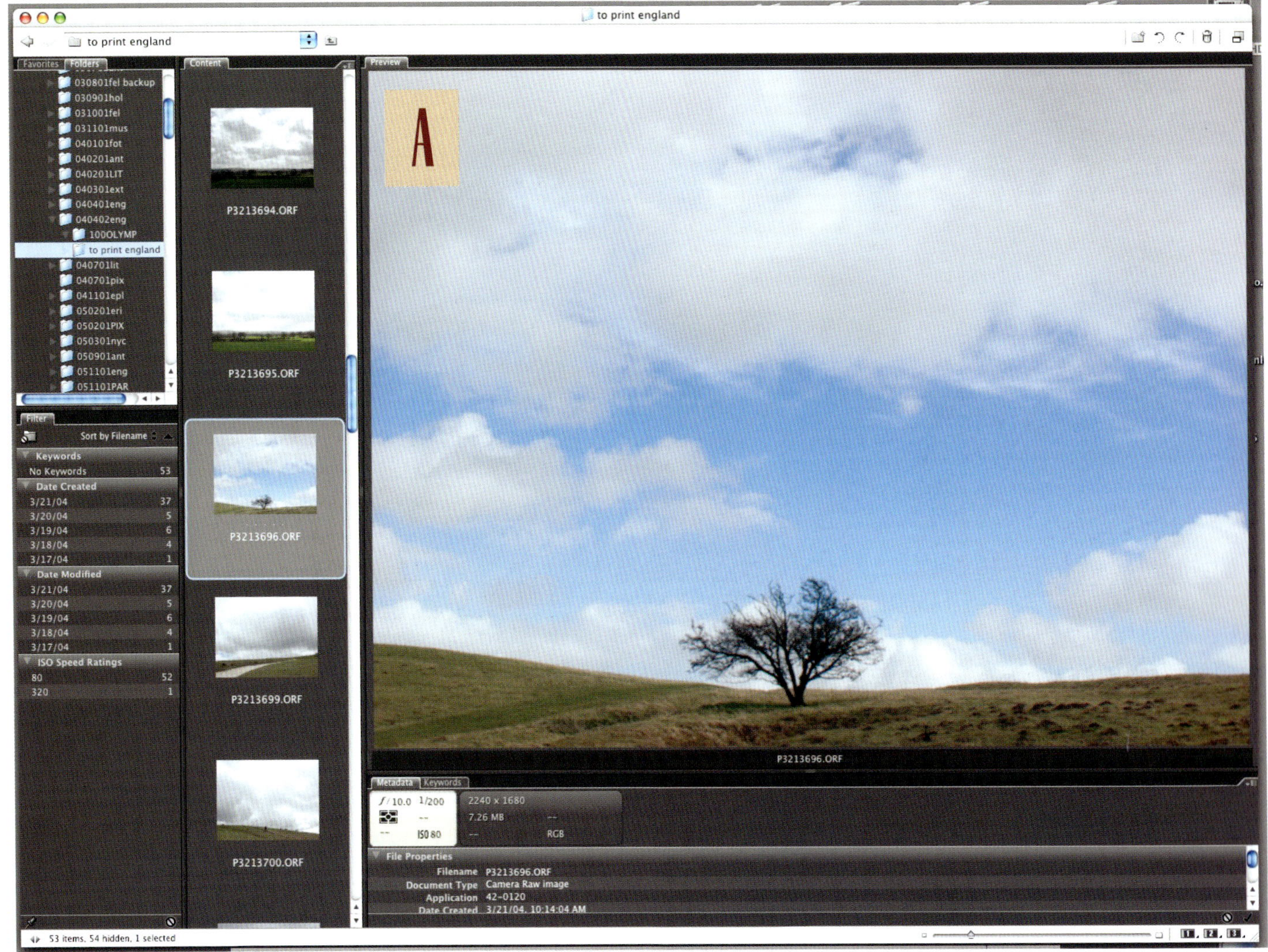

look at files, the next thing I know I'm flagging and sorting files, pretty soon I'm managing my metadata, applying RAW settings, and goodness knows what else.

Again, this is like learning to type. Start at the "home" position, and your fingers learn where to go. Start in Bridge, and you'll learn a good workflow.

Here's how it opens: In Photoshop, go to File>Browse. Just about everything here needs to be changed, in my opinion. In the lower right corner of the window you have preset views, and you can drag the borders of the panes around to suit your taste. Right off I select the "Folders" tab in the navigation window at the top left and slide my panes around to get this (A).

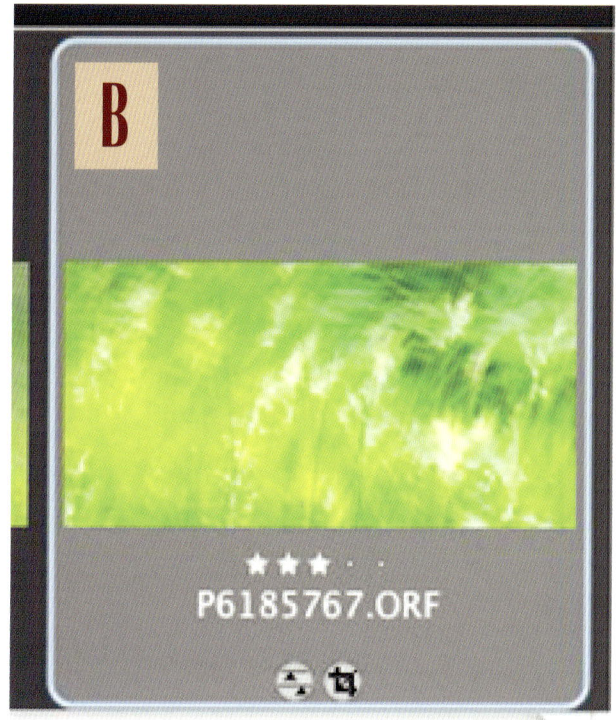

The one to five-star rating system in Adobe Bridge makes it easy to narrow down your images quickly, without the hassle of writing down the file name or opening them individually in Photoshop.

This gives me a nice vertical row of thumbnails and a large preview. It makes me happy. You can set it up however you choose. Just slide those panes/borders around, mess with the controls, and under "Window" you can save the Workspace (Window>Workspace). Then, if someone moves your stuff around, you can go right up to Workspace, load yours, and be happy again.

If I double-click on an image in Bridge, it opens in Photoshop. If it is a RAW file, it will open in Camera RAW. I can move files around simply by dragging the thumbs to the target

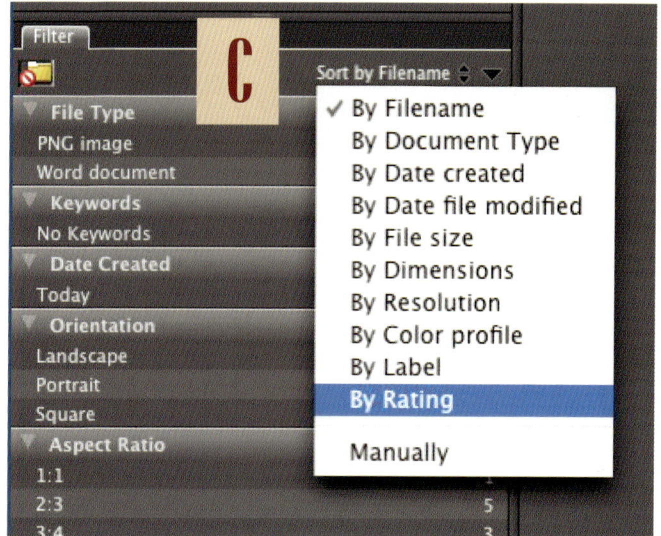

There are a number of ways for organizing a large number of image files in Bridge, as shown in figure (C). This is the list of options available under the "Sort by" drop-down menu.

folders in the navigation pane at the upper right. I can copy them there, instead of moving them, by holding down the "Alt" key while dragging them. How cool is that?

The other feature you need to know about for getting started is the flagging system. Notice the three stars and the two dots on the file shown. I've flagged this file (B) with three stars simply by clicking on the dots—if you want two stars, click two dots. This works whether you're adding or deleting stars. Click five dots and you get five stars. Go back and click the third star and the rating drops to three stars.

How do you use it? If you go to the top, you'll see a button labeled "unfiltered." Click it, and this is what you get (C).

This menu gives you the ability to choose which images you see, and thus quickly sort through them. Let's say I bring in a bunch of images with a "no star" rating. I pick out the images that are decent and give them three stars. Then I use the "filter" to hide all the unstarred files—I've sorted out the keepers without deleting or moving anything. I can continue and flag the ones I really want to work on by giving them a five-star rating, filter for five stars, and bingo, I select my five-star files and open them.

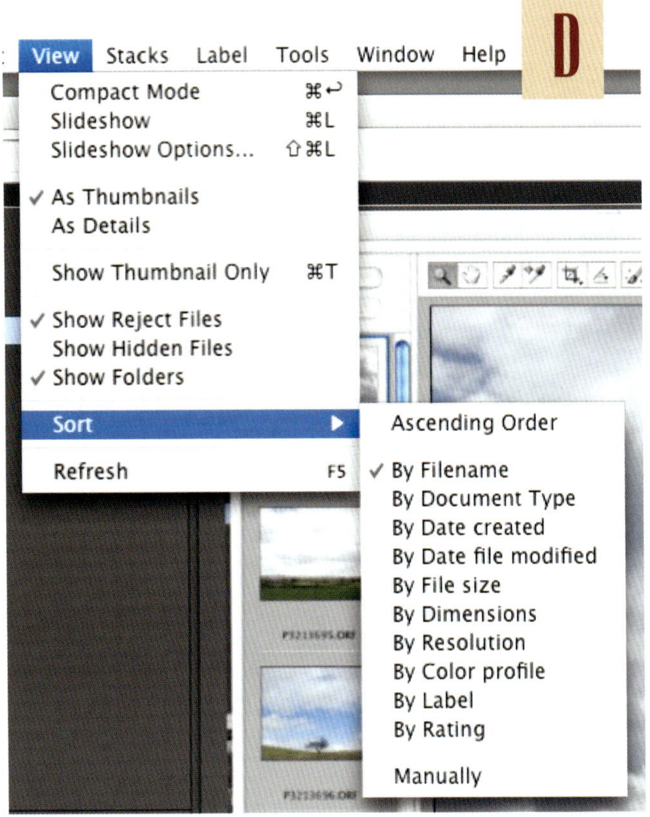

You can also sort your image files through the View>Sort menu option, as well as the "Sort by" drop-down menu in Bridge.

This is about rating first, then sorting by making the images viewable or not. Once you get to where only those you want are viewable, you can edit and work on them.

Another way to sort is through View>Sort (D), and you'll see a whole host of options—my personal favorite is "Manually." Sorting manually allows you to sort images like you would on a light table, dragging them around and ordering as you choose.

Automation with Bridge: Did I get to Automation through the Bridge yet? Go to Tools>Photoshop>Batch, and there you'll find your friendly "Batch" dialog, except now you can set the source to "Bridge."

See how this works? See your files. Rate your files. Sort your files. Select your files and run an Action on them, all through the Bridge.

This should get you started. There's a raft of other stuff here, but again, if you can get into the habit of going here first instead of using some program outside of Photoshop, you're going to start on the right foot.

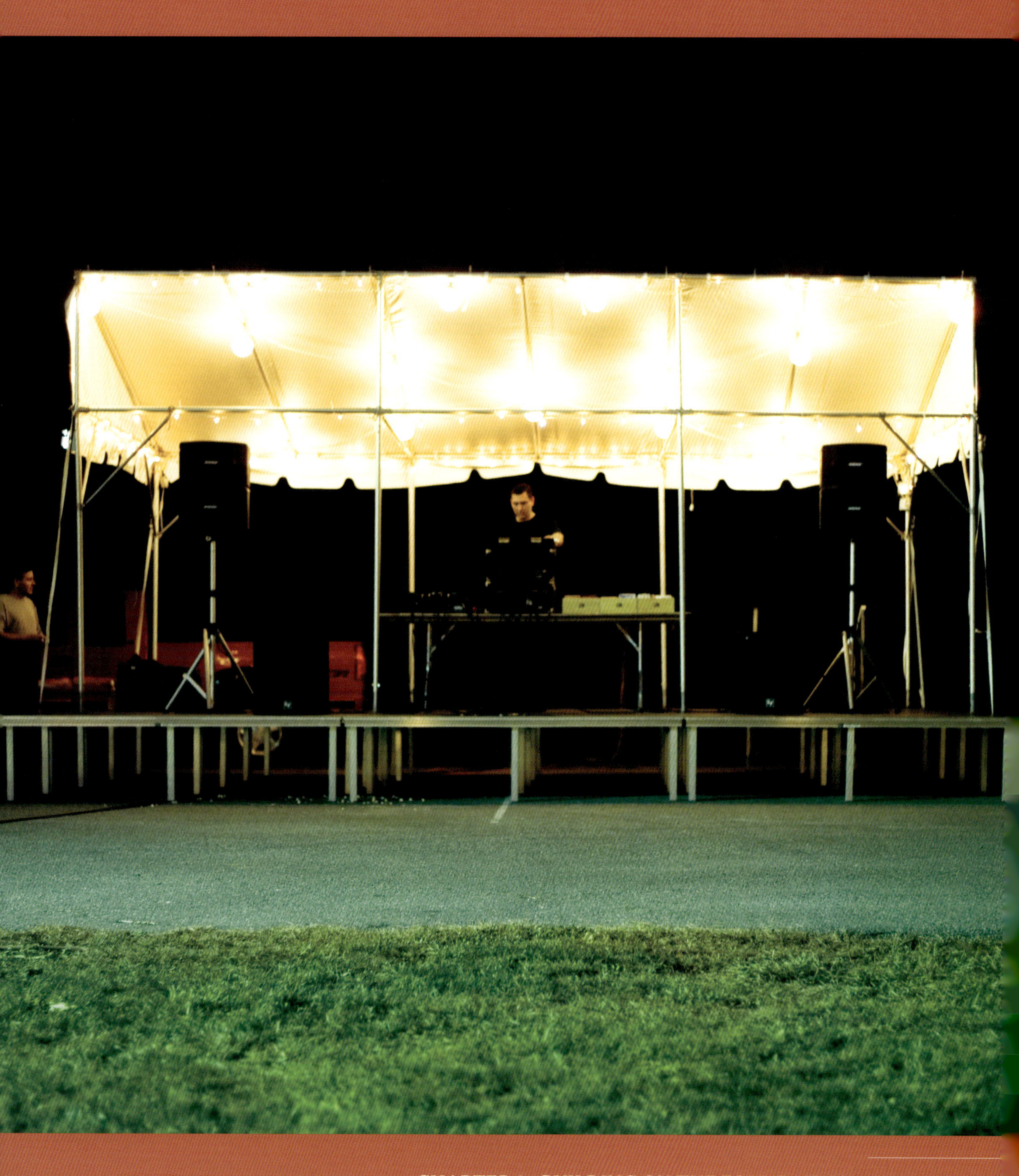

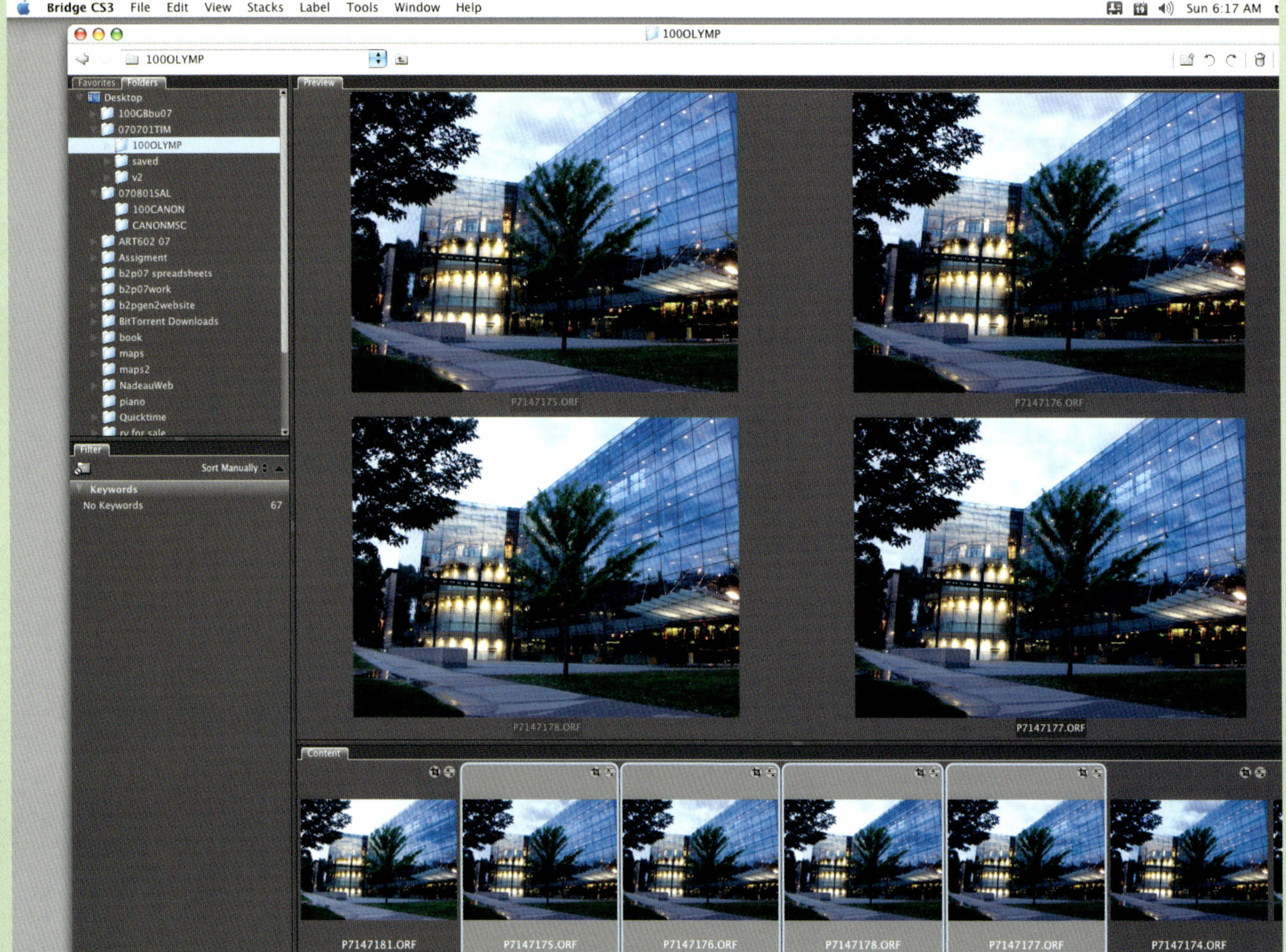

Stacks

Stacks are a way of making a pile of similar files in Bridge and placing your favorite image on the top of the pile. If you want to go back in, look at the similar images, and possibly change your pick, its as easy as finding the Stack, opening it, reselecting the pick, and stacking it back up.

Here's the issue. In all my sorting, ranking, picking, and copying of files, I may be separating out my main "pick" files from the "outtakes." Suppose I make a decision to call one file my pick, and copy it to a folder. I print this and finally decide that I want to see the outtakes again, because I'm not too pleased with some part of this file. I have to then go back into my folders, find the files, figure out which were the outtakes, and then decide which one to use.

Here's another example: I do a portrait shoot, pull out the files that I think the client will like, and show them to the client. The client says, "I kind of like this one, but do you have others like it?" I have to rummage through all the outtakes again, find the sequence, and show the options. That sequence may not be very accessible, or it may be stored on a remote drive. Solution? Stacks.

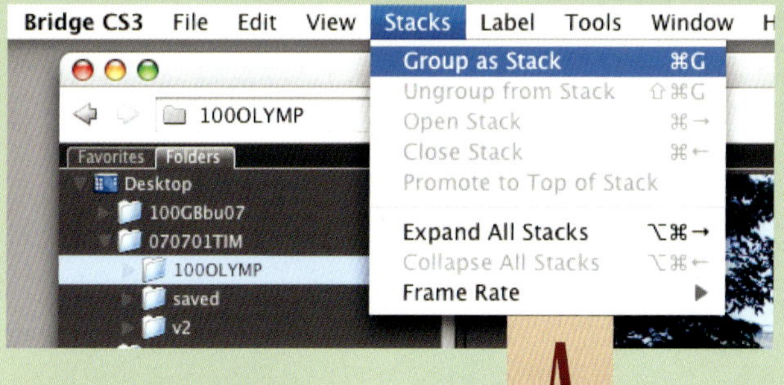

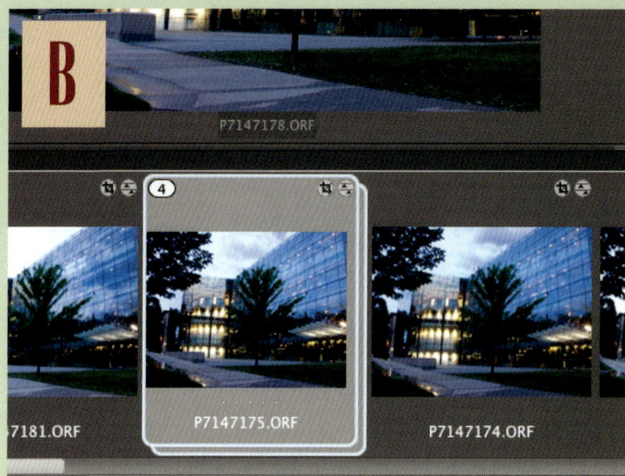

Using Stacks

First, in Bridge, sort and select the images you want to stack. The first image in the series will be the one at the top of the stack—it will be considered the "pick." Go to Stacks>Group as Stack (A), and you'll see a little pile with a number in the upper corner indicating the number of images in the Stack (B).

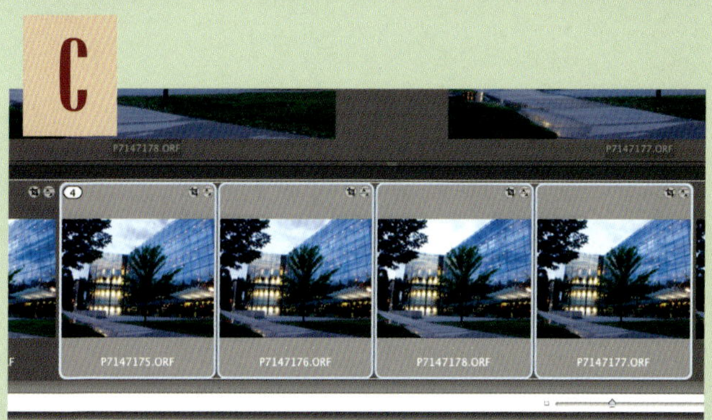

Changing the "pick" of the Stack is really simple. When the Stack is open (C) (double-click the little number to open and close the Stack, or select Stacks>Open Stack), select the image you want to be the "pick." Go to Stacks>Promote to Top of Stack, and when you restack the Stack, that image will be the visible one (D).

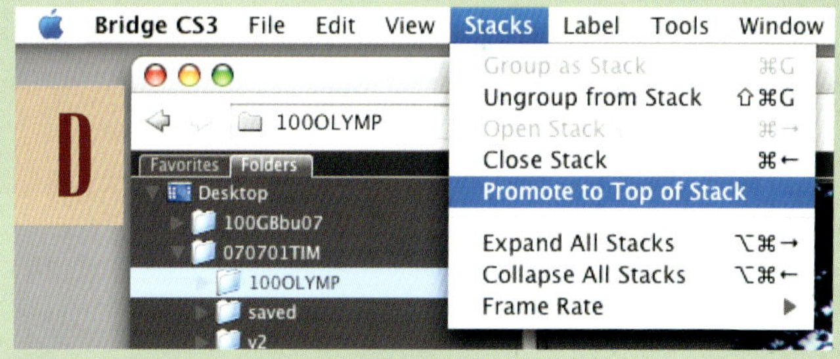

All of your images in the Stack can be moved and copied as one image—simply grab the stack and do what you will with it, just as you would move a pile of stuff around your desk. For those of us that use the "pile" file method (aka the "filepile") in the office, the Stack is a natural, fast way to organize your work and keep your options close at hand.

If you want to un-stack your files—that is, not to just open the Stack, but to take them out of the Stack entirely—go to Stacks>Ungroup from Stack (E).

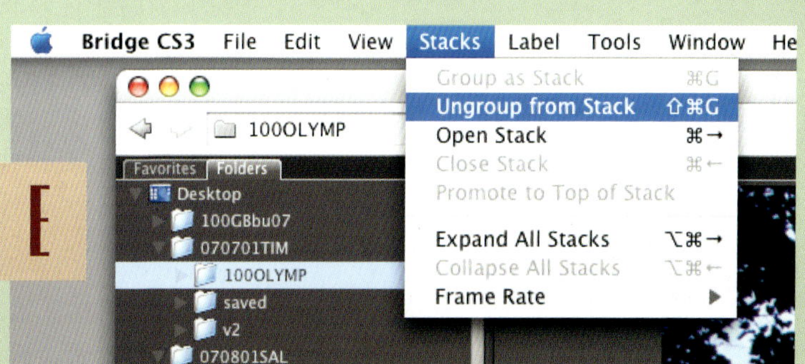

Adobe Camera RAW

As a plug-in for Photoshop 7, Camera RAW opened up a new world to the serious photographer. When Camera RAW hit, every photographer I know at least tried shooting in RAW, if not converting to it totally.

The RAW file represents the light that fell on and was recorded by the sensor, pure and simple. You can't alter that file—the data is the data. Even if you have your camera set to JPEG, it has to shoot RAW and process the file to JPEG. You can go back and process the RAW file in many different ways, but you always start with the same basic data.

For that reason, the RAW conversion process is a constructive process—building data, rather than a destructive or selective "massaging" of data. Once you have a TIFF, for example, all the Curves and Levels you apply are only able to move data around at best. Most often you're throwing data away.

I'm going to give you quick tour around the Camera RAW window so you can get started, but I go into the greatest detail on how to really use the RAW file and work in a bulletproof RAW workflow in Part 4 of this book. If you really want to know about every feature in Camera RAW, go to Bruce Fraser's *Real World Camera RAW* to start.

Go to the Camera RAW window simply by trying to open a digital camera's RAW file. I use an Olympus E-10, which makes an "Olympus Raw File" (file extension ".orf"). Clickety-click, and it opens this window (A).

The big pane shows your preview. The small pane to the right shows your image adjustments. Note that you have tabs with icons for each function: Basic (Adjustments), Tone Curve, Detail, HSL Grayscale, Split Toning, Lens, Camera Calibration, and Presets. On the bar with the name of the tab is a cryptic little icon that takes you to your "Settings" menu. Below the Preview pane is the "Workflow Options" link. Finally, at the bottom left you have "Save Image," on the bottom right "Open Image (or Object)," "Cancel" ("Reset"), and "Done" buttons.

The Preview pane shows the image with the adjustments you've made as long as the "Preview" box is checked. You can easily do a "before and after" comparison by checking/unchecking the "Preview" button. You can zoom in, zoom out, and move around the preview using the same tools and shortcuts we use in Photoshop. The Zoom tool is found in the upper left. There are little arrows at the top of the Histogram window—with a click they show you a gamut warning if your highlights or shadows are being clipped.

In the bottom pane (B), you can click the "AdobeRGB," etc. link and you have the "Workflow" options. Make sure you are set to AdobeRGB 1998, working in the color depth you want (most often 8 bit), and set the "Resolution" to

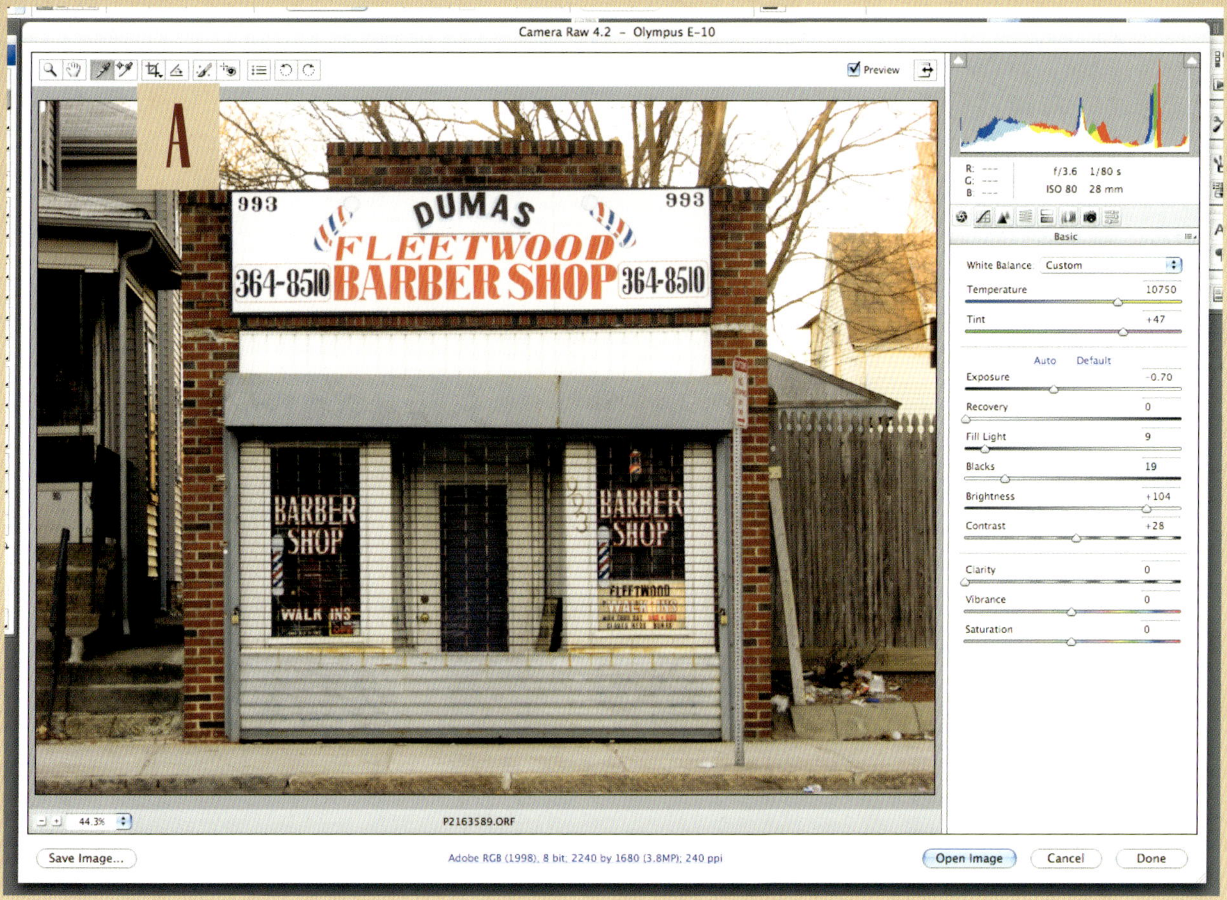

Adobe Camera RAW is a key piece of the RAW pipeline. Here is where you decide how your RAW image files will be processed, and this is a very powerful tool. As we delve further into the workflow, you will begin to see how important it is to familiarize yourself with Camera RAW, and why it is so powerful.

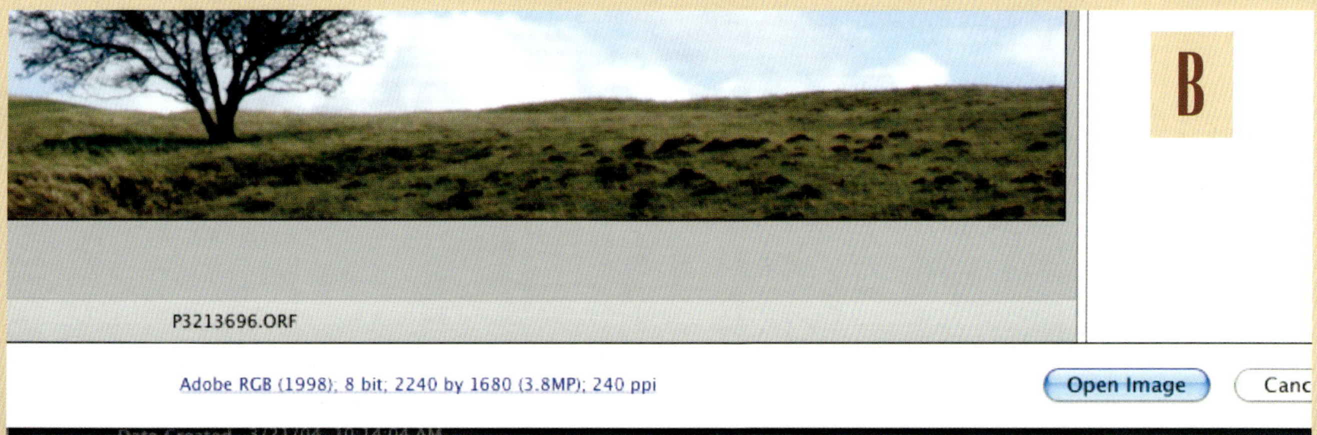

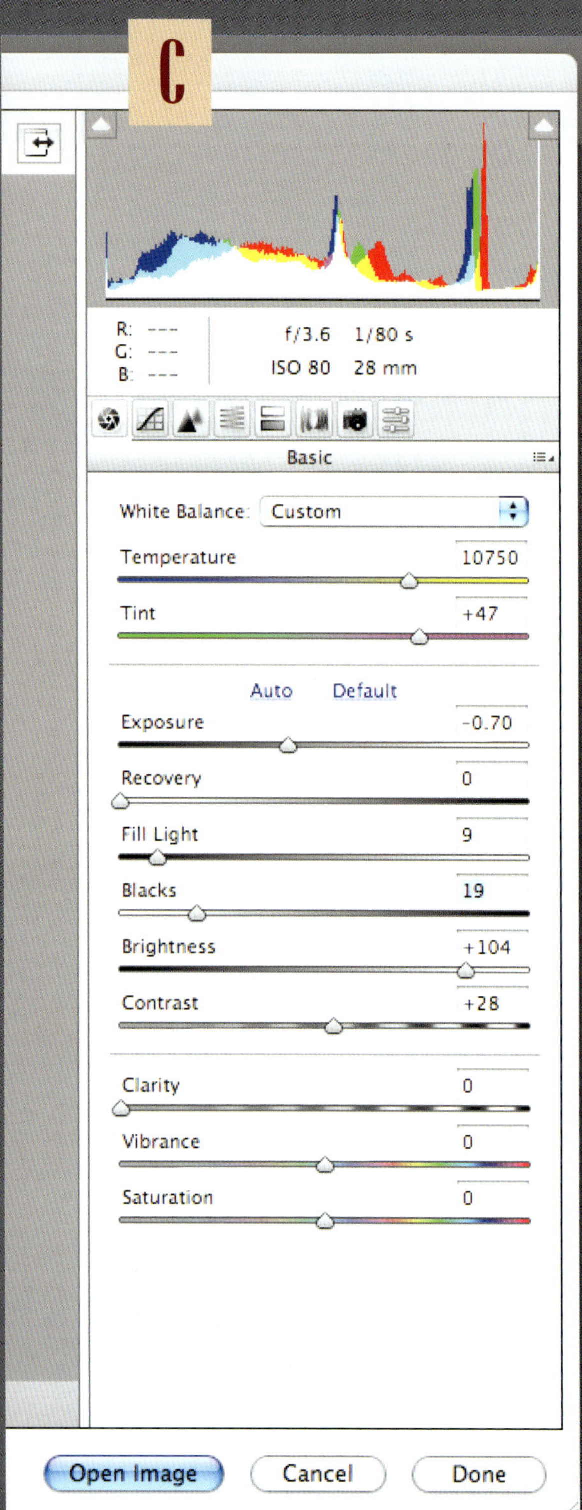
C
R: ---
G: ---
B: ---
f/3.6 1/80 s
ISO 80 28 mm
Basic
White Balance: Custom
Temperature 10750
Tint +47
Auto Default
Exposure -0.70
Recovery 0
Fill Light 9
Blacks 19
Brightness +104
Contrast +28
Clarity 0
Vibrance 0
Saturation 0
Open Image
Cancel
Done

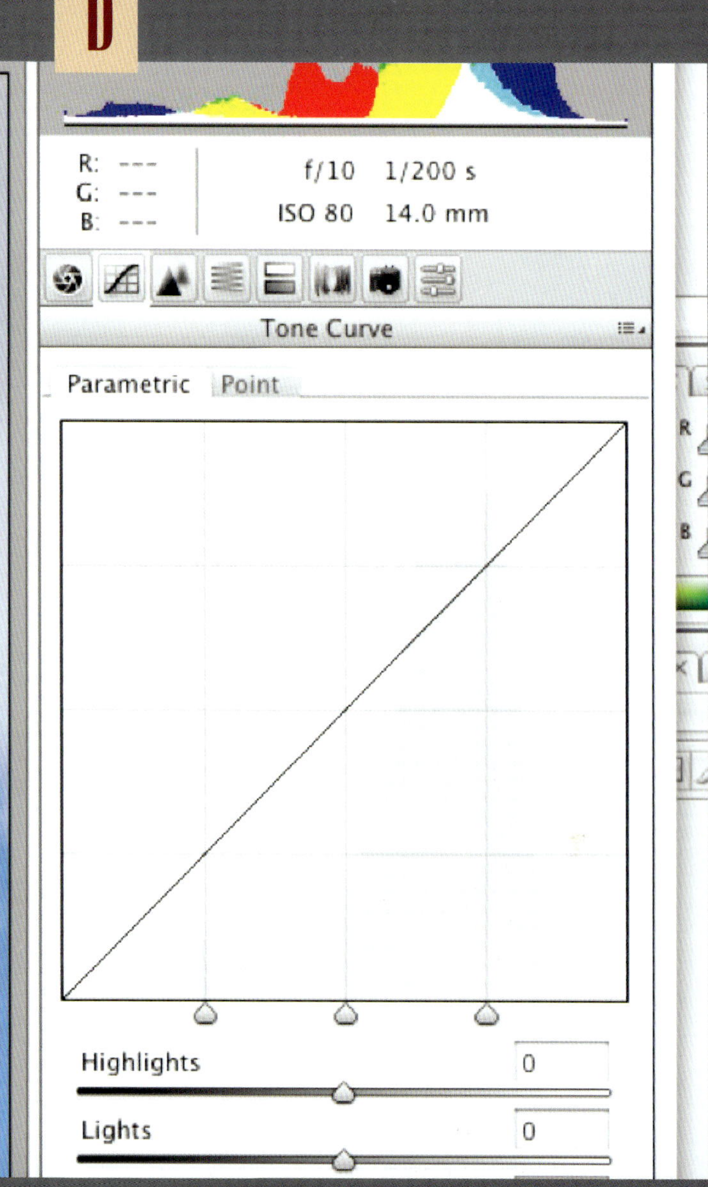
D
R: ---
G: ---
B: ---
f/10 1/200 s
ISO 80 14.0 mm
Tone Curve
Parametric
Point
Highlights 0
Lights 0

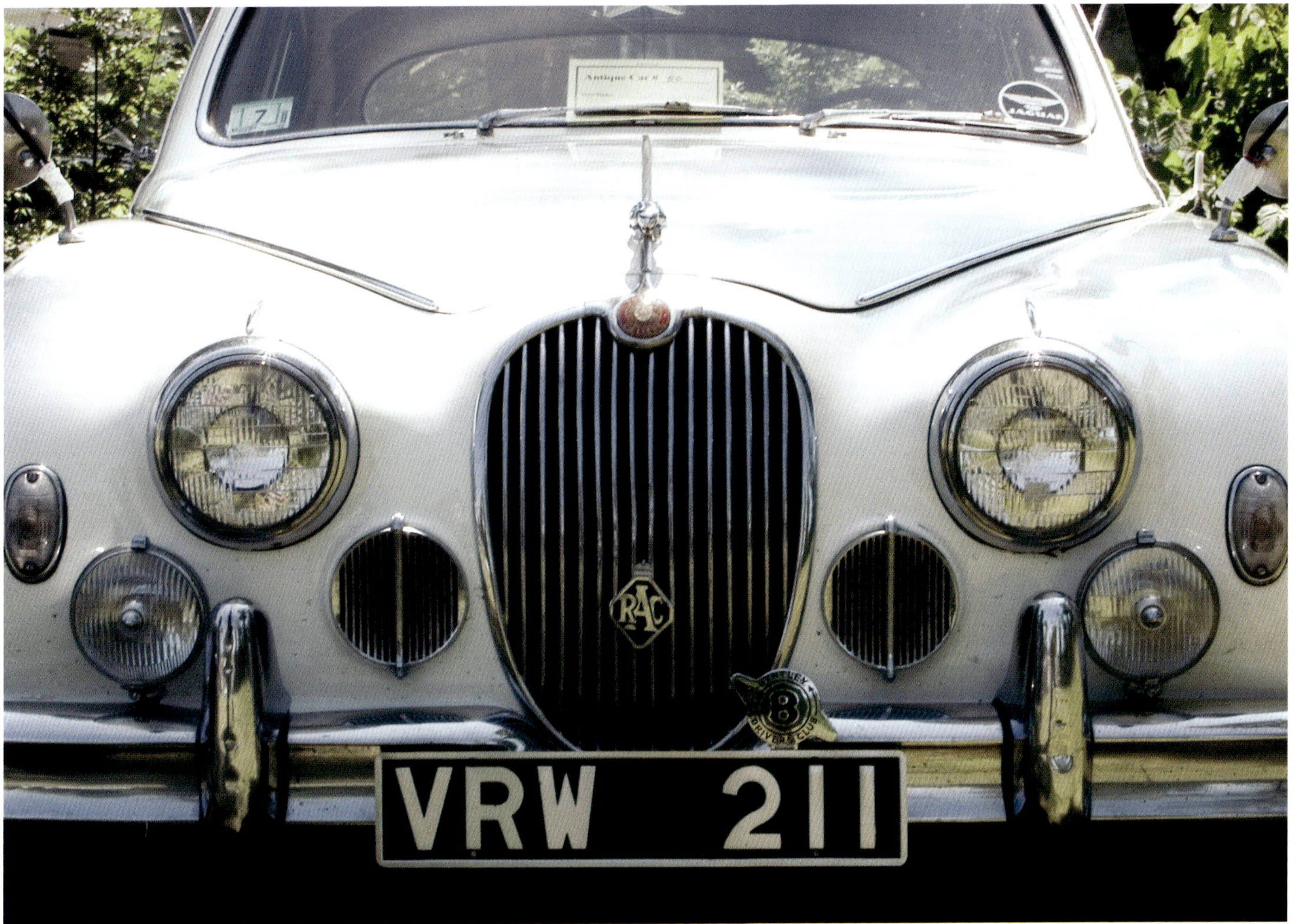

the number you like for the "Document" resolution. The "Size" is where you can set the file size before completely processing the RAW image—sized up, down, or kept at its native size. This is a nice way to move toward a final image size, because first, it's working on the RAW pixels to build the file up, and second, it only gives you mathematically harmonious sizes to go to. It doesn't force the pixels to do something they don't want to do.

The image adjustments are where you do most of your work (C). The first tab is what I like to call the big hammer, where you tap the images into the neighborhood, using the White Balance pane to dial in color, and the other sliders to take care of contrast and tones. Once that's done, I usually go to the Camera Calibration tab, the little hammer, to fine-tune the colors. There I can take each of the three basic channels, (R, G, and B), and control their hue and saturation.

The Tone Curve tab (D) allows me to precisely adjust what I've done with the Contrast and Tone settings in the Basic tab. I make my Basic tab settings first, then go to the Tone Curve tab and do a little redistribution if it needs it. Finally, the Detail tab is where I can apply

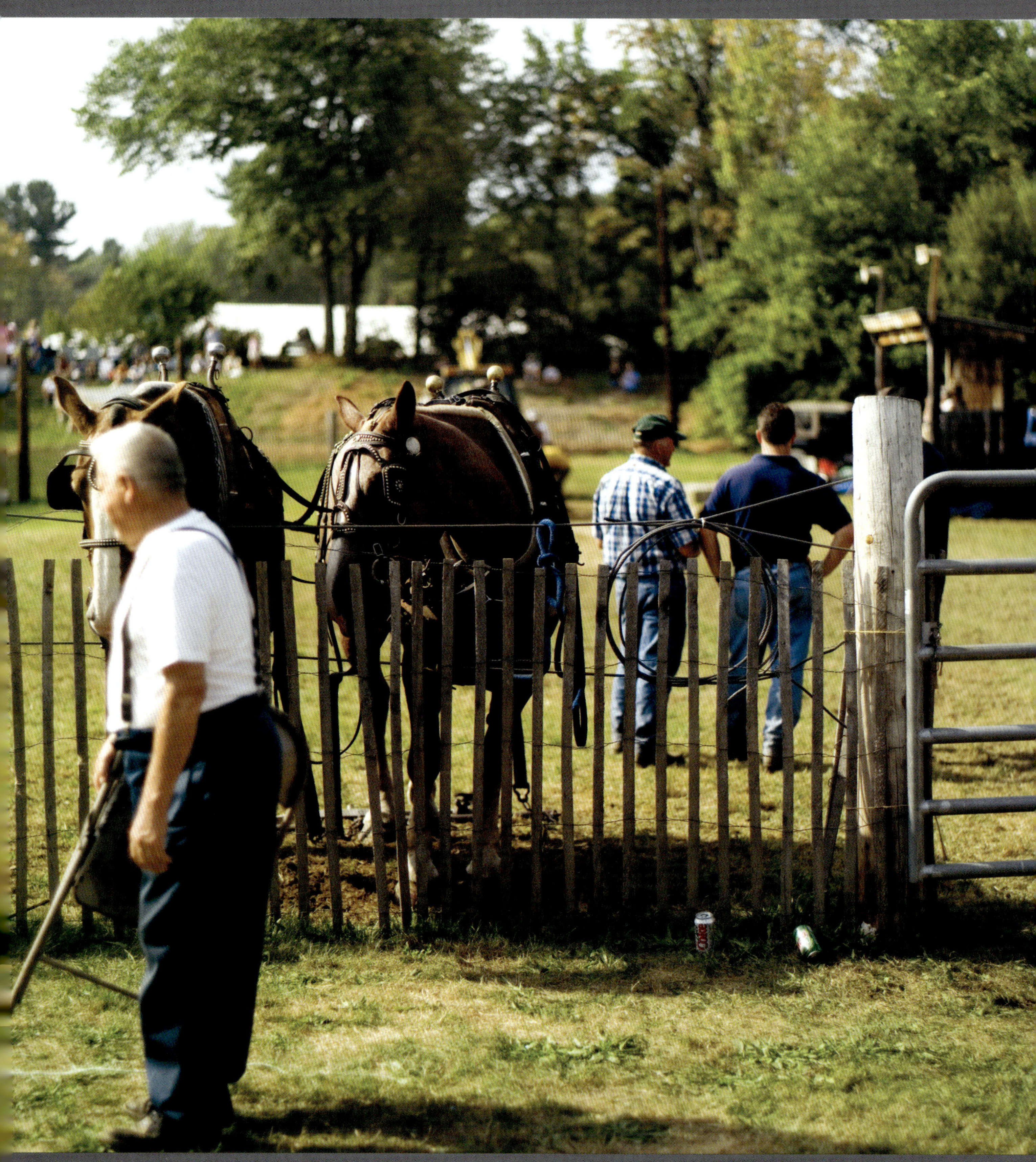

Sharpening, Smoothing, and Noise Reduction. The Lens tab is, in my humble opinion, gratuitous, but fun nevertheless.

When you go into Bridge and select a few files, instead of just one, these files now show up as thumbnails in the Camera RAW window. When you select a few files in the Camera RAW window (here we've selected all four), we can "Save 4 Images," which allows us to process and convert these four images to TIFFs, JPEGs, or whatever, to a target location in one fell swoop.

Again, with the Bridge: view, rate, and sort the images (see page 113-116); select your finals; and open them in Camera RAW. Go through each one and make your adjustments. Select them all, and Save them as TIFFs in your "Work" folder. How much better could life be?

Smart Objects

Smart Objects were introduced with Adobe's Creative Suite 2, and are part of a "non-destructive editing" push. They really are a big deal.

Basically, what a Smart Object does is allow you access to all the attributes of the original source of the layer (say, for example, a RAW file). When you drop a Smart Object into an image in Photoshop, it looks and acts like a layer. Much of what you can do with a regular layer, (for example, mask it, control opacity, control the order) you can do with a Smart Object. The difference is you can get right back to the source of that Smart Object layer (in our case, the RAW file), simply by double-clicking the icon on the layer.

Think of it like this: the Smart Object is a layer in your image that is a little container holding another file. It's a box holding your RAW file in its original state. It holds all your RAW data, as well as all the edits and changes you've made. (This is usually stored in the .xmp file that hangs along with your RAW files; you may have seen them.) In a Smart Object layer, the .xmp file is built right into the layer. It actually ends up in the header information in the file (the "code" that is the actual computer language that makes up the file). Smart Objects give you all that—without having to go outside Photoshop or the image—so you can rebuild the layer from the source, rather than re-edit it.

My theory, and it's only my theory, is that they made Smart Objects to make the Creative Suite workflow more streamlined. You can work Illustrator files into your Photoshop workflow, and it can be done in a non-destructive way. I'm not really sure that they were thinking RAW files here; in fact, more than a few instructors I talked to were unaware that RAW files could be handled as Smart Objects. In CS3, however, we see Adobe stepping up to the plate and supporting the RAW/Smart Object process in a big way, and it is certainly no mistake.

Working with Smart Objects

Smart Objects are not images, by strict definition. They have to be "placed" in images in Photoshop, and in CS2 the only way to do that was to open a file (creating a "target image") in Photoshop, and then going to File>Place>in Photoshop from Bridge (A). (Well, it was not the only way, but the only truly practical way.) With the release of CS3, it's clear Adobe has a handle on the needed workflow—they built a few more practical ways to work with Smart Objects.

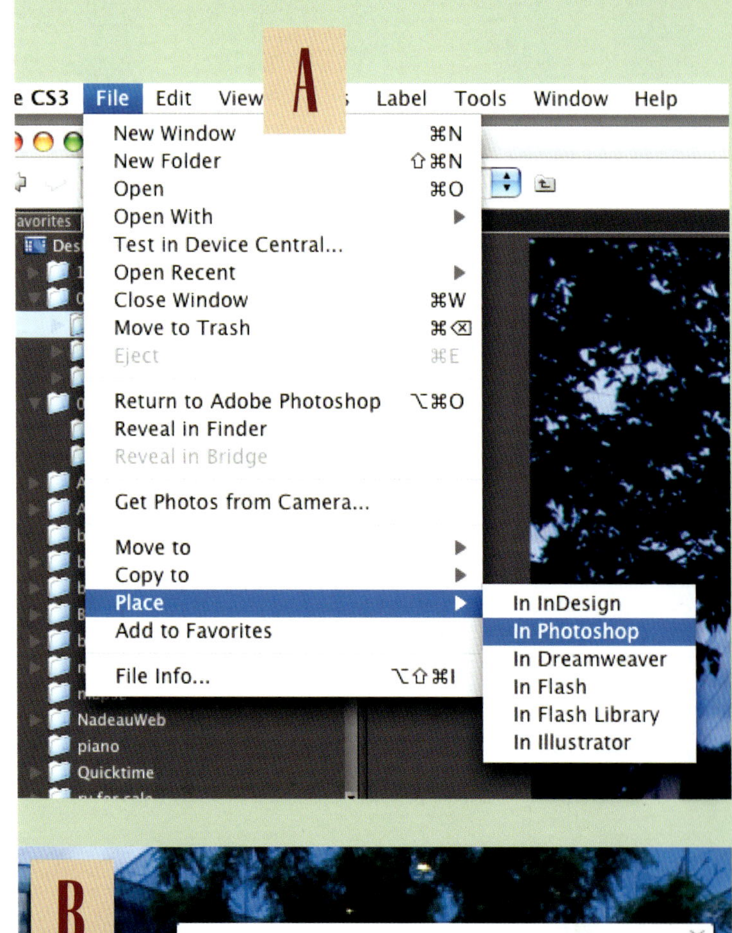

You can still do File>Place>in Photoshop from Bridge, and that takes you right into Photoshop without opening the Camera RAW dialog. You used to be able to do a little adjustment in Camera RAW when you "placed" this way, but no more. That method just takes you right to Photoshop, and you get a layer with a Smart Object icon (B).

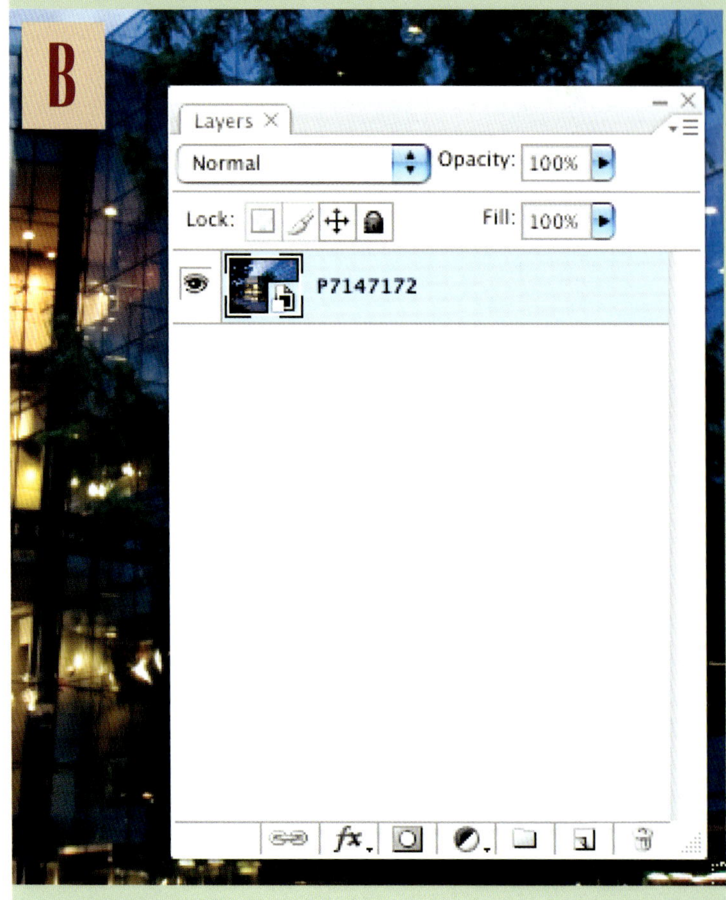

I'm not too fond of this method for general practice, because CS3 has given me a much nicer option. In the Camera RAW dialog itself, under "Workflow Options," I can set Camera RAW to open RAW files as Smart Objects automatically and still retain access to the adjustments in Camera RAW.

In the main window of Camera RAW, look at the very bottom (C). There is what looks like a web link in the middle, under the Preview. Click that, and it takes you into the "Workflow Options" dialog. Check the box next to "Open in Photoshop as Smart Objects," and you're all set (D). Every RAW

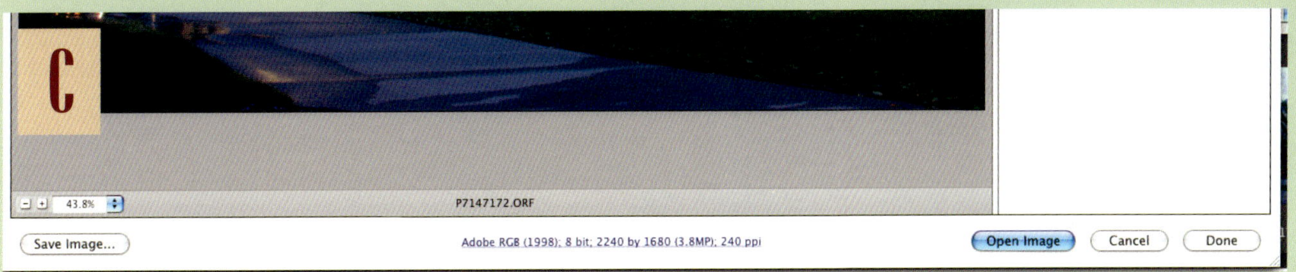

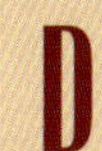

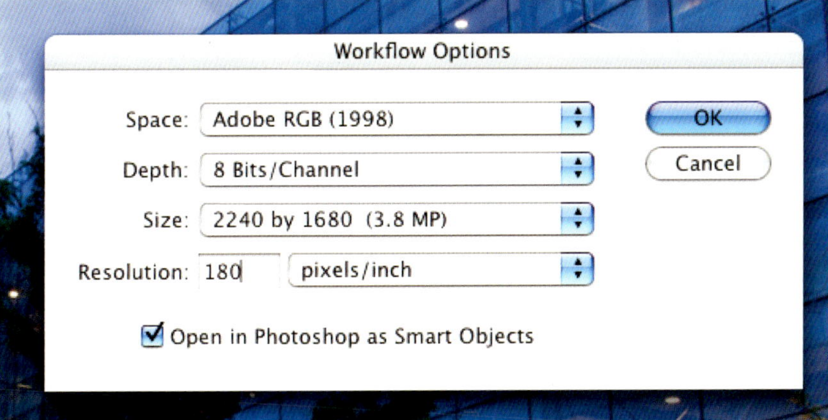

file you open will be a file with a Smart Object layer. This will stay set like this until you change it, so keep that in mind if you want to work on some images without using Smart Objects. (Now, why would you want to do that?)

Once you do that, the dialog button at the bottom no longer says "Open Image"—it says "Open Object" (E) (which is a good reminder that you are in "Open in Photoshop as Smart Objects" mode in the Workflow Options).

There is one other, well, *fairly* useful way to get an image into Smart Object mode, and that is direct from the File> dialog in Photoshop. Go to File>Open as Smart Object (F). This will open a file, you have to navigate to it using the Finder dialog, and it will open up the Camera RAW window.

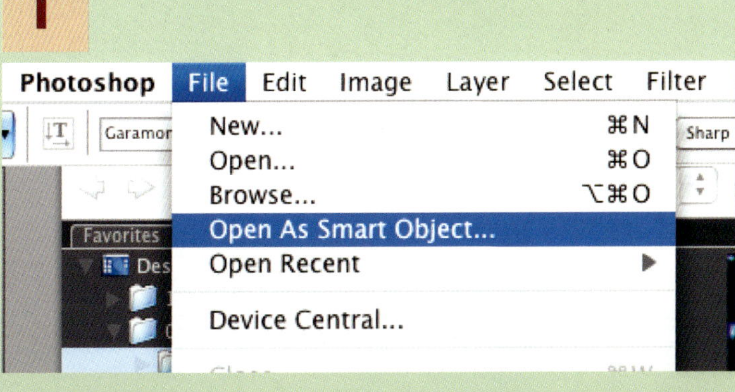

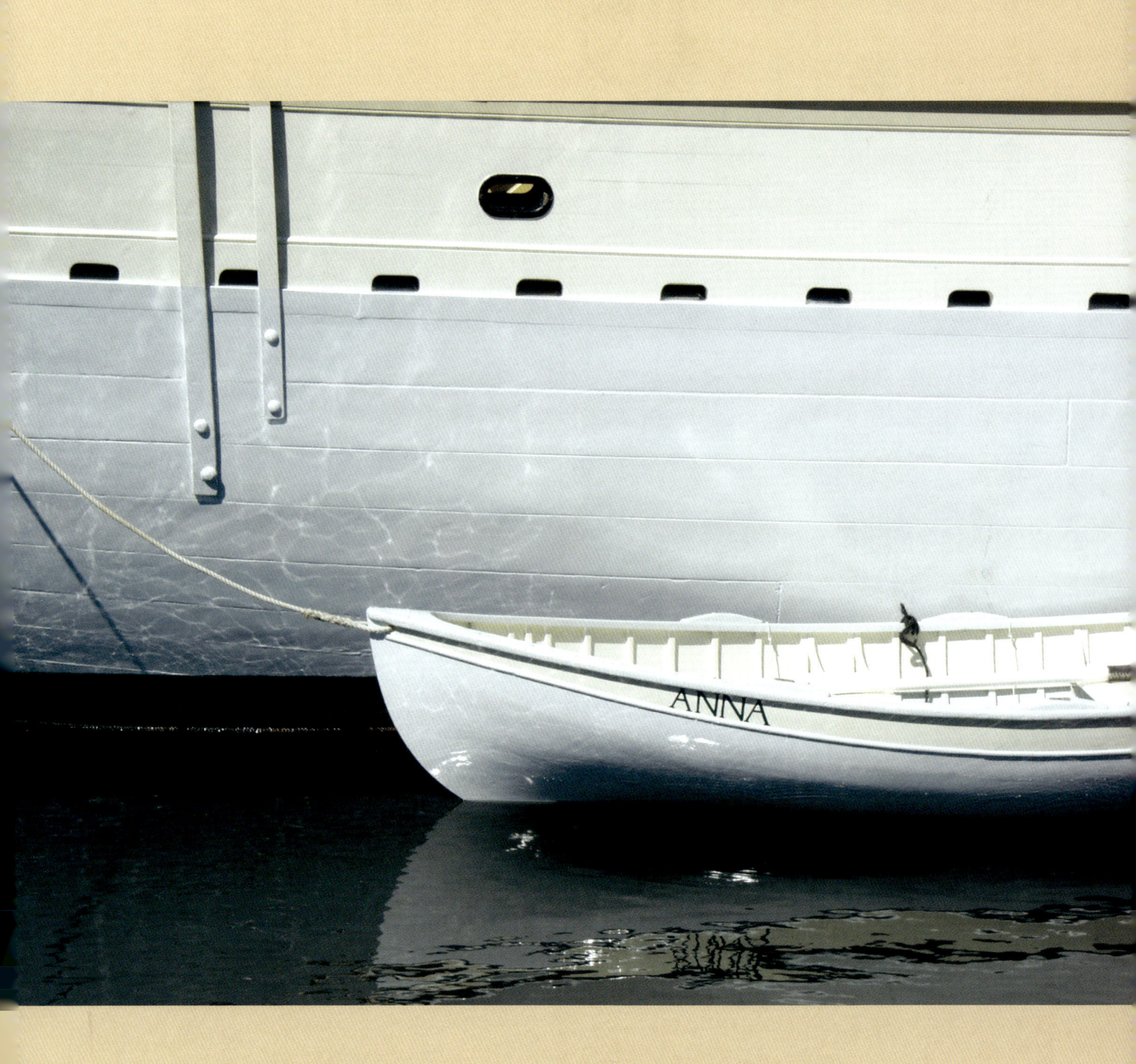
ANNA

NOTE: I try to discourage people from using this method, just because I like to get you in the habit of using Bridge for everything. It is so integral to all the aspects of the workflow, and by going back to Bridge for everything you are simplifying your process and eliminating random efforts.

Duplicating Smart Object Layers

The trick to adding Smart Object layers is to NOT use the "Copy Layer" function. This will simply create another Smart Object that is linked to the original. Whatever you do to one layer will be done to the other. You have to make a distinct, separate Smart Object. You do that by going back to Bridge and using the File>Place>in Photoshop method we used to open it in CS2, or, from Photoshop, simply go to Layer>Smart Object>New Smart Object via Copy. This will build an entirely distinct Smart Object that you can adjust to your heart's content without changing any other layers. (For those of you that are using a right-clickable mouse, your right-click on the Smart Object will give you that menu option as well.)

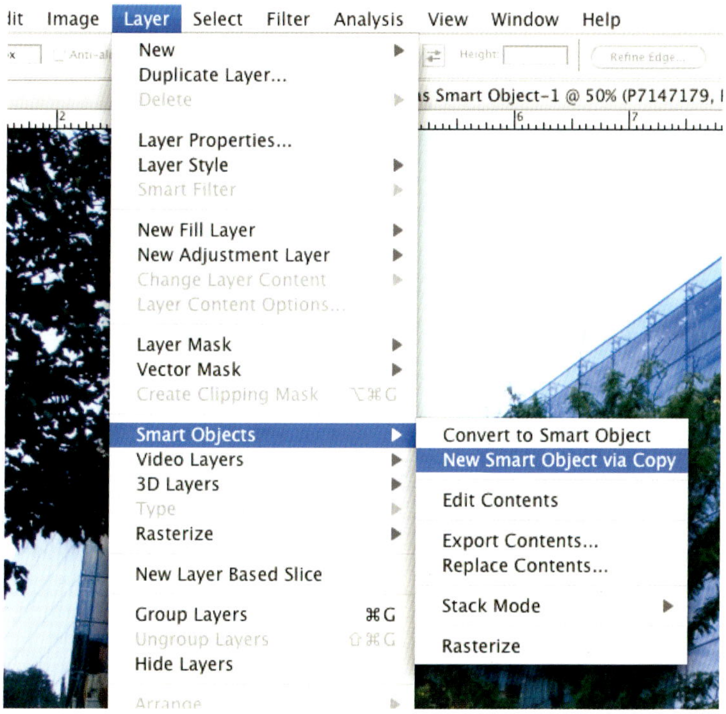

Now you can work away on your image using your Smart Object to get back to the RAW file and all the rich information it has in it. You can also use all the tools that Layers allow—you can mask, re-order the layers, control opacity, specify sharpening, and all the other good stuff we've talked about. We're using the same, simple sets of tools we used before, only this time on a Smart Object.

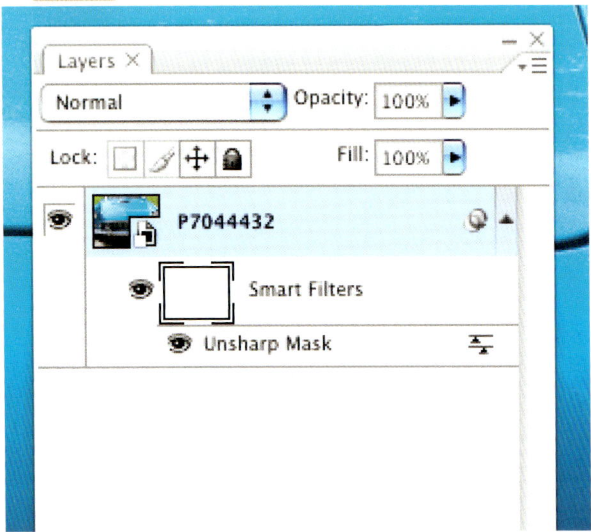

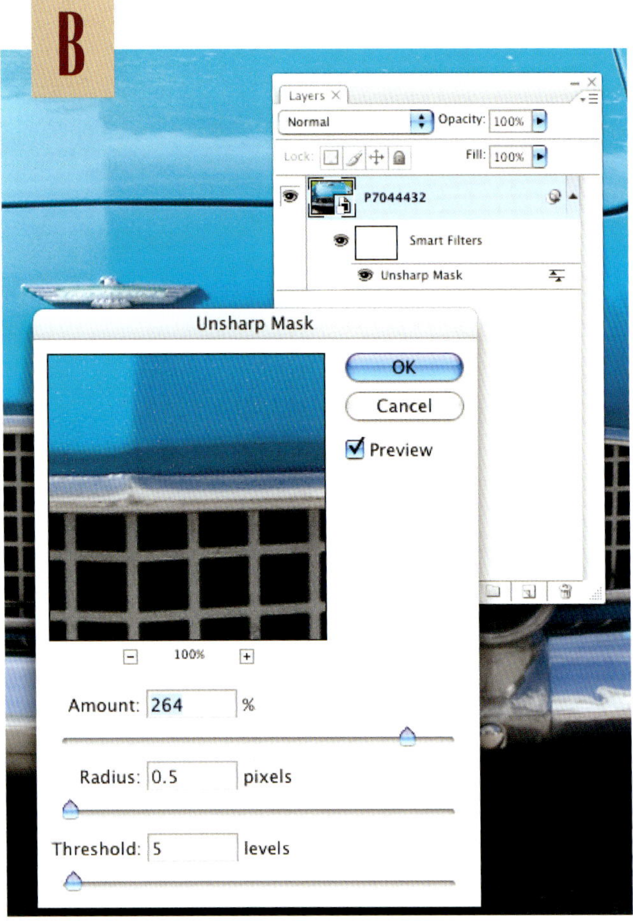

Adding Smart Filters

CS3 added one more twist to the Smart Object arsenal. If you are working on a Smart Object Layer and you add a filter, it gets added as a Smart Filter. That is, you can go back and re-adjust the filter, too. You can also treat it like any other layer. You can mask it, adjust the opacity, copy it, move it—whatever you can do to a layer, you can do to a Smart Filter.

Start by making a Smart Filter on the Smart Object layer. To do this, make sure you're working on that layer, and ask for a filter. Here we're using Unsharp Mask (A). The first thing you see is a mask with "Smart Filters" as a name, and it has the standard "eye" which activates and deactivates it. Under that is the actual filter.

To the far right of the layer you see the adjustment icon. Click that, and you get right back to the Unsharp Mask filter settings dialog (B).

This is an entirely new tool in the Smart Object workflow. It eliminates part of the need for a "Merge Visible" layer as we're used to doing as a last step—instead we can use the Unsharp Mask Smart Filter on every layer. We can duplicate it for the burn, dodge, and spot color correction layers, and even use it for selective sharpening Smart Filter layers.

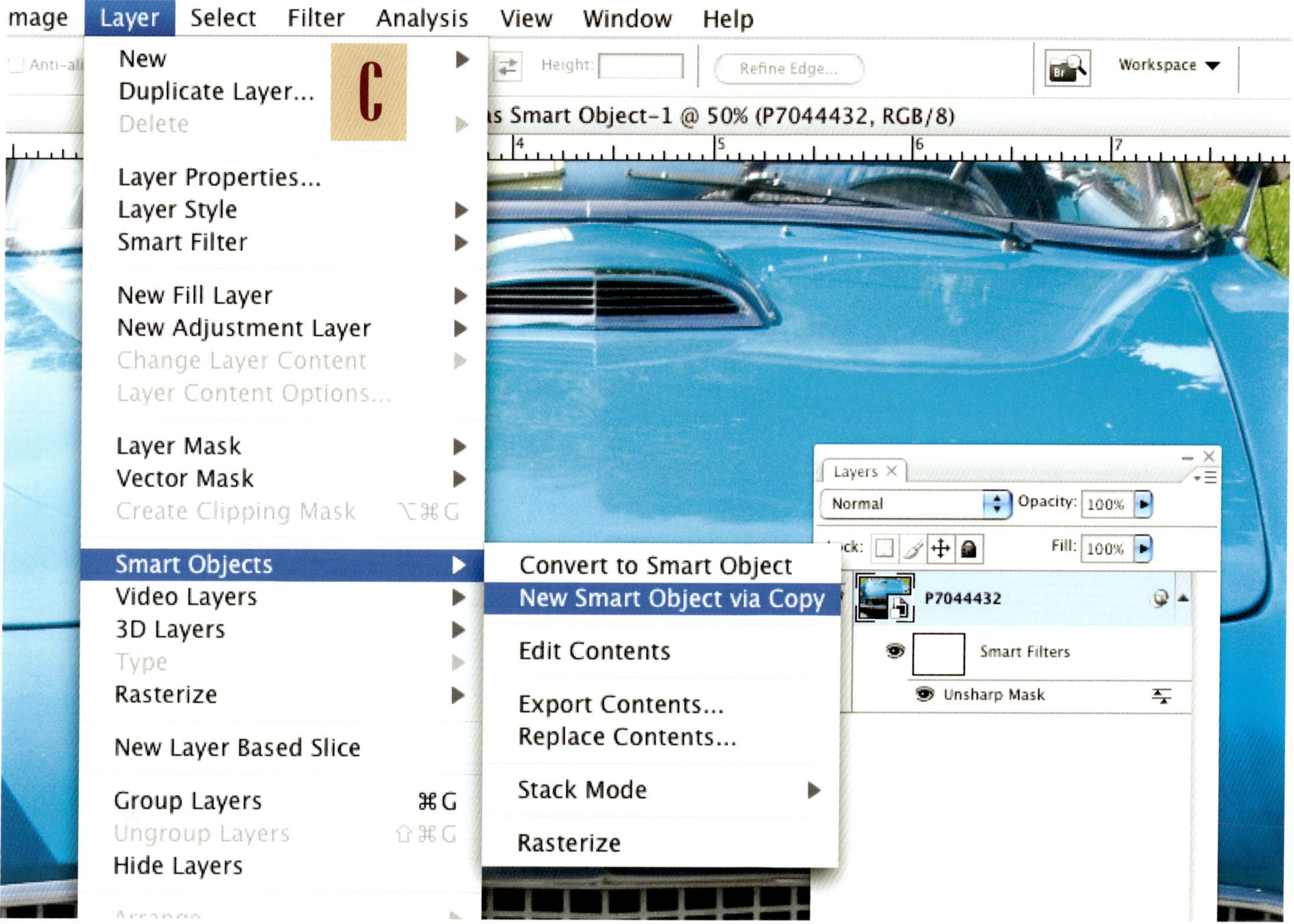

Working Smart Filters into the Process

As we've seen, applying Unsharp Masking is an essential step in our printing process. Applying it as a Smart Filter allows you to adjust sharpening on a layer-by-layer basis. The question is, how do you work with it? My solution is to build it into every layer with basic "default" settings, and then go in and change those settings when I start seeing work prints.

If you start off with a layer that has a Smart Filter attached, you can simply use Layers>Smart Objects>New Smart Object via Copy to make a duplicate of the entire set of adjustments (C). When I start working on an image, I usually go to the first Unsharp Mask layer and do a standard setting. I then disregard the filter until later. I'll go along and do my usual set of adjustments—burning, dodging, and spot color corrections—and won't revisit the Smart Filter until the very end when I get to my final sizing step.

You can, however, handle the layer in the usual ways. If you do one setting in the Smart Filter and want to apply it to all your Smart Object layers you can do so with Option+drag, and drop the Smart Filter wherever you need it (D). You can also mask it, and Option+drag the masks from one Smart filter to another, just like on an Adjustment Layer or Image Layer.

Here you can see the complexity of the available masking techniques (E). On the second layer I've done a burn adjustment in my Smart Object and applied Unsharp Masking as a Smart Filter. I've masked out a small area of that Smart Filter in the center, because that happens to be a place that has some objectionable noise. Unsharp Mask (USM) exaggerates that noise, so I can minimize it by electing to not apply USM to that spot.

As the tools become more powerful, the workflow gets—well, maybe not simpler—but at least more elegant. I'm using Smart Objects to simplify and minimize the layers I need to get a tuned, corrected, and modifiable image. I can resize and adjust my sharpening at will using Smart Filters. There are still parts of the process that we need to approach in the old, traditional, pre-Smart Object ways, but who knows what we will see in Photoshop CS4, or even CS5?

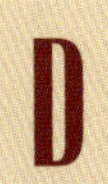

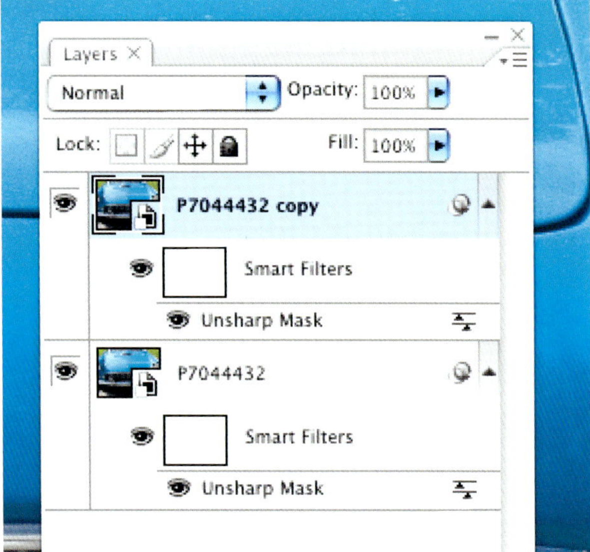

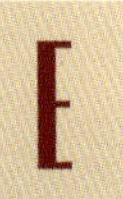

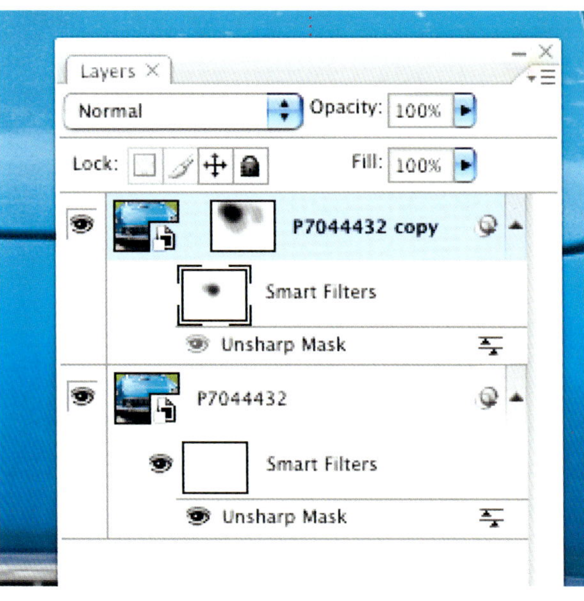

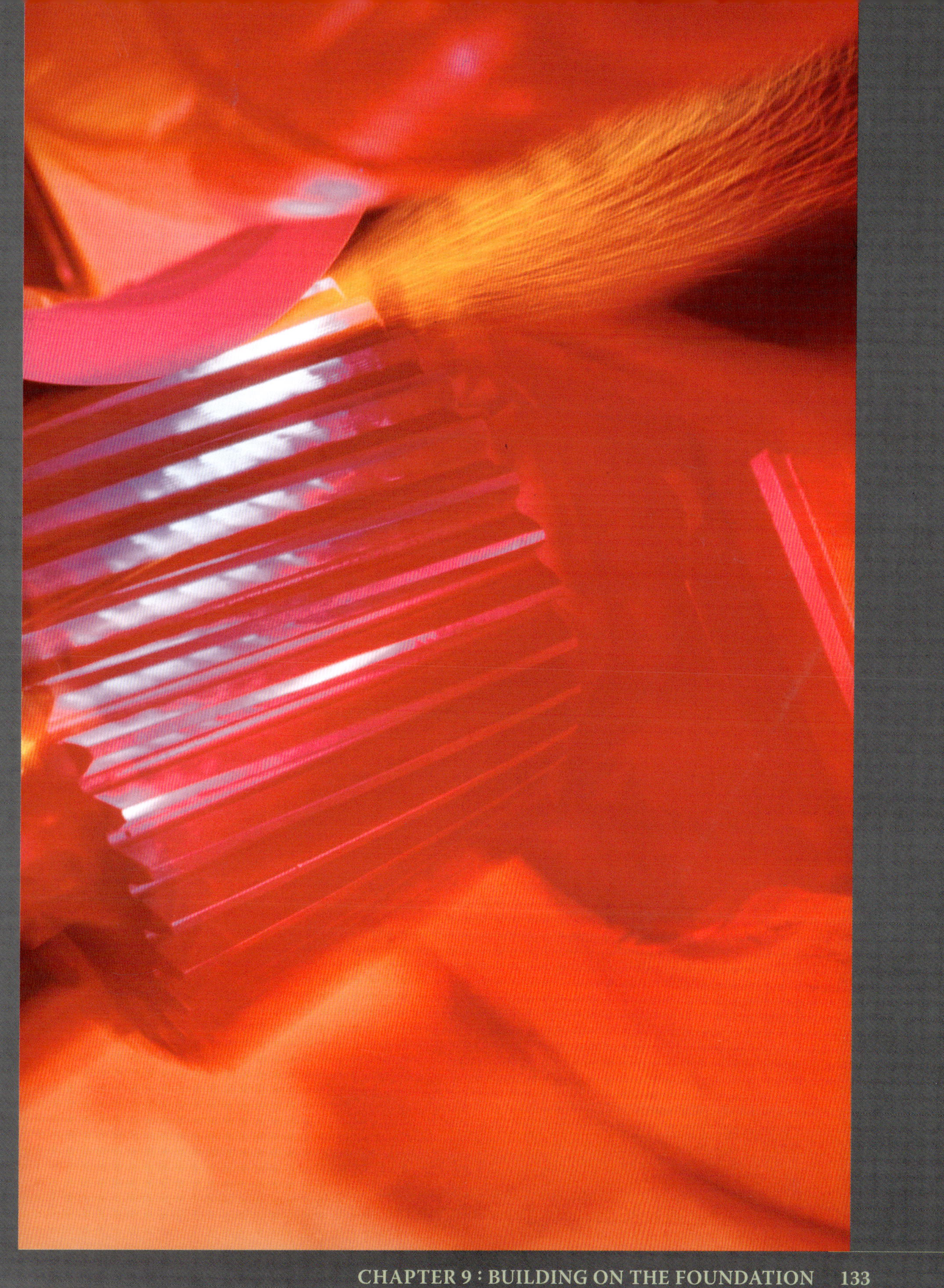

A

070601SAL
Network
Macintosh HD
BU_disk2
BU_disk1
Desktop
teddillard
Applications
Documents
Movies
Music
Pictures
100GBbu07
070601SAL
070701TIM
070801SAL
ART602 07
b2p07 spreadsheets
b2p07work
b2pgen2website
BitTorrent Downloads
book
finals with changes
RAW
1 item, 16.5 GB available

B

Macintosh HD
BU_disk2
BU_disk1
Desktop
teddillard

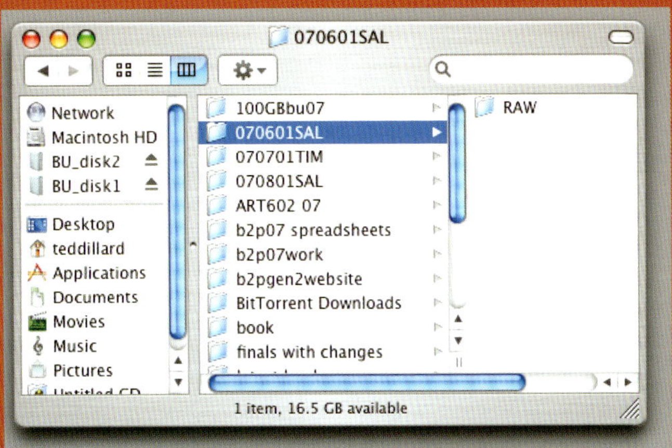

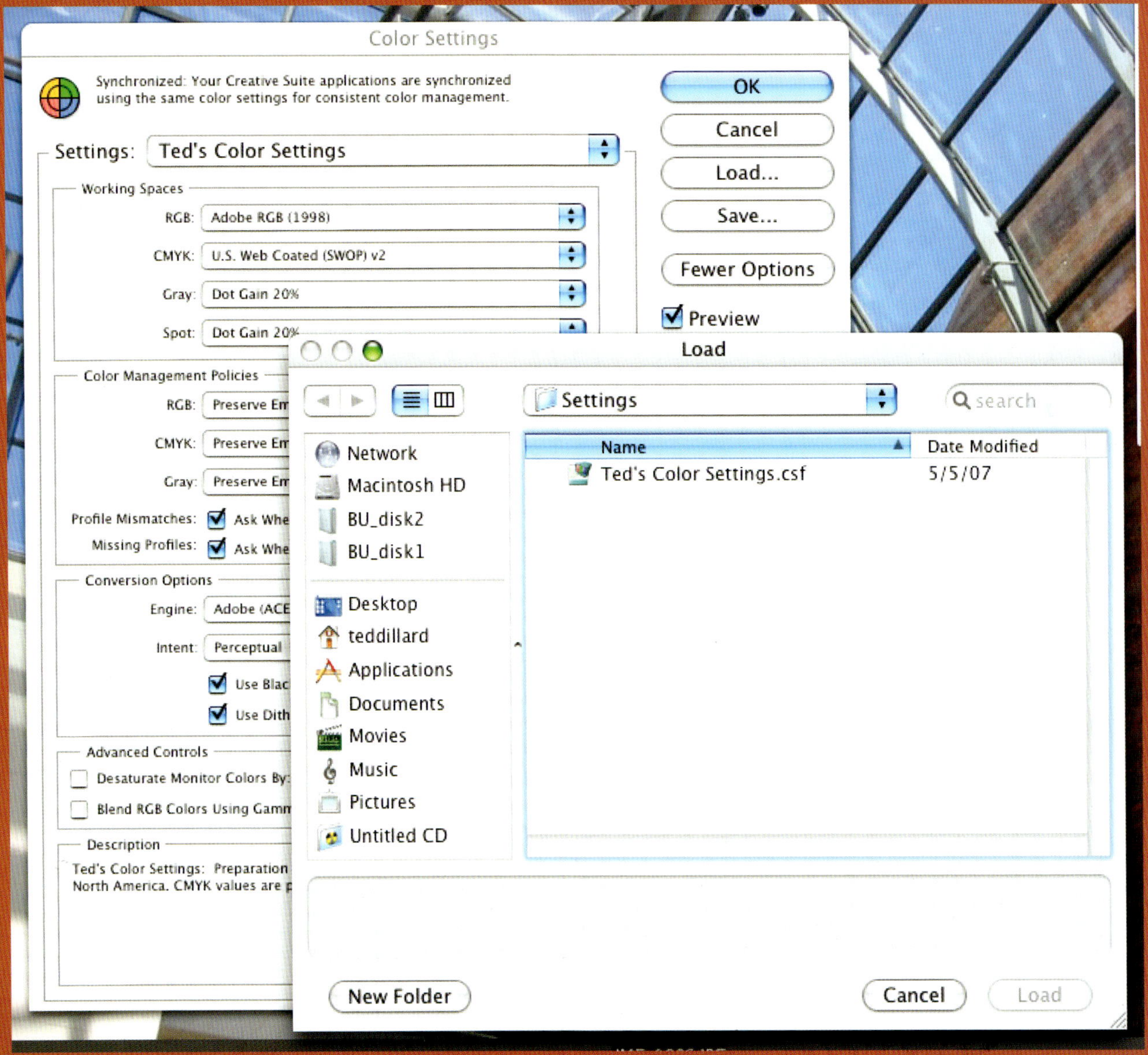

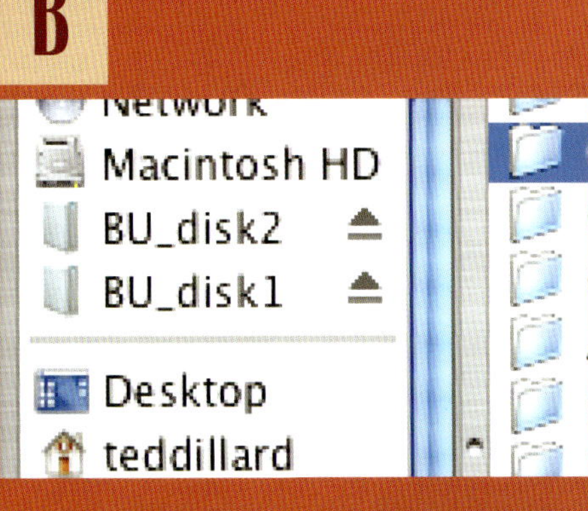

C

Workflow Examples

So, let's go through some examples. I'm going up to Salem, Massachusetts, to spend the day. Before I leave the house, I make a folder on my computer called "070601SAL" for the images (A). Inside it I create a subfolder called "RAW," and since I don't have any idea what I'm going to shoot, I leave it at that.

When I get back from shooting, I plug in the card reader, drag the images to the RAW folder, and eject the card reader from the desktop. I then drag the entire folder "070601SAL" to the backup hard drives, "BU_disk1," and "BU_disk2 (B)."

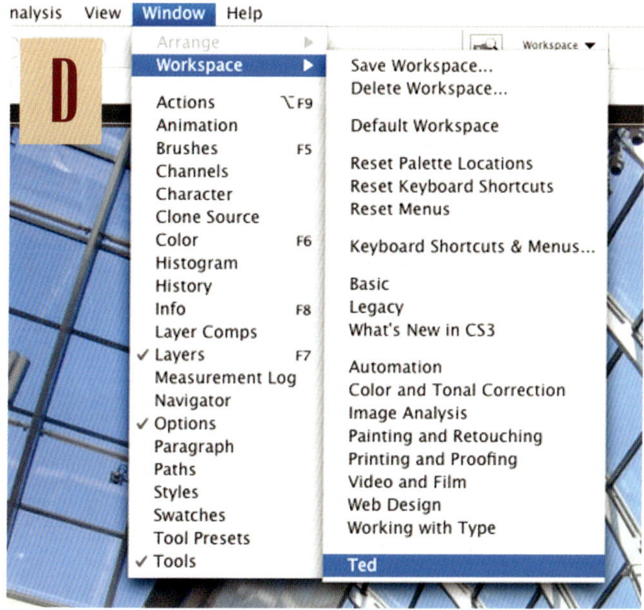

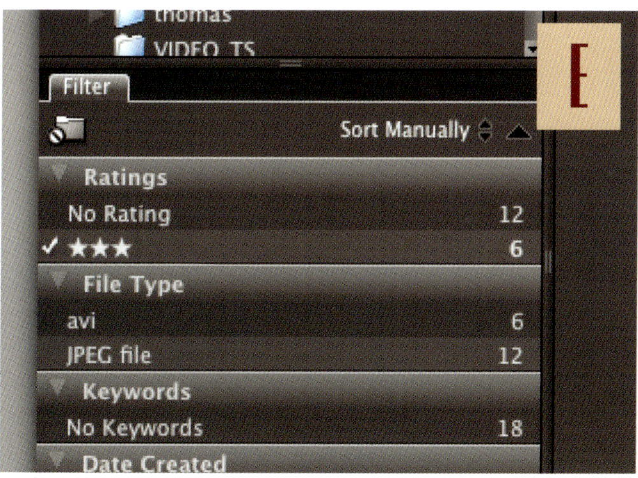

If I'm ready to start working, I close the door to my workroom, close down my IM, email, and web browser, and turn my phone off. I open Photoshop and check my Color Settings (C) (Edit>Color Settings)—sometimes I change them using "Load"—and set my Workspace (Window>Workspace>Ted) (D).

Photoshop is ready to go and I'm ready to go, so now I get into Bridge. I point it to my folder and decide what images I want to work on. I rank them using a simple star system—three stars is a keeper. Apple + 3 (Cmnd + 3 for Windows) gives any selected image a 3-star rating. I click Filter>3-star rating (E), and now I see only the 3-star images. I select them, double-click them, and they all open in Camera RAW.

Normal Adjustment Layers Workflow

Let's start with just a normal, non-Smart Object example. The images I gave a 3-star rating are all open in Camera RAW on the "filmstrip." I go

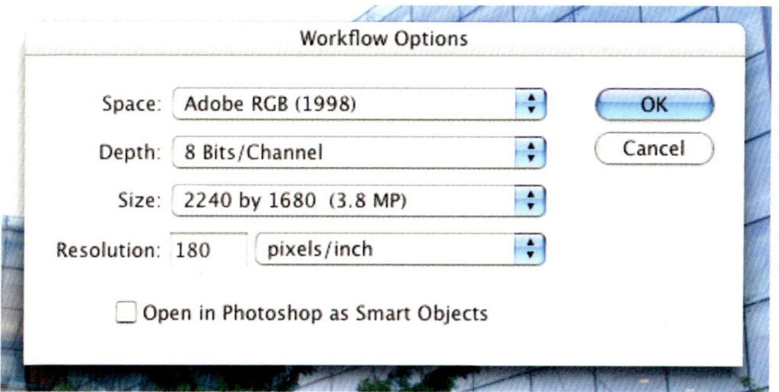

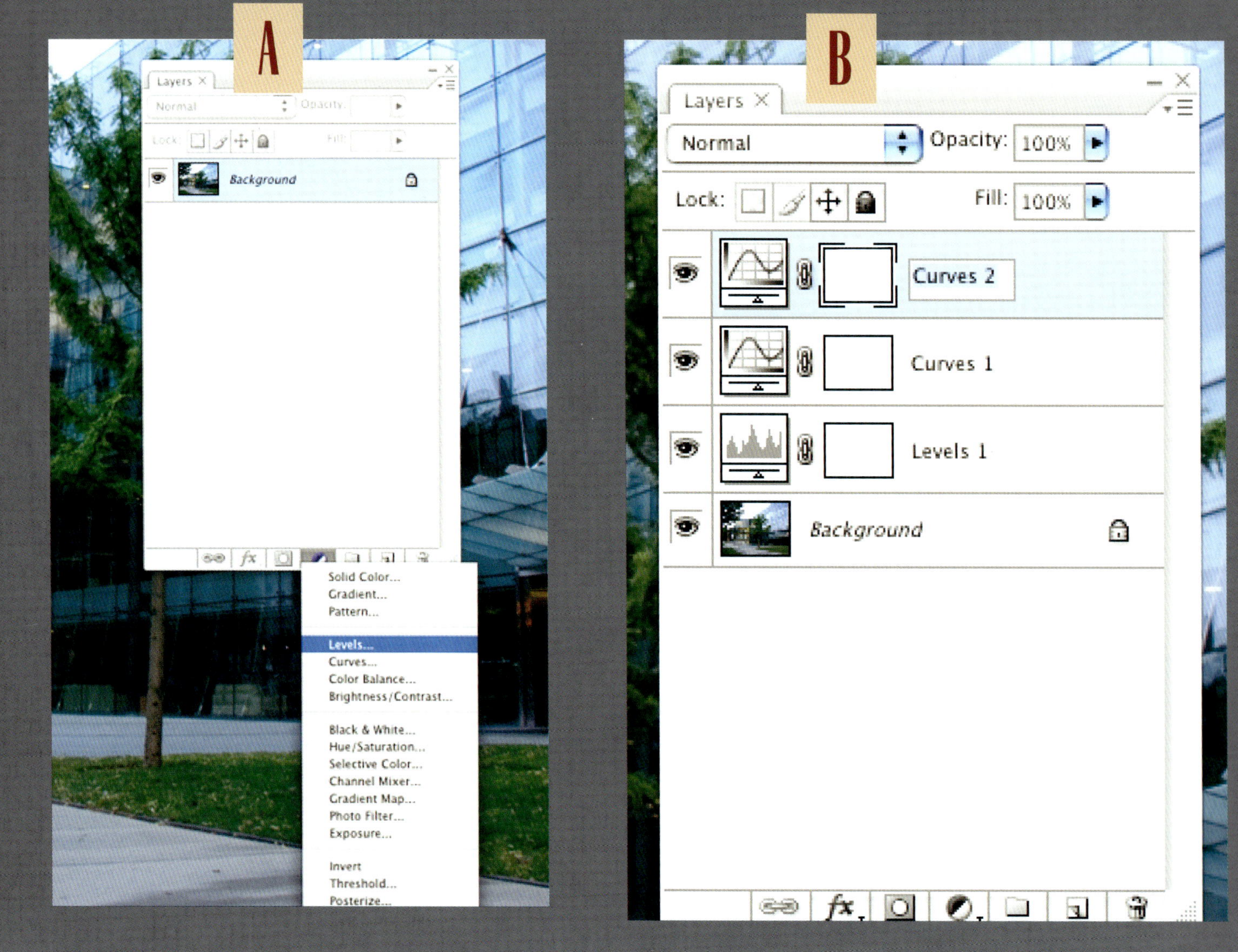

through each one and make it as pretty as I can, and then select them all. I remember to check my "Workflow Options" and uncheck the box "Open as Smart Object," hit OK, and then go back to Camera RAW. I select everything on the Filmstrip, and push the "Open Images" button, and they all open in Photoshop.

Adjusting the Image Using Layers

I now have my images open in Photoshop, and I want to do some final tweaking to make them just right. I click the Oreo cookie-like icon (A), access my Adjustment Layers dialog, and start with Levels to make the basic black point and white point adjustments. I then go to Curves (Oreo cookie-like icon again) to adjust the overall brightness (B), and finally hit Curves again to do a color correction using separate channels. (I always rename

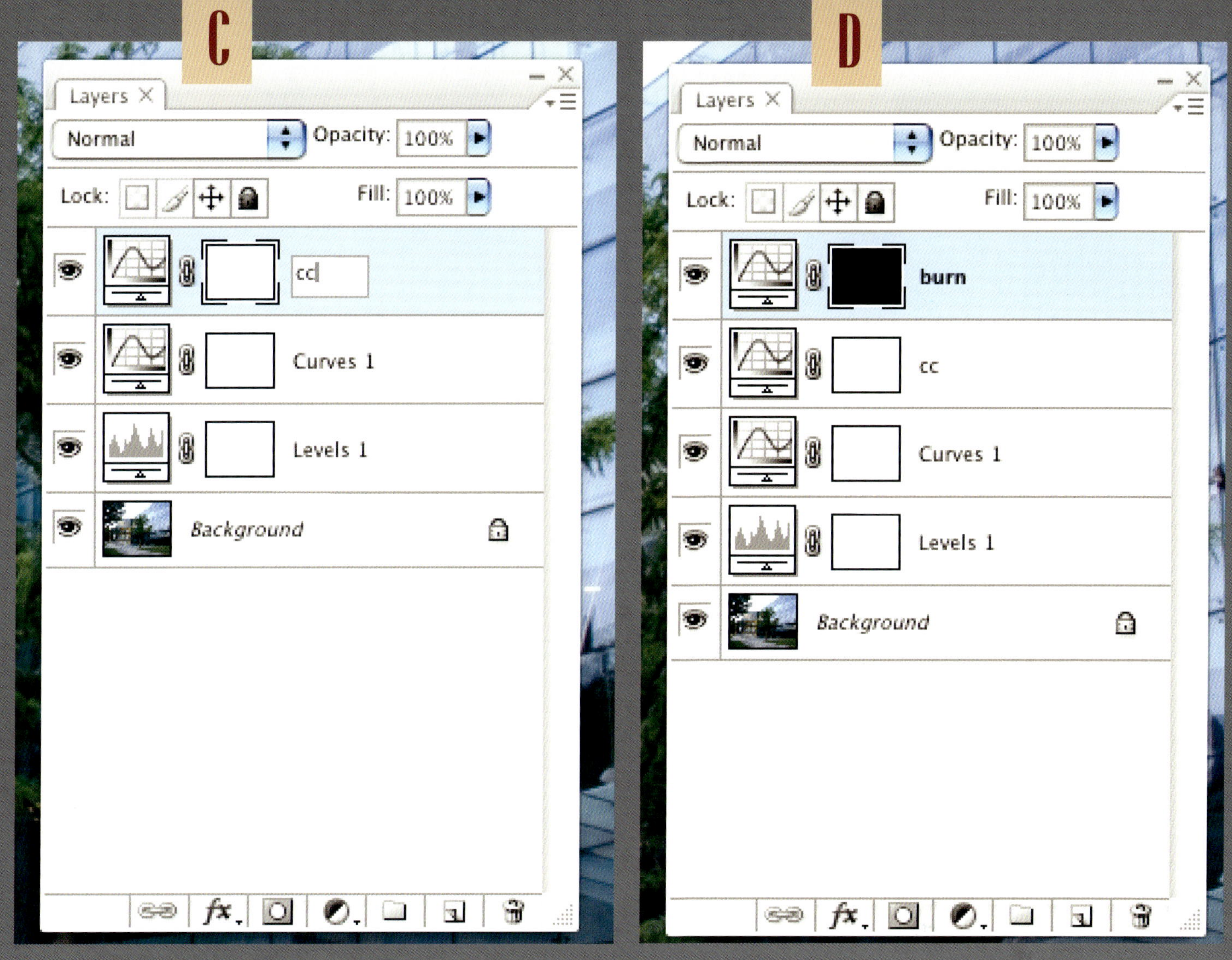

that last Curve layer "cc" (C) to remind me what it's doing, which is color correction.)

Burning and Dodging Using Adjustment Layers and Masks

Now I want to burn, or darken, the foreground. I make a Curve layer, pull the Curve down to make it dark, and name the layer "burn" (D). I select the mask that is generated automatically, and hit Apple + I (Cmnd + I for Win) to invert the mask to black (all opaque, completely masking my burn adjustment).

Here comes the fun part!

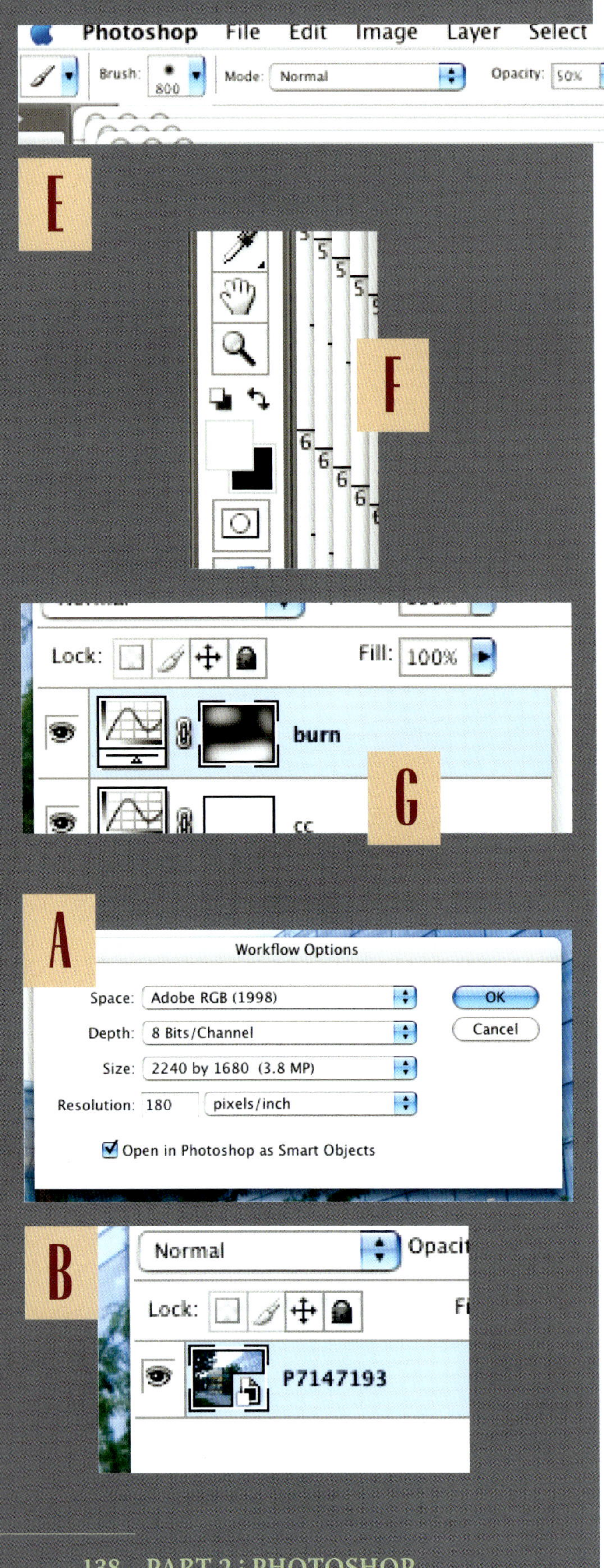

Controlling Areas Burned Using the Brush Tool

I confirm the Brush tool settings (E): Mode: Normal, Opacity: 50%, Flow 50% Background color: Black, Foreground color: White (F).

I double-check to make sure I'm on the Mask, not the Image, by clicking the Mask icon on the layer. I choose the burn tool from the toolbar and simply "paint" white on the black mask, opening up the areas I want to "burn" (G). I'm actually selecting the areas of the mask that I want to be more transparent, just letting them show through. If I make a mistake, I just switch the Foreground color to Black (Keyboard shortcut "X") and paint back over the white area. Now we're done and ready to print.

Smart Object Adjustments Workflow

If I want to work with Smart Objects, back in the Workflow dialog in Camera RAW, I select the "Open in Photoshop as Smart Object" box (A). My button changes from "Open Image" to "Open Object," and when I hit that button I get into Photoshop with a little Smart Object icon instead of a plain Image icon (B). I make my basic, overall adjustments by double-clicking that icon and it opens up the Camera RAW dialog again.

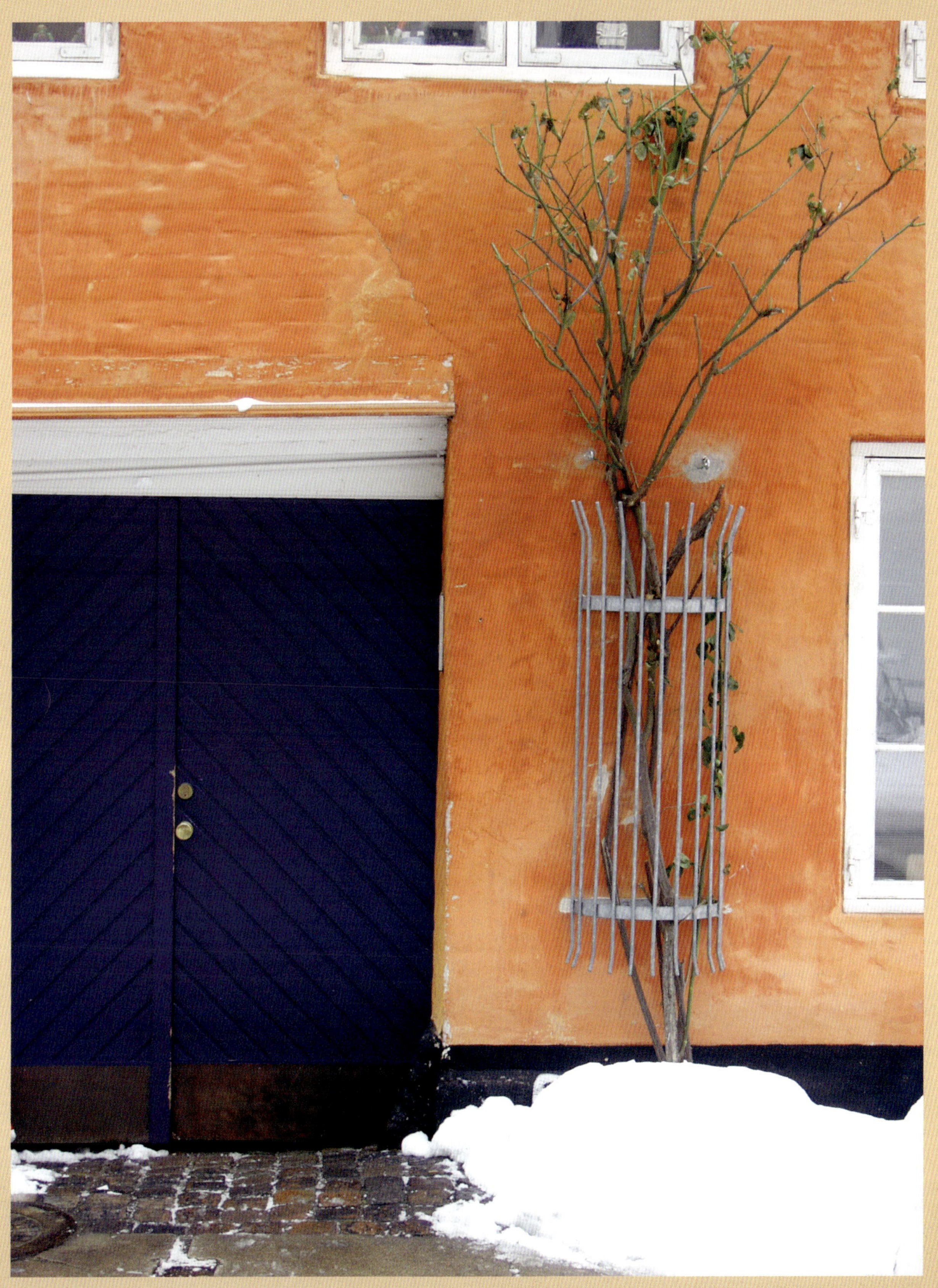

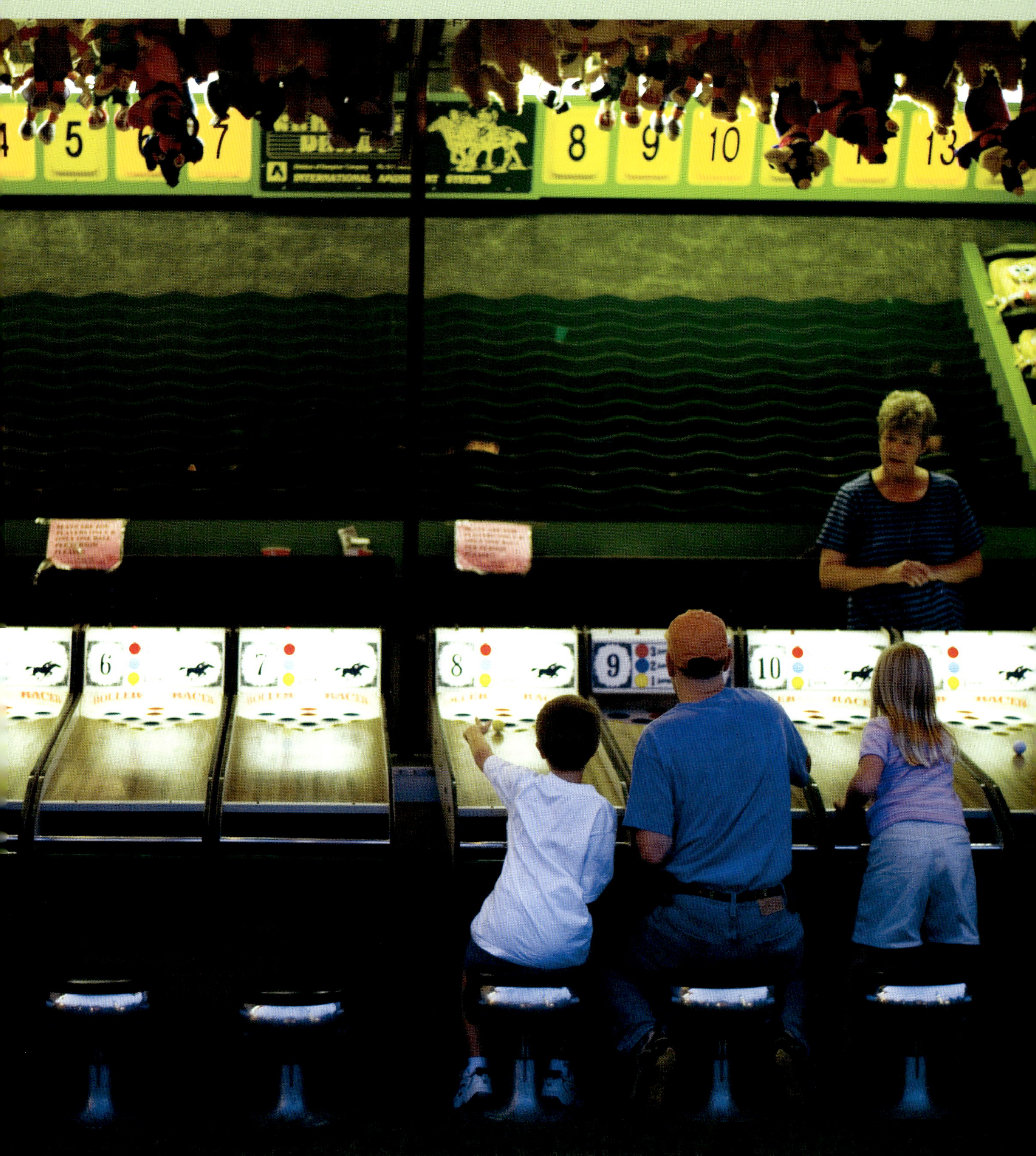

5
7
8
9
10
13
6
7
8
9
10
RACER

Burn with Smart Objects

Now I want to do my burning. I make a new Smart Object Layer by going to Layer>Smart Object>New Smart Object via Copy (A). I double click the little Smart Object icon on the layer, opening Camera RAW, and make my adjustment there (darkening the image). I hit OK. This time, I have to make my mask, because one is not created automatically. I do that by hitting the "Mask" icon (the circle within the rectangle) on the Layers pane (B). I then work the Mask the same way I did before, and I always rename the Layer "burn" so I know what it is.

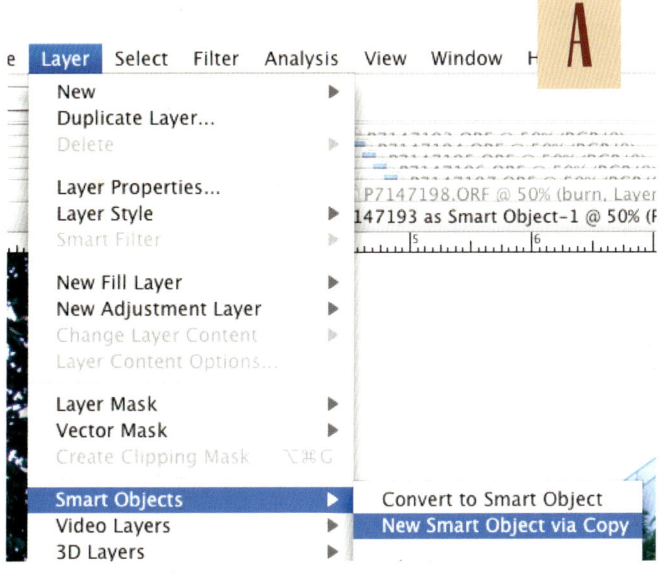

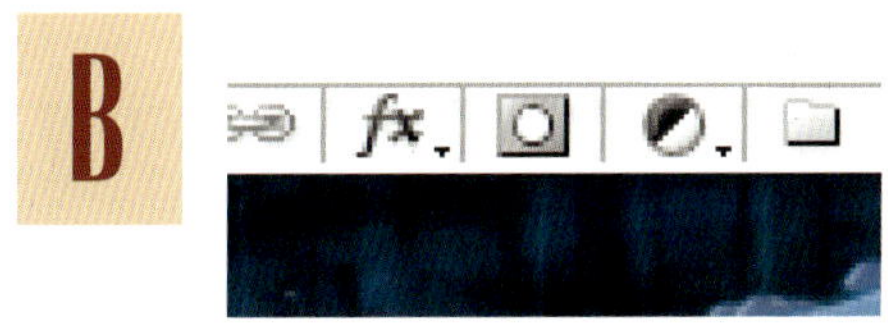

Conclusion

I don't think I've taught a class yet where there hasn't been someone that has offered a different way to do something I'm talking about here. There are about a dozen different ways to do anything in Photoshop, but my answer is always, "bear with me; there's a method to my madness."

By limiting yourself to a few tools, you're allowing yourself to develop a habit. The secret is that those tools can do almost anything you need to do.

Give it a try before you decide. Use Bridge to sort and view your images. Use Layers to make your adjustments, and Masks to make your selections. Allow yourself to develop a rhythm in your workflow so you can appreciate the process. As I tell my students, "for this semester, I want you to do it my way—after that, you're on your own." (Always accompanied by rolling eyes and groans.)

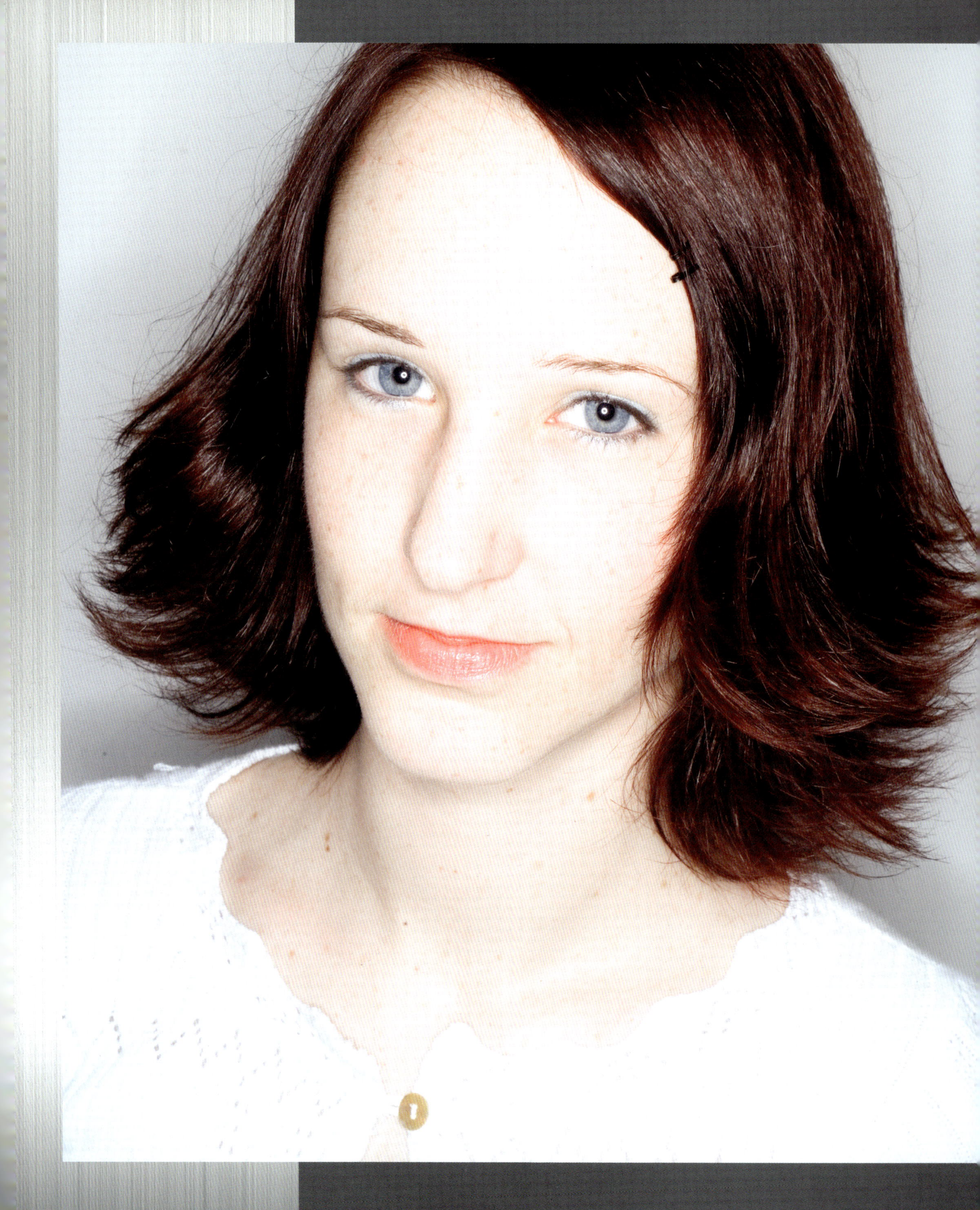

PART 3: FINE DIGITAL PRINTING

introduction

It seems that a large percentage of the photographers I've met, studied, or read about, are frustrated musicians. One of my all-time favorite quotes about printing is from Ansel Adams: "The negative is the score, and the print is the performance." (Before he was a photographer, Ansel was a concert pianist.)

This section is about how to understand the basic processes you need to go through to get the image from the camera's sensor to the printer; or to use a musical metaphor, learning and practicing your scales. I'm starting with a much more detailed description of color management, as well as some essential set-up and organizational discussions. I'm then going to show how to apply color management to interpret and control the color rendering of the printer, expressing the vision of the photographer.

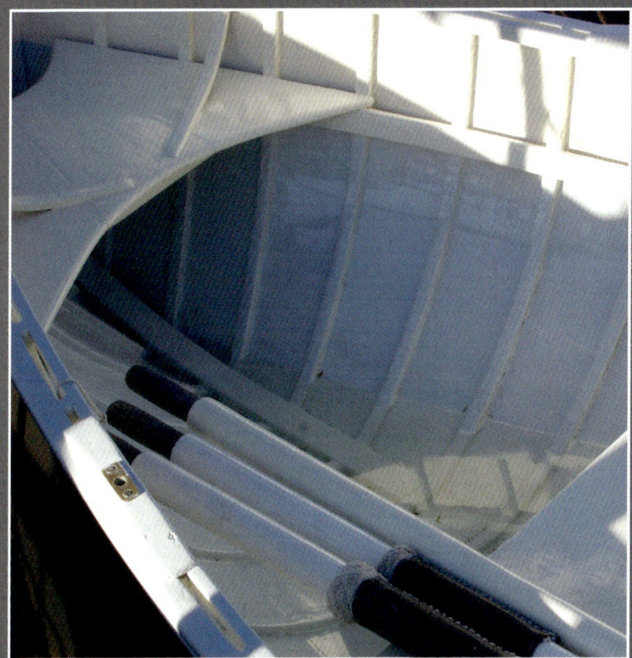

The "desktop darkroom" (if anyone has ever used that term before) makes photographic printing accessible to people who have never printed photographs, never used a darkroom, and may or may not understand the basic principles of color and black-and-white printing. It is crucial that you understand that what you're doing is making a fine print, and that a large part of learning this process has nothing to do with the desktop darkroom. You are a victim of the same limitations and principles that anyone who has ever tried to make a print has labored under: limitations of color gamut, rendering from additive to subtractive color, and the physics of the color wheel.

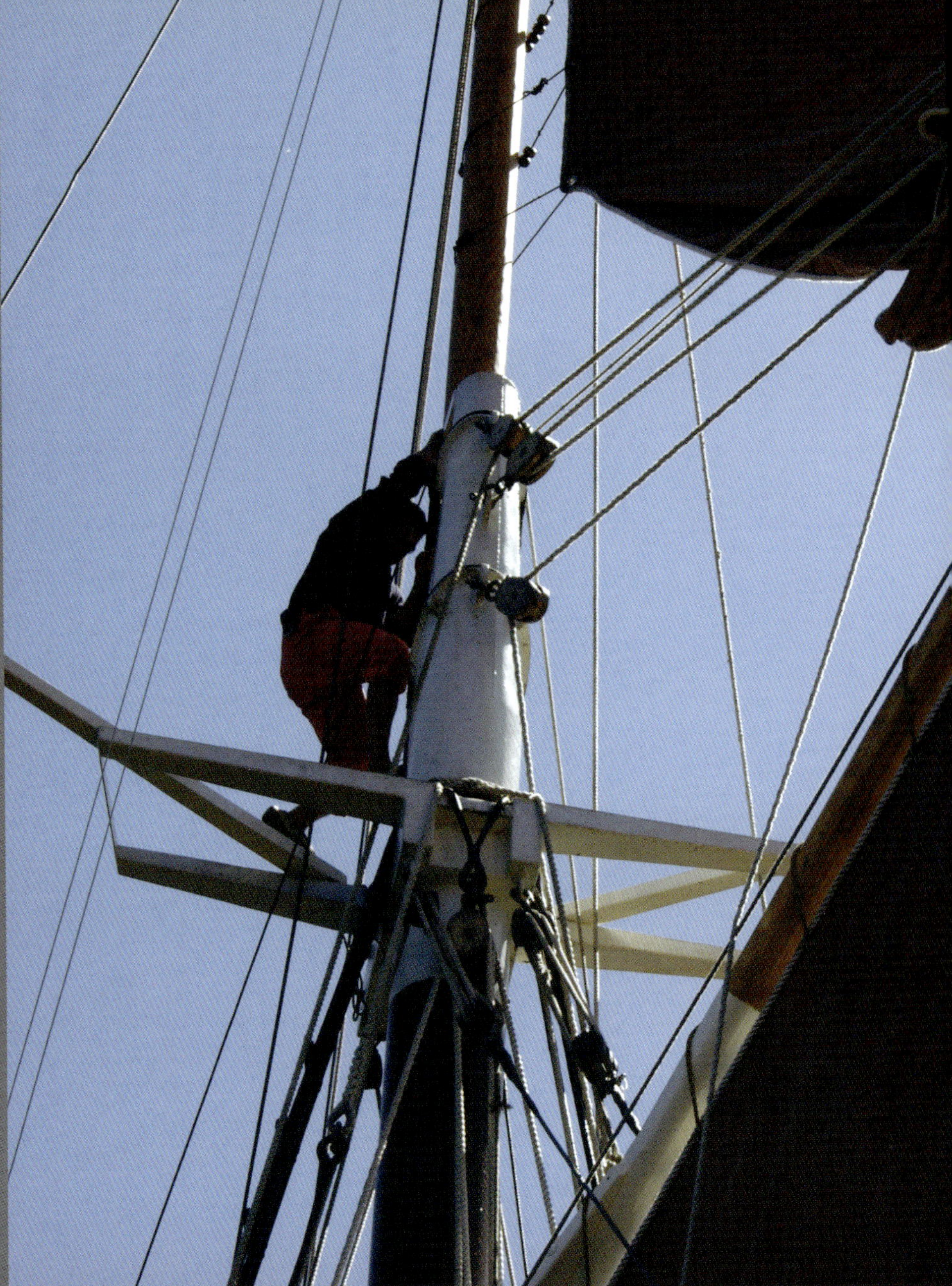

The good news is learning how to print is much more efficient in the desktop darkroom than the traditional darkroom. The results are immediate, your images print much faster (saving more time), and experimenting is less time-consuming. The commitment to issues like standardization, calibration, and the qualities of a fine print, however, remain unchanged.

One more bit of advice. I never learned so much about printing as when Jack Walas, (my yearbook advisor at the University of Maine), handed me a couple of 250-sheet boxes of paper and said, "when you run out of that, just call the annex and get more." It was totally liberating. You learn to print by printing, and you have to use paper and ink, almost with no regard, to learn. To end with one more quote from my father, "the film (for us, the paper and ink) is the cheapest thing you've invested in this whole thing. Don't limit yourself by cutting corners there."

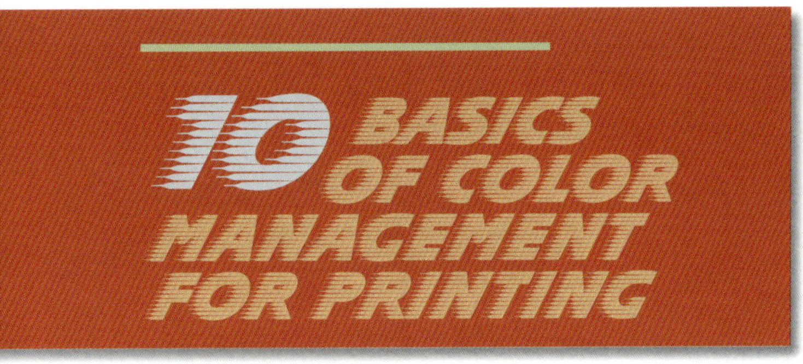

The Working Color Space

One of the problems in understanding color management is that everyone talks about ICC (International Color Consortium) profiles (ICM profiles in Windows), as though they're all the same. ICC profiles, in general, are used to describe the color attributes of a device (printer, monitor, image editing software, etc.) by defining how that device reads and reproduces color. There are some very important distinctions within these profiles, and the first, and probably most important, are the ICC profiles called "working color spaces."

The working color space is what defines your available color spectrum. It decides what colors you can use, and how they are distributed and displayed. It is like your film—it takes all the colors of light that come through the lens and renders them in its own individual way, according to its own rules.

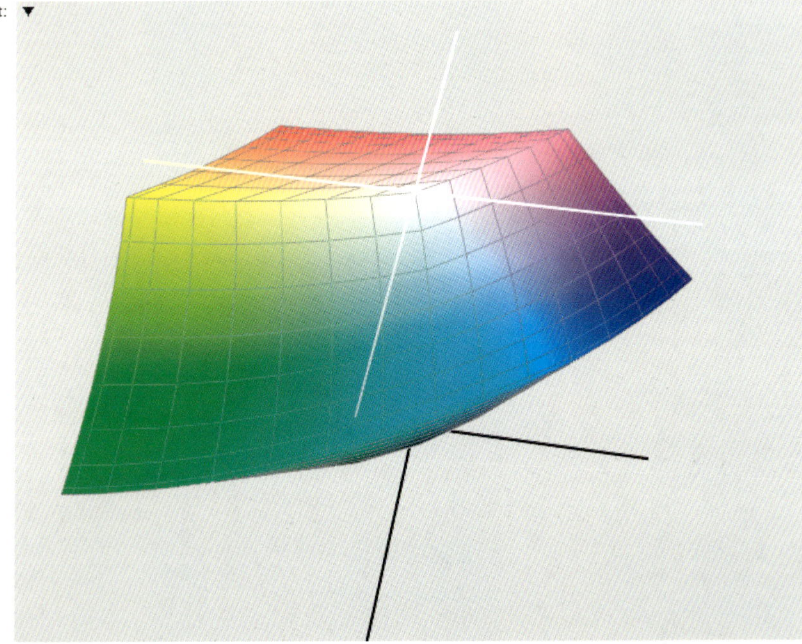

The difference between film and a digital color space is user control. With a color space, we can manage how colors are defined using math. That math, in essence, is calculated by Photoshop using a color engine: ColorSync on Macs or ICM in Windows.

To the left is an illustration of the Adobe RGB 1998 color space. There are a few things to note. First, it's shown as a three-dimensional volume. Strictly, the three dimensions

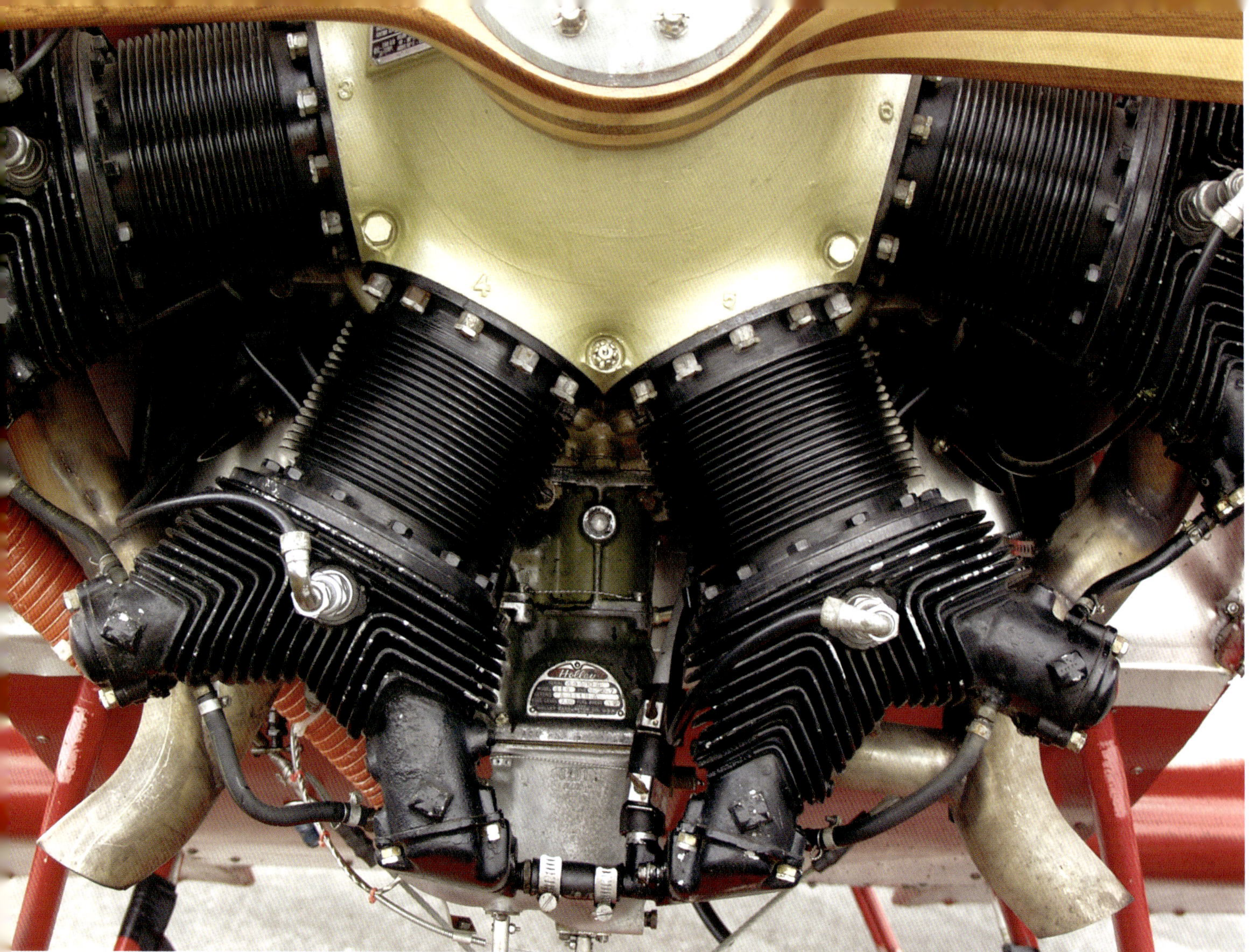

shown in LAB color (otherwise known as "machine color," or "device-independent color") are channel A, channel B, and Lightness. The colors contained within Adobe RGB are plotted on those axes. It's important to understand that color is a three-dimensional concept, a "space," because we are vitally concerned with what is contained in that space and what falls outside that space.

The second point is that different color spaces fill different volumes, and we are dealing with an increasing reduction in color spaces as we move from our initial photograph through the process down to the final print. This, of course, is no different from working with film in the darkroom, where the eye sees all the visible colors, the film captures a small slice of that, and the print reproduces an even smaller piece. The artistry of the print, after all, is managing that reduction so the final print—for all of its limitations—vividly recalls the expression and feeling of the original vision.

Finally, we have a vast number of tools to digitally manage this reduction in color spaces. With film, there is a limited ability to control how a particular emulsion is going to render contrast, tonal values, and colors. In the desktop darkroom—especially with a digital camera file—there are a staggering array of options to determine what remains in the final image and what gets lost in the translation.

Think of the working color space as your center, your enlarger table in your digital darkroom. You bring information into the color space, the monitor displays it, you edit it, and then the output device such as a printer produces it. The working color space manages everything.

Calibrating the Monitor

Once you start to understand the concept of a working color space, the importance of having a good quality, well-calibrated monitor becomes very clear. You want to make sure that your monitor displays color accurately and consistently. The system is playing by the rules of the

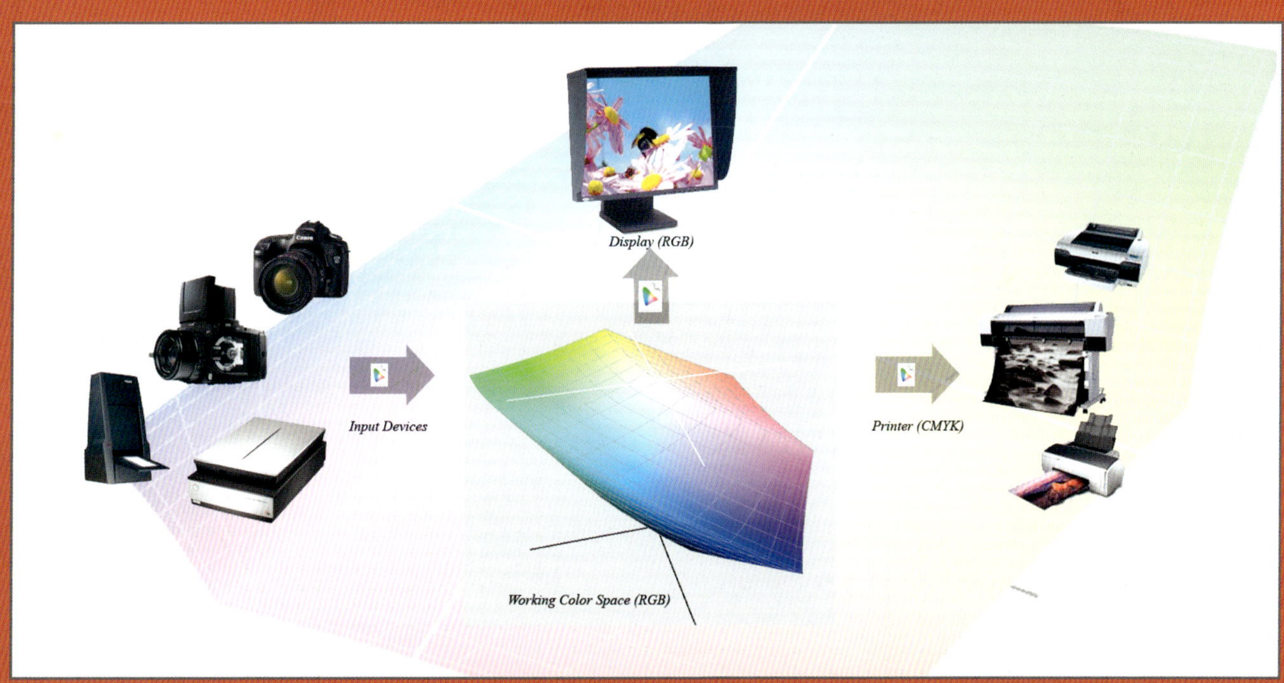

Color management is vital to achieving consistent results, especially for photographic prints. Each part of the process plays an important role is designating how the color of an image is perceived, processed, and rendered.

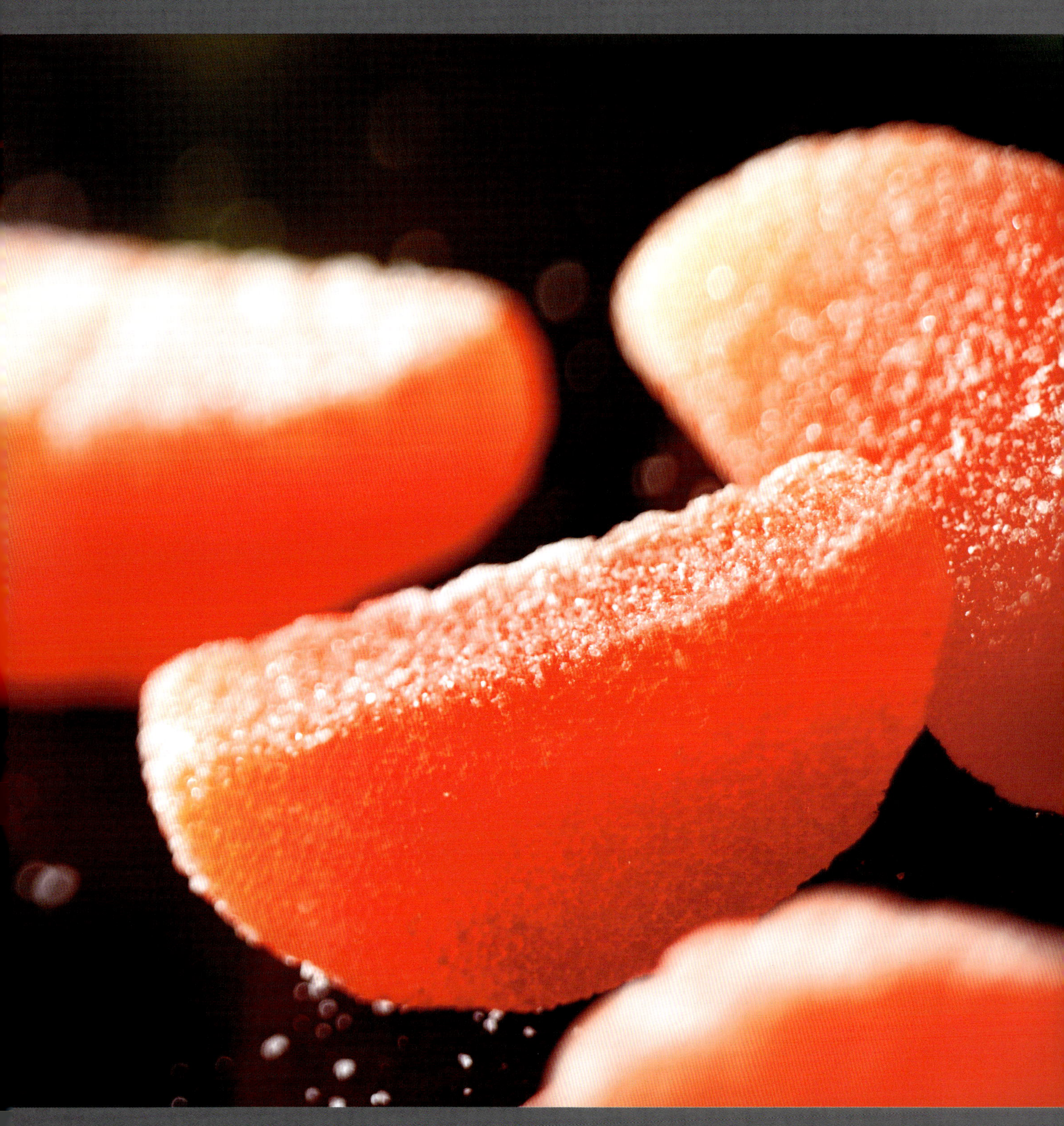

color space; it is crucial that the monitor is adjusted so that it is playing by the same rules of the system and the color space. You want it to create black, white, and gray when it's told to.

If you try to calibrate a monitor that is old and worn out, one reality of monitor calibration becomes painfully clear: if the monitor can't recreate the color, no amount of calibrating is going to help. You need to run on a good, graphics-quality, monitor. Some monitors are good for other applications, but simply can't recreate colors accurately. Once-good monitors can wear out, fade, or become uneven. Again with a musical analogy: if you have a set of speakers that can't project bass notes, you're not going to hear the bass. You can't adjust the bass if you can't hear it. And you can't adjust the colors accurately if you can't see them accurately.

Assuming you have a good monitor, use a calibrator and software to ensure it's accurate. The calibration process is quite simple. The color calibration software sends color to the monitor, the calibration device reads the actual colors the monitor displays, and the software makes up the difference, correcting the actual colors to match the expected colors. This is a pattern in any calibration procedure: send known samples, read the resulting sample, and correct to match the actual expected values.

When you calibrate the monitor using any hardware calibration systems, you will need to know your target values for two things: Gamma and White Point. These values have pretty much been standardized industry-wide as a Gamma value of 2.2, and a White Point value of 6500, or D65. In some cases, with LCD monitors, you have to choose a "Native" setting on the White Point, mostly to overcome the limitations of the software or the monitor, but the "Native" White Point of most LCD monitors is pretty close to 6500.

The rationale behind these values is a source of much discussion and confusion. In the simplest terms, these settings make sure you are closely synchronized with what the monitor was designed to do and how a computer's operating system processes color information. This is all an effort to display colors accurately and predictably in a way that your eye can see.

For the record, this is called a "display profile," and along with the working color space, is an ICC profile.

Input and Output Profiles

More fun with ICC profiles! Input profiles and output profiles are also ICC profiles, but perform a different function. Input profiles adjust the numbers that define the color information to bring a file into a working color space accurately; output profiles adjust the color-defining numbers to send that information out

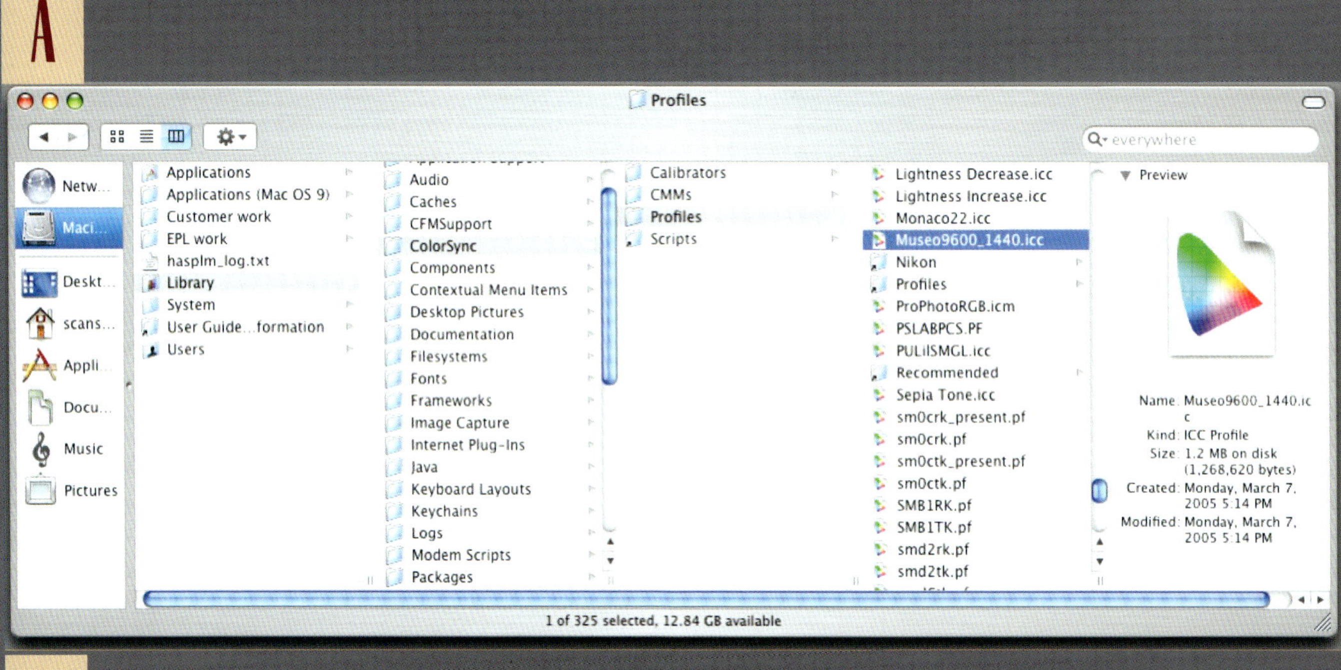

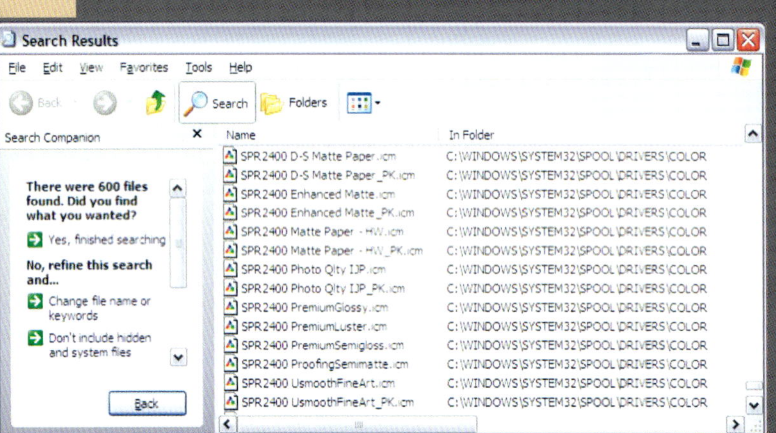

It is important to keep all of your printing profiles in the same place so that you can access them whenever you need them. Finding where your printer places its own profiles is a good start. If you decide to build custom profiles, label them in a way that is easily repeatable and easy to understand.

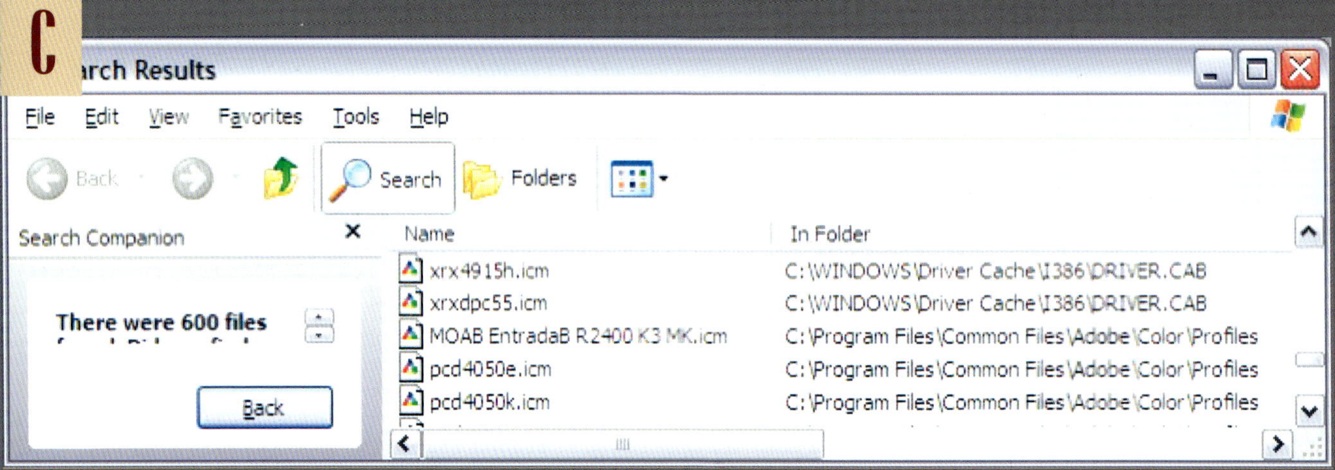

accurately. To narrow the discussion down to the printing side of the equation, an output profile takes the colors from Adobe RGB 1998, as it's being (accurately) displayed on the monitor, and applies the necessary corrections so that it gets translated accurately to ink on paper.

Output profiles for any decent printer are installed when you install the printer. In Mac OSX, you have to execute the "Add Printer" procedure in the Print Center to load the necessary profiles. You can also load other profiles—for instance profiles from paper manufacturers like Crane and Ilford—by placing them in the correct system folder. Finding that folder can be tricky. Here (A) is where they go in the current version of OSX, which will probably change by tomorrow.

Windows profiles are buried pretty deep too. This search (B) shows where the 2400 profiles are, and there's another spot where you can load them too, shown (C) (see MOAB EntradaB R2400 K3 MK.icm).

Probably the easiest way to figure out where to place profiles when you download them is to search ".icc" in a Mac and ".icm" in Windows, and put the other profiles in the same folder with obvious paper and printer profiles. You need to restart Photoshop for them to show up.

You can also build your own profiles using any number of available products. You might want to do this for two basic reasons—first, because you want to print on a paper that does not have an available profile, and second, you might want to try a different profile to render an image depending on your original interpretation or individual preference.

Profiles now are starting to resemble film. Generally, the difference in two profiles is subtlies in tones, colors, hues, and how they are reproduced on paper. Building your own printer profiles allows you to experiment and tune your printer to render your images to your specific wants.

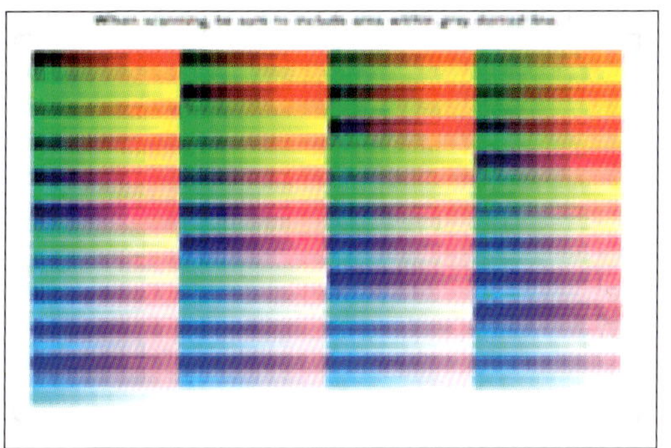

A color target print will give you a good idea of how your printer and chosen profile will render color.

Building a profile has been greatly simplified. Whatever the software, it will instruct you to print a target (see above). Print the target in a completely un-calibrated state to reduce your variables. When you read the printed target with your calibration device, the software builds a correction file. It wants to see certain colors in certain spots, and if it sees variation it program a correction.

If you've worked in the darkroom, think of this as a filter pack. You take a known film and start with a basic filtration to get to a starting point.

Here, you have your Adobe RGB colors that you see on the screen, and send the printer a correction so that what it produces is close to what you saw on the screen.

RGB Additive Color vs. CMYK Subtractive Color

Of course, therein lies one of the big problems in any printing process. Light creates color through what's called an "additive" process. No light is pure black. You add colors and quantities to make your light brighter. Total intensity is white. Additive light uses what amounts to three basic channels, RGB. However, printing uses ink, and any ink, pigment, paint, or dye process uses a "subtractive color" process. Subtractive color starts off with white; the paper with no ink. As you build up ink, you build up density, and total ink coverage is pure black. Subtractive color uses four channels, CMYK, or cyan, magenta, yellow, and black.

There is simply no way you are ever going to match what you see on your monitor with what you see in your print, because they are two different media, operating within a different set of rules of physics. One is transmitted light, using additive color; one is reflected light, using subtractive color. The best we can hope for is to come acceptably close, and that's what can drive us nuts.

You need several things to close the gap between the additive and subtractive processes. The first thing you need is a consistent system response, so you can predict and control the elements (monitor calibration). The second thing you need is decent (preferably excellent) color matching, and that becomes an issue of personal tolerance and taste. Some printers can look at an image, make a few corrections, and nail the print on the first shot despite that the image on the monitor does not come close to the print. Others have their color management so tight that even within the restrictions of the CMYK process, the prints match the display remarkably well.

The first goal of a color management consultant is to determine the "color taste tolerances" of the client. That is, how picky the client is about color matching. That ought to tell you something.

Print-Viewing Light

The viewing light for your desktop darkroom is critical. Any good lab will have viewing booths set up to simulate different lighting scenarios for viewing prints. If you are printing for a gallery, chances are you will show the print under quartz incandescent spotlights. If the prints are for an office, they will likely be viewed under cool-white fluorescent. If you don't know the ultimate viewing light, a safe bet is 5000k daylight conditions.

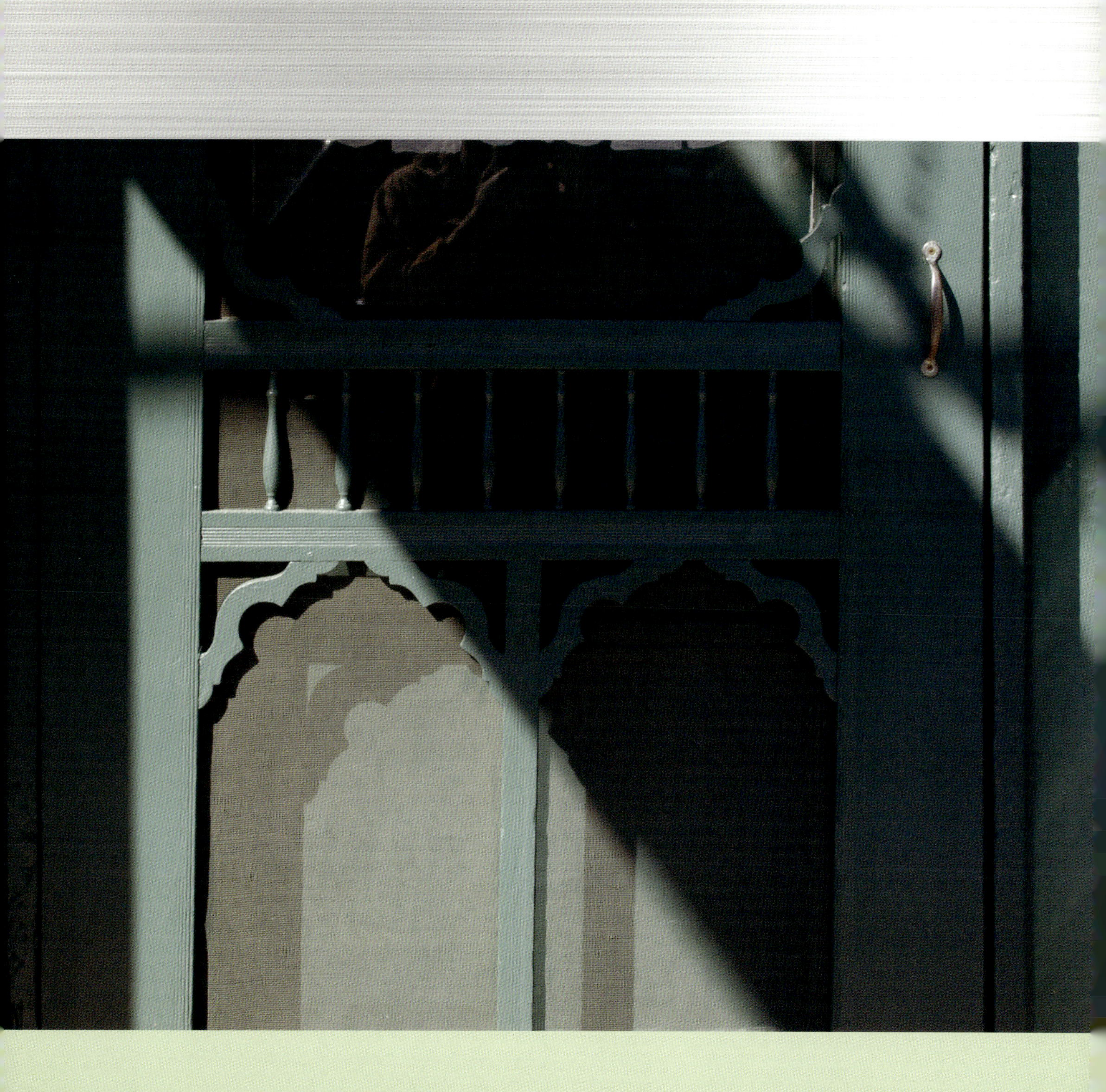

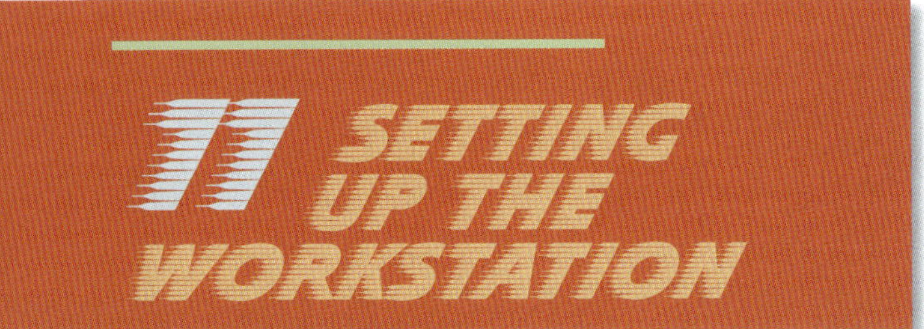

Calibrating the Monitor

I generally suggest calibrating your monitor with the room lighting you normally work in. The hidden message here is that you should really work under low-glare lighting, which amounts to dim room lighting. So the final word is that you should calibrate under fairly dim room light. If you work in an environment where you cannot control the lighting and it's brighter than that, I suggest you use a monitor hood (you probably should anyway) and calibrate with the lights off or down, then use the monitor at your normal room lighting. You still might have problems from the glare, but not because of the calibration.

Make sure you calibrate your monitor after it's had a chance to warm up, usually a minimum of half an hour. An LCD monitor, especially, changes dramatically with temperature differences.

Again, basic calibration of the monitor depends on the monitor being able to create colors accurately. From there, it's a relatively simple procedure, as shown here. Once the software is up and running, be sure to set the target values at 6500 for White Point and 2.2 for Gamma.

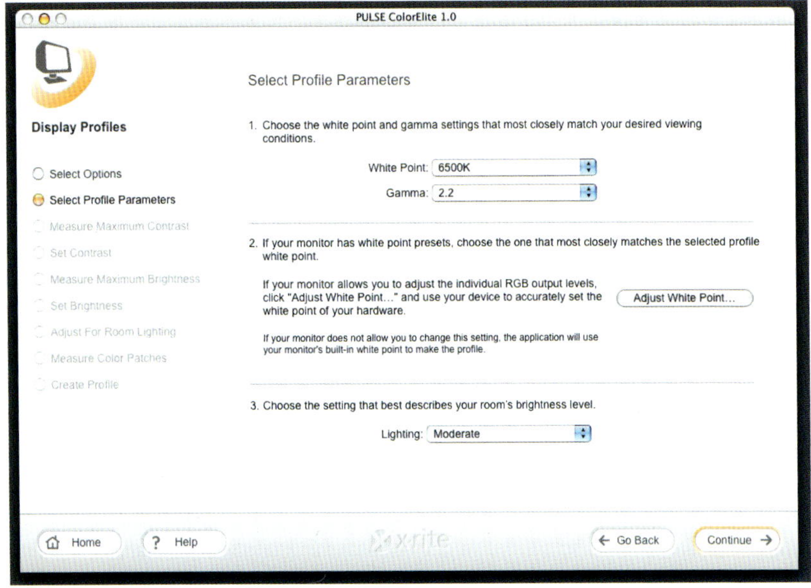

Color Settings in Photoshop

This is where we see the importance of the Color Settings dialog we discussed on page 60. Now we can see how files are brought in to Photoshop and how they're managed in Adobe RGB. We'll also see how Photoshop, the printer driver, or a RIP translates that color information to tell the printer exactly what to do. I'm showing the dialog once again, here (A).

A

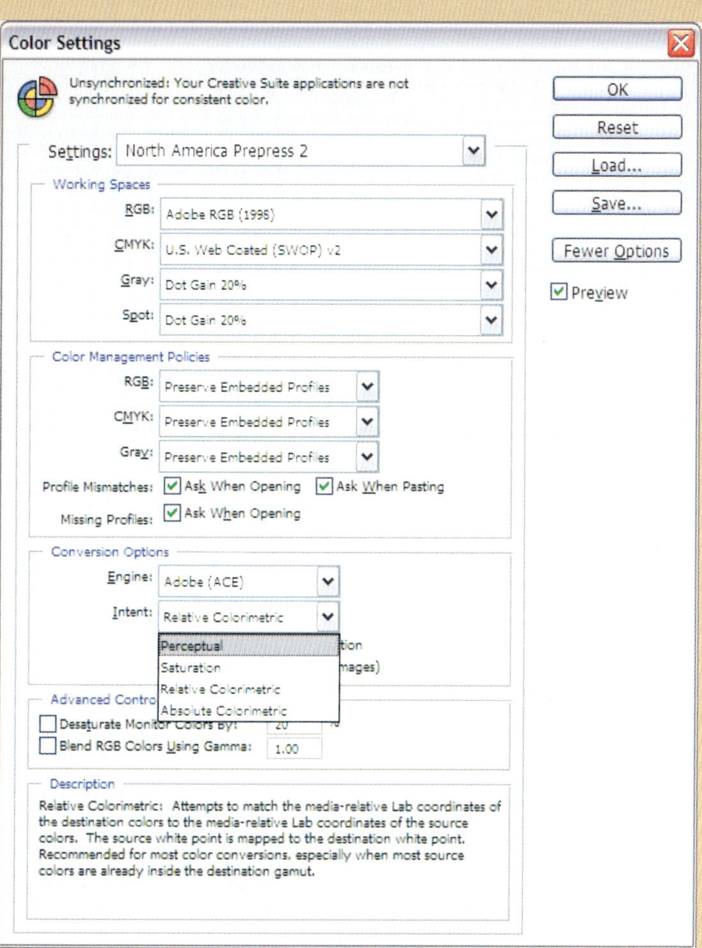

Once you've established that your monitor is accurately calibrated, you must set up Photoshop to work within that standard. Go to Edit>Color Settings, and click the "More Options" button. Your entire detailed policies of Color Management are there for you to see. From the top pull-down menu, select "North America Prepress 2." Go down to the Conversion Options pane, and under Intent select "Perceptual." Close the dialog and you're done.

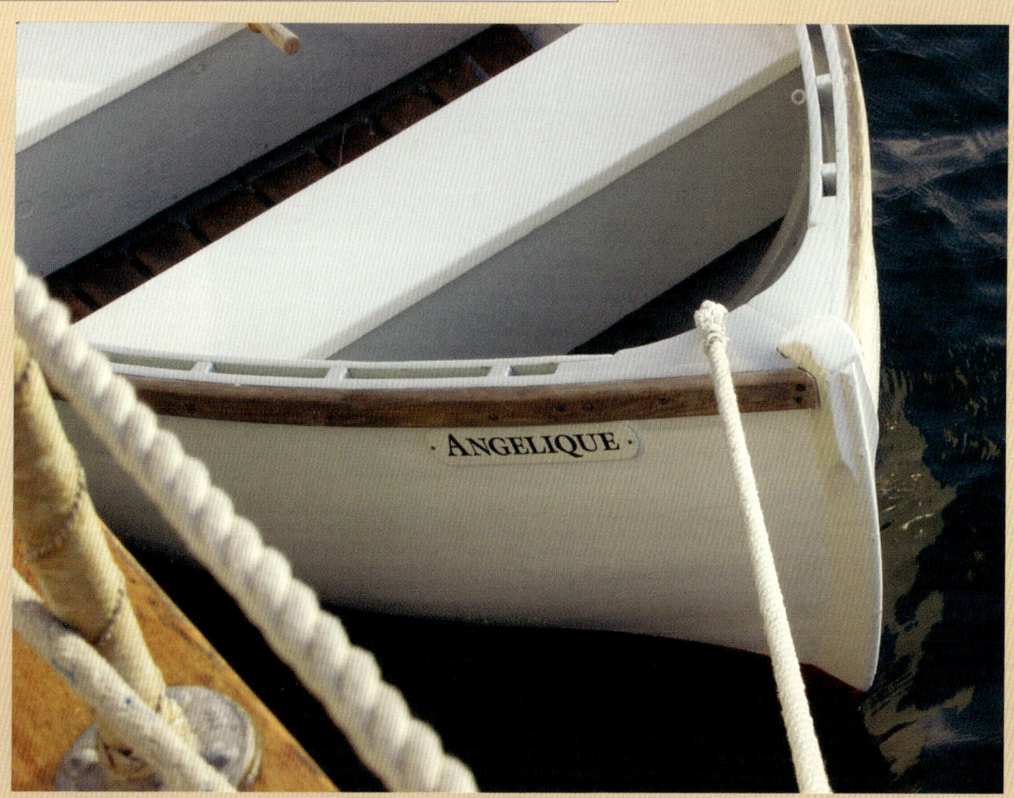

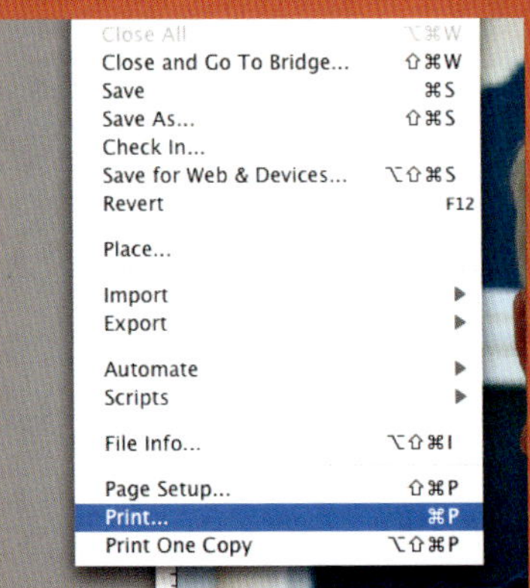

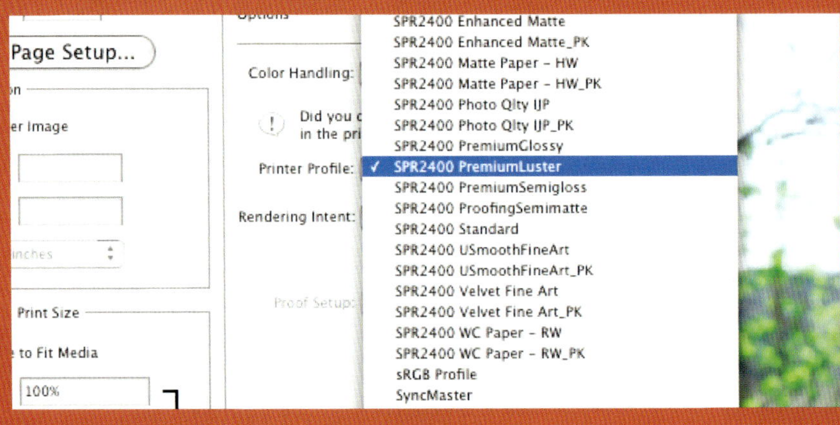

Choose the paper that is close to what you want to print on in the "Print" window. All paper has different thickness, whiteness, and luster, and these make a difference in how your printer applies the ink to the page.

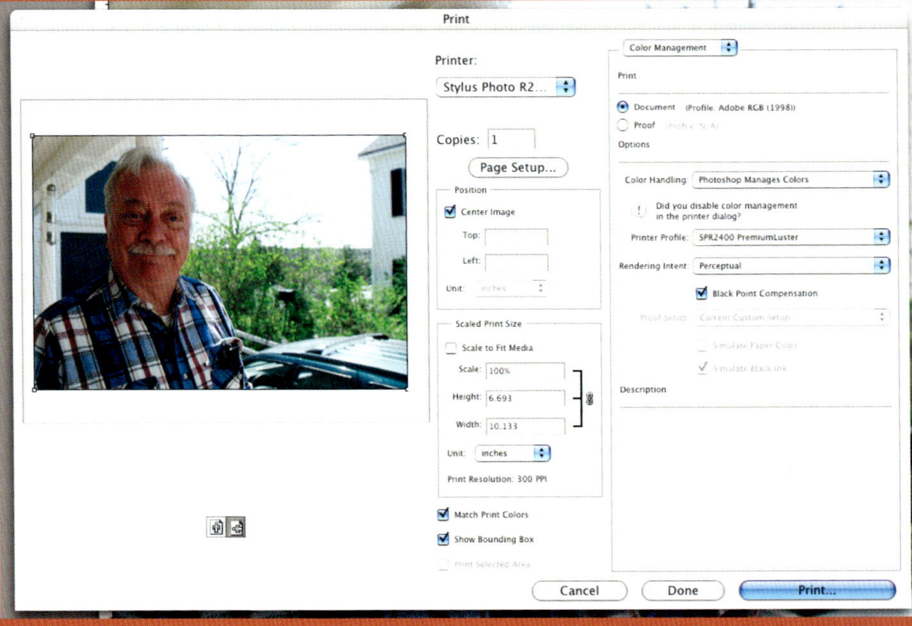

Sending the File to the Printer: Basic Color Management in Photoshop

We have our image, we're in a good, color managed environment with a calibrated monitor, and the settings in Photoshop are correct. We want to print the image, and because we've done all this setup and preparation, we expect the print is going to look like what's on the monitor.

The first step is to change the colors in the image into information the printer understands. To do this, you must assign a printer/paper profile, in the "Print" command in Photoshop. (I'm going to show you the Mac setting; the Windows dialog is different in but the same in theory.)

In "Print," go to the Color Management pulldown menu and choose "Let Photoshop determine Colors." You then tell it what paper/ink combination you're using. This is assigning the output profile to the image, converting the

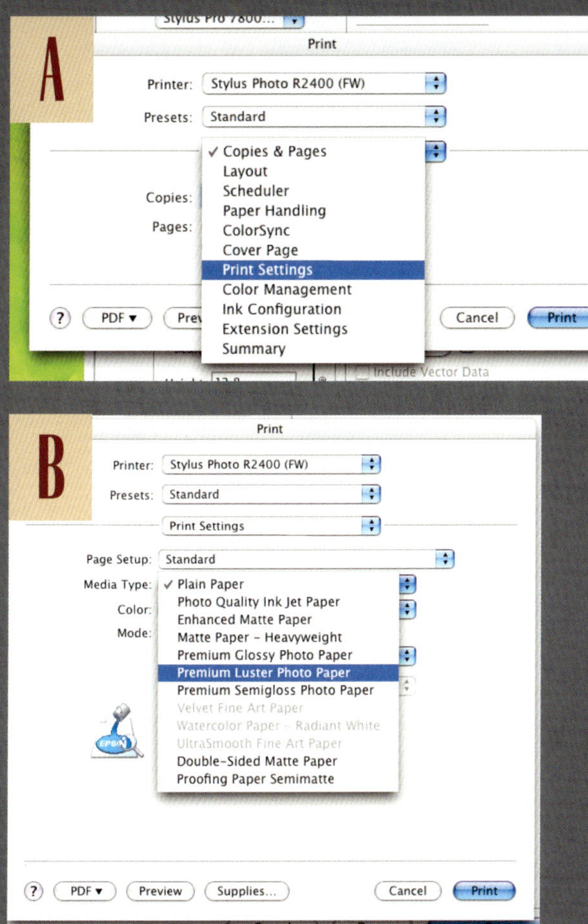

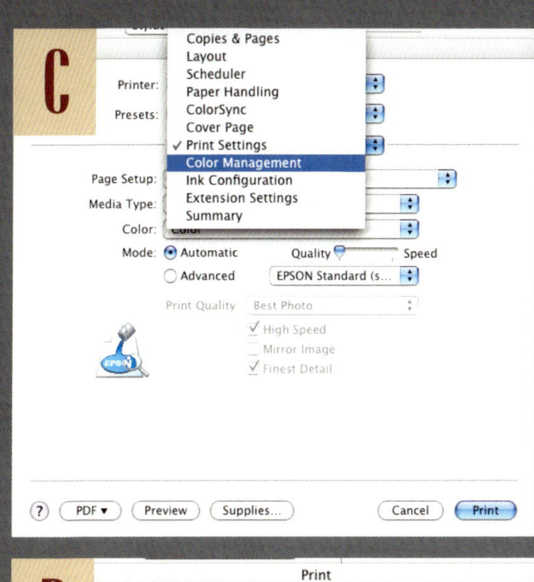

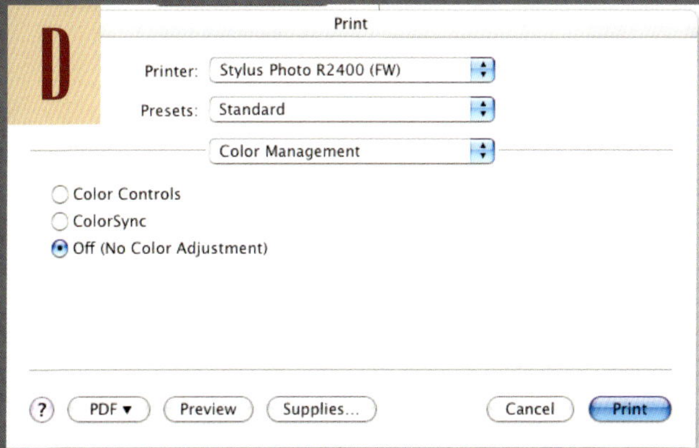

colors from Adobe RGB 1998 to whatever the printer needs to print those colors as they appear on the screen. When I hit "Print" I am going into the printer dialog (in this case I'm using an Epson printer), and I have to start by setting up the paper in the Print Settings dialog (A) and (B). I then go into the Color Management dialog, and here I turn the Color Management off by selecting "No Color Adjustment" (C) and (D). We have already done color management in the "Print" window. If we do it here, we're double correcting, first with Photoshop and then with the printer.

Let's go through the steps in a Windows environment. Print; Let Photoshop determine Colors; set printer/ink profile; hit Print.

When you get the Windows printer dialog, choose "Properties." Right off, go to the "Advanced" button at the bottom right.

That will take you to the Color Management dialog and there you can set all the important things. Select the paper feed ("Sheet" in this case), the paper type ("Premium Luster Photo Paper") and the resolution or the droplet size, of the printer ("Best Photo"). You then want to go to the Color Management pane and check "ICM." Then select "Off (No Color Adjustment)."

Hit OK, and OK, and get happy printer noises.

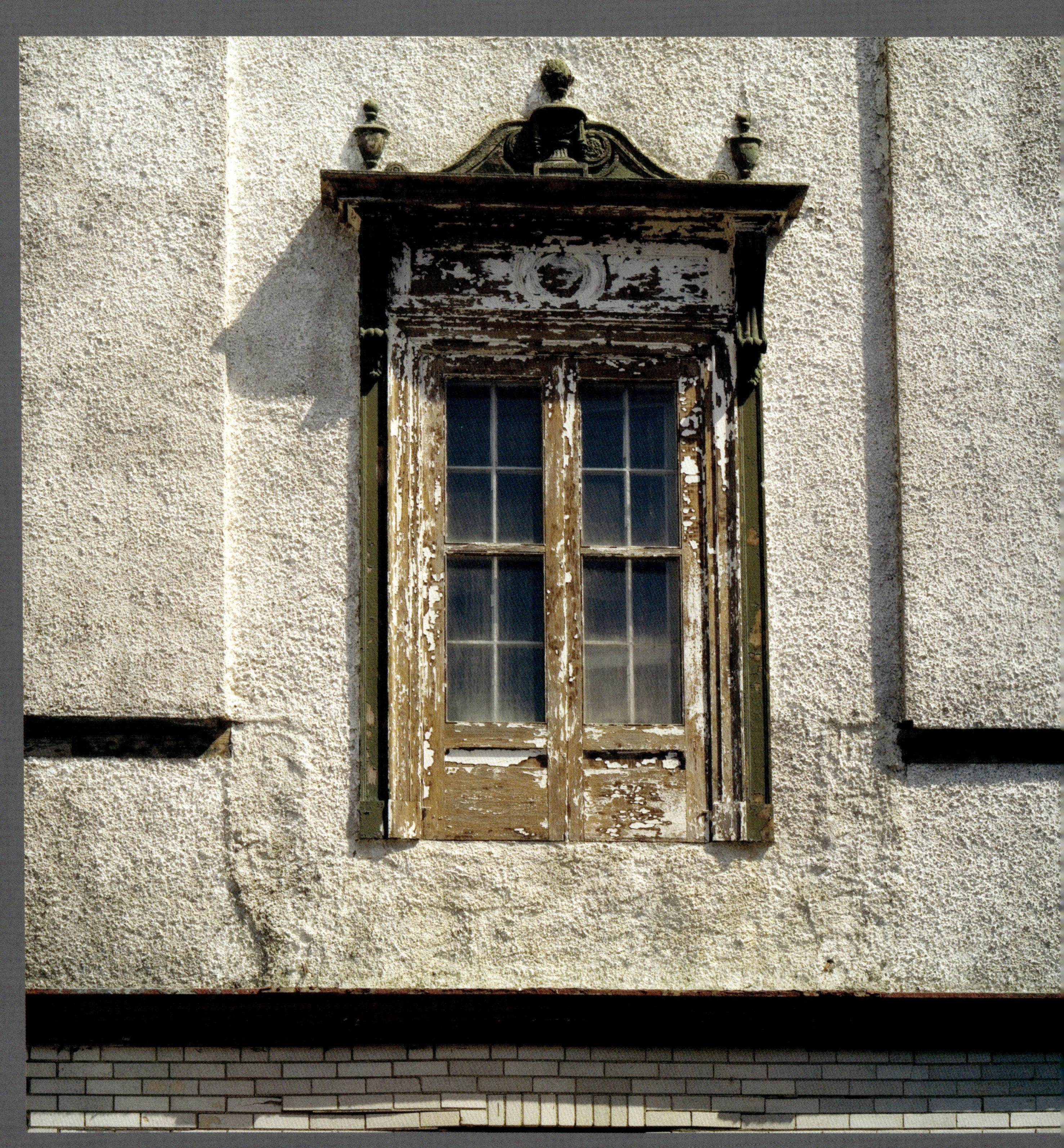

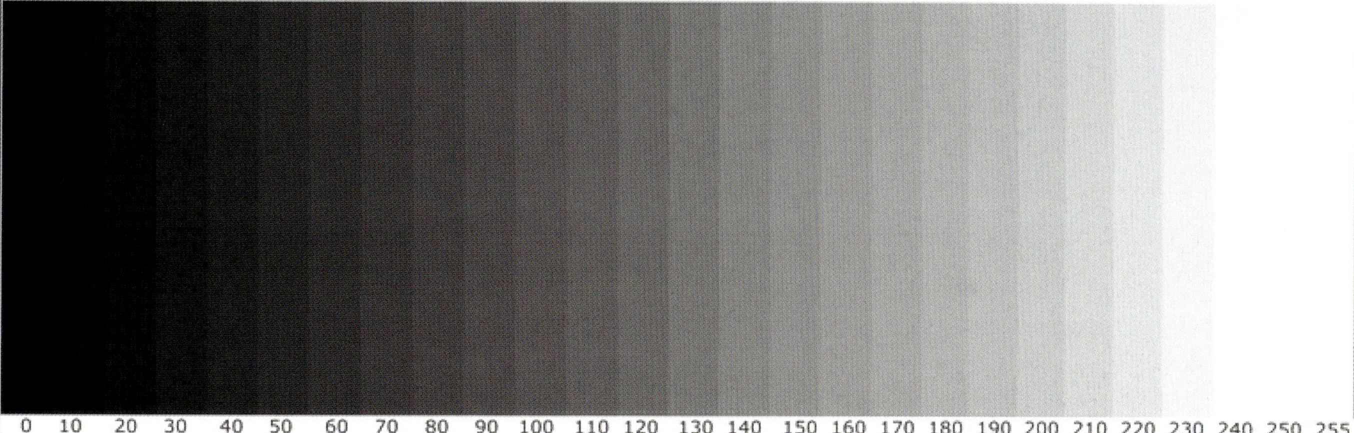

The above image is a grayscale step target—a fairly common printing device. This target shows how your printer renders tonal detail, especially towards the black and white ends of the spectrum. This device gives you an idea of where you should set your black and white points in the RAW conversion process, so make sure you keep this in mind when optimizing an image for printing.

The Grayscale Step Wedge: Printing the Wedge

After everything is all said and done, we still have a major issue to contend with. Regardless of how accurately the monitor and system handle and display our tonal range from black to white, the printer will still have it's own little way of rendering those tones. For example, most Epson printers like to block the black values, giving you no separation between RGB values starting at 15 or 20 all the way down to 0. On the other end, they like to hold a little dot in the highlights, not printing a pure white until you get all the way up to 250 – 255. They may or may not track up through the tonal range evenly, either. They may shift colors slightly at, say, 120 or so. How do you know what your printer is doing to the RGB values you see on the display?

Simply put, you print a step wedge. The target above, which you can get from www.rawpipeline.com is a 27-patch target broken into increments of 10 in RGB values. If you simply print this out using the standard printing procedure outlined above, on the paper you will use, you will see exactly what your printer is doing. Every different paper, profile, or ink you use will produce a subtle difference in the target. Once you know what your printer does, you can adjust and compensate for it.

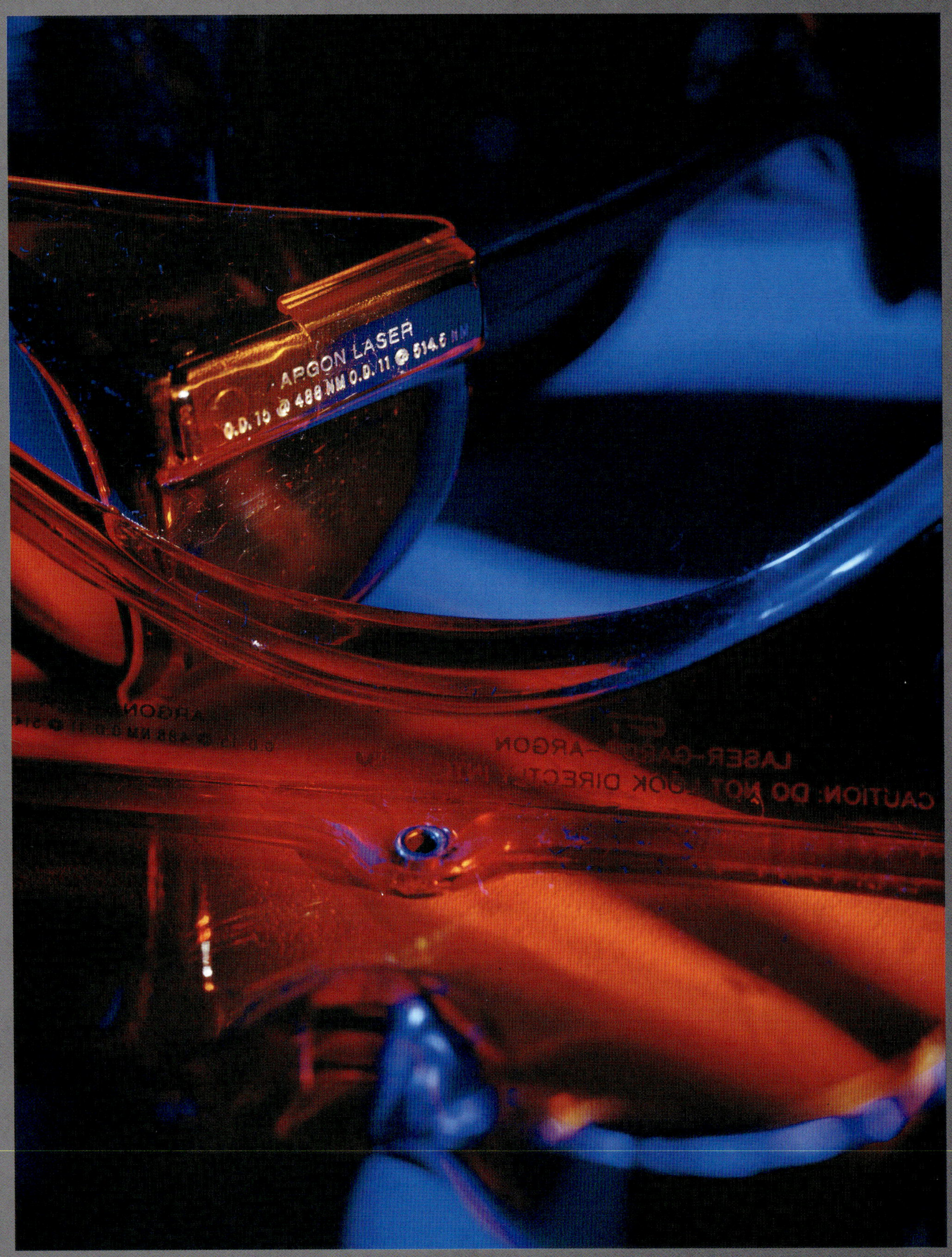
ARGON LASER

Evaluating the Printed Target

Look very closely at the 10 patch, just to the right of pure black. Can you see a difference between that and the 0 patch? If not, the 10 patch is printing as pure a black as the 0 patch, and values in your image that have detail at 10 will simply print as black without detail. If there is a difference between the two patches, you know that the detail in your image at 10 will be retained in the print.

The same concept applies to the highlights. Is there a tone at 250? If so, the values at 250 in your image will hold their detail. If not, they will blow out to pure white. You also use the wedge to evaluate the tonal rendering throughout the scale. You can clearly see if your printer, with the paper and the profile you're using, prints tones from black to white evenly and consistently. If there are abrupt changes among tones or color shifts through the grays, the printer is not rendering the tones throughout the scale smoothly and evenly, and once you know this you can compensate.

Using Levels to Preview the Print

Once you know how your printer renders tones, how do you locate and adjust tones in your image? There's a nifty little trick in Levels that allows you to see what values are where, by using a gamut warning. A gamut warning is just a color flag that Photoshop uses to show specific color value areas (gamuts) of the image.

Open Levels (as a layer, of course) and go to the black point on the "Input" scale (A). Hold down the "alt" ("option") key, and grab the black point. Slide it up to 20 or so, and you'll see a gamut warning in all the areas of the image that fall at that point or below.

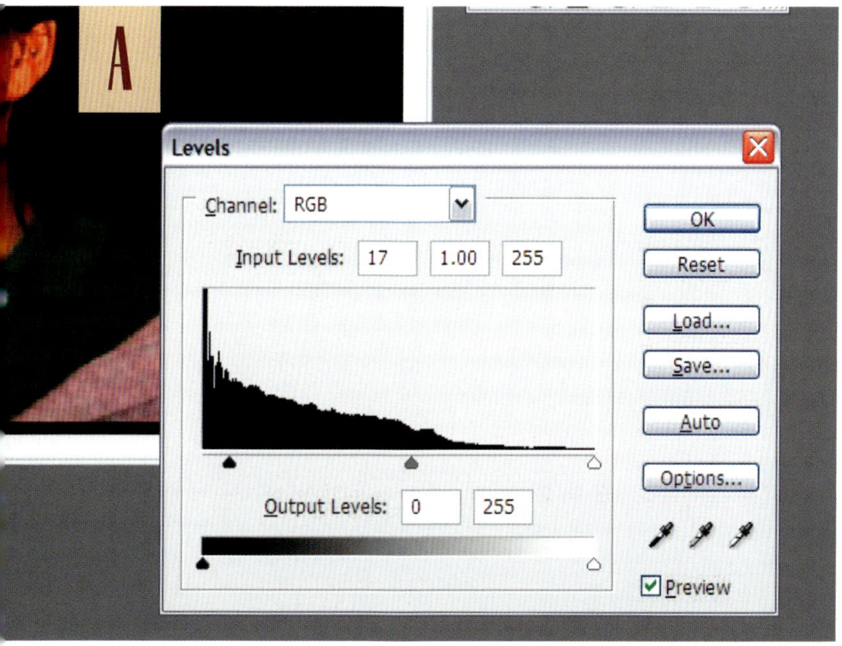

Follow this reasoning out. I've run a grayscale wedge through the printer and seen that for values of 20 and lower I get pure black, regardless of what shows up on the monitor. I may have detail at 10 on the monitor, but the printer can't reproduce it. Now I want to see where in my image the areas are falling at 20 or below, to see what I am going to lose to pure black. I open Levels, grab the black point, hold down "alt" ("option"), and slide it up to 20. Everything that gets blocked in by the gamut warning is going to be pure black, so I can decide how I want to compensate.

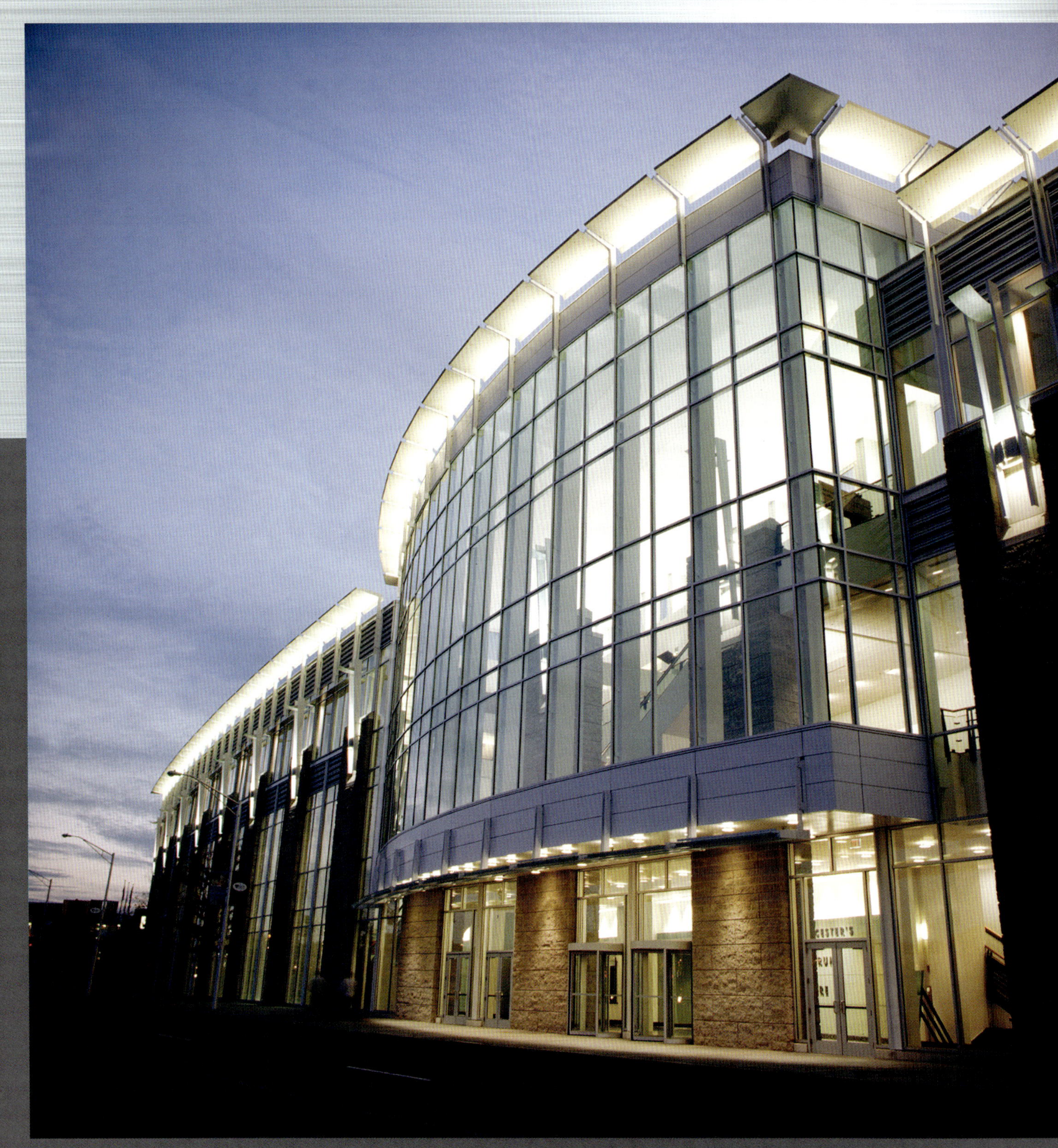

Understanding Papers and Inks

It's important to understand that the paper/ink combination in inkjet printing has very specific parameters, and will respond in very different ways (depending on variables such as printer settings, rendering intents, and general color management). When a profile is built for a printer, it is attempting to eliminate variables, so the source space, printer settings, and ink types must be standardized. If you build a printer profile that runs at 1440 "dpi," it may perform differently if you apply it using 2880 dpi, for example. A profile built without color management is going to work differently than if it was built in Adobe RGB.

The point here is that the profile you use has to be applied very specifically to the paper and ink combination, and in the way the profile was built. Usually a custom profile will have instructions for its application, and if you build your own profile, you must apply it as you built it.

Beyond that, know that just because two papers look and feel the same doesn't mean they will respond the same way to a profile. Just because Crane Museo looks a lot like Epson Textured Fine Art doesn't mean one profile can be used for both. Sometimes you can shortcut things by using a similar profile, but it's unpredictable at best.

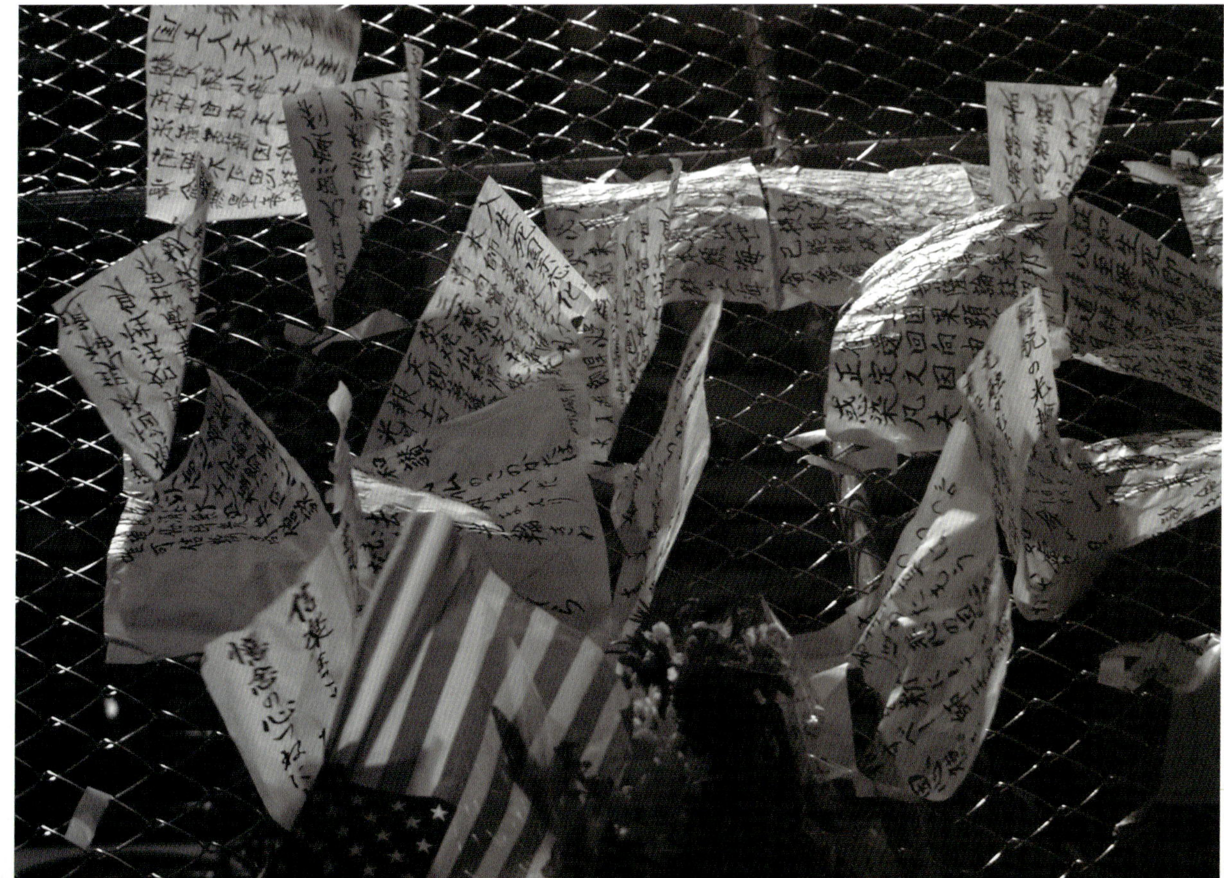

Bill Atkinson and Building "Bouquets"

Most of us who dive into building custom profiles either do it to fix a nasty printer or one that does not have good "canned" profiles, we're using a paper that does not have profiles for our printer, or we want options in how the printer is going to reproduce colors. I look at it like printing in my old darkroom. I have a particular photograph that I think would look good on a certain type of enlarging paper. (One of the great tragedies in the mid-1980s was the dramatic change in Kodak's classic Kodabromide paper. That stuff was beautiful, and made a deep, rich, and powerful print, while holding subtlety and nuance in the deepest of blacks.) Custom profiles give us some rendering options and some personality to our printing pallet.

You usually start by simply going through the routine that the software takes you through. Everyone suggests you should make the target prints and then let them "dry down" for 15-20 minutes, but I know only a few people who actually wait, especially with the fast drying times of current inkjet printers. Most people will print the target, measure it, make a profile, load it in the ColorSync folder, give it a try, and decide if it works or not.

Not Bill Atkinson.

This is a case study on how it's done by a pro. Bill became a household name in the inkjet printing community when he posted his own profiles for the 9600 series and 7600 series printers through the Epson support page. Bill knows his way around color printing. He was one of the original development team of many of Apple's graphic programs, as well as a driving force behind ColorSync, Apple's color engine. Today he prides himself in challenging the industry to do better—much of the reason for why Epson is where they are today is because of Bill's insistence to rise to the demands of photographers.

First Bill talks about linear printing. Working with a printer that is linear—that is, performs in a predictable way throughout it's range of colors and tones—is absolutely essential to being able to profile it, and the 9600 series of Epson printers were good, but still challenging. Bill describes it in a mathematical way—if the printer is not linear, the computations that are needed to profile it go through the roof. The number of adjustments becomes unmanageable. With the introduction of the 9800/7800 series printers, Epson responded to the demands of Bill, and the market. The 9800/7800 series printers, are, as Bill describes it, the closest thing to linear, and the closest to the performance of the "Great Mother Epson Printer in Japan."

So we have a printer that does the same thing every time, as well as doing a nice job of holding consistency throughout the tonal range it prints. What next? Bill starts with designing his own custom targets. His feeling is that his targets—built on a graded ramp of color patches rather that a scattering of different patches—allows the measuring device to smoothly move from one color to the next. It can measure the patches without having to adapt to dramatic changes. Also, after you build the profile, it is easier to see

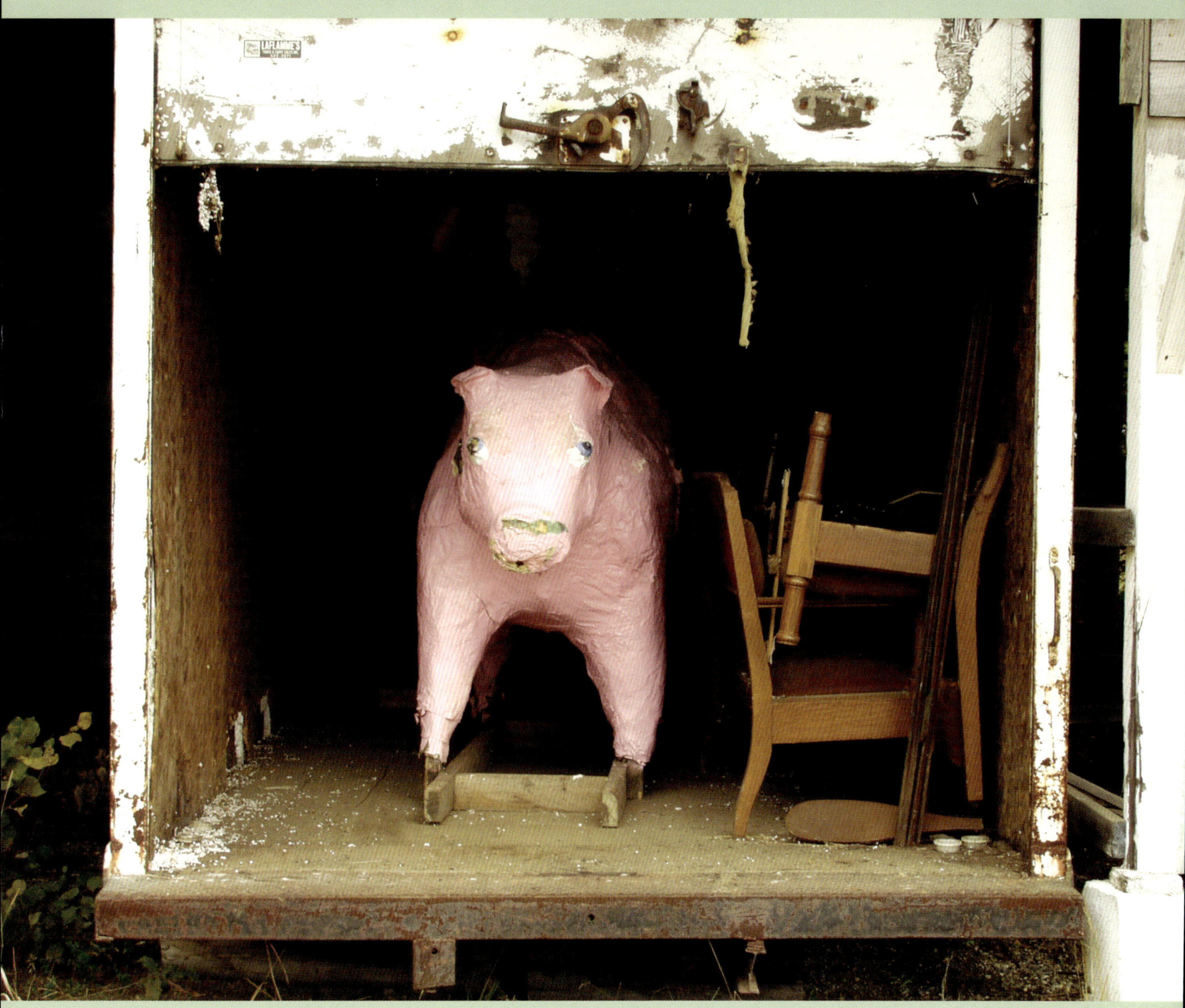

the profile's unevenness if you print the targets. If your blues are all blocked up, for example, you know you have a problem.

Bill prints the profile targets and lets them sit for two weeks before measuring them, allowing them not only to dry, but to "gas out"; that is, letting all the fumes and vapors of the inks dissipate. Not only that, he will print at least three targets—in most cases five—to provide a nice, general sample base. Because he's a good technician, he measures the targets a number of times, and then averages the readings again to correct any random errors.

Here's where it gets interesting. Bill will do this with several different software packages. He has also written and tried out his own profiling software. He describes putting in 1200+ hours and doing over half a million spectral measurements to put these profiles together. The result is a selection of profiles, a "bouquet," as he calls it, that allows us to try different renderings and strategies to see what we like best, and what suits our images. These profiles, at the time of publication, are available at Bill Atkinson's sitefor you to download and try:

http://homepage.mac.com/billatkinson/FileSharing2.html

Far from pure science, this shows how much of printer profiling and color rendering is an art, but, like all artistic disciplines, is founded on a basis of practice and experience. By eliminating many of the variables and errors along the way, Bill is able to give us a true picture of what the sofware and profile can do when used properly. The painter selects the pallet of colors with understanding and a specific intent. The "bouquet" of printer profiles allows us to make our choices just as deliberately. Good technique and good science gives us a good handle on what our tools can do.

Supplied Profiles and Custom Profiles

Only a short time ago, the profiles for Epson printers were totally inadequate. Building your own profiles, or hiring a color-management consultant to build custom profiles, was really the only way you could get these printers to perform to their potential. As Epson and other manufacturers have come to understand the photo market a little better, they have realized that if they build good, solid profiles then their printers will ultimately sell better. The profiles with the latest printers are very good, and because the printers are more consistent (or at least more linear), their profiles perform better in practice.

Having said that, there is probably as much art as there is science to building a profile, just as there is as much art to designing a film emulsion. Building your own profiles is more affordable than even a few years ago. Granted, it may be less essential, but custom profiles give you a whole new array of tools for rendering your image. Each system interprets and builds the profiles in it's own little way, to the point that some photographers are building "bouquets" of profiles (see page 164). These are bunches of profiles, built to his rigid specifications, with different software and hardware for a single printer/paper/ink combination.

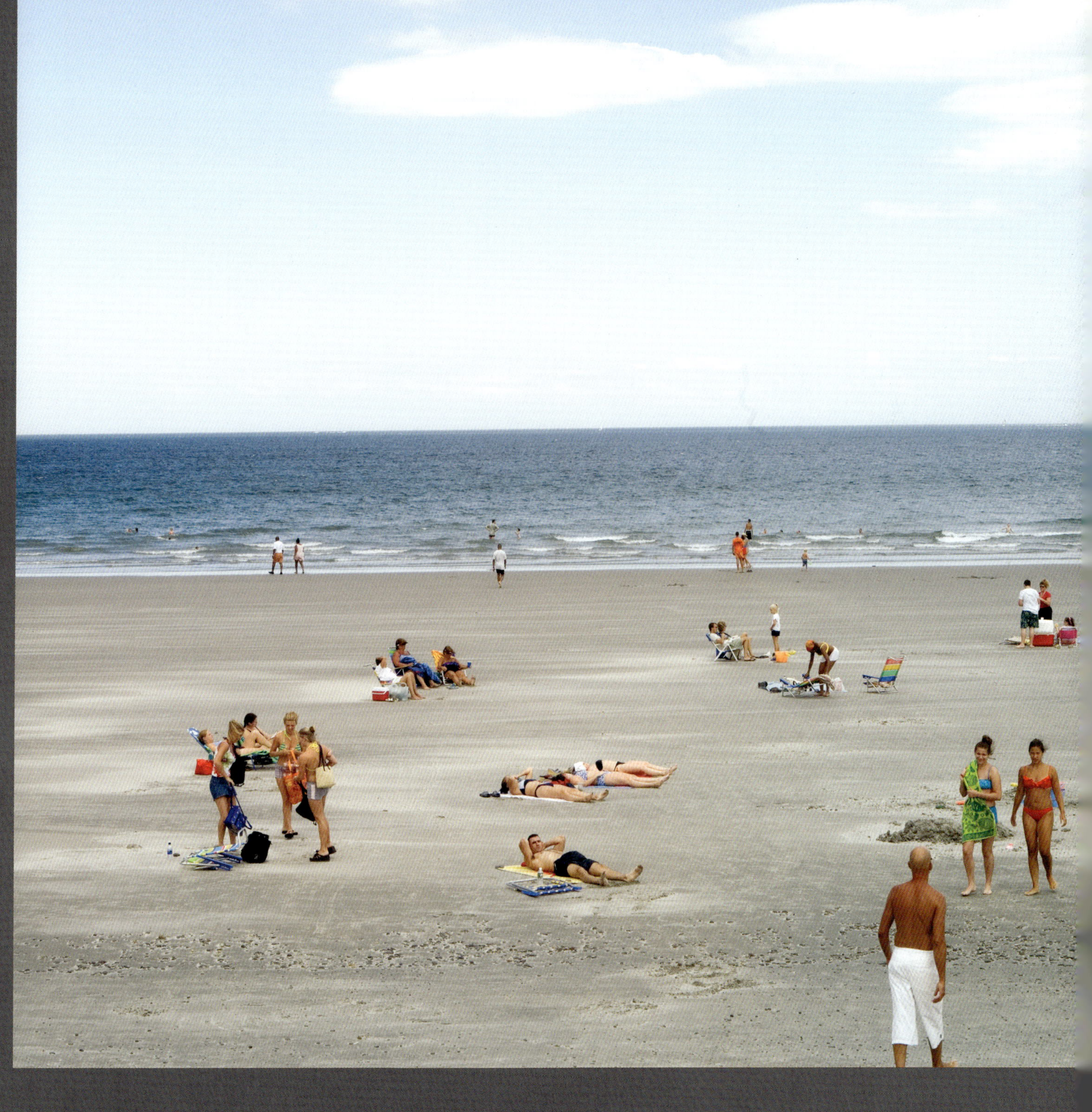

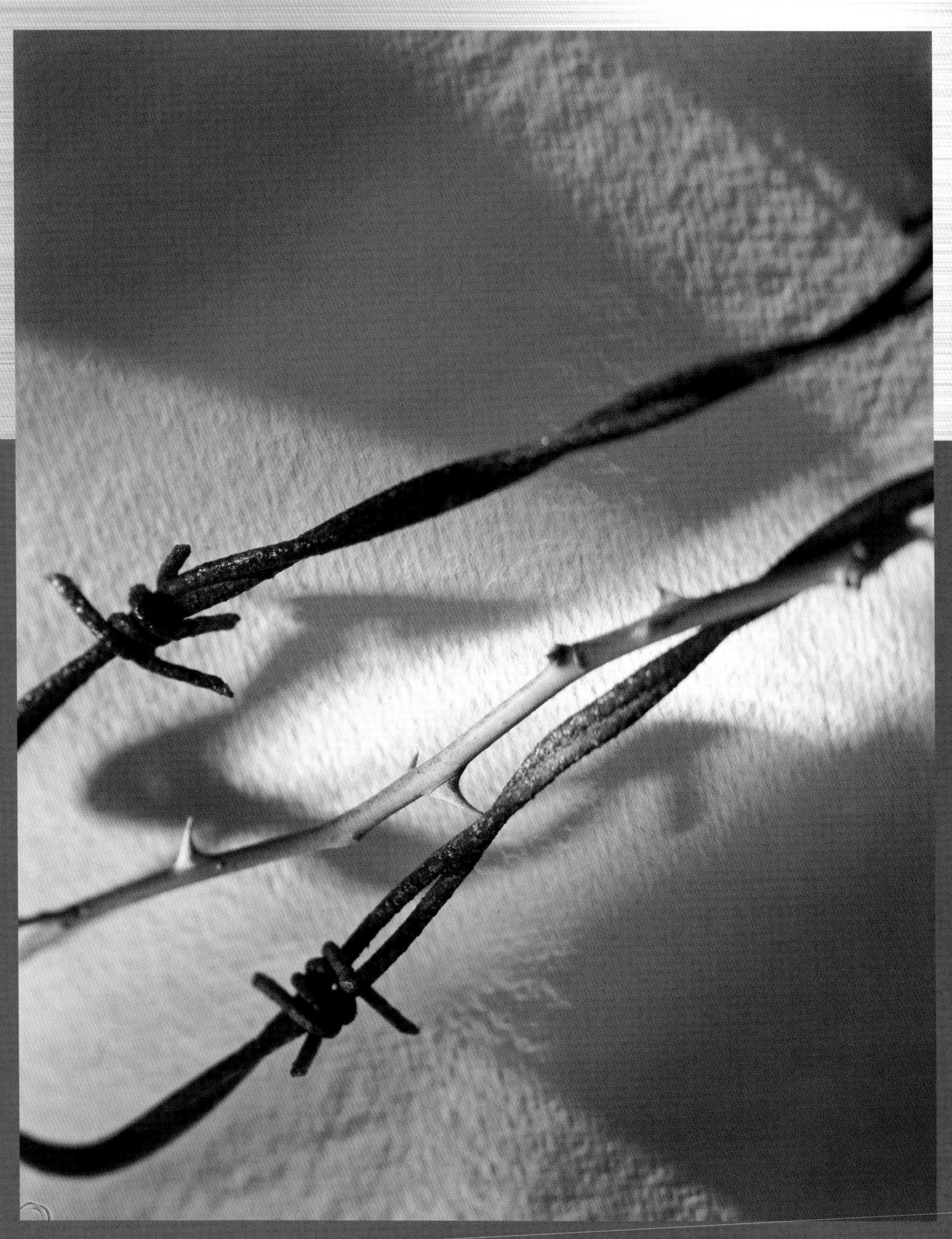

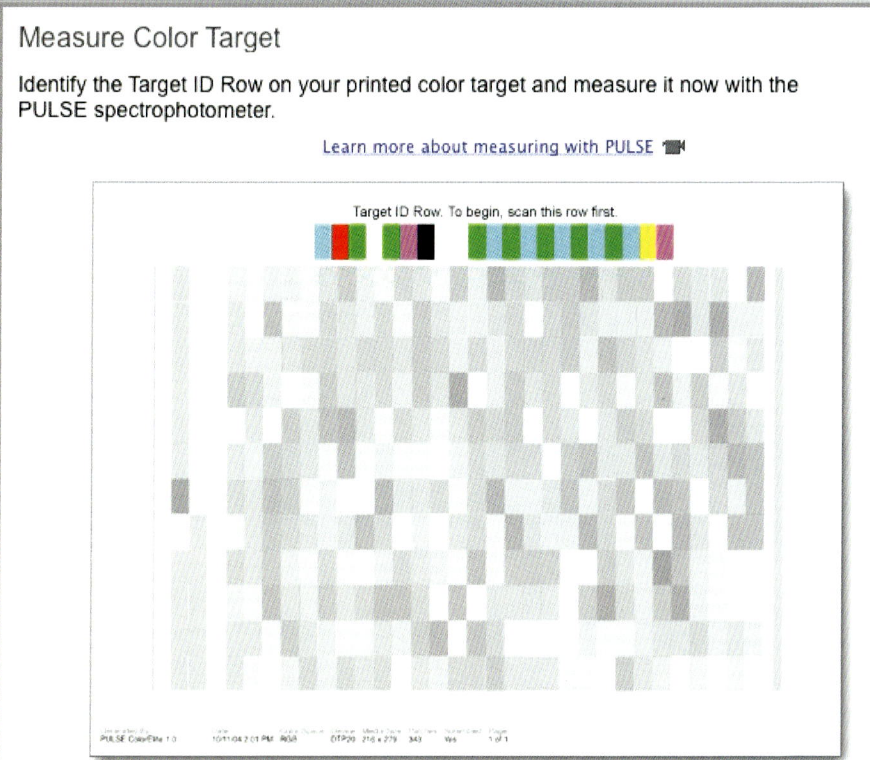

A

Building Profiles

Building your own profiles can be quite easy now. The software is user-friendly and the hardware is very accurate and affordable. Like everything else, what used to cost $10,000 and didn't work very well now is $1500 and actually fun to use.

The procedure is just the same as any other calibration process. Start with known values, see how they are rendered, and measure them. Take the actual rendered values and correct them to be closer to what you want. The figure shown (A) is the initial reading screen in Monoco Pulse. It shows a diagram of the target that you've printed, and is telling you which row you need to read with the spectrophotometer. Simply follow the directions and you've built a printer profile.

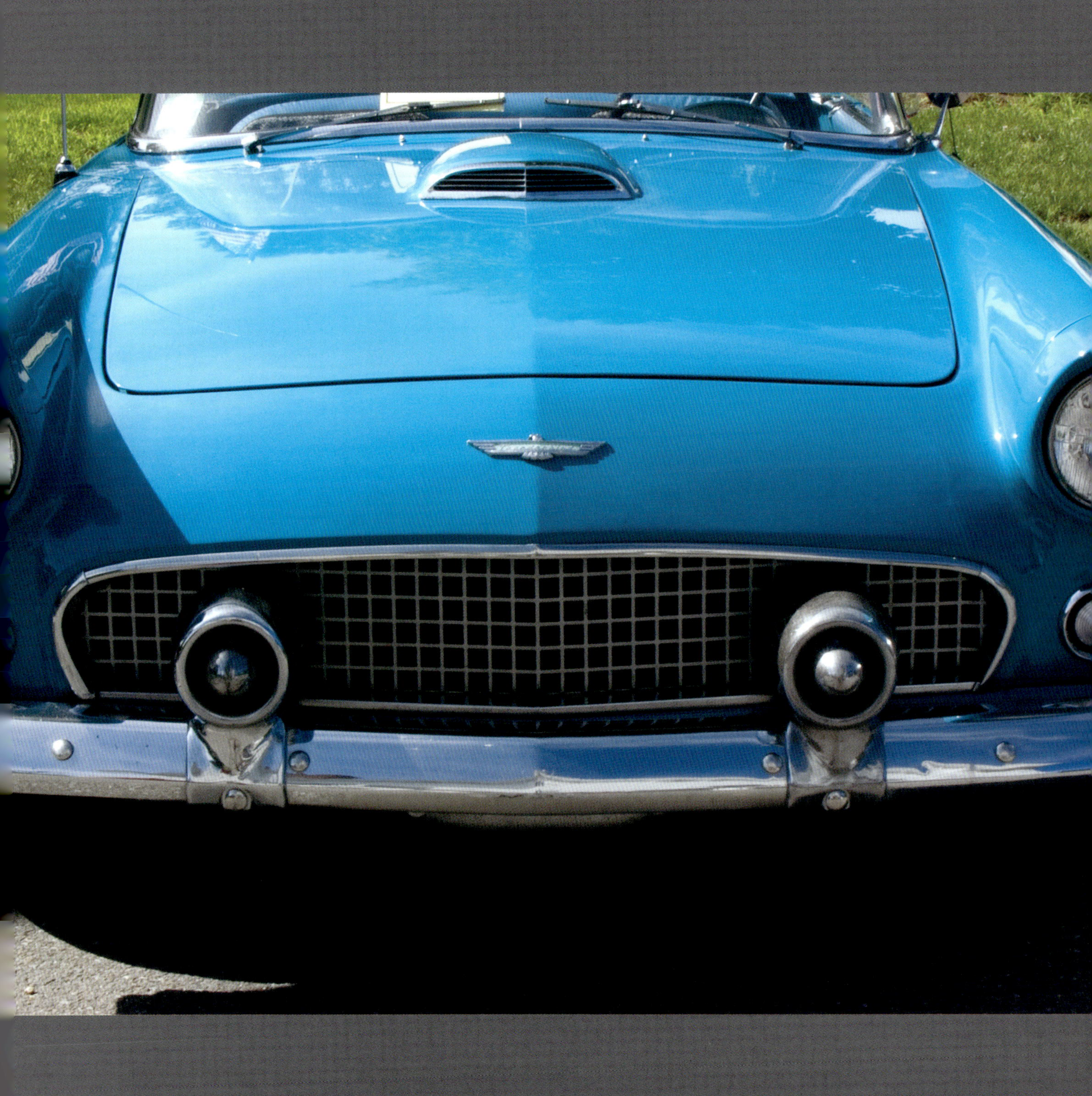

Soft Proof Profiles: Proof Setup and Gamut Warning

The soft proofing technique is a helpful guide; it give you a general view of how a printer will render your image, and whether that printed image will have the necessary detail.

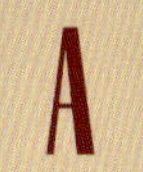

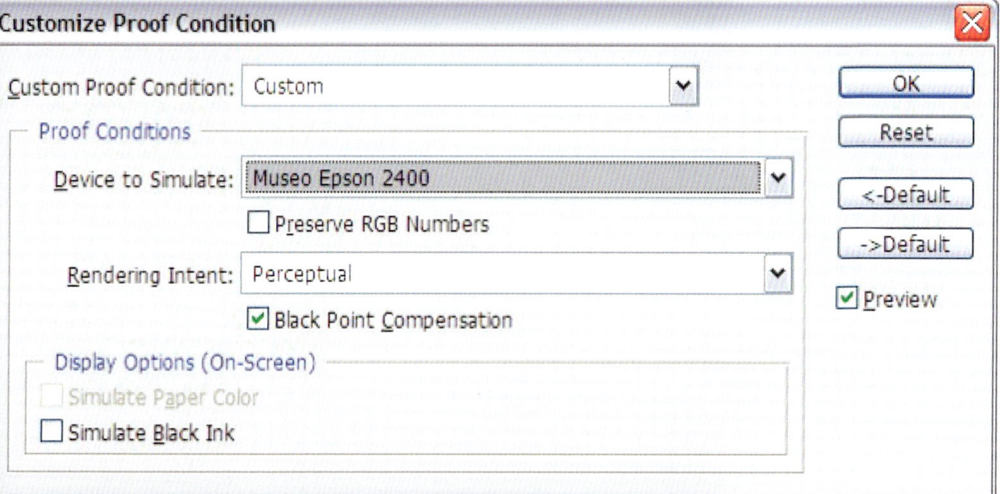

Now that we understand the tools and the process, how do we evaluate all this without actually running a few million prints? Simple: use Proof Setup along with Gamut Warning. Go to View>Proof Setup>Custom. Here I've set the Proof Setup to show me what Crane Museo is going to do on the Epson 2400 (A).

With the Preview selection, I can see how that paper and ink combination is going to respond. I can use this to flag problems such as lack of separation in color areas, blocking, uneven transitions, and other gamut-related issues. I don't, however, adjust the color based on my soft proof until I start the Gamut Warning view. To do this, go to View>Gamut Warning.

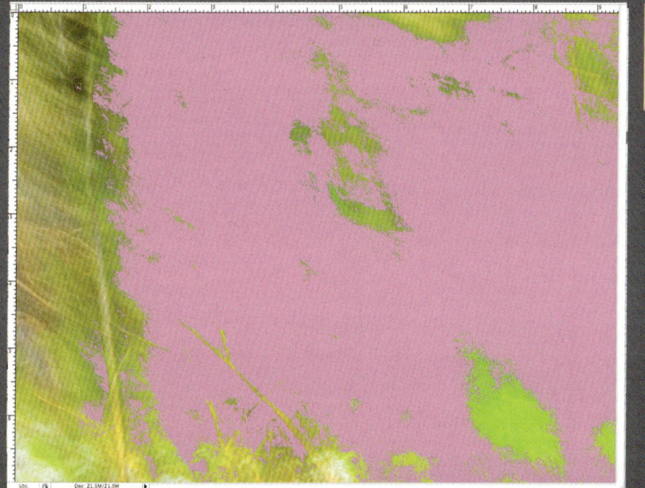

B

Pay attention to the areas highlighted by the gamut warning view. If these areas are important to your final printed image, then you must compensate for that in your image adjustments.

The image shown (B) has an area of color that will fall outside the gamut of the paper/ink combination.

This gives me very interesting information. By looking at the Gamut Warning with various Proof Setups for the same printer/ink/paper, using different profiles, I can judge which profile to use. I can see which profile best handles the colors on the edge of my gamut, and which profiles just dump the colors with no rendering.

Using Proof Setup and Gamut Warning to Choose Papers

This tool allows me to see and judge which paper is best for the image. I can use Proof Setup to emulate a smooth matte, a high gloss, or a luster stock and see which paper renders that specific image best, with the least loss to gamut.

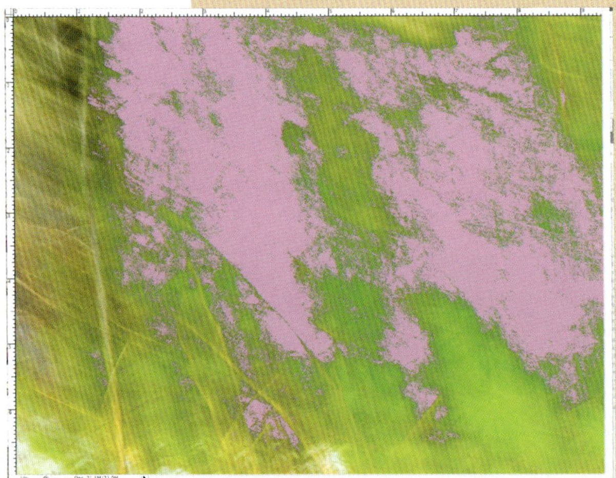

Different papers will render the image differently, so try the gamut warning view with several types of paper to see which one gets closest to your final vision.

The image you see here is the same file, but with a Proof Setup for Epson Premium Luster paper, and it's quite a surprise. This coated, photo-style paper actually has a more reduced gamut than Crane Museo, a watercolor stock. In this case, if the shadows and tones in the right center of the image are important, I'm going to try Museo over Premium Luster.

I find Proof Setup and Gamut Warning to be an efficient way to see how the paper, profiles, and printer are going to respond. This helps target a paper, however, nothing can really show you on the monitor how the printer is going to print, and nothing can replace simply running a print.

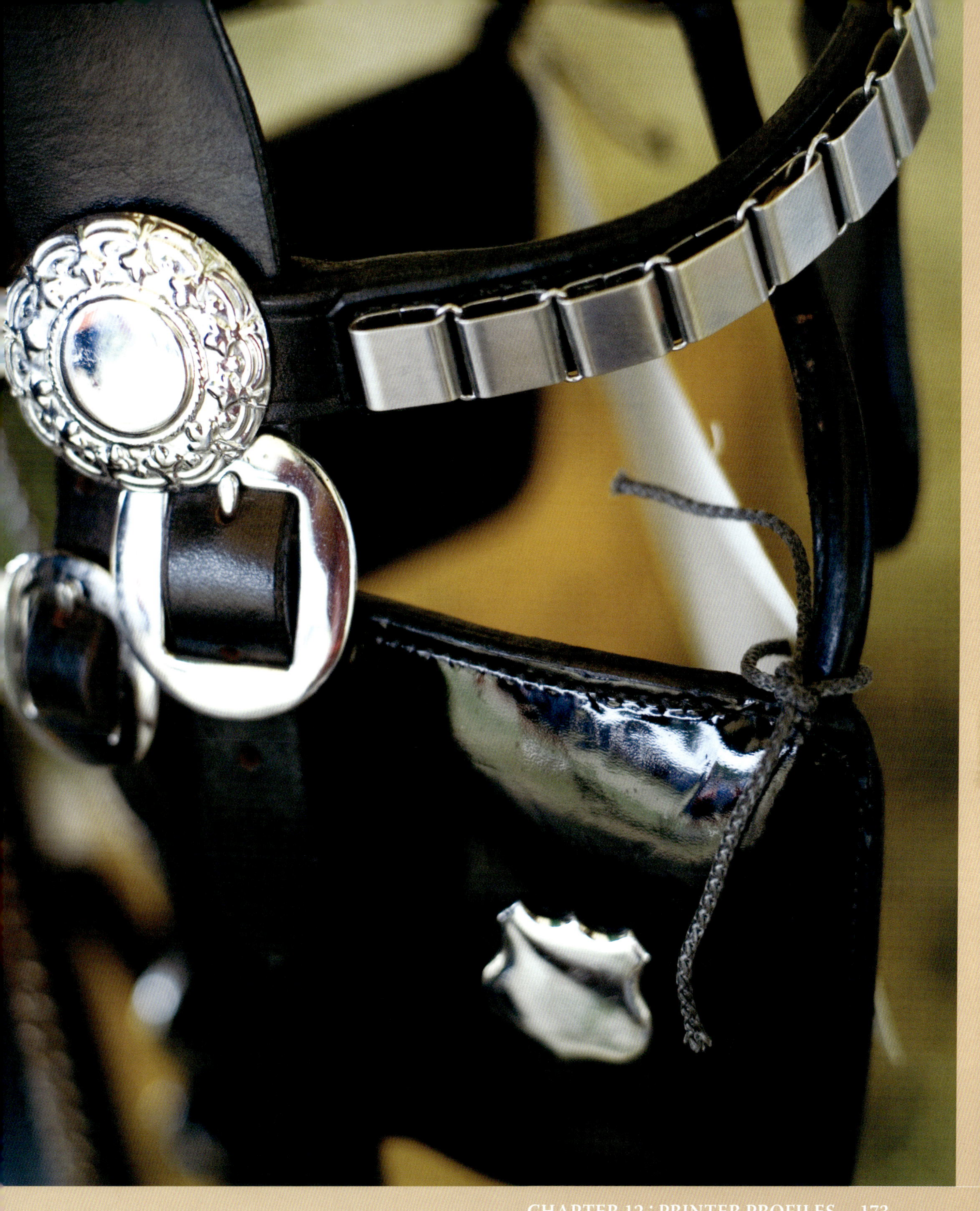

13 EXCEPTIONS AND ADVANCE PRINTNG METHODS

Epson's "Advanced Black and White"

Now that I've got you ignoring the Epson print drivers, I have one more thing that will be the exception that proves the rule. After ten years of building printer drivers that didn't work too well, Epson decided to throw caution to the wind, and actually make a black-and-white printer driver that runs better that anything else out there. Who'da thunk it?

To use this, the first step in the Print window is to select "Let Printer Determine Colors." We now have to allow the Epson print drivers to do their job, since Photoshop is not going to do the color management (A).

Once you hit "Print," you see the familiar Epson driver window (B). Start off by going into the Print Settings pulldown menu of this dialog. Once you select the proper paper type (shown is Premium Luster Photo Paper), go to the Color window and select "Advanced B&W Photo."

Next, go back up to the Print Settings pulldown and now select the "Printer Color Management" option.

This opens up the Advanced B&W dialog that allows remarkable control over how the printer renders the image (C). Generally, you would select the "Normal" rather than "Darker" tone, and apply a preset warm, cool, or neutral tint. You can also apply a custom tint by selecting a point on the color-picker wheel.

For the first time, not only does the printer produce a fine black-and-white print, but it does this with ease and consistency. The prints produced by these printers in Advanced B&W mode are as good as any other printing method, including silver.

A

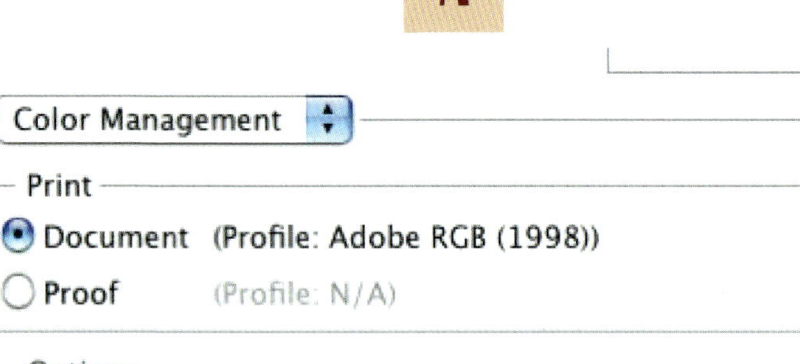

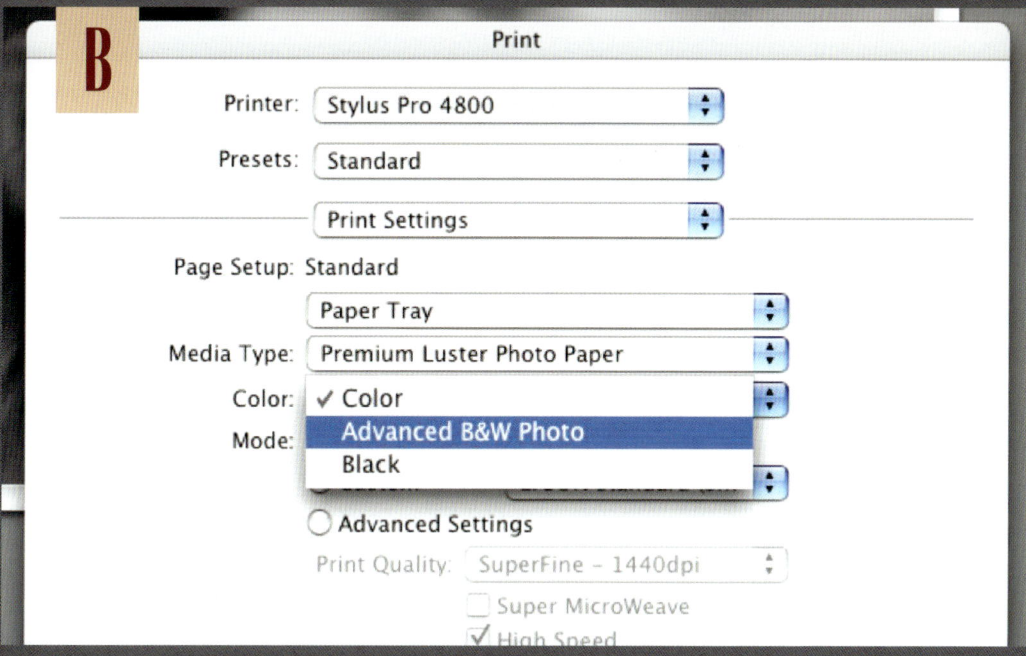

Because of the demand for accurate color and black and white print rendition, Epson has stepped up it's game with its built-in profiles. The "Advanced Black and White" printer profile is one that has certainly hit the mark.

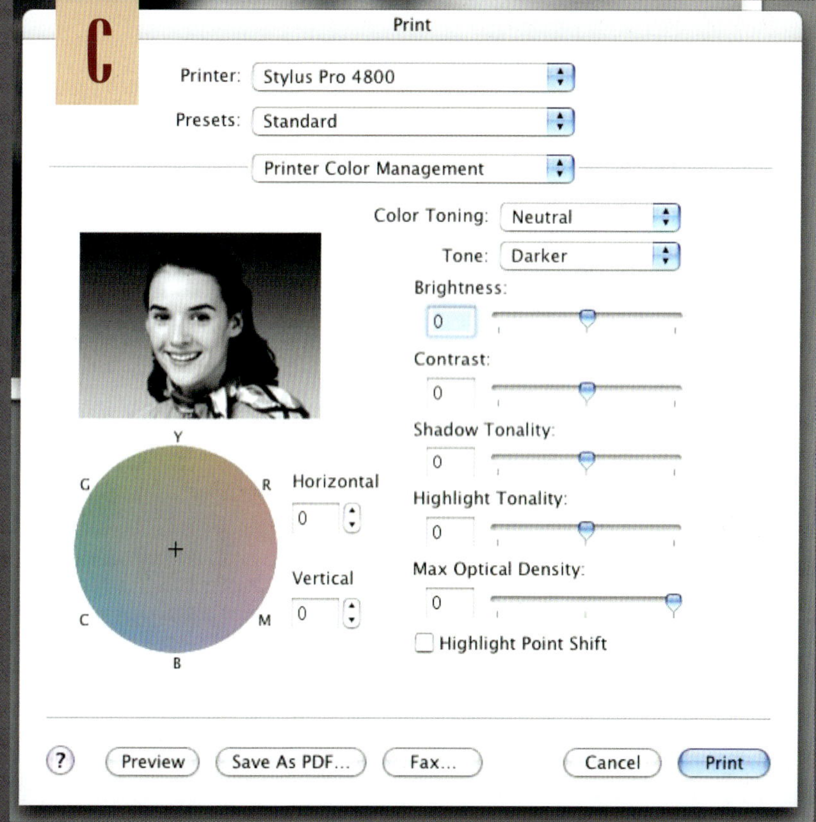

Look through the options available in the "Advanced Black and White" print dialog. Even here, Epson has created excellent control over the rendering of the printed image. The custom tint wheel is also a great creative tool.

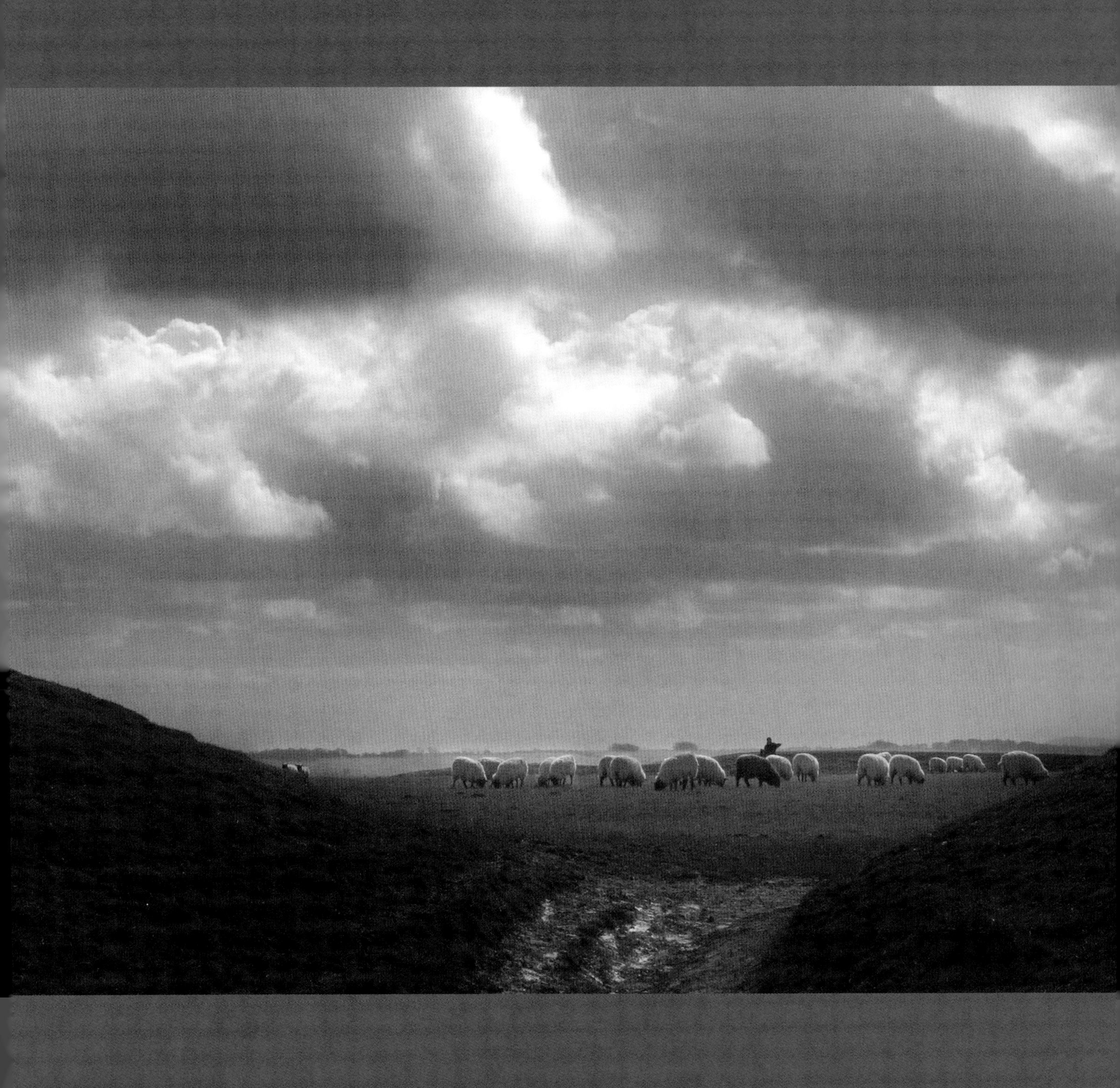

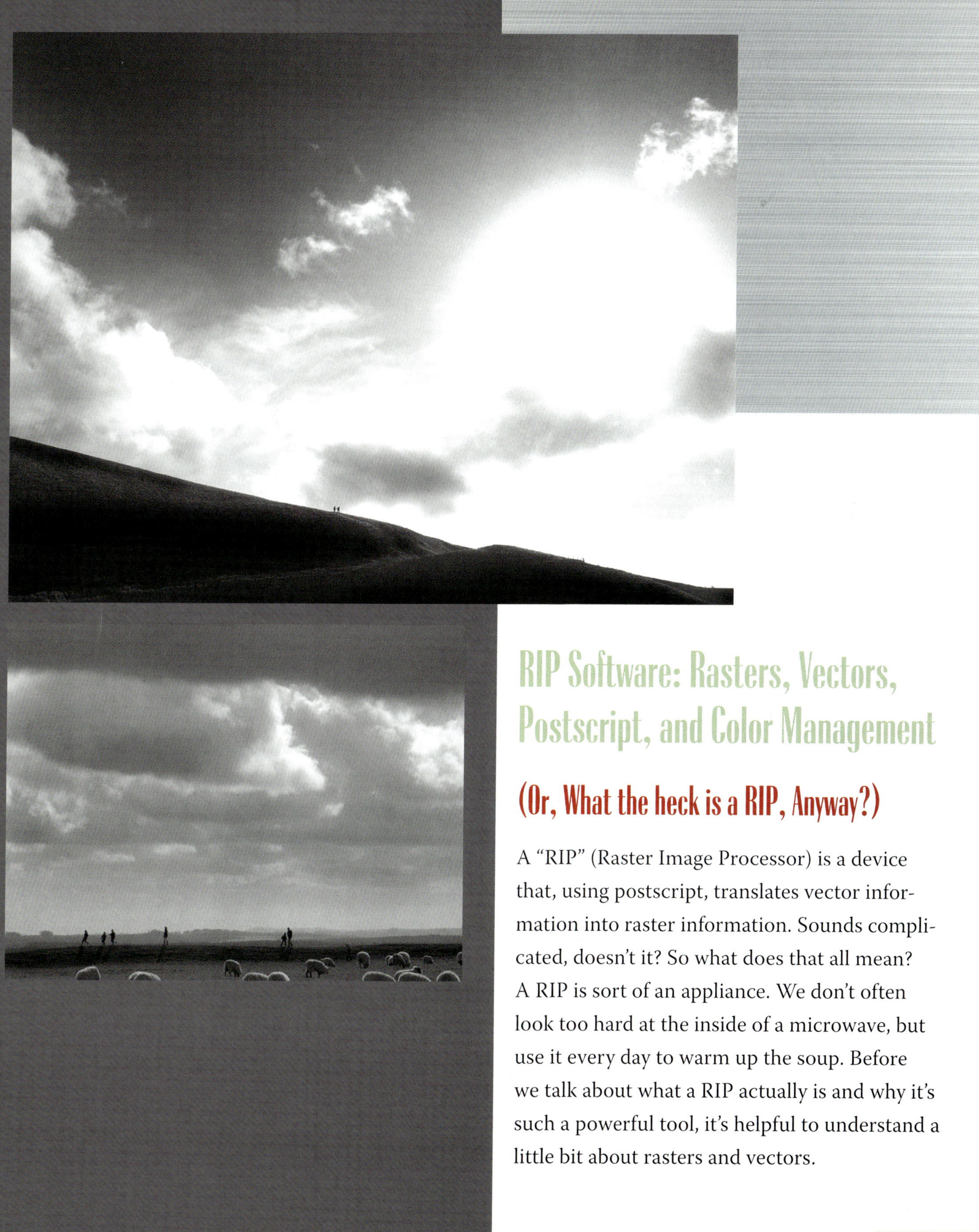

RIP Software: Rasters, Vectors, Postscript, and Color Management

(Or, What the heck is a RIP, Anyway?)

A "RIP" (Raster Image Processor) is a device that, using postscript, translates vector information into raster information. Sounds complicated, doesn't it? So what does that all mean? A RIP is sort of an appliance. We don't often look too hard at the inside of a microwave, but use it every day to warm up the soup. Before we talk about what a RIP actually is and why it's such a powerful tool, it's helpful to understand a little bit about rasters and vectors.

Rasters, Vectors, and Postscript

Let's start with the difference between a raster image and a vector image. A raster image, otherwise known as a "bitmap," is just that—a map of the bits of information in a document. Thinking in terms of pixels in Photoshop, each pixel has a location and a color. The larger the document dimensions and resolution are, the bigger the file is. Your printer, to continue the example, wants to know how much ink to put down and where. Thus, a raster image literally translates the image into a map of the pixel information.

A vector image, on the other hand is more like a sheet of directions. It doesn't specify individual pixels, rather it uses line and points to create a general shape from the pixel information of an image. This makes it easier to change the overall size of an image; the ratio of the image stays the same, regardless of its actual dimensions. Typeface, for example, is a vector image, because a font needs to be able to be resized without making the actual file bigger. Postscript is the computer language by which these vector images are described. The vector image is converted to a bitmap for monitor display or for printing.

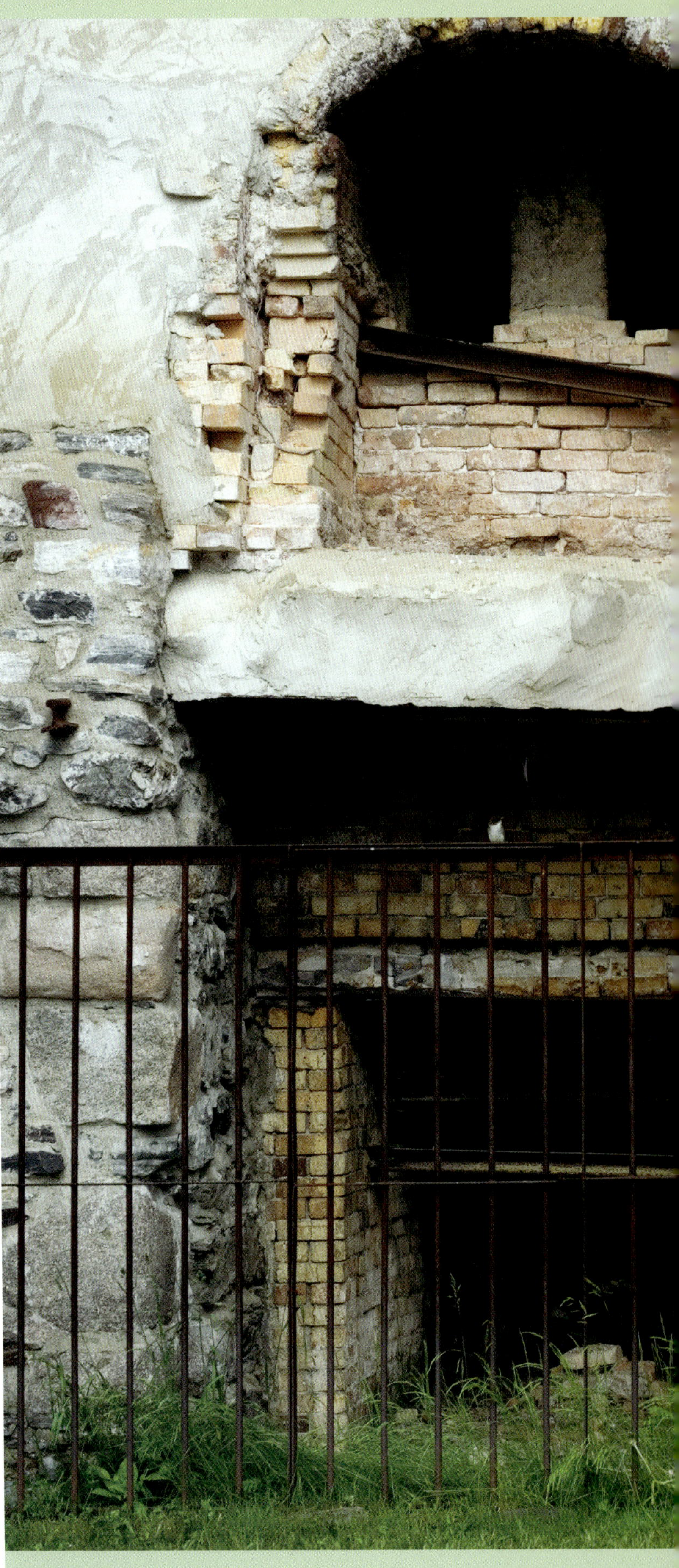

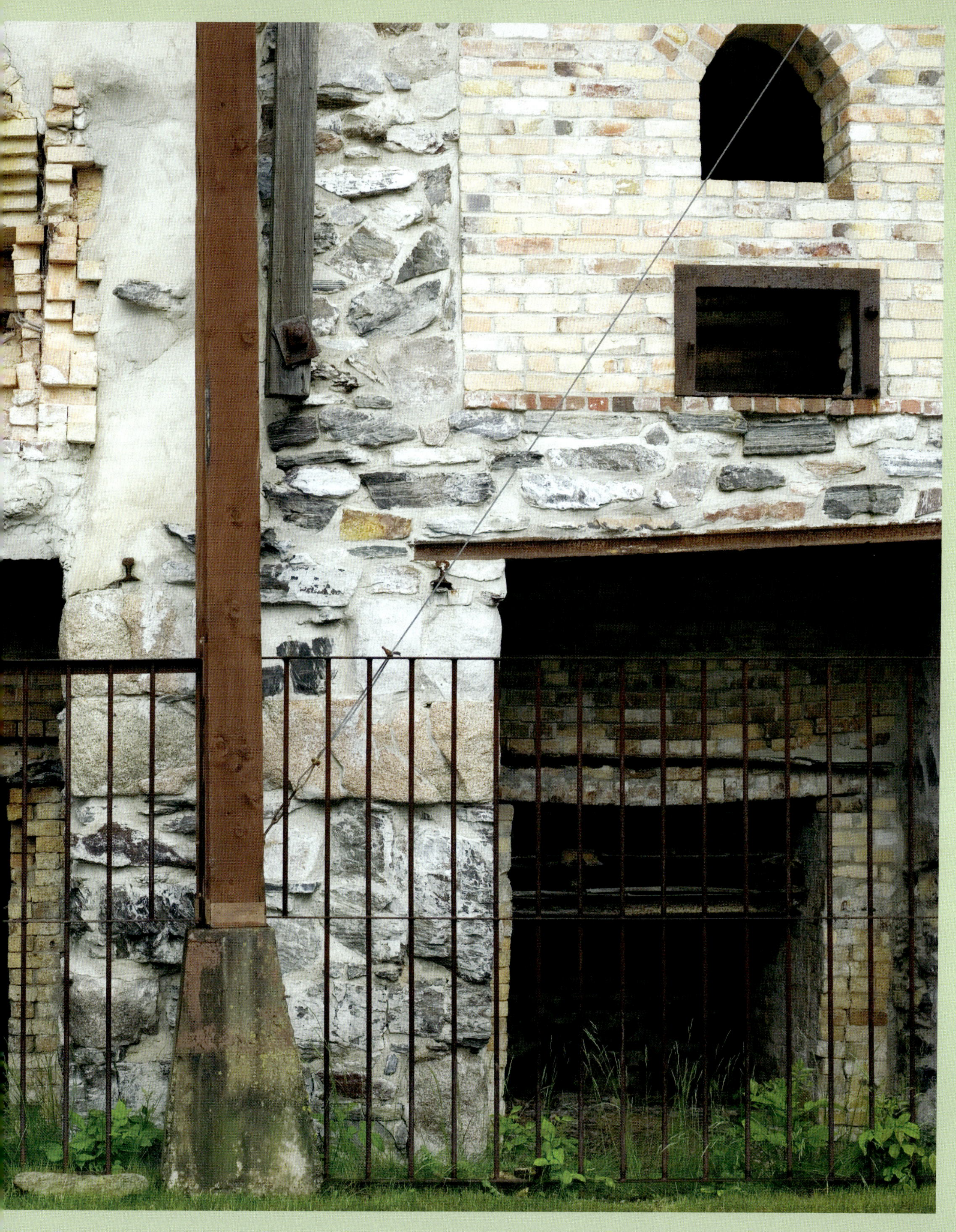

Suppose you have a friend standing in a field. You tell them to walk forward a random number of paces. Then you tell them to turn to the right, and walk exactly the same number of paces, whatever that was. Have them do this two more times and they have made a square. This square, or "image," isn't about the actual number of paces, it is simply defining the shape. If your friend chooses to make the first "leg" ten paces, then the image is ten paces square. If they choose to walk a mile, then the image is a mile square. Keep in mind that the biggest message here is based on the direction they walk and the ratio between the "legs" they walk. If you say, "walk forward, then turn right and walk twice that distance," then you're making a rectangle with a 1:2 aspect ratio.

So, the RIP uses the postscript and translates the vector information into raster information.

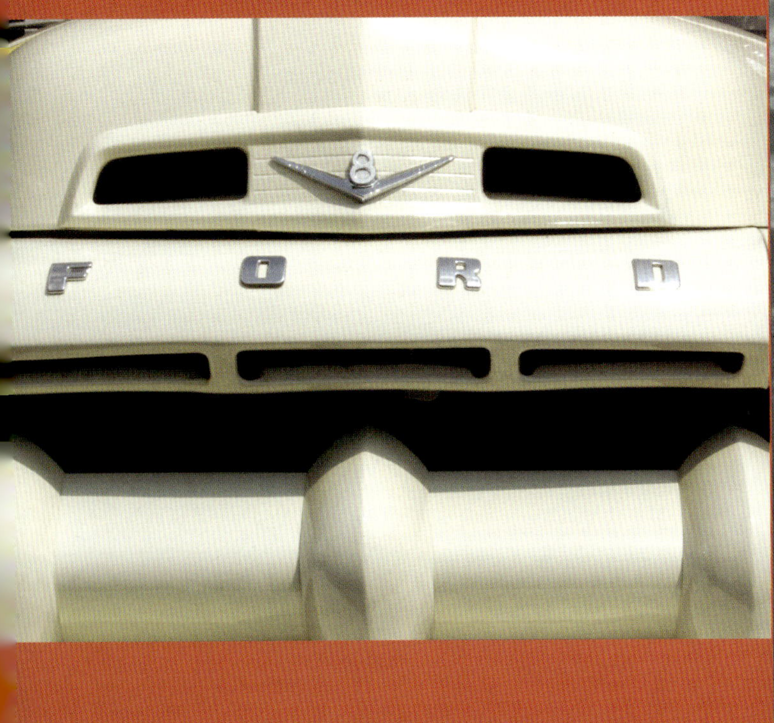

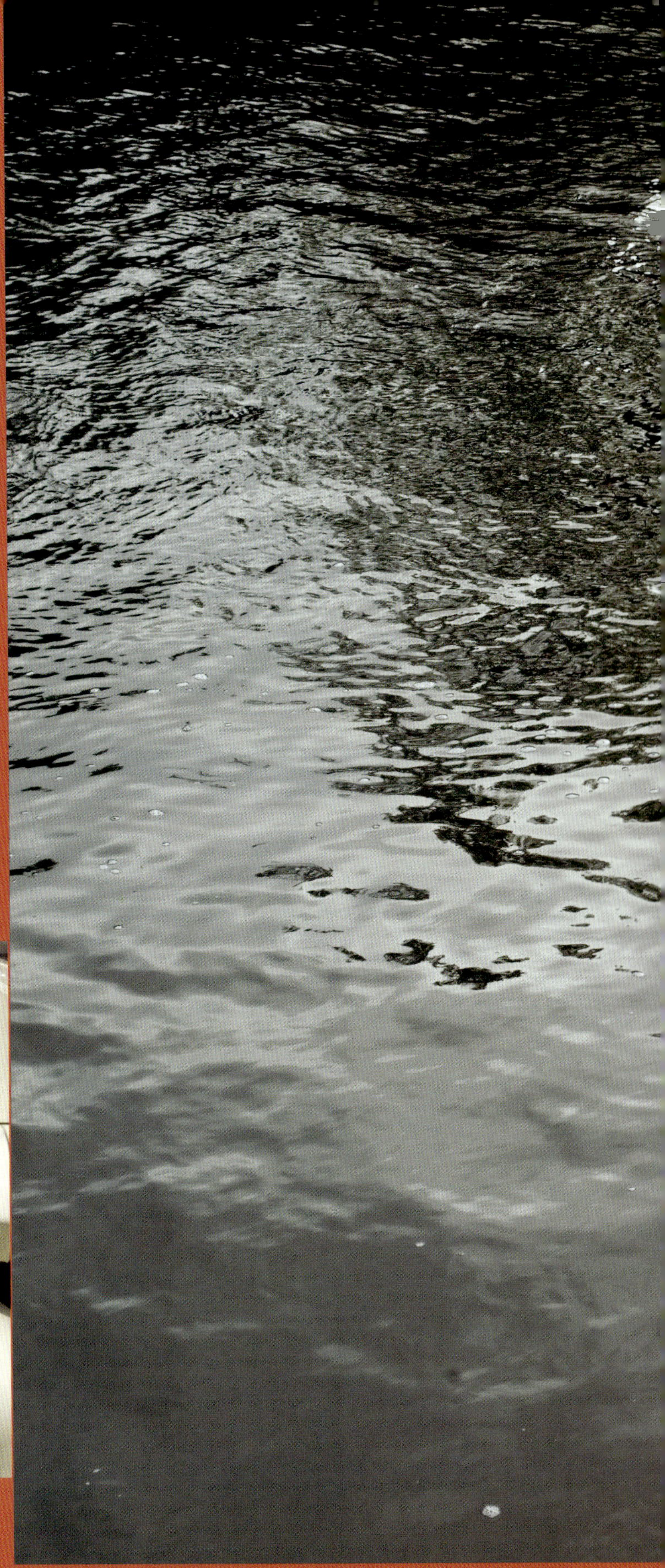

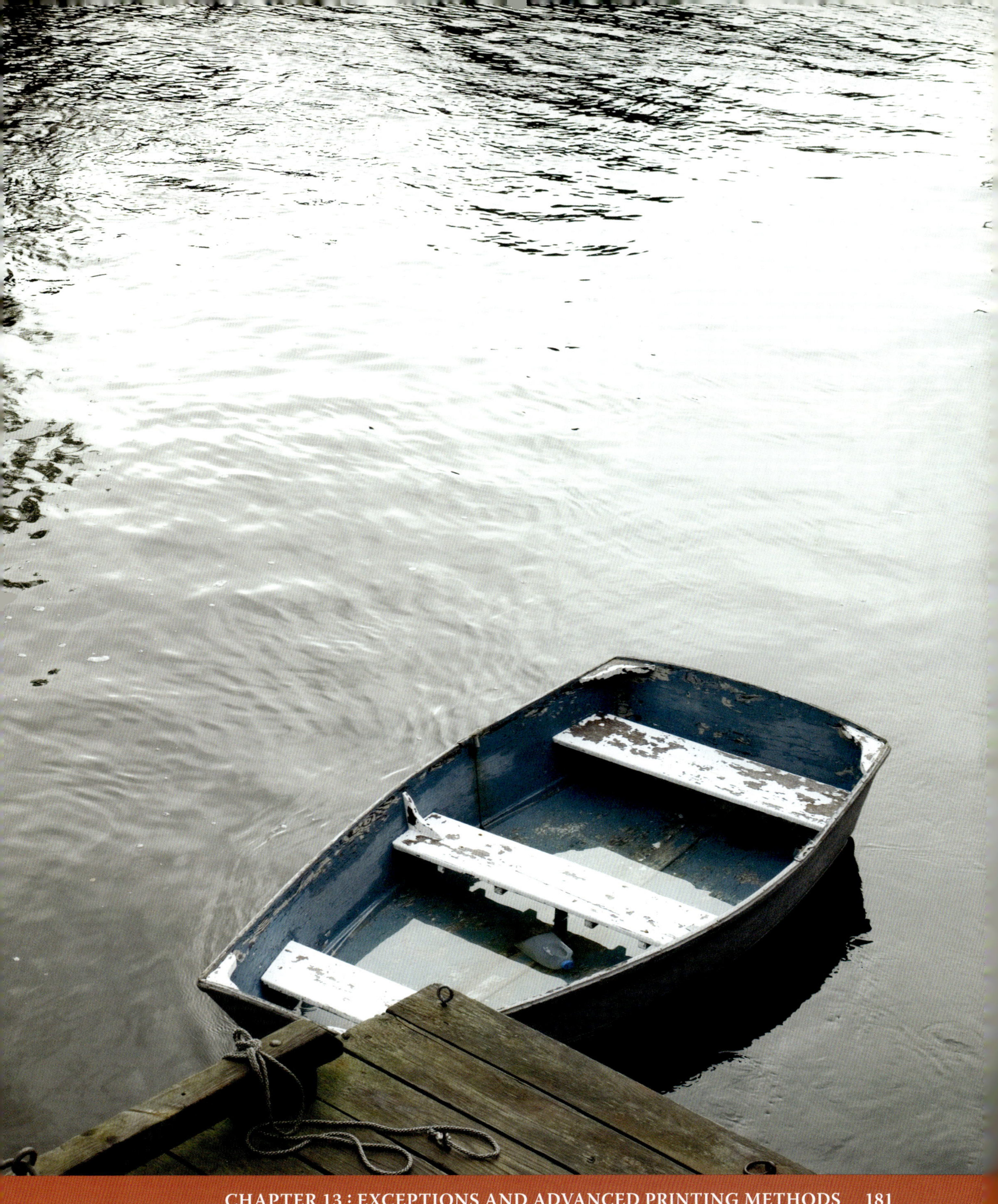

It takes these "directions," feeds in the size and resolution, and makes a map of the specific pixel information so the printer knows where to put ink down.

Here's the interesting thing (and, by the way, the point of this discussion): whatever RIP you're running takes over the functions of the printer driver. The regular printer driver doesn't know what to do with vector information, and the RIP basically tells the printer driver to stand aside and let it drive. Since it is taking full control over the printer, you have a chance to work some real magic with exactly how you drive that printer's individual color channels, the way it mixes color, and the size and pattern of the dot.

Essentially, we're talking color management, here, not raster/vector issues. Most RIPs, almost as a by-product, started allowing some very refined color management policies. Now, RIPs have evolved to include incredibly accurate press proofing, as well as high-quality photographic rendering and profiling.

RIP Control

The dangerous part of this is not knowing the controls for the RIP, or not setting them correctly. If you're only concerned with rendering your postscript files nicely, maybe it's not so much of an issue, but if you are concerned with the accuracy of the color, you have to know and set the RIP settings very specifically to match your output requirements. Like any incredibly powerful tool (whoa, watch out where you're pointing that surgical laser there, Sparky!), when the settings are right, you're going to get

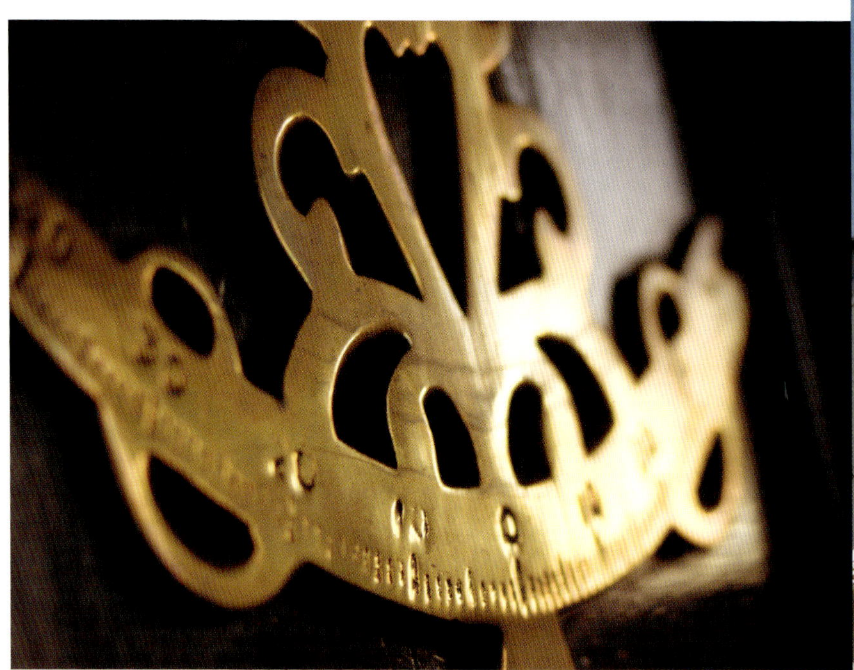

beautiful results. When they're wrong, it can create a problem.

At this point in RIP history, much of the RIP can be controlled by a relatively simple interface, the profiling, dither, interleaving, ink limits, and all the rest are set simply by choosing the right paper and ink setting. It was not always this way; back in the old days it felt more like

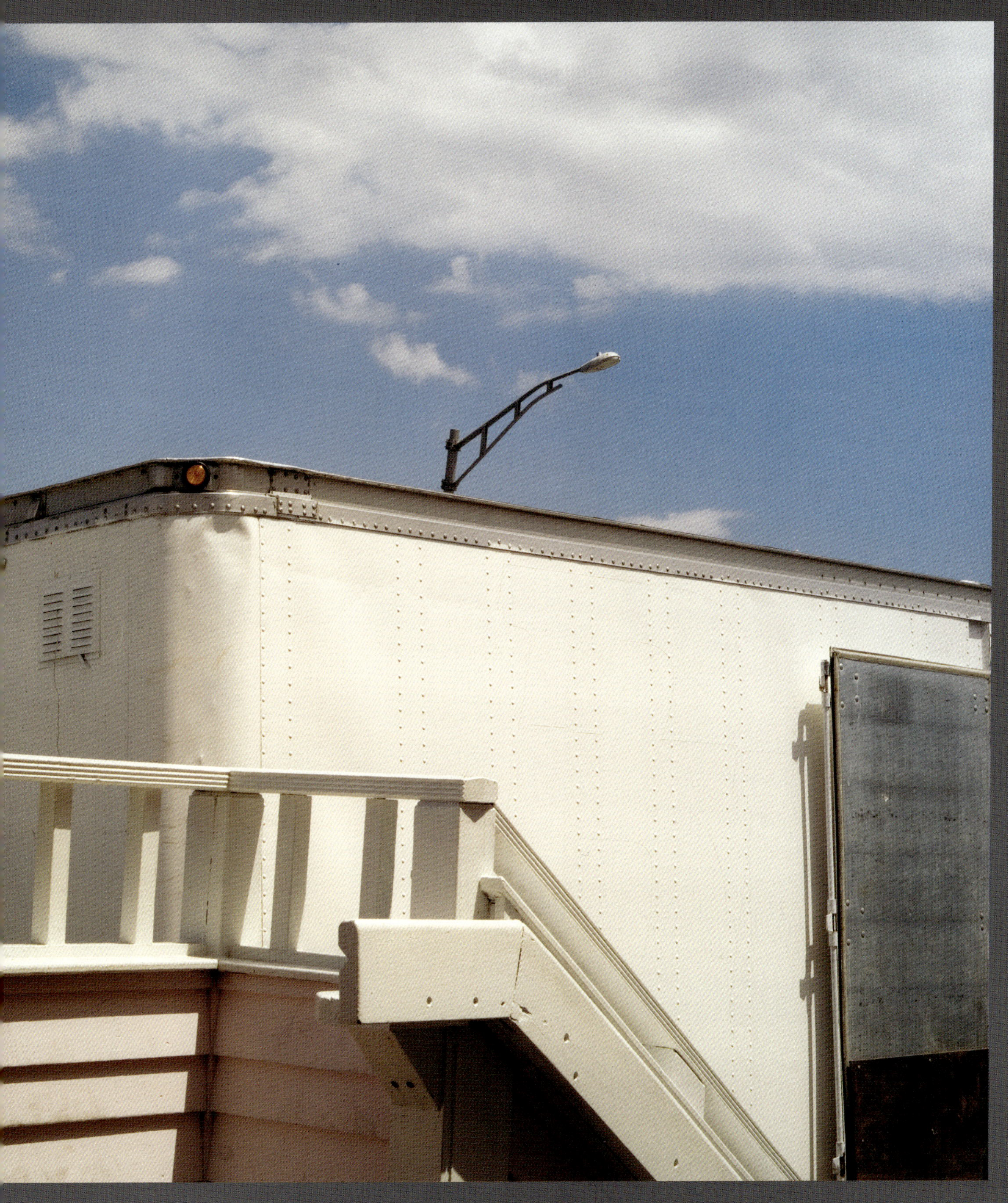

programming. Whether you're running the common RIPs we work with, like ColorBurst, EFI, PowerRip, or another product, make sure you have your settings right, and if you can't find them, get help. The key is to remember they are there, and you can get your RIP to perform to it's fullest potential by using them correctly.

The RIP (such as the Colorburst and ImagePrint RIP) is just another tool in your toolkit. Like a custom profile, the RIP can give you an alternative which may be moderately, or even infinitely preferable to your standard printer driver, depending on your image and your needs.

Having said that, I don't much use RIPs anymore for fine printing. They add another level of complexity in my process, and for the printers I use, the standard drivers have evolved to a remarkable level of performance. As with many tools in digital imaging, the RIP started out as a fix for inadequate factory tools, and now that the factory has stepped up to the plate the RIP has become more of an option than a necessity.

Interestingly, since it handles all the color management issues, the RIP receives files through the "Printer Color Management" dialog. The RIP becomes the "virtual" printer, if that makes you feel better, and, like the Epson Advanced Black and White driver, we allow it to do its job. "Print" goes right to the printer driver, in this case the RIP, with no color management. The RIP, on the other hand, must be told precisely what to do.

Advanced Methods: Working with ProPhoto RGB

Here's where things get interesting.

Up until now, I've suggested that you set up to work in Adobe RGB 1998, and for most of your commercial work I'll stand by that. Adobe RGB 1998 is pretty much the industry standard for photography and prepress, and is a nice, large color space. I'm going to cross over to the dark side now, and suggest that, in any case where you want to get the absolute most from your file, process the files to ProPhoto RGB.

To understand the issues, let's talk a little more about this particular color space. Think in terms of a color space being your box of crayons. The working color space defines all the colors you have, and the rules with which they are handled. To put it into perspective, ProPhoto RGB contains almost all the colors that your eye can see. Essentially, sRGB contains the colors your monitor can shoot, but your printer can only handle a fraction of those. Adobe RGB 1998 falls somewhere between the ProPhoto RGB color space and the sRGB color space. From the great big world of radiation out there, your eye sees only a fraction of the colors, your film captures a piece of that, and the print you make in the darkroom is only a piece of that. It's a reductive spiral down to the medium you are printing to, right?

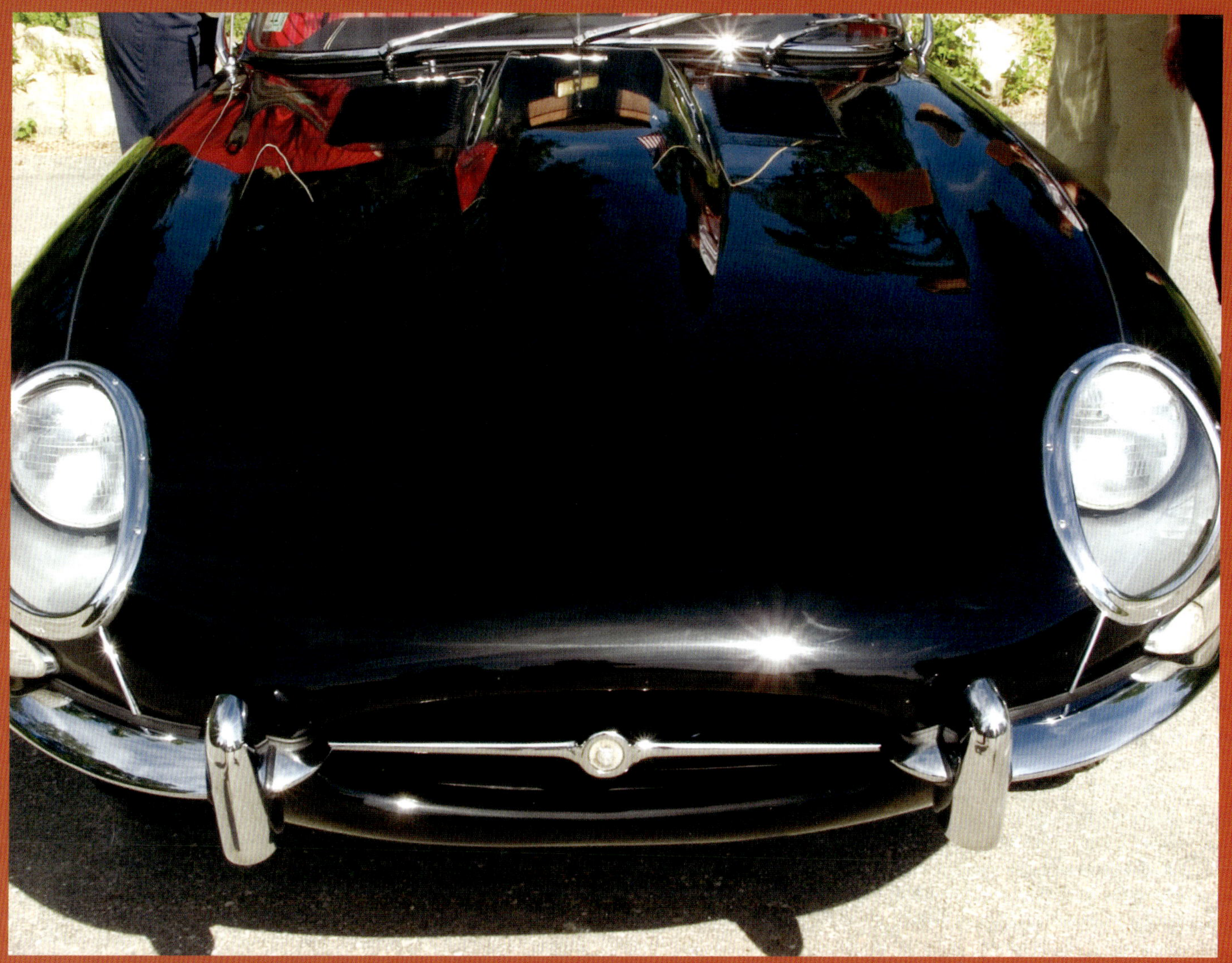

This is nothing new. A painter works with the same issues. Everything the artist sees is interpreted to fit within the pallet of their paints, and this is precisely what makes art expressive. We love pencil renderings because, in spite of the limitations of the pencil, through skill and sensitivity the artist can express what was seen and felt.

Here's the punch line. Your digital camera captures colors that fit pretty well within the ProPhoto RGB color space. If you process the RAW file right into Adobe RGB 1998 you're throwing away a pretty significant amount of color right off the bat, and with no control. You're just telling the machine to dump the colors that don't fit. If you process the files into ProPhoto RGB, you're keeping the colors intact, and you can handle and interpret them yourself.

Remember, though, that your monitor can only shoot sRGB. You can't even see Adobe RGB 1998's crayon box, never mind the larger ProPhoto RGB gamut. The challenge is to develop a way to work with these invisible, but available, colors.

A

Customize Proof Condition
Custom Proof Condition: Custom
OK
Reset
<-Default
->Default
Preview
Proof Conditions
Device to Simulate: Adobe RGB (1998)
Preserve RGB Numbers
Rendering Intent: Perceptual
Black Point Compensation
Display Options (On-Screen)
Simulate Paper Color
Simulate Black Ink

B

Adobe Photoshop
File Edit Image Layer Select Filter View Window Help
PC255262.ORF @ 33.3% (RGB/8*/Adobe RGB (1998))

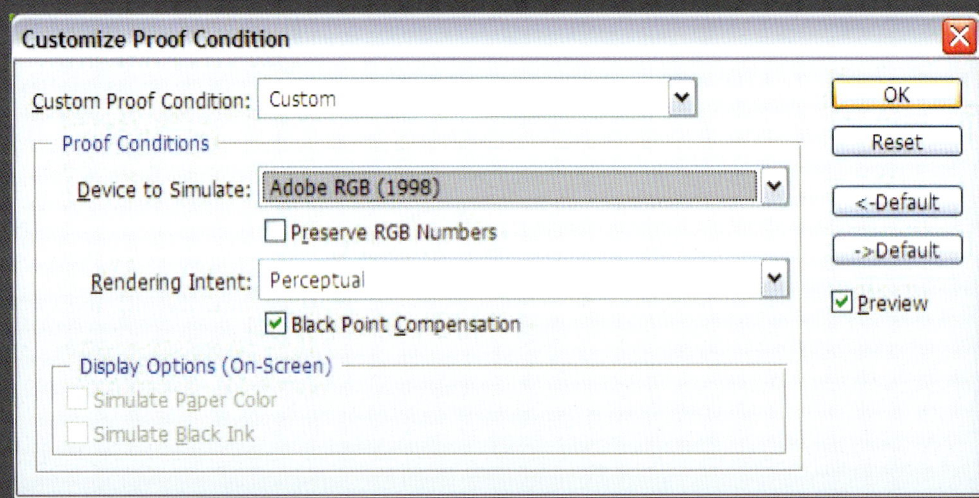

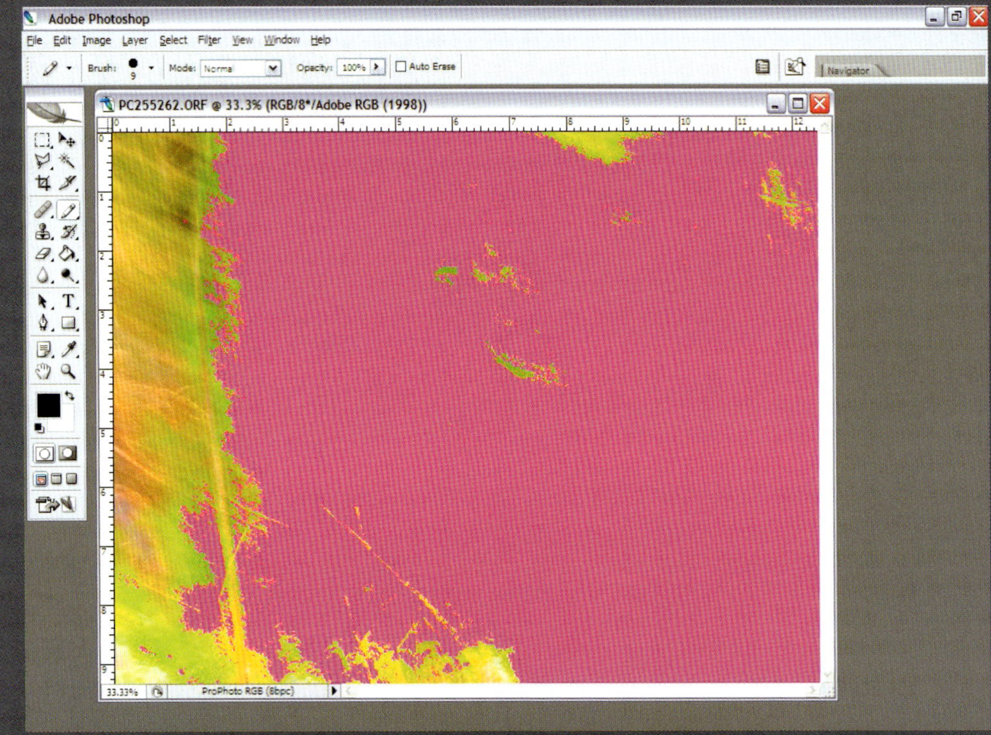

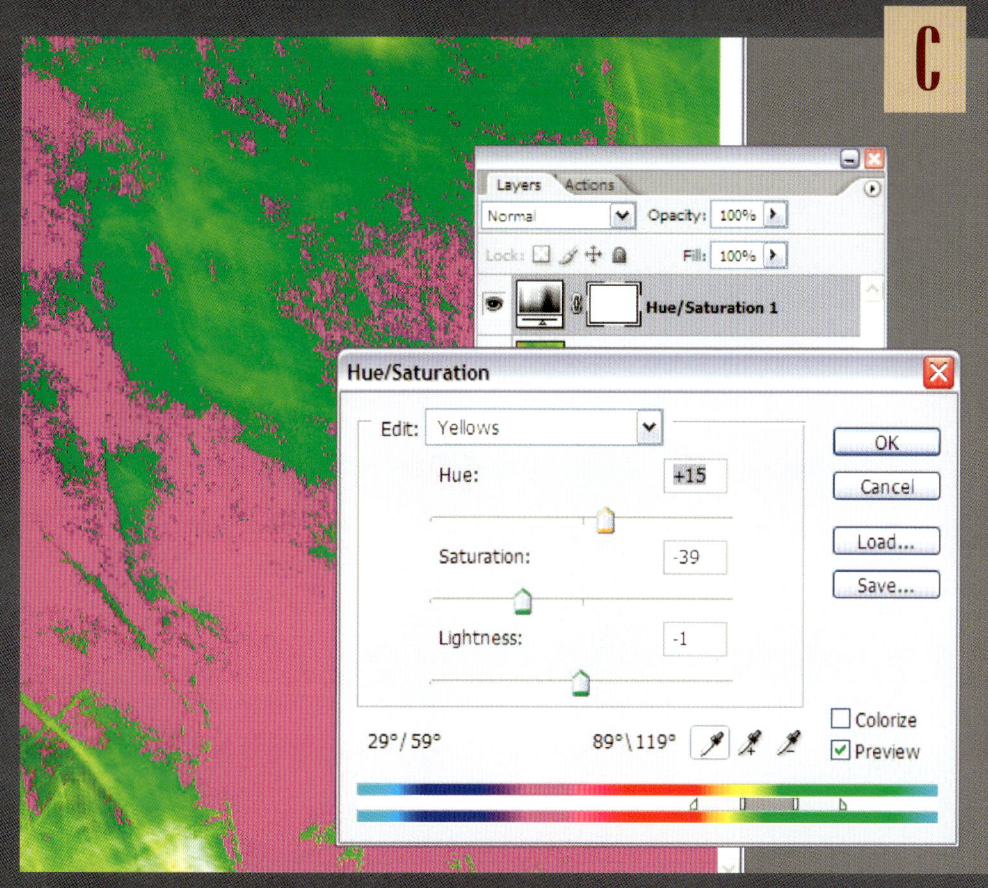

Your answer is, again, "Proof Setup" and "Gamut Warning."

Open a file and make sure your color space is set to ProPhoto RGB. Go to View>Proof Setup>Custom and you'll get this window (A). Set the "Device to Simulate" to Adobe RGB 1998 and hit OK.

Now, go to View>Gamut Warning, and activate it. What you're going to see is your image with a funny color overlay, showing all the colors that are in your file (in ProPhoto), that are "out of gamut" or wiill be lost when you move to Adobe RGB 1998 (B).

Now that we can see them, we can track them in, and for this I'll use the only slider I ever use: Hue and Saturation (C). By selecting the specific colors that are in the Gamut Warning and adjusting the Hue, Saturation, or Lightness, I can manually push the colors around until they're in gamut, but rendered the way I'd prefer. I've selected the "Yellows" and found that I can reduce the saturation a bit and move the hue to the Cyan range, and I pick up more than half my gamut in a very pleasing way. I'm not at the mercy of the machine, and I'm getting every drop out of my camera.

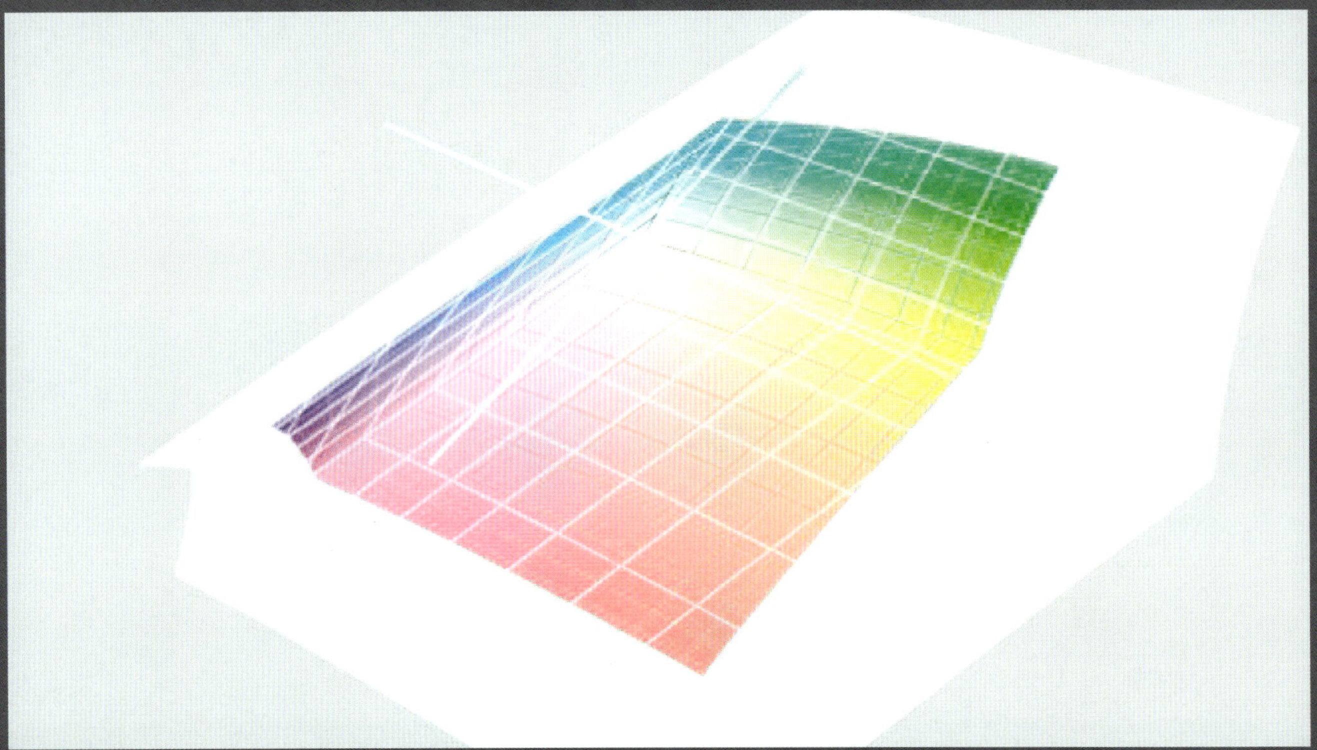

What I'm showing here are screen shots from the Apple Colorsync Utility, with Adobe RGB superimposed over ProPhoto RGB. Check it out. ProPhoto compared to Adobe looks like, well, Adobe compared to CMYK. Ha!

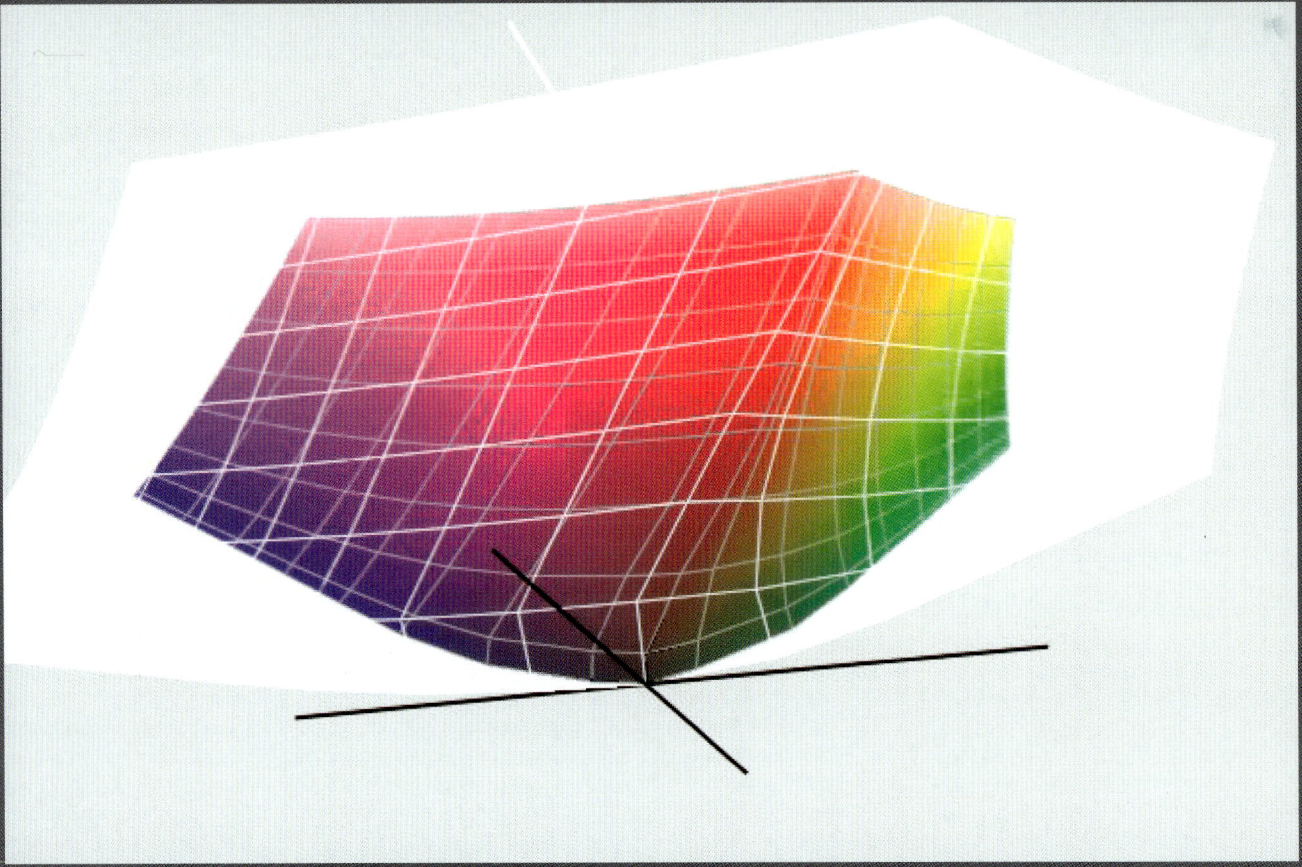

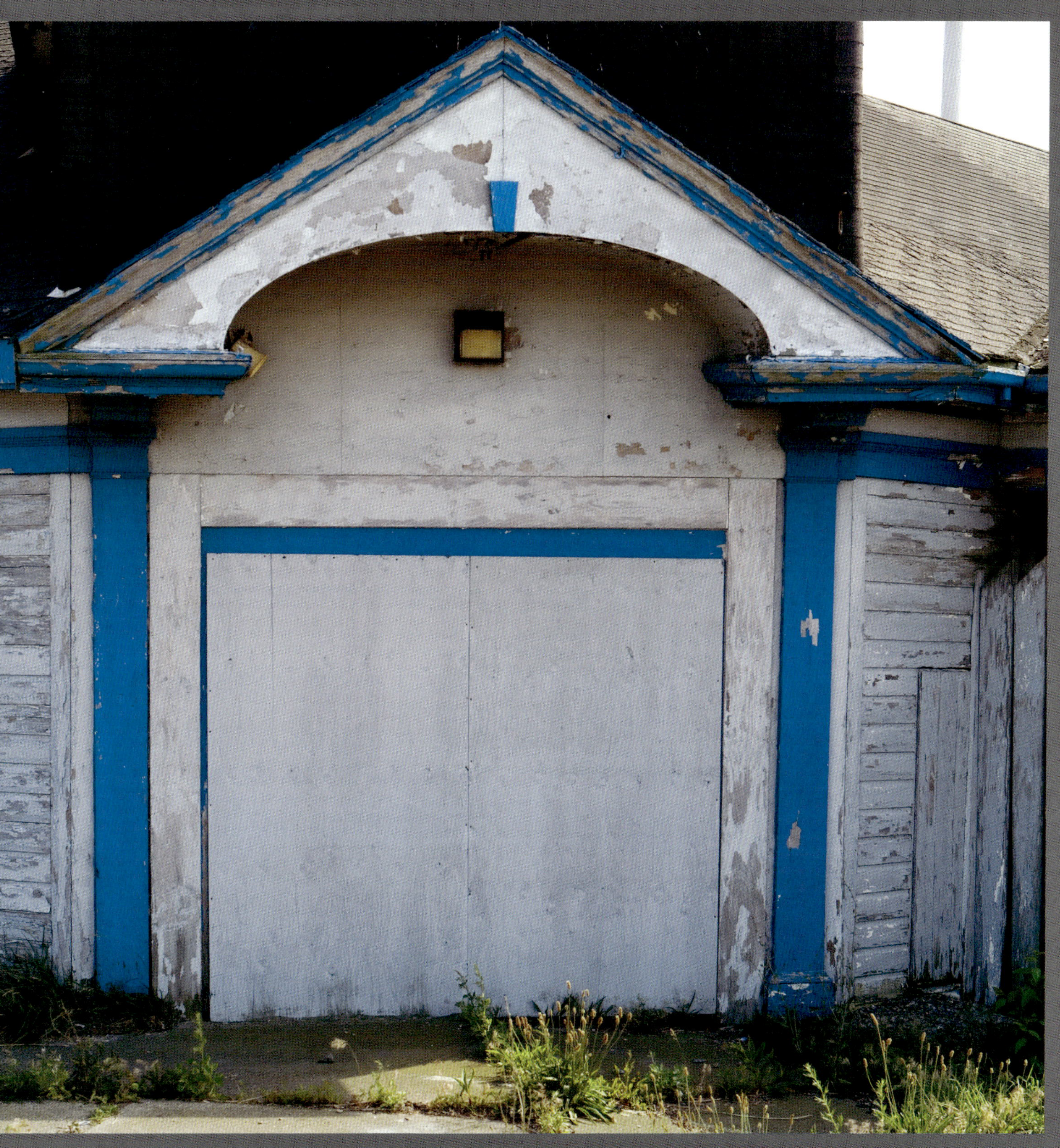

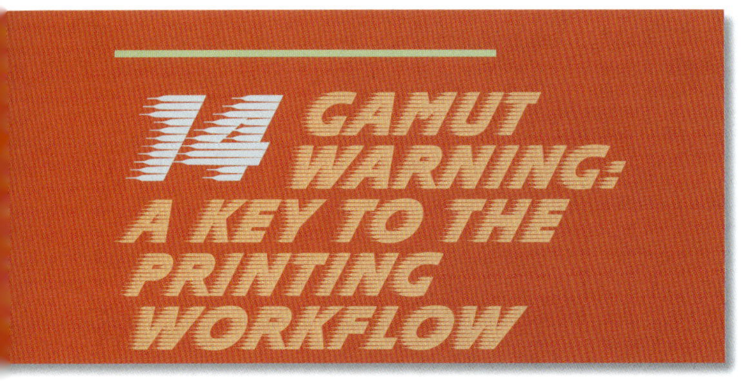

14 Gamut Warning: A Key to the Printing Workflow

I want to show you an example of how to use gamut warning in the printing workflow.

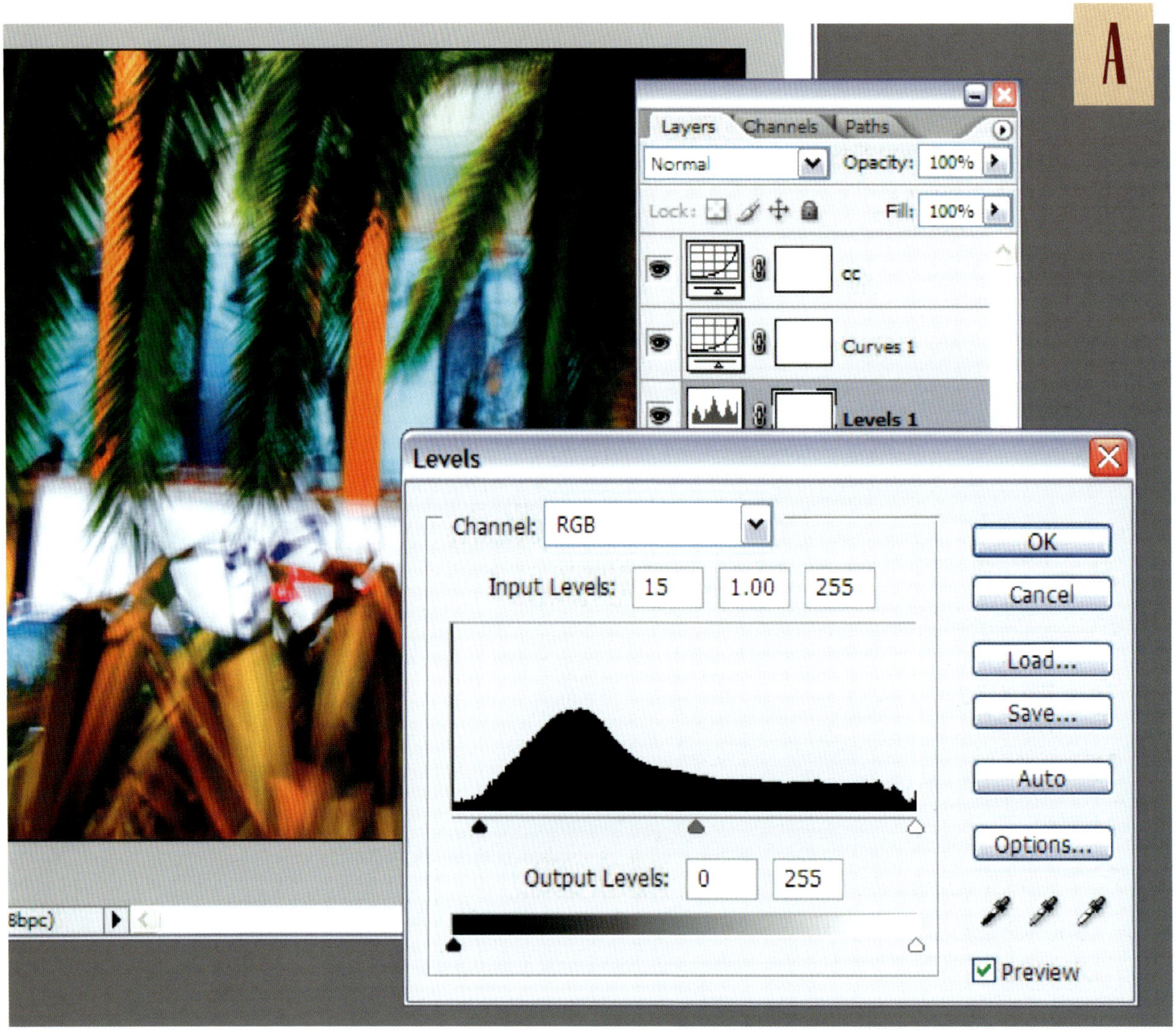

I'm going to start out by opening a RAW file from my Olympus E10, an .orf file. I go right in and build my standard adjustment layers, first a Levels layer, then a global Curves layer, and

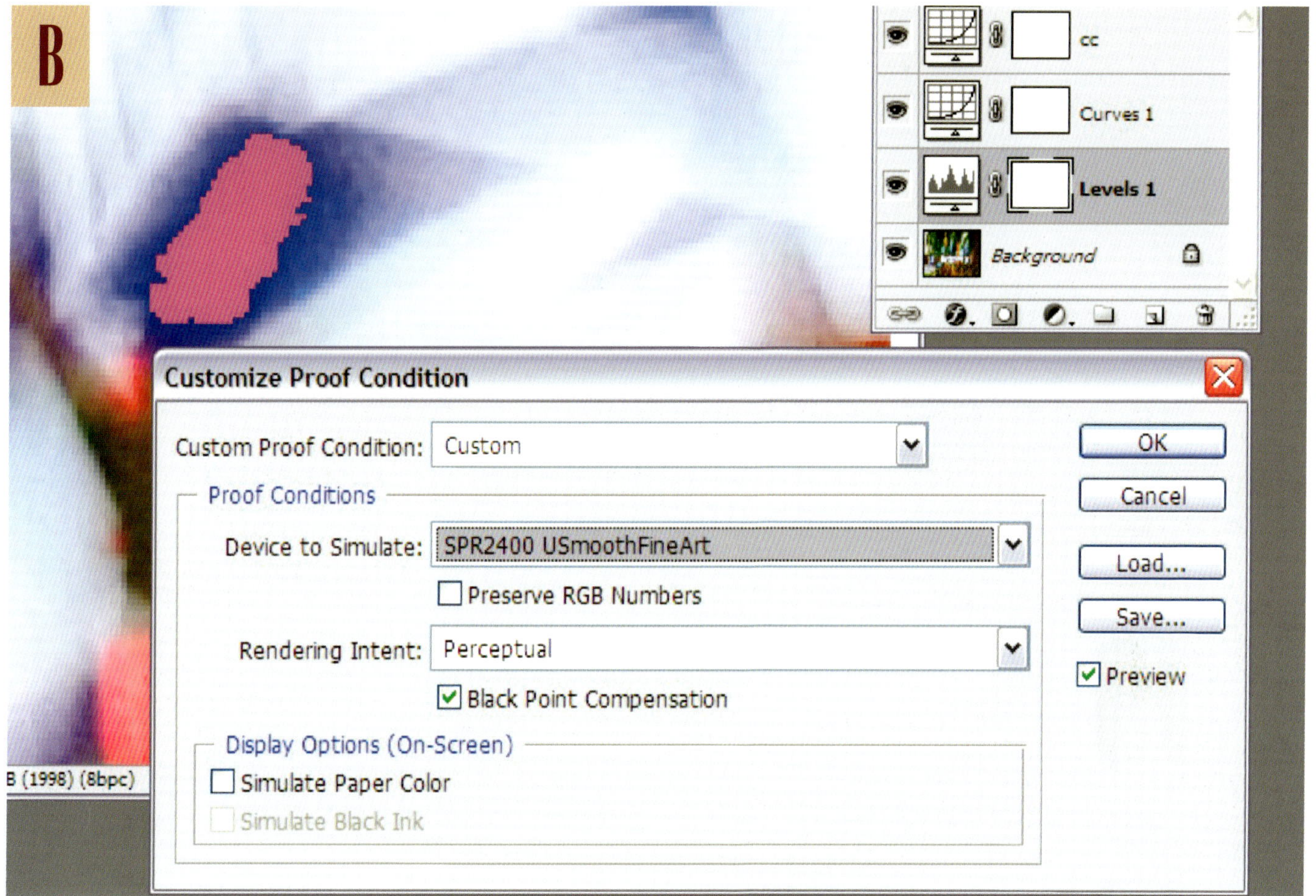

finally a color correction Curves layer labeled "cc." I quickly look at my Levels layer (A) and check to see what areas are going to block up as black or get blown out as pure white, by clicking the curser on the black point or the white point and holding down the "alt" key, and I get a gamut warning showing what is falling at 20 and under, and what is falling at 250 and over.

Now I want to check my gamut, so I can decide what paper to print on. I go into View>Proof Setup and start with Crane Museo. I toggle the Gamut Warning on and off using a "Shift-Ctrl-Y" keyboard command to find spots that are out of gamut. I then check my second choice paper, Epson UltraSmooth Fine Art (B).

Notice that this paper shows a gamut warning in the deeply saturated blue areas. For the most part, that paper is what I want to use so I'm going to deal with the gamut issue.

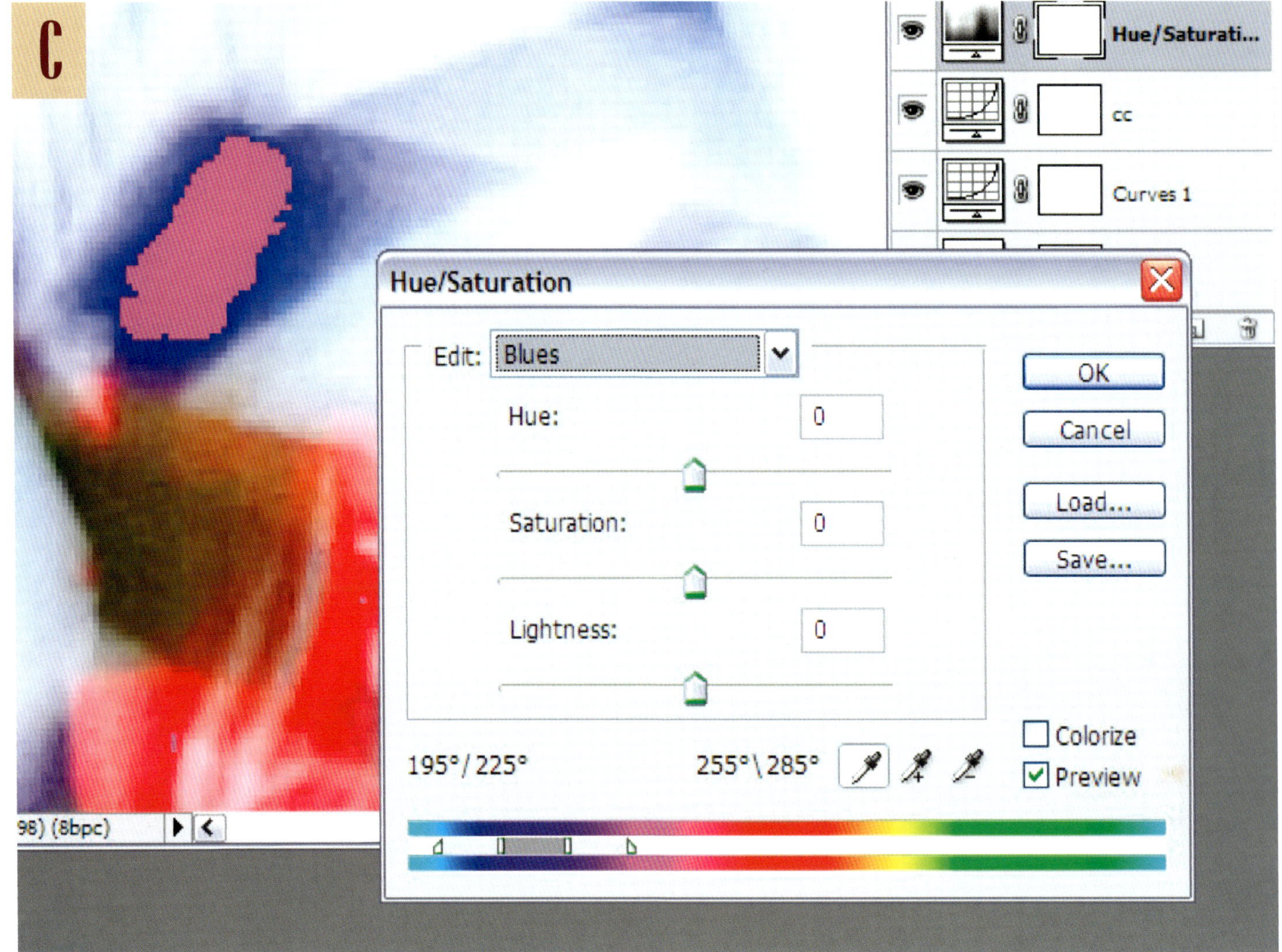

I've built some profiles for this paper with Monaco, so I'm going to try them using the same gamut-warning methods. For the sake of argument, I don't see a difference, so, because I know from experience that I like the rendering of the Epson profiles for green (which there's a lot of here), I'm going to live with the blue and try to fix it.

Now, here's a nice little trick. Create a new Hue Saturation adjustment layer (C) and select "Blues." By using the sampler eyedropper, you can click in the offending blue area on your image. You can literally track pushing the blue into gamut range by adjusting the Hue, Saturation, and Lightness. If I take down the saturation and boost the hue into the cyans a bit, I can take all but a tiny part of the blue into gamut (D).

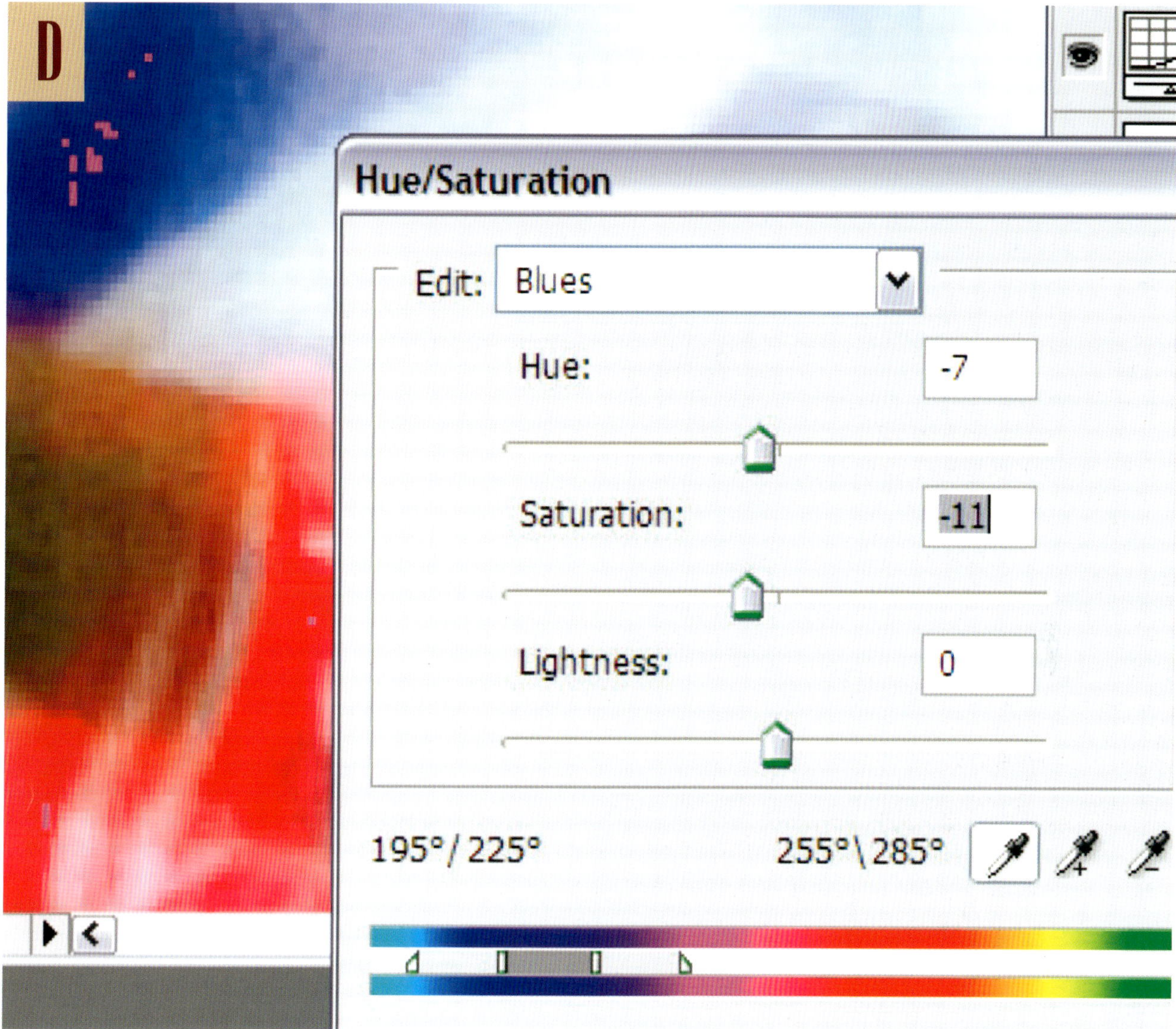

This is important! I have made the decision, based on the indications I have from Photoshop, to render the blues a little more yellow and a little less saturated to get the print I want. This is very intentional; I'm not letting the machine do it's thing.

Of course, I make a few work prints, and if I want to change the rendering I can go in to the adjustment layer and re-adjust, mask, change the opacity, or whatever, because I'm using adjustment layers! Woohoo!

I go to the "Print" window and convert the file from Adobe RGB 1998 to Epson Ultrasmooth Fine Art 2400 MK (the profile for the 2400 paper), and Matte Black inks (MK). I select "Print", go to my Print Settings and set the source for the Manual Feed slot. Next, in the Color settings dialog, I turn color controls off.

Finally, I look at the print in my 5000k light booth. I then hold it up under the track lighting in my gallery to make sure it looks right in the source under which it will be shown. How much better could life possibly be?

Conclusion

Making the print is when color management becomes tangible. The image you visualized, the tiny picture you saw on the camera, and the vibrant rendition you saw projected on your display—becomes ink on paper.

I sat in on a class where an instructor was explaining LAB color. He explained LAB color as a way of describing color independent of a device. We always think of color in terms of the perception of color, and that becomes "device dependant"—through your eyes, the camera, the printer (even wavelengths)—the typical description of color is describing color in the context of light. LAB color is an abstracted, mathematical description of color that is independent of any device. By removing the context of a device, it gives the computer operating system a way to manage it.

The instructor made the statement that LAB color is "real world" color, where other ways to describe color were, well, not. My first reaction was that this was absurd—how could this abstracted, artificial description be in any way "real?" Once I considered the problem, I realized it was no different than any other scientific description; it's a way to abstract a problem so that you can work with it.

There you have the difference between art and science. The artist feels that the world around him is real, the scientist, by developing a method of describing a world that is beyond our senses, finds a way to manage it. Making the print is the elegant threshold between the science of color and the art of photography.

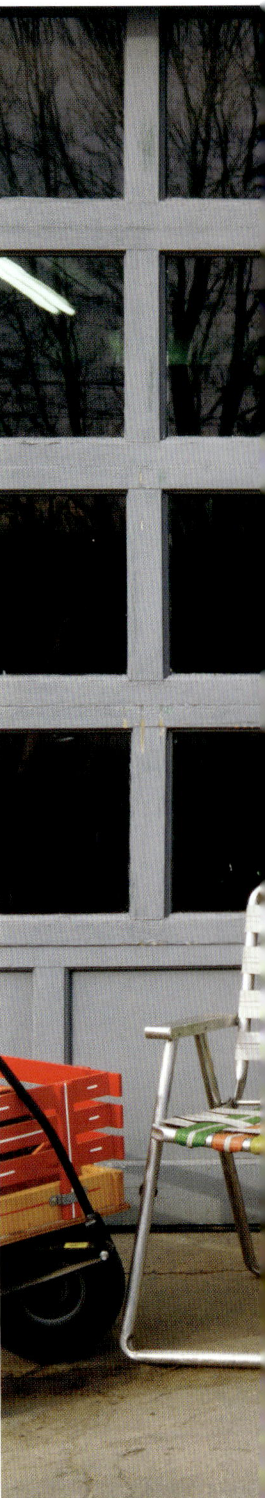

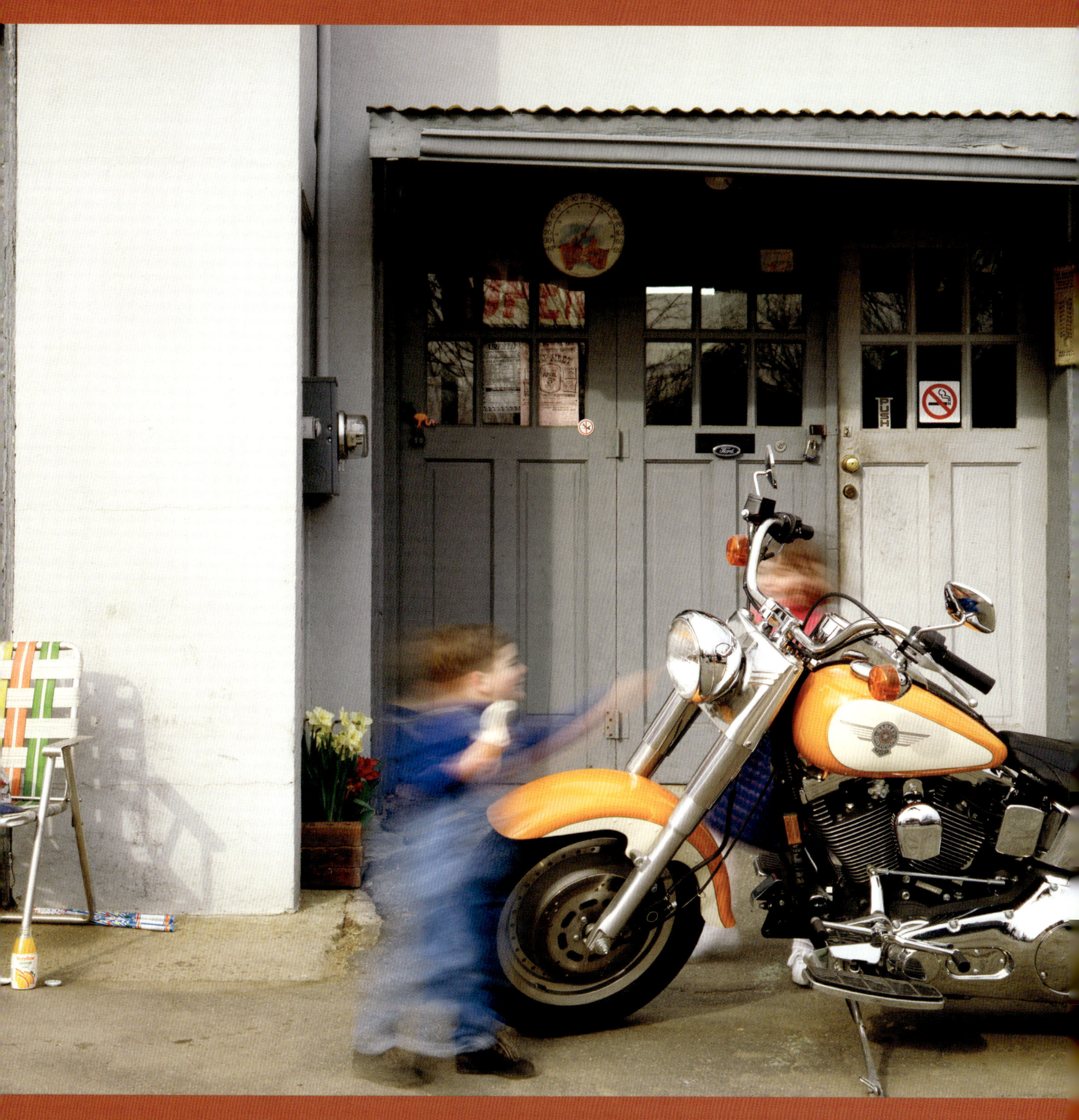

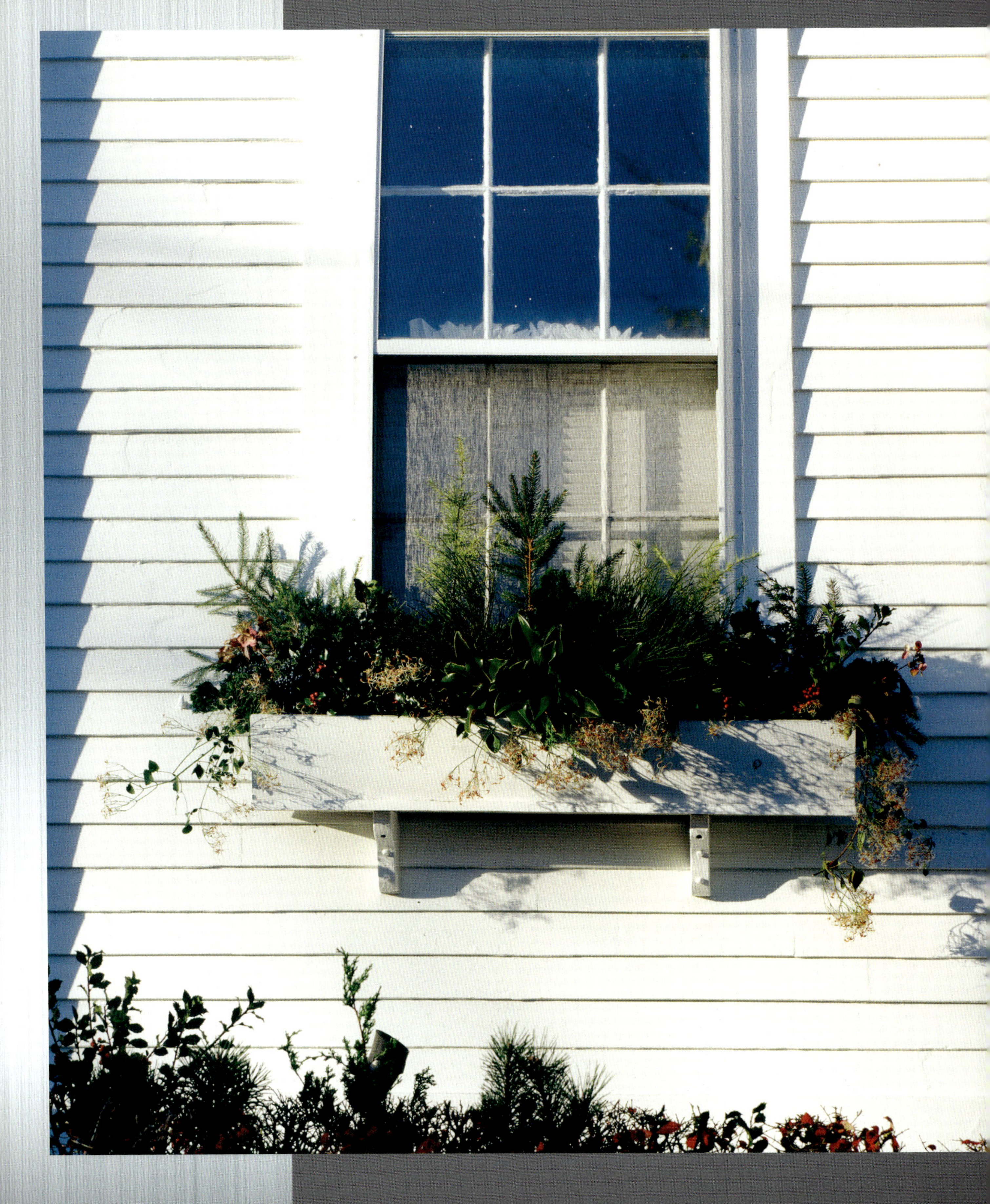

PART 4: THE RAW PIPELINE: STREAMLINING A WORKFLOW

introduction

"The negative is the score, and the print is the performance." This statement, beyond belying Ansel Adams' training as a classical pianist, describes the task of the traditional photographic printer. In the negative you have the score, the path laid out by the photographer, which can be interpreted in many ways. Adams went so far as to donate his negatives so that students would have an opportunity to render them, and "perform" (print) them in their own ways.

The digital file is more the "composition" than the "score." Because it can be built from several images or several components, each of these parts may be interpreted on their own to produce a unique print.

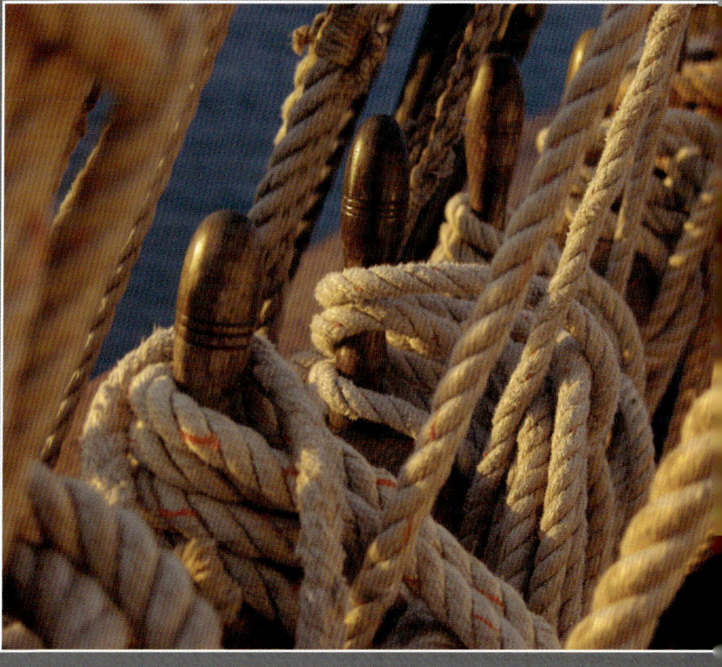

The daunting task in working with this rich composition becomes developing a system to manage it. In a medium where almost anything is possible, developing this system is about limiting and defining your tools and methods. The following describes a number workflows that—once the tools of layers, masks, color management, and gamut are understood—become powerful and efficient ways to streamline the RAW process. What I use is my "recipe." This will point you in the direction of creating your own workflow—your own recipe—to produce the prints that fulfill your photographic vision.

Developing a Constructive (vs. Destructive) Workflow

First are the Layers, and then the ability to Mask the layers and control almost every aspect with which the layer is going to be applied. Next is the huge amount of available information in the RAW file. We've got all our housekeeping under control, are well color-managed and are protecting our data. So how does this come together into a system?

Now that we have the tools in place we can put it all together. The mantra of this process is "Go Back to the RAW." Instead of making destructive edits and massaging a limited amount of image information, we're going back to the source, reinterpreting it, and layering it into our file.

The basic outline of the process is this:

- Start with the RAW processor and do the best you can to adjust the file.
- Once you have it open in Photoshop, save it as a TIFF, and start working on it. You might make some color and density adjustments and you might do some "burning" and "dodging" (as layers, of course)—all the standard work you'd normally do to make a fine print.
- Make a work print.
- After evaluating the work print, you'll probably make some more changes to the image. Using Adjustment layers allows you to do this easily, by going back to your basic adjustments and finessing them. After some more work and some more testing, you will get to a point that you're satisfied with the print. Here's where it gets interesting.
- Go back to the RAW file. Reprocess the RAW file, but process it to more closely match your final working image. Use the speed and consistency of Layers to do the preliminary work that can be recreated with the RAW process.
- Bring that reprocessed image in as an Image Layer to replace the Adjustment Layers you used to make the initial print. If you made global color and density adjustments, make global color and density adjustments in Camera RAW. If you're making spot adjustments—like burning down a highlight—do the same thing in the RAW process and use the same mask to select that area. Process the data to build the image you want and substitute it for the destructive adjustment you made.

There are two things at work here. First, in thinking about the entire image, if you go to the RAW process and target the information you need, you will get a better interpretation of that information. For example, if I process a RAW file to have more contrast, I'm building a full histogram out of the data. If I edit a TIFF file to have more contrast, I'm selecting a portion of the histogram and stretching it out to fit the contrast range I need, throwing away the high and low range of my image. In the RAW process I'm building a histogram; in the TIFF I'm tearing it apart.

The second thing, in thinking about the image in detail, is that I'm adding information. If I want to burn a highlight in a TIFF file, my only choice is to take the highlight values and try to bring them down, removing file information. I'm not adding detail—I'm just working with what I have. If I go to the RAW file and bring the exposure down, I will see a whole lot of detail and tone that was not in the TIFF.

This can be used in very simple ways, as described above, to recreate adjustments that you have already applied. It gets a little more complicated—and powerful—when used with burning and dodging. Once you've mastered the skills, however, it gets very interesting. You can use this to do selective sharpening of an image, or noise and aliasing processing using an array of layers and varying degrees of mask opacity. For example, you can process an image in Nikon Capture for the enhanced shadow detail

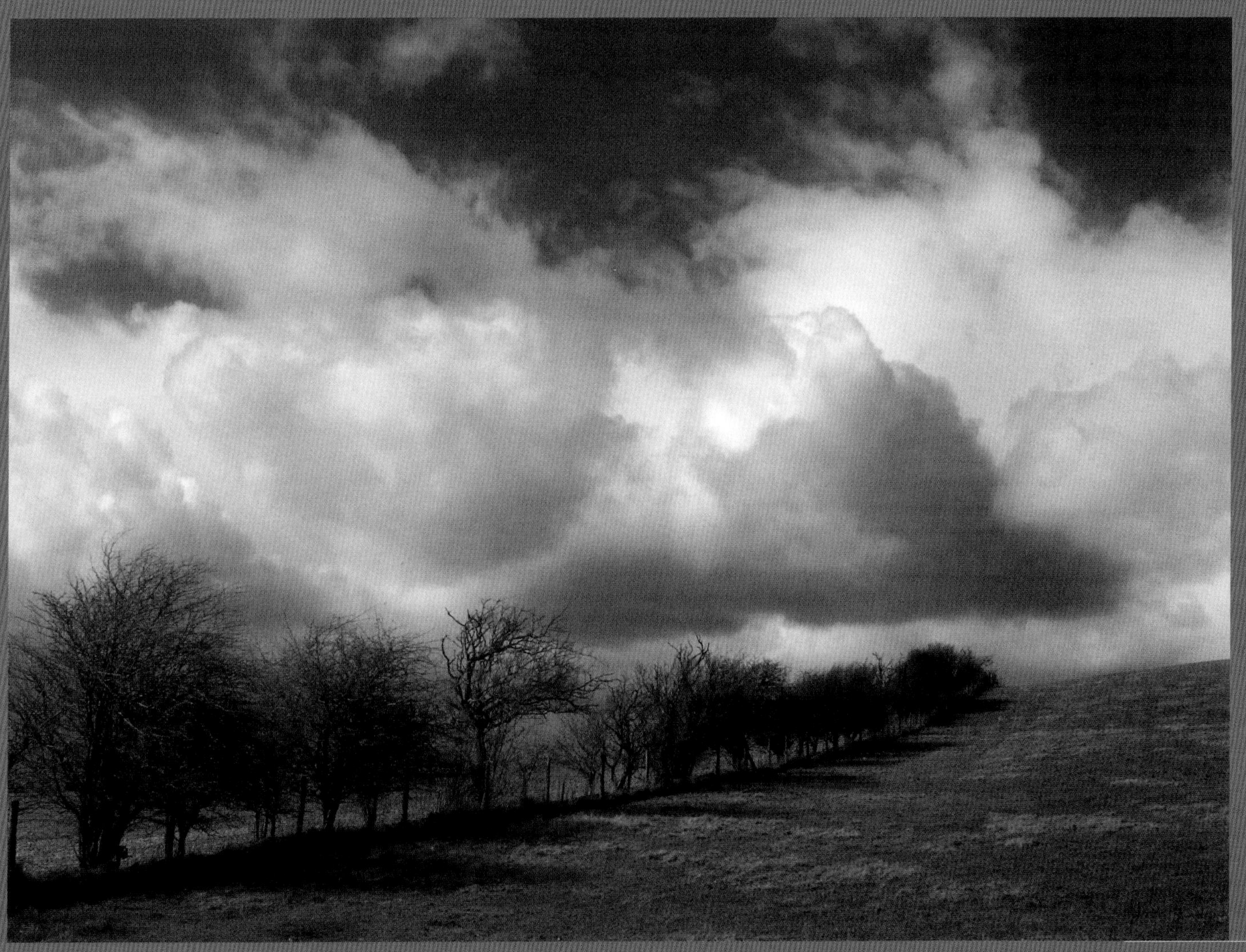

and deep-tone transitions, and then reprocess it in Camera RAW for the additional highlight detail that Adobe gives you. The control is astounding, and the options are almost unlimited.

Learning the Process: Step-by-Step

I want to go through three examples of workflows. In Step One, I am simply making Adjustment Layers and duplicating that work with a RAW version of the same adjustments. Step Two is an example of making Masks to burn and dodge, and applying those Masks to the RAW Image Layer. Step Three brings the process together, starting with a basic image, making adjustments, duplicating it in RAW, then burning and dodging using the same tools. Step Four finishes the process with applying Unsharp Masking, spotting, handling noise, and sizing for final output.

Step One: Adjustment Layers and RAW Image Layers

Let's start with building an Adjustment Layer, making the same moves in the RAW file, then bringing them together.

Create a new Adjustment Layer (A) (click the oreo cookie-like icon at the bottom of the Layers palette). I pick a Levels layer, make the Levels

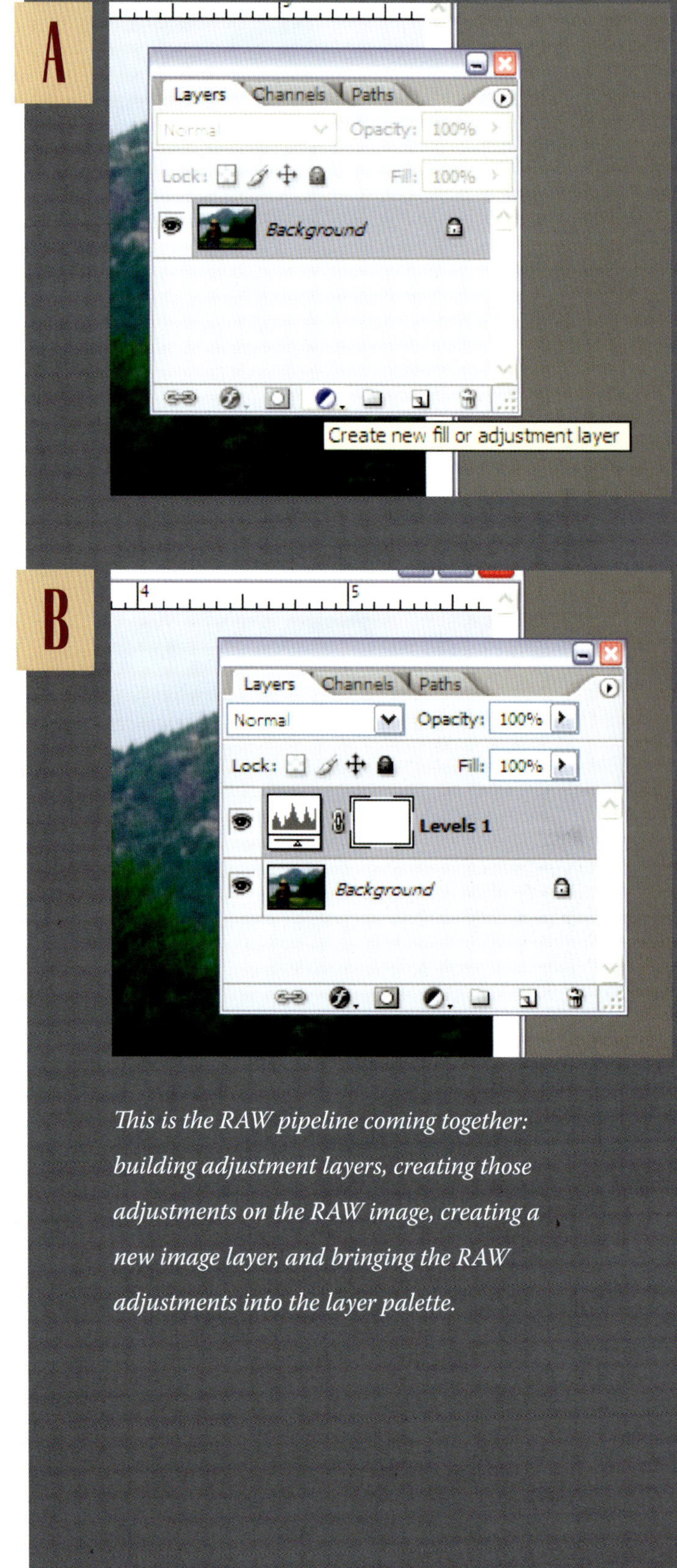

This is the RAW pipeline coming together: building adjustment layers, creating those adjustments on the RAW image, creating a new image layer, and bringing the RAW adjustments into the layer palette.

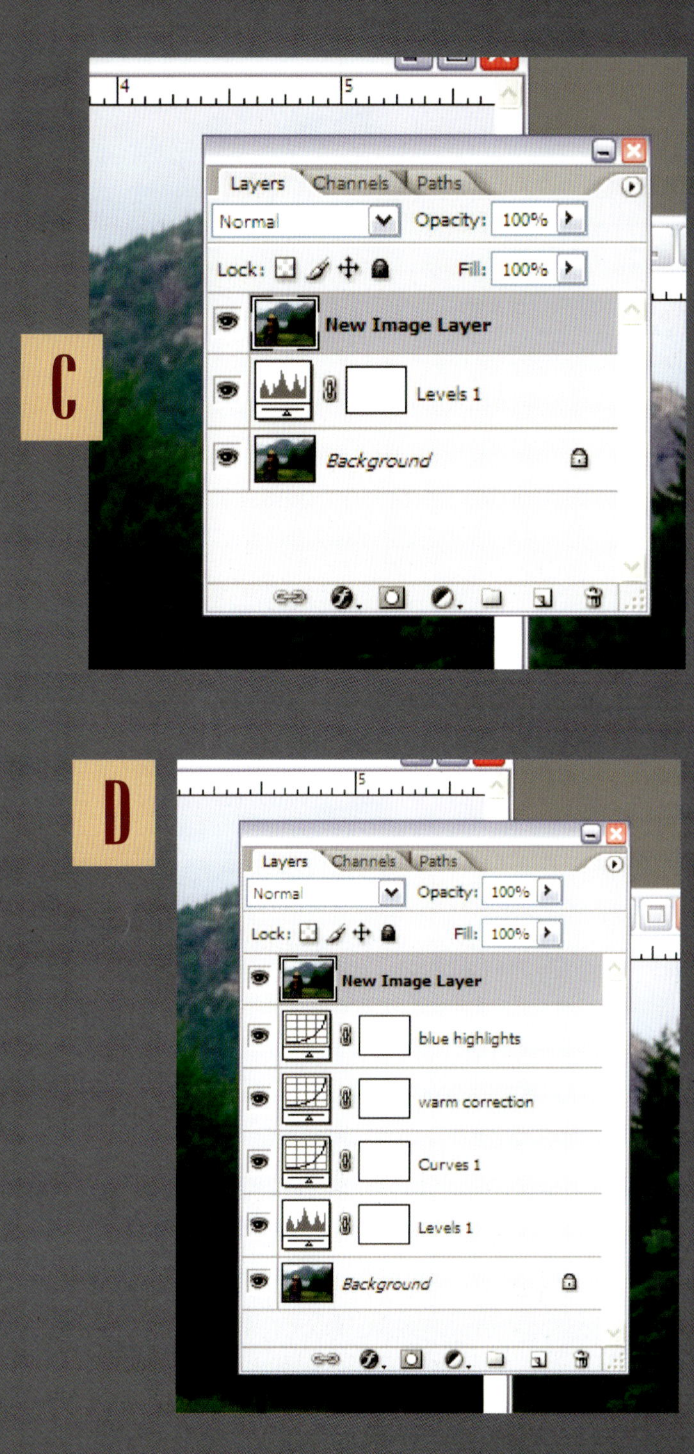

adjustment I want, and OK it (B) (it gets placed into the file as a new Layer).

Now to bring in an Image Layer: I've made a few changes in Levels, so I want to duplicate them in the RAW process and drop that new image in place of the Levels adjustment. I go back to the file, re-open it in Camera RAW, and make the adjustments to match. When the file opens, I simply Move it to the first file to paste it in as an Image Layer (C). To get it registered correctly, hold the Shift key and Move it. The new Image Layer is dropped on top of the Adjustment Layer, perfectly aligned, and has no Mask.

This is a basic example of the first step in learning the process: make an adjustment and duplicate it in RAW. Use Adjustment Layers because they're fast and editable, and then set up the RAW file in Camera RAW for that specific adjustment. Instead of making destructive edits to the file, (as any adjustment is), we're going back to the source to build the original file to exactly what we want.

Typically, an actual work file will have several Adjustment Layers that are ultimately duplicated by one Image Layer (D). I often start with a Levels and a Curves adjustment, and then do some fine-tuning of colors with a few more Curves layers. Once the image is where I want it, I'll drop in the Image Layer from the RAW file. Notice that this is where labeling Layers leaves a nice trail of breadcrumbs for me to follow.

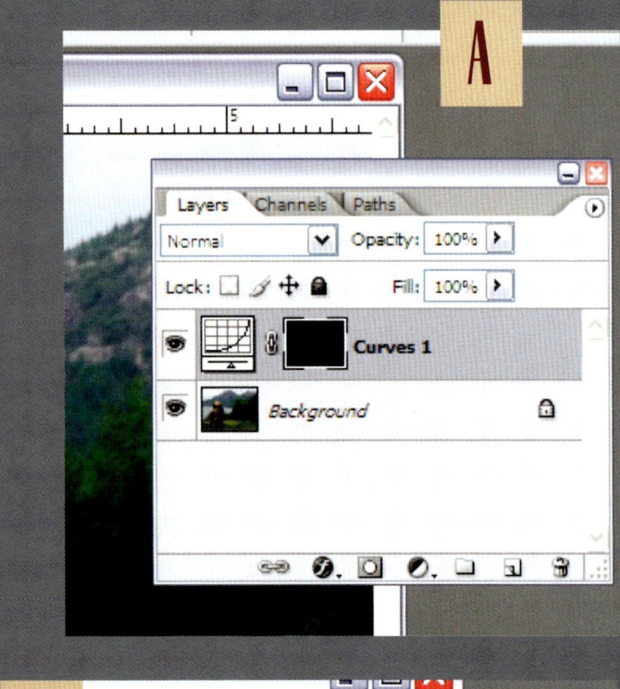

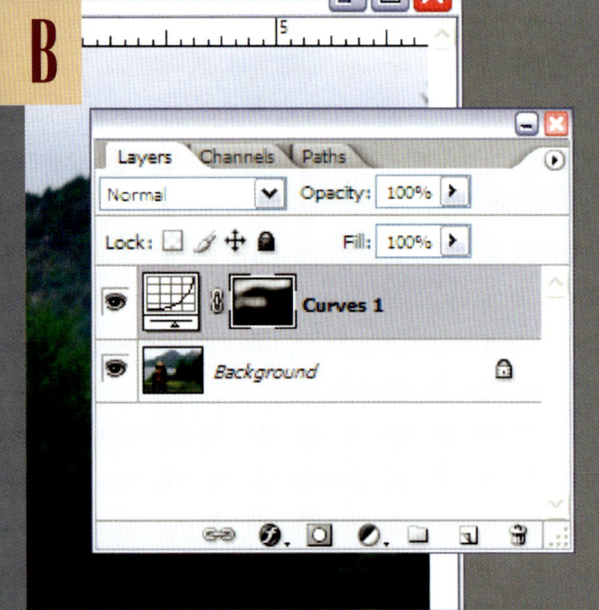

Using masks for selective adjustments gives you complete control—you can choose exactly where you want the adjustment to appear. Make a mask on an adjustment layer, reveal the areas you want adjusted with the paintbrush tool, and then—using the mask adjustments as a guide—go into the RAW image file to make your additive adjustment.

Step Two: Using Masks

Now that I've made global adjustments to the color and tones, I want to do my selective edits—burning, dodging, and selective color adjustment. To do this I need to select specific areas of the image, so I use Masks.

Here's a simple example: I have a file with a specific area to burn down. I build a Curve Adjustment Layer and pull the curve down to darken the sky, for example. This applies to the whole image, which I don't want, so I will mask it. Any Adjustment Layer automatically creates a mask (the little white rectangle to the right of the Curves icon). I want to turn that black—to make it opaque—so I click on the mask and hit Command "I" to invert it to black. This blocks the entire Curve adjustment (A).

To reveal the areas I want, I paint white on my black mask. I select the paintbrush, set the opacity and flow to around 50% to control the amount of transparency of the mask (thus controlling the adjustment), and use the paintbrush just as I would burn and dodge in the darkroom. I move it over the area, change the brush size, and go over areas repeatedly to build up the density of the adjustment. This shows in my mask as white areas in the black mask (B). If I go too far, I switch the paintbrush to black and paint back over the areas I want to fix.

Now, I go back to the RAW file to make the constructive adjustments rather than destructive. I re-open the file and make the same moves (in this case, bringing the sky down using

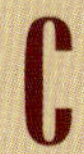

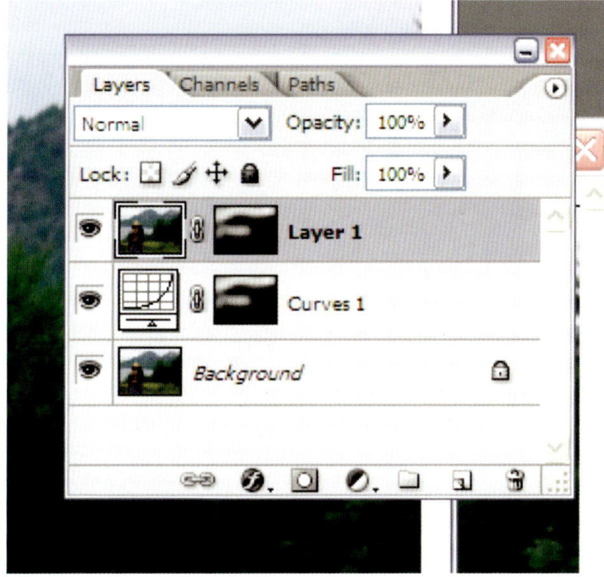

Exposure and Brightness). I use Shift+Move again to bring the image in as an Image Layer, just as in the previous example (C). To mask my Image Layer, I simply Alt+click on my mask and drag it into the new image layer, where it is duplicated. I end up with a new Image Layer replacing my Adjustment Layer, with the identical mask.

I do this for each specific area I want adjust. I may make a burn of the sky and a dodge of the shadows. I could create color shifts in the highlights or skin tones. This is where the technique really starts to become powerful: I can build tones and colors that weren't in the original file.

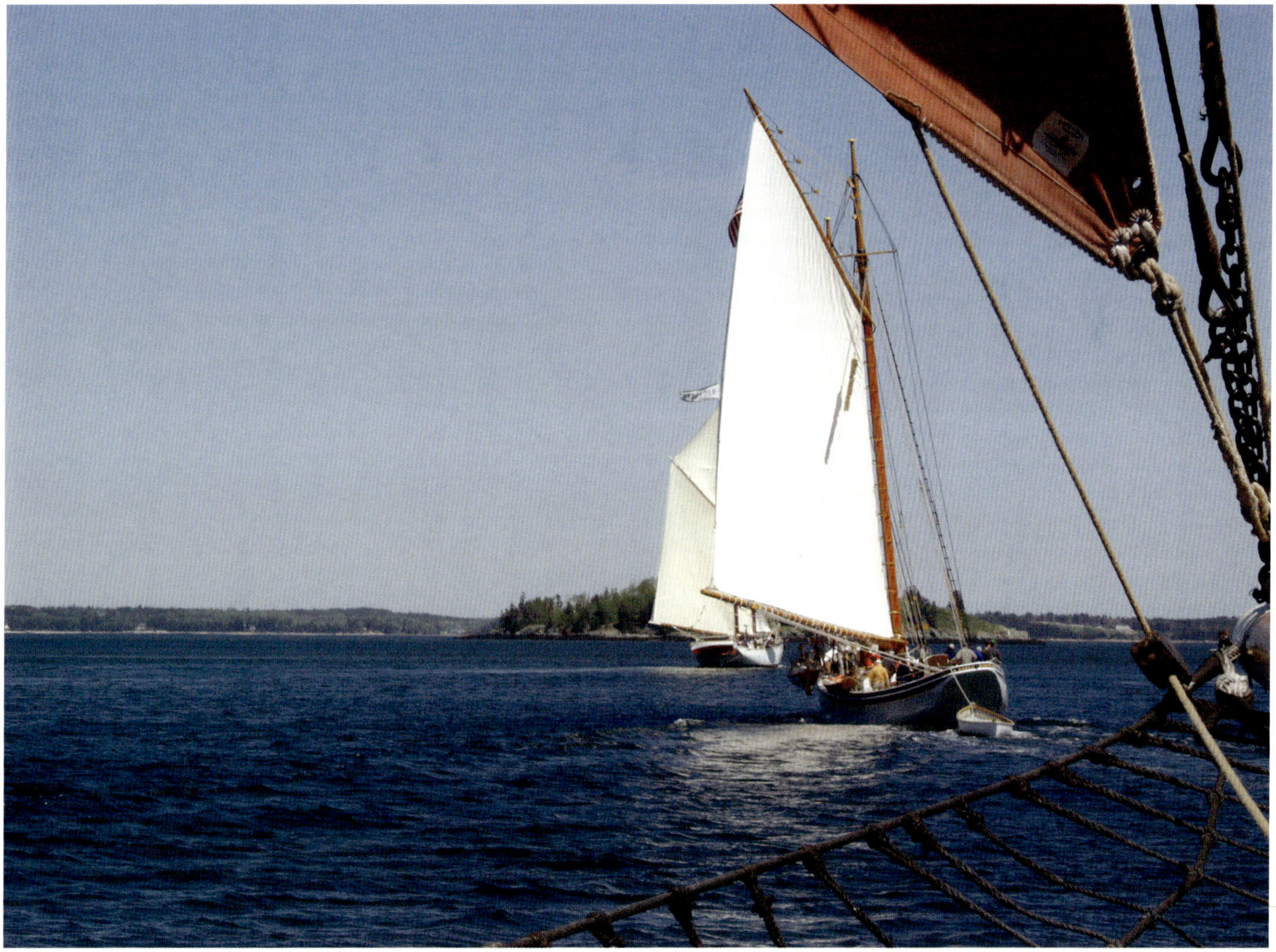

A

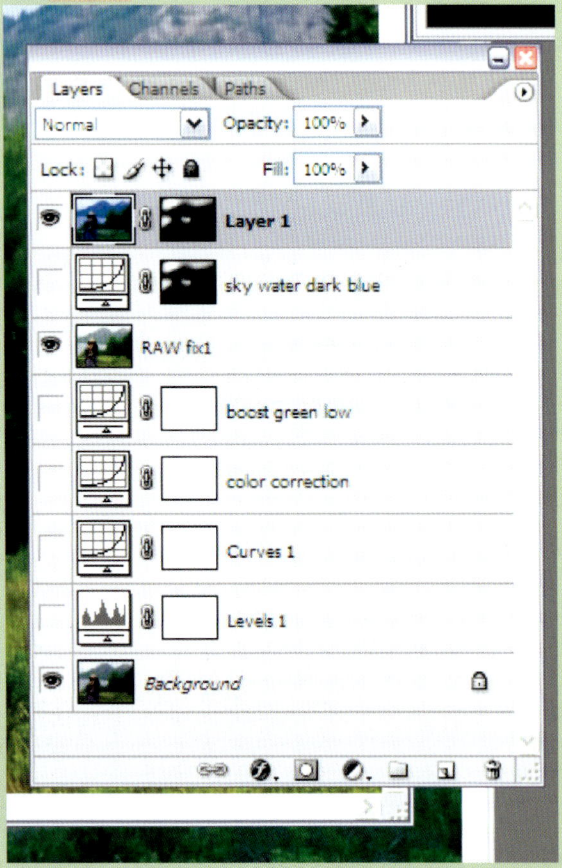

B

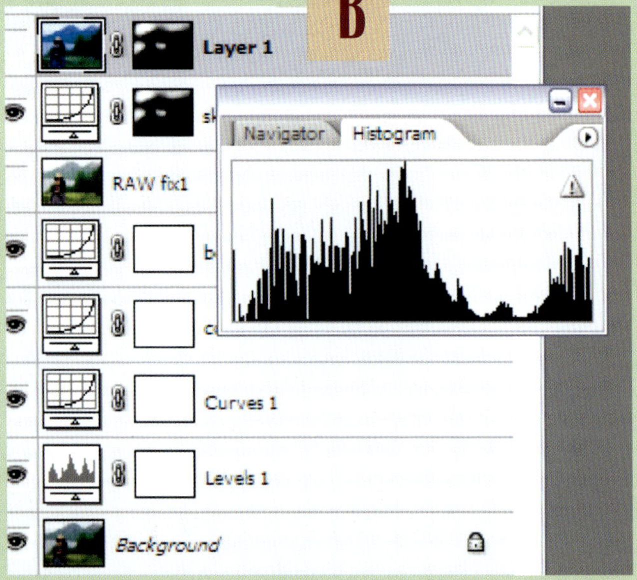

Step Three: The Process

How do we put this all together?

First, as in Step One, I open a file and edit my working Adjustment Layers. I duplicate them in the RAW process, drop the Image Layer in, and turn off the Adjustment Layers. Next, as in Step Two, I use Adjustment Layers and Masks to burn and dodge working prints again. I duplicate those edits in RAW and drop those Image Layers on top. I copy the mask from the Adjustment Layer and drag it to my Image Layer (A).

With practice and skill, my RAW layers will match my Adjustment Layers. They will be deeper, richer, and have better color values than the adjusted file. This is where the differences between what you've done as an adjustment and what you've done in RAW really show.

Do you want to know why we do this? Look at the histogram (B). The first histogram I'm showing you is the adjusted file with no RAW adjustments. The second is the file with the Adjustment Layers turned off and the RAW layers turned on (C). The gaps in the top histogram are missing colors where there are holes in the data. This shows in the print with banding, posterization, uneven and weak tonal gradations, and thin color rendition.

The RAW histogram shows a rich, deep file without holes. This prints with better transitions and better color—a rich, deep print. First, I'm making the most of the information that is in the RAW file, and determining what adjustments I need. Second, I'm duplicating those adjustments in original RAW file and layering it in. Not only am I preventing holes, I'm filling in holes by layering in color and tone.

I've simplified this example, but you can see that it can be taken much further. Almost every step that I apply as an edit can be duplicated in the RAW conversion. I can, when working in grayscale, layer in gray tones from a variety of grayscale renderings, and I can bring files in from any number of RAW conversion software systems. In effect, I can go back to the light that fell on the sensor and change the film and developer it to suit my needs. The RAW file is not the "digital negative." It's the "digital latent image."

Step Four: Wrapping Up A Sharpening, Spotting, Noise, and Sizing

Since we're adding Image Layers on top of Image Layers, anything we've done at the start to the Image Layer—like sharpening or spotting—will be hidden when we add a new RAW processed Image Layer. Consequently, we do this last.

I start by building a new, empty layer. I select that layer, and, holding the Alt key, go to the Layer Options and "Merge Visible." This takes all of my work and flattens it into my new layer without flattening any of my layers (A).

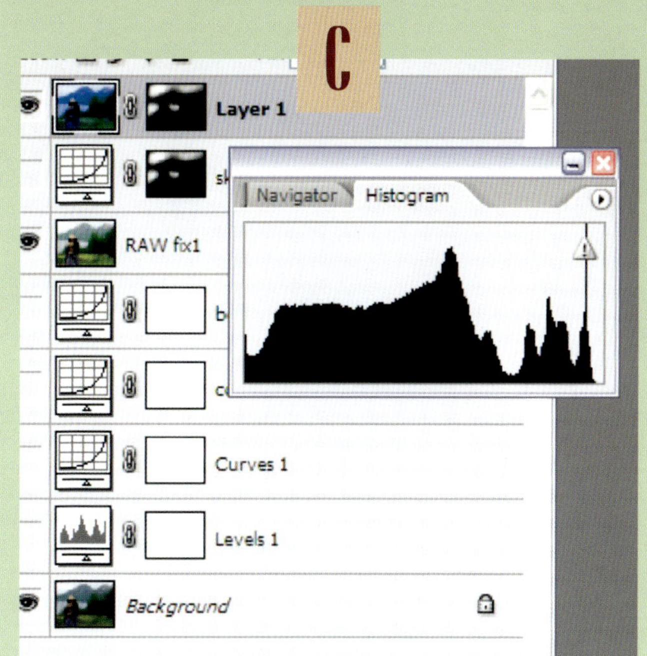

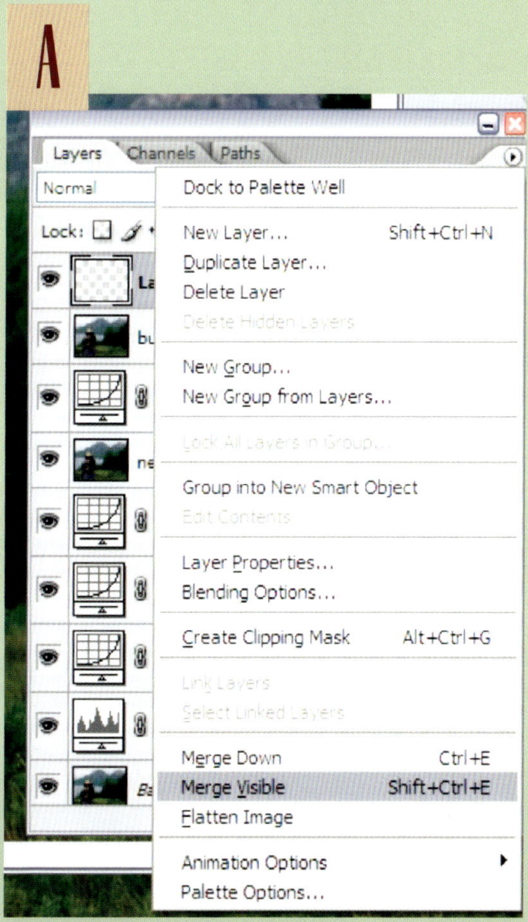

I usually start with any spotting or retouching I need, then, if I want to add Noise, I will build a new "Merge Visible" layer and add that, generally in that order. These multiple layers allow me to adjust the intensity of the filters by using the layer's opacity capability and to go in and select, delete, or re-do a filter if I don't like it.

In the previous process, since I have had to keep the size of the image intact (to make sure the imported reprocessed RAW files align correctly and easily), I have not sized the final image. Until now, I have been doing my work-print sizing in the printer driver. After I determine a final image size, I resize my file using Image>Image Size, using "Bicubic Smoother" to size up or "Bicubic Sharper" to size down, and then apply my Unsharp Mask or Smart Sharpen in a new "Merge Visible" layer.

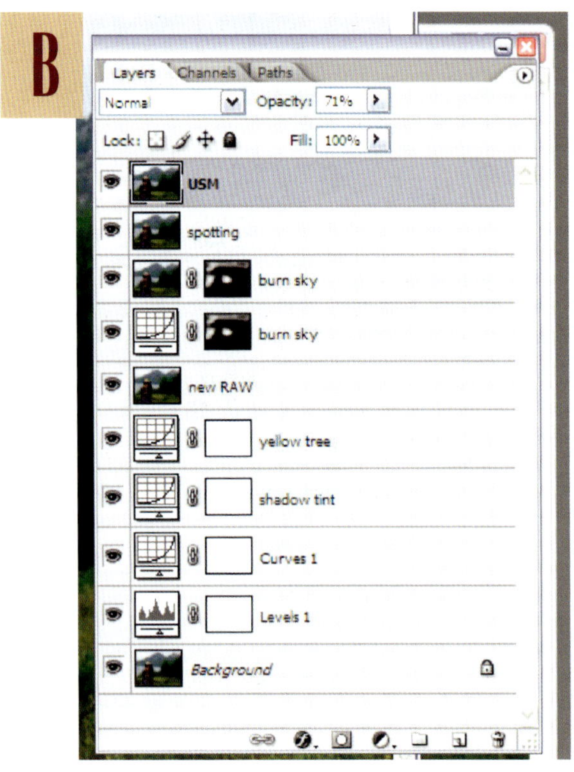

Here is the final file (B). There are the Adjustment Layers, the Image Layer on top of those, the burn and dodge Adjustment Layer with the Mask, the Image Layer with the same Mask, and the final spotting and USM layer sitting on the top. Everything is labeled—I can go back and change anything I want. The layers are arranged in a pyramid of work, so I am not putting big changes on top of small changes (the big changes would cover the small ones). I pretty much do the same thing every time, so this structure is familiar to me, and I can see where I've done things even without the labels. I have a fast, easy, and repeatable workflow in a process that yields an incredibly high-quality result.

Tricks and Tips

1. Work so your layers reflect an increasing amount of refinement as you go up. That is, start with big changes and make each more refined change on top. Create a pyramid of fine-tuning.

2. Adjustment layers can be moved from one work file to another by clicking and dragging.

3. Using Alt+levels and holding on a shadow or highlight point on histogram will preview detail loss in print.

4. Command(Apple)+click on a masked layer before creating a new layer to duplicate the mask, or, simply Option(Alt)+click on a mask to drag it to your target layer.

5. Save your layered file, even with layers you've turned off; these are your notes.

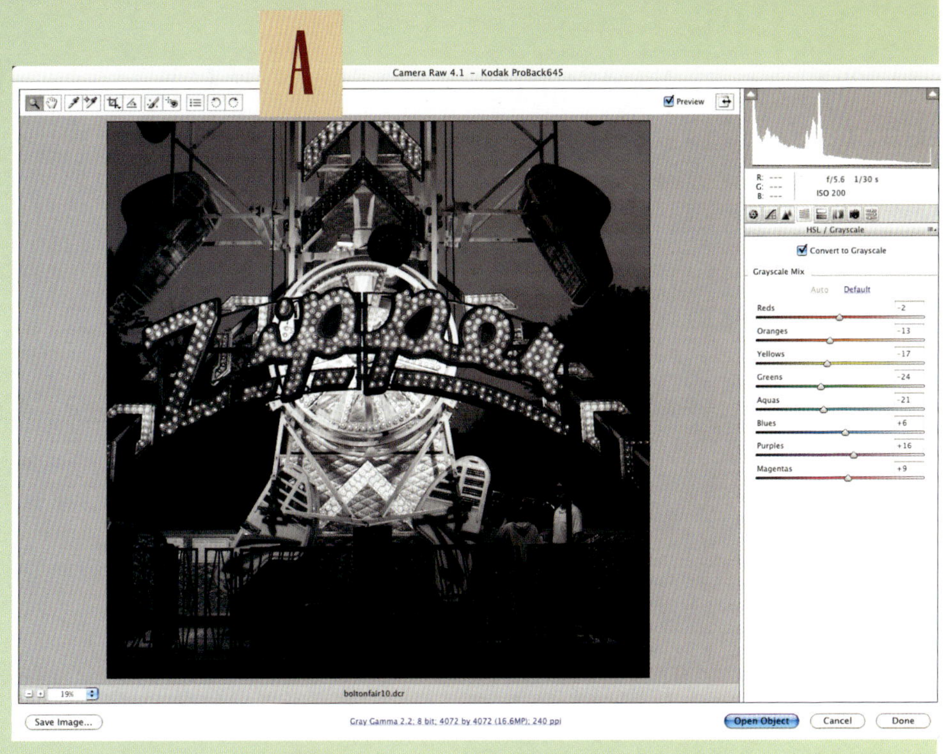

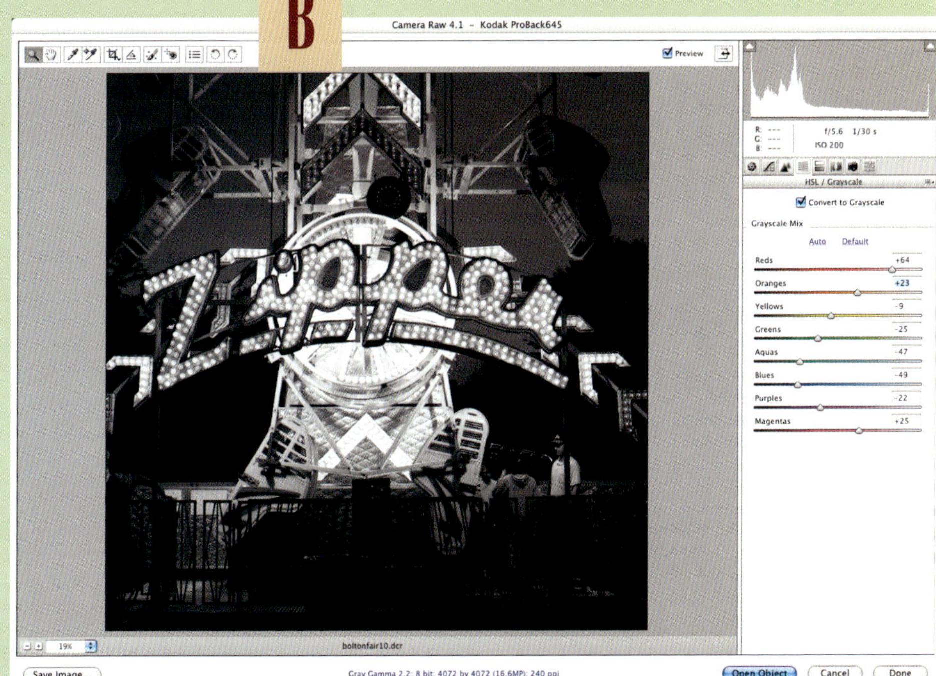

In Camera RAW CS2, we could still do the "Saturation" grayscale conversion, but with less satisfying results. Figure A is the default "Saturation" conversion, figure B shows the conversion with the red channel boosted, and figure C shows the conversion with the blue channel boosted. None are very clear, and the tonal changes seem clunky.

Revisiting Grayscale

We've talked about using an Adjustment Layer for Channel Mixer, in Grayscale mode, to take a color RGB file and convert it to a black-and-white image. You might suspect that I'm going to go off on some thing about converting to grayscale in RAW, mightn't you? Well, you are right.

In Camera RAW CS2, we had few options for converting to grayscale, other than the fairly inelegant process of simply running the "Saturation" slider all the way down. Once that was done, you could then try to ramp up the main colors in "Tint" and "Temperature" to feed the Saturation slider different colors (or different channels), but it really wasn't a great solution (see figures A, B, and C). One of the things that I really liked about Apple's Aperture program was that, in their RAW process, you could use a device similar to Channel Mixer to make black-and-white conversions right there in the RAW process, in a very familiar way. Well, Adobe cherry-picked some of the coolest

C

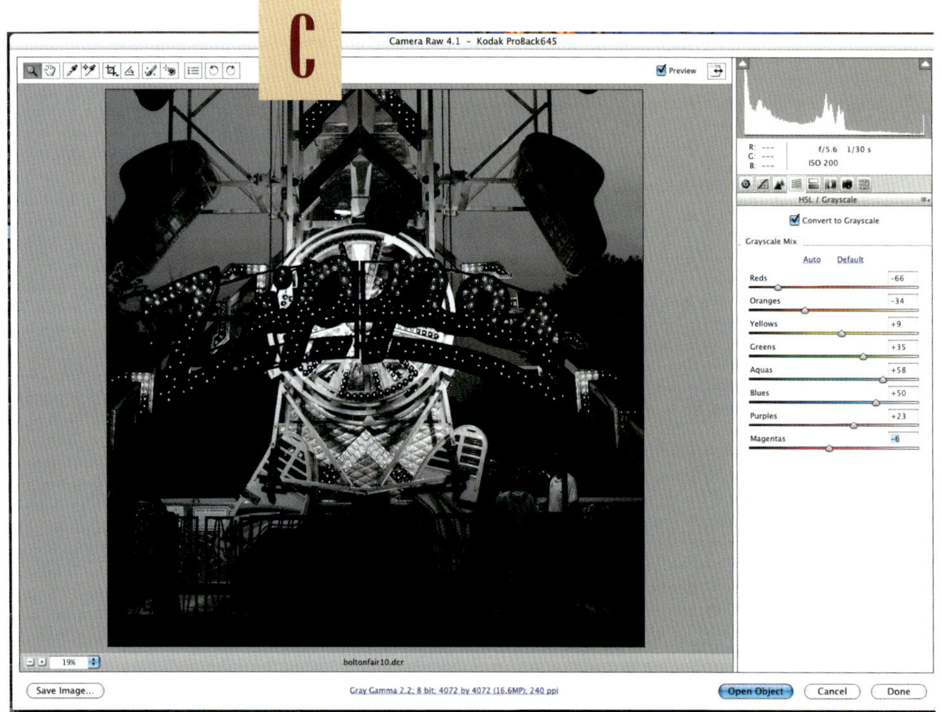

D

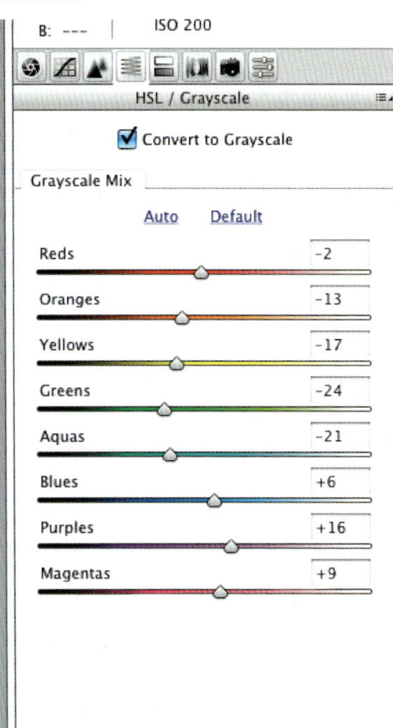

features of other software and gave it to us in CS3, which brings me to the HSL/Grayscale tab.

Why does this matter? Why can't I just use Channel Mixer as an Adjustment Layer for the simple, humble, and fairly tiny Grayscale mode? Once again, the information I'm using is built from the sensor. I'm starting right from that Red, Green, Blue, and Luminance (RGGB; the second G channel is for Luminance) and building my Grayscale information directly from there, not by scavenging information from a file that was built in RGB.

HSL/Grayscale

CS3 introduced the HSL/Grayscale tab (D). In color images, it gives you access to Hue and Saturation controls, but when the "Convert to Grayscale" selection is made, it essentially becomes a Channel Mixer in RAW. The example shown here is the default de-saturation. Note that it gives me a nice, graceful transition from the reds, through the greens, into the blues and magentas, and back into the reds. When you adjust these sliders, keep as much of that gradual movement from one channel into the next to maintain a nice tonal ramp.

Here I'm showing a conversion setting that I like to use (E). It heavily favors the red channel, and balances out by toning down the blue and green, much as my basic 80/20/20 setting in Channel Mixer (see page 98). I've made it into a gentle curve from the boosted red, down to the lowered green and blue, back up to the magenta and red.

If, by making this move, I lose separation in a certain area of my image, I can make another conversion that holds the detail I want, drop it in as a layer, mask it, and bring it out as I see fit. Once again, I'm building in data from the RAW capture, not trying to massage a bad conversion. (I once had a student who made grayscale conversions to burn and dodge in this way, shooting with a Nikon D70, and he had, at one point, 16 layers of images, every one holding a bit of detail that he then layered and masked into the image. Over the course that the print was up in the gallery, a number of seasoned professional photographers ask if the print was from a 4 x 5 mm film camera—it looked so rich, full, and detailed.)

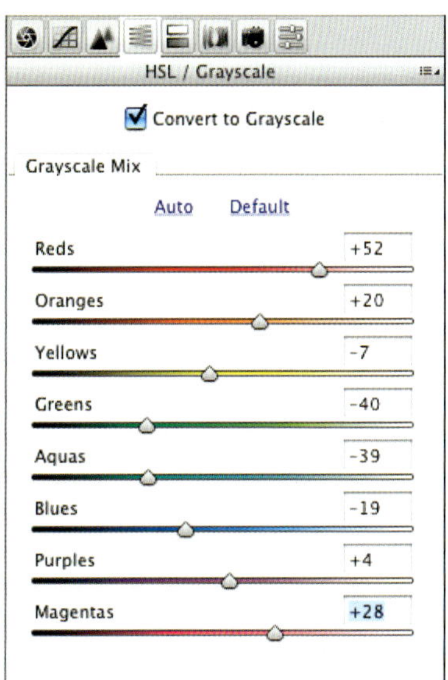

"Burning" and "Dodging" Black and White

As in color images, I will burn and dodge a black-and-white image using the RAW process. I can make standard lightening and darkening moves in processing the files and simply bring them in as layers, but I have a lot of other options available, too.

I could process files out using a color balance that amplifies detail in areas. In Camera RAW, I could use the Saturation slider to simply de-saturate the file, converting it to grayscale. I could, after making that move, go into the Calibrate tab and adjust the Hue and Saturation of each of the three channels to separate out detail and tones in specific areas. This is a rabbit hole of trial and error, but you may find a combination of settings here that gives you detail and separation in an area you've been unable to work with before. My experience is that if you make dramatic adjustments here, the file quality goes downhill fast. I suggest you use this only for specific problem areas and not for a general Grayscale conversion, but I've had students go off the deep end with this method and make absolutely beautiful prints.

Every RAW processor has different saturation and channel controls, and CS3 has some truly profound improvements in the Black and White conversion part of the RAW process. You can also try incorporating any of the other methods of Grayscale conversion out there, if you're of that persuasion. One very powerful method, developed by Nick Wheeler, is separating out each channel (channels are nothing but grayscale images, after all) and copying them as layers into your image. With this method however, adjusting the opacity of the layer controls the amount that layer is contributing to the conversion. This gives you a many interesting options.

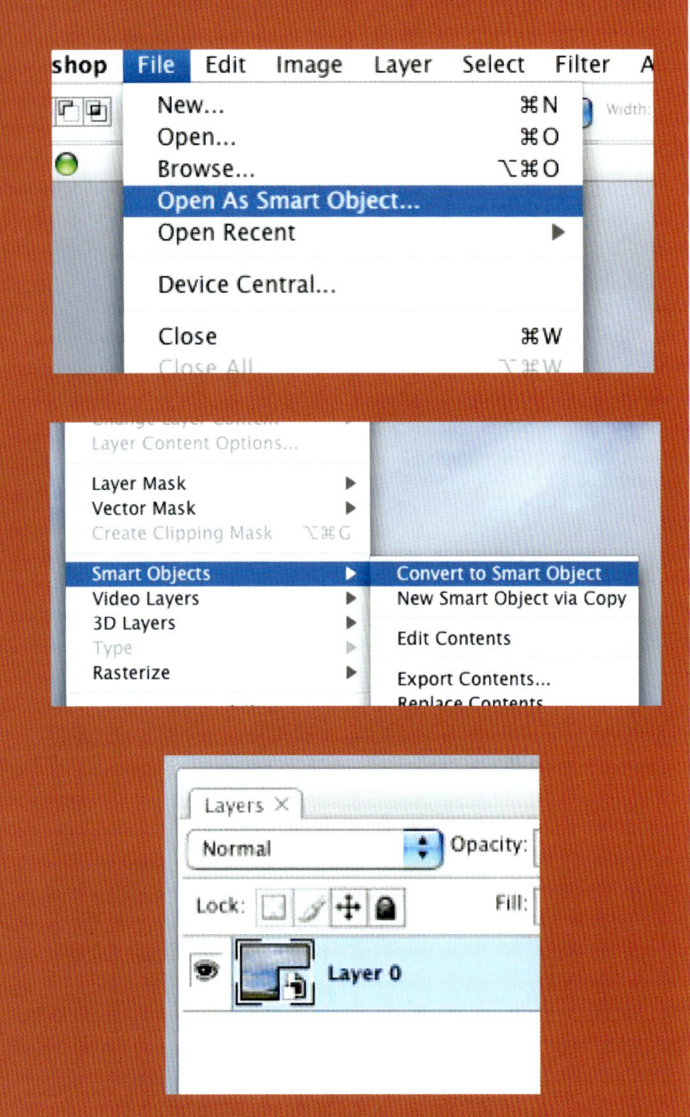

Explore and experiment, research, be aware of the methods available, and try to understand the differences in their results, but always keep in mind the strategy of returning to the RAW file for more data. Remember, the main goal is to standardize your method.

Advanced Methods: Smart Objects

Adobe developed a way for you to imbed, for example, an Illustrator file into a Photoshop file as a layer, yet keep the ability to re-open the file in Illustrator. This was introduced in CS2, and called the "Smart Object." This was the idea: working in Photoshop you can "Place" an Illustrator file in as a layer, and you get a layer with a funny little icon. If you double-click the icon, you get right back to Illustrator and the file, and can edit it as it was originally, a vector-based graphic file.

RAW files, I suspect almost by coincidence, can also be handled as Smart Objects. This is huge (and, curiously little-known in the photography industry). The processes I've set out in the preceding chapters show a repetitive sequence: adjust, replace with RAW, adjust, replace with RAW. The RAW file imbedded as a Smart Object allows me to simply re-open and re-process the RAW file. With the release of CS3, there is a much smoother incorporation of the Smart Object into the workflow, as well as the addition of "Smart Filters"—filters that can be re-adjusted after they're applied.

Let's take a look at the basic Smart Object. I can open the RAW file as a Smart Object directly with File>Open as Smart Object. I can also open a RAW file normally, and then convert it to a Smart Object using Layer>Smart Objects>Convert to Smart Object. Either way, I get a layer with a funny little icon. Double-click that icon, the Camera RAW dialog kicks right back up.

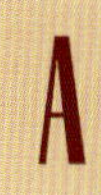

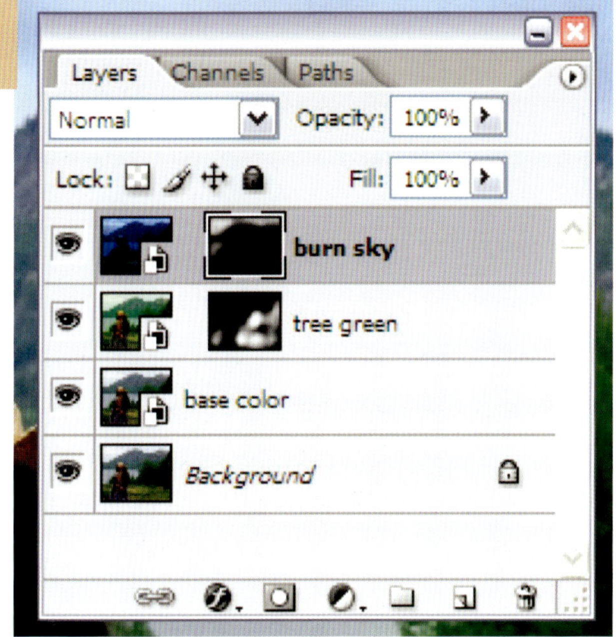

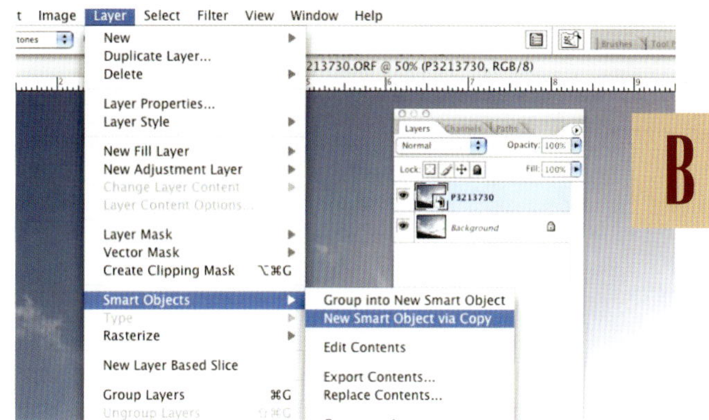

The Smart Object icon, shown in example (A), makes it much easier to access the RAW image file to make your additive adjustments. You can be in Adobe Camera RAW, and then back to Photoshop, in a snap.

The old, CS2 way—which still works—is to use Bridge and select an image. First, open it up into Photoshop, go back to Bridge, select it again, and go to File>Place>In Photoshop. This will take you through the Camera RAW dialog and put that funky little icon in your layer again.

You can do anything to the Smart Object Layer that you can do to a conventional Image Layer, but additionally you can re-open the Camera RAW dialog with a simple click of the icon.

This means I can treat the RAW image layer with the same flexibility and control as I would an Adjustment Layer. If, after making work prints, I want to do fine adjustments and tweaks of specific areas, I can simply reprocess the RAW and change whatever I want. The framework is the same: open the file, save it as a TIFF, "Place" the RAW file, Mask, Adjust, Print, and reprocess the RAW files (as Smart Objects) as needed.

What follows is an example of using the Smart Object workflow. It's incredibly simple and clean, and you waste very little time trying to match the adjustments you've done with Levels and Curves to the controls in Camera RAW, since you're just working in Camera RAW. Because you don't have a pile of inactive Adjustment Layers, there are fewer layers to confuse you.

The Smart Object Workflow

Once we understand the process and workflow of Adjustment Layers, Image Layers, and Masking, utilizing Smart Objects is a walk in the park. Instead of bringing in Adjustment Layers, I simply "Place" an Image Layer as a Smart Object (A). I open the file, save it as a TIFF, go back to the Bridge, Place the file as a layer in the TIFF, then Layer>Smart Objects>New Smart Objects via Copy to build in a few working layers (B) (I usually start with three).

I do my basic global adjustments as usual, on the first layers, and then work up to burning, dodging, and specific color correction using a masked Smart Object Layer. When I want to tweak the layer, I double-click on the Smart Object icon on the layer and it opens up the Camera RAW dialog again and I make my changes. Easy!

The same strategies apply to the end of the process, like spotting and sharpening on a "Merge Visible" layer, and final sizing. This just allows me to go back to my RAW file much more easily.

This is the logical progression of the process. Adjustment Layers, reprocessing the RAW controls in Camera RAW, understanding Layers, masking, and editing your mask are all essential groundwork to working effectively with Smart Objects. Once this is mastered, you have a truly elegant workflow.

Notes of Caution

NOTE: You cannot simply copy the Smart Object Layer using normal layer copying methods. When you do that, each change you make to

Note of Caution: The Rosenholtz-Sanchez Effect

A very interesting thing can happen when you make new Smart object layers this way, which was pointed out to me by students who work in multiple Layers, with several overlapping Masks. The students shall, due to ego-containment factors, only be known as "Rosenholtz and Sanchez."

When areas of several layers, duplicated from the layer below them, overlap, Sanchez pointed out that you get a compounded edit. Of course, this is impossible. How could a full, opaque Smart Object image layer possibly compound the edits below it—complete drivel! Well, the truth is it does, and here's why.

When you work on a Smart Object and apply edits to that Object—including filters—it essentially creates a complete package in that Object. When you use that Smart Object to make another with Create New Smart Object via Copy, it creates a new Smart Object, and everything from the source layer is incorporated into the new Smart Object, including Filters and anything else you've done to it. It's takes all the changes you made, contains them, and then sets them up again creating a compounded edit. That's fine, if you work like I do, where almost none of your edited layers overlap. For Rosenholtz and Sanchez, it's a problem. One solution is to simply create new Smart Object Layers from the bottom layer, your "core source" Smart Object.

Be very careful about which Smart Object layer you use as a source, and be very aware of where and when your layer masks overlap. If you're getting effects that seem to be amplified, what you may be seeing is the Rosenholtz-Sanchez Effect.

one Smart Object applies itself to the duplicated layer. (It's Smart, remember?) You have to go back to the Bridge and bring it in fresh, as a new Object, or perhaps the best way is Layer>Smart Objects> New Smart Object Via Copy (see figure B on page 211), so that it behaves independently.

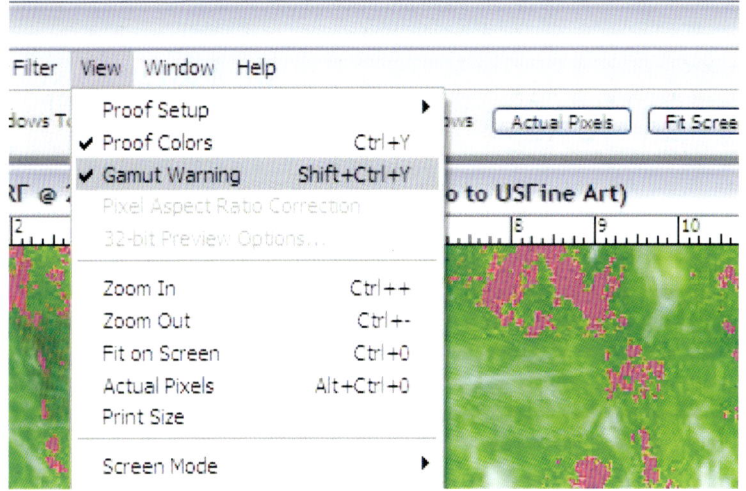

NOTE: The Smart Object layer gets centered on the window you have open. If you have the window zoomed in on something that is off-center the Object will be out of registration. Zoom out to full view to make sure the new layer is registered correctly.

NOTE: If you've selected something other than the image on the target layer, such as a mask, Photoshop will give an error message. (The error is kind of confusing, something about not being able to make an import this object.) Make sure, in your target file, you've clicked the image icon, or the layer itself on the layer to which you're building the Smart Object, and all should be well.

NOTE: Your file is going to get enormous. It's the price you pay!

ProPhoto and the Smart Object Workflow

Here's where it gets really interesting. Think back to how the camera is capable of capturing colors contained in the ProPhoto working space. A good way to work with these colors, instead of in a Hue/Saturation Adjustment Layer as described before, is using Smart Objects.

Here's an example:

In Bridge, open your file. When Camera RAW opens, make sure your Color Space is set to ProPhoto RGB and click OK.

Back in Bridge, with the file selected, go to File>Place>In Photoshop. Once you click, you'll get the RAW dialog—here is where you should make your adjustments. I'm going to saturate the greens here. (It's what I want the file to look like, but I know it's going to cause trouble.) Click "Open." You'll see the "Preparing Placed Document" message, and then you'll see the image with a diagonal "X." A double-click sets the new Smart Object.

Now set up your Proof Colors. View>Proof Setup>Custom takes you to this dialog. Set the "Device to Simulate" box to your printer/paper profile, and hit OK.

Go to View>Gamut Warning, and you get a lovely overlay—in this case hot pink—of the colors that are in the file but lost to the printer. Adjust the colors by going back to the Layer with the Smart Object and double-clicking the Smart Object icon. This re-opens the Camera RAW dialog and allows you to readjust the colors to play within the gamut of your particular printer and paper. You can do this globally, or make a duplicate Smart Object Layer so that you can mask it and burn in the offending colors. (Layer>Smart Objects>New Smart Object via Copy). No matter how many times Adobe releases CS, the basic framework will probably remain the same. Because of its simplicity and structure, the RAW process and Layer/Masking workflow adapts to whatever we throw at it.

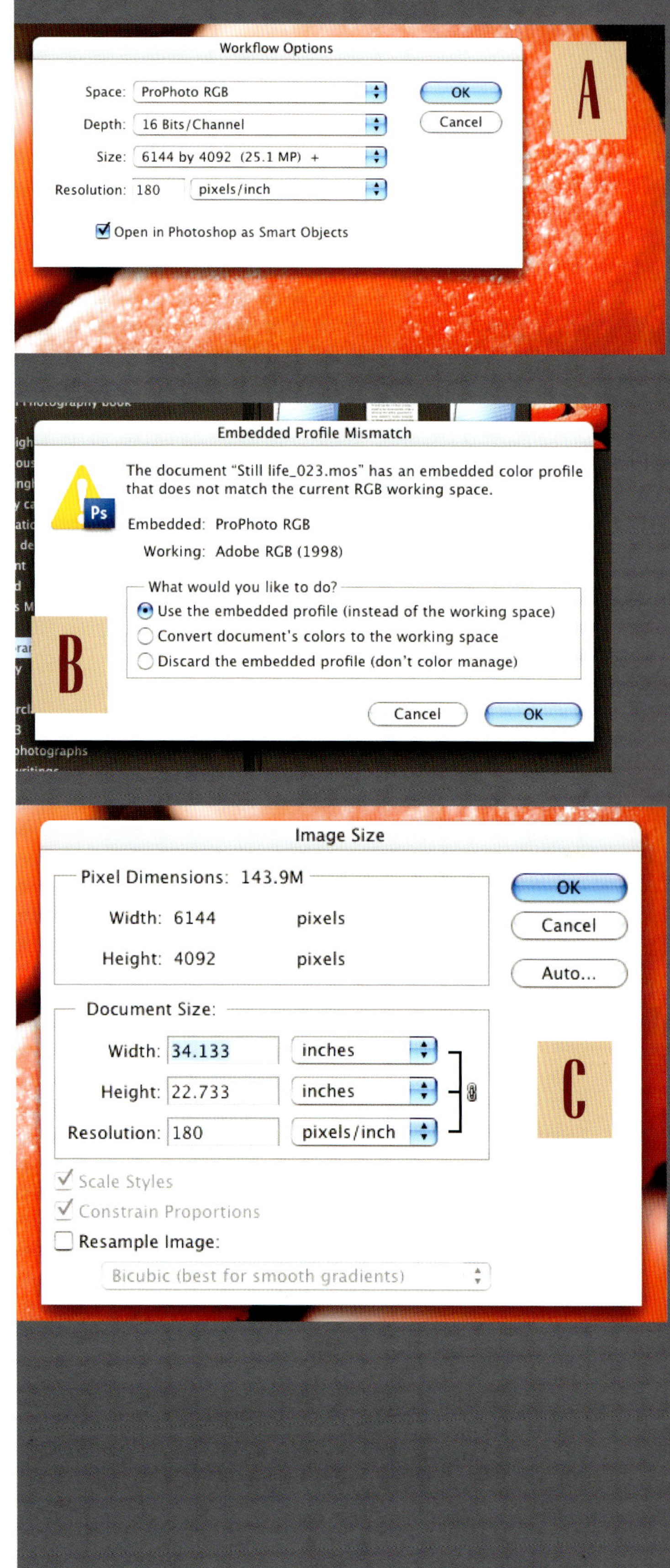

Smart Objects, Smart Filters, and the ProPhoto Workflow

There's a lot here to distill into a coherent method. I'm showing this as an example of how I generally work, but it's intended as just a pointer. The tools and methods go together in any number of ways—an unbelievably powerful workflow. Use this as just a starting point and build on it to fit your vision and images.

I'm picking an image that is going to challenge me on all levels. The color is tough to handle for both the camera and printer. I want to make a big print, and the texture of the subject is

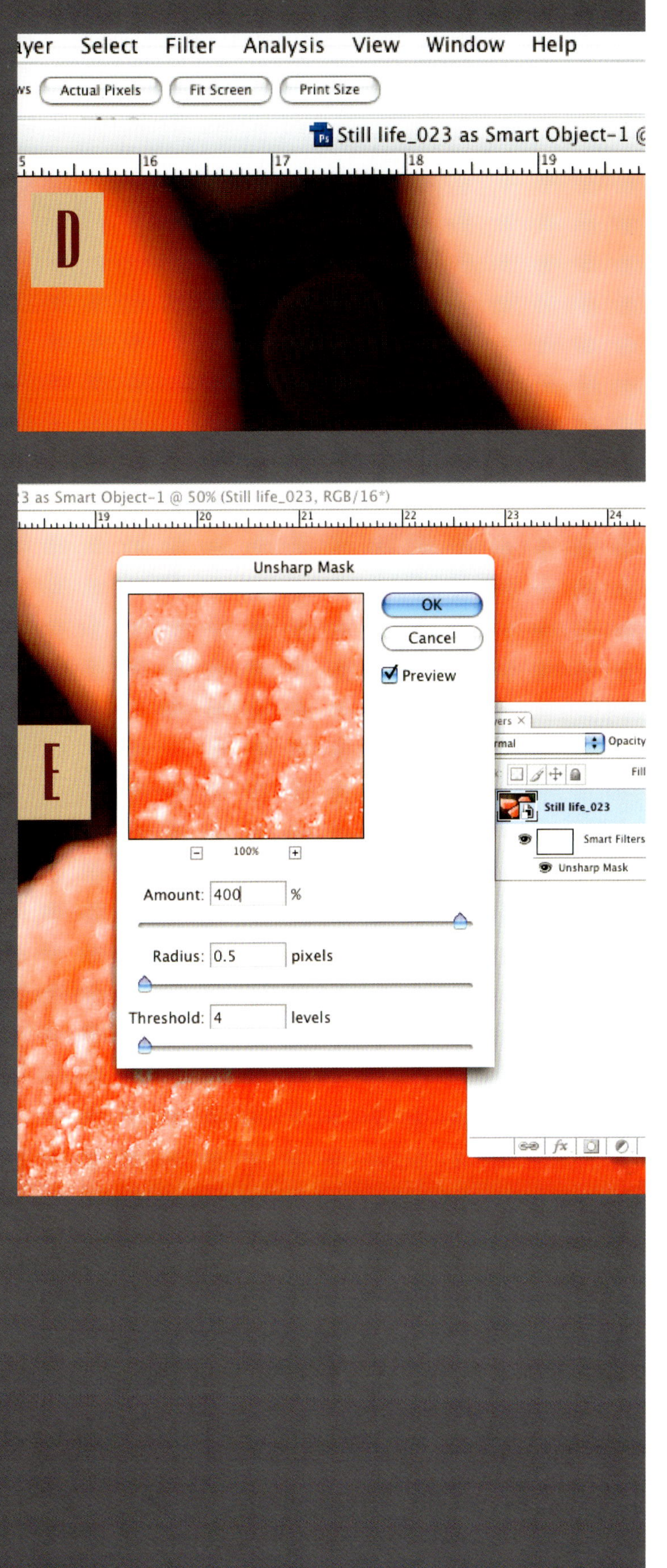

going to need some special work in applying Unsharp Mask.

I'm going to handle this using Smart Objects, ProPhoto RGB, and Smart Filters to work selectively on the areas I need to control from the RAW file.

Step One: ProPhoto

In Camera RAW, set the Color Space to ProPhoto RGB, the bit depth to 16 bit, size up, and select Open in Photoshop as Smart Object (A).

This will give you this message (B); choose "Use the embedded profile."

Working in ProPhoto RGB gives me the opportunity to maintain and control all the colors the sensor recorded. Instead of allowing the system to remap the colors (the "Convert" or "Discard" options), I will view the colors that are a problem and map them as I want them mapped.

Step Two: Sharpening with an Unsharp Mask Smart Filter

First I check the image size (C) and make sure I'm viewing it at "Print Size" (D). Then, by selecting Filters>Sharpen>Unsharp Mask (E), I can create an editable "Smart Filter."

Building a Smart Filter on this layer establishes the filter settings for all the subsequent layers.

I try to get it as close as possible, based on the size for which I'm aiming (I can always go back and change it).

Because the file is huge and will print at over 30 inches, I'm applying a very high Amount (400) but keeping the Radius at 0.5 (E).

Step Three: Gamut Warning and Hue/Saturation

Here I check the ProPhoto gamut against the paper gamut. I set the Proof Setup to the paper I'm using (F), and turn Gamut Warning on (G)

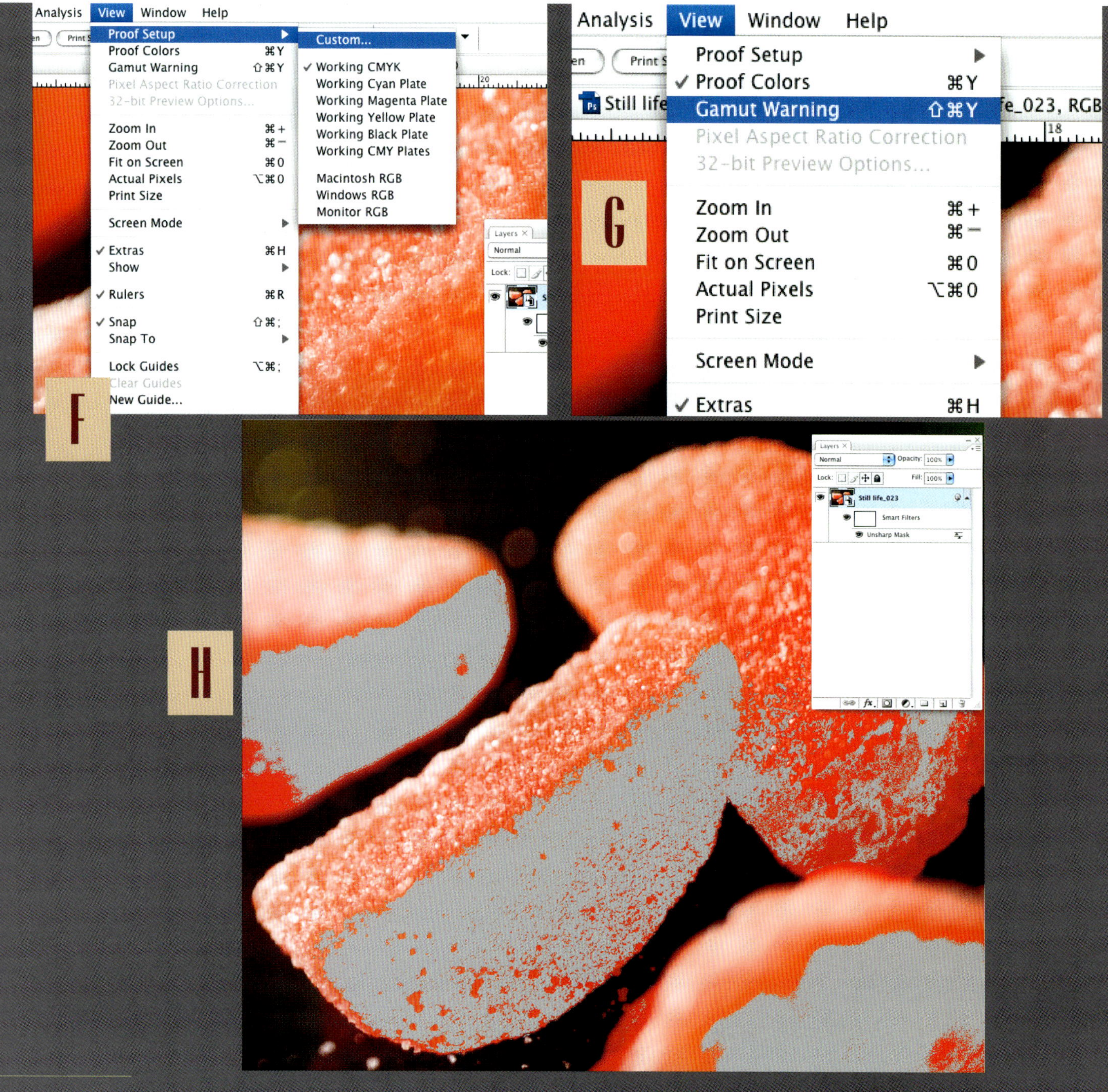

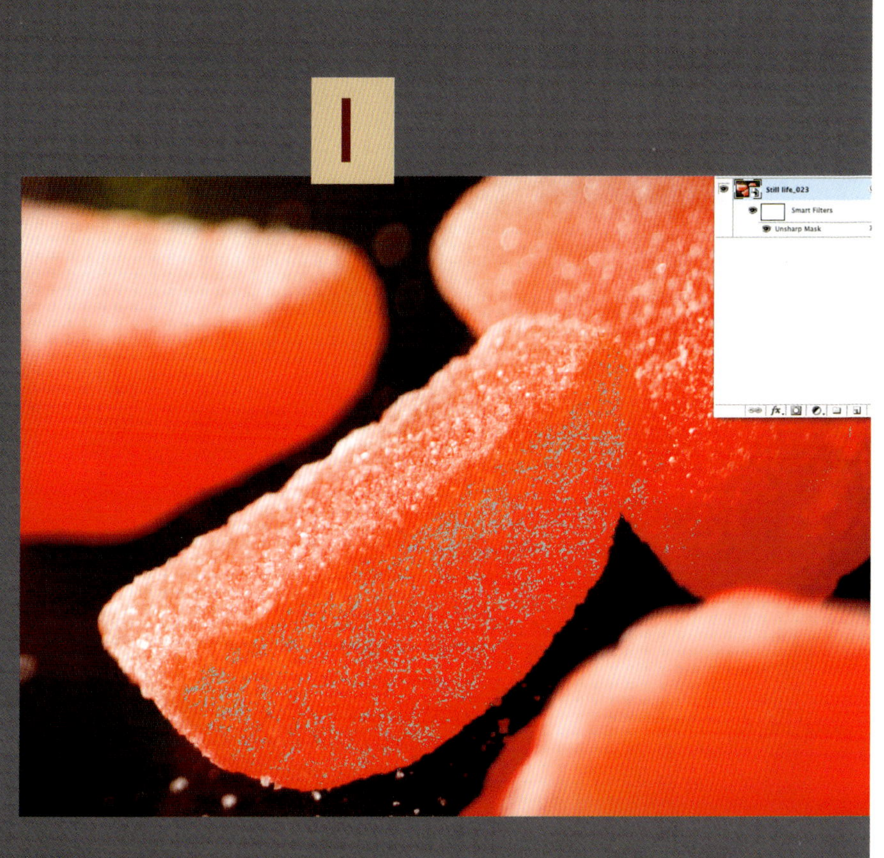

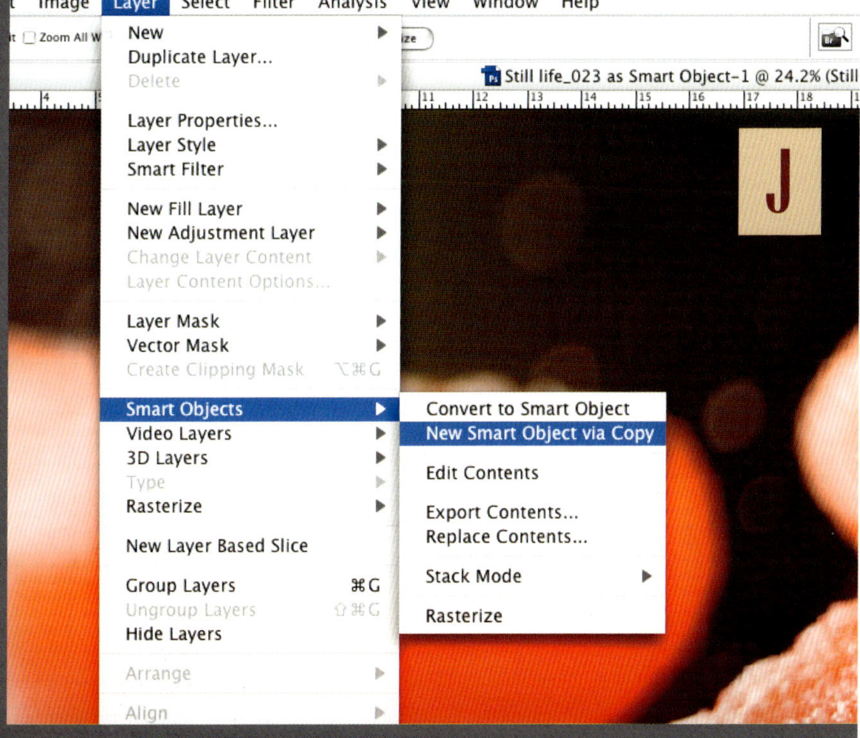

to view the out-of-gamut colors (H). I then go back to the RAW, adjust the hue and saturation, and track those changes with the Gamut Warning (I).

This step allows me to see which colors are held in the ProPhoto RGB color space, but will not be visible with the printer and paper I'm using. I can, by using Gamut Warning, go back and forth between Camera RAW and the Gamut Warning and make the adjustments I feel will best reproduce the image as I want it.

Step Four: Burning, Dodging, and Spot Color Correction

We've used the Smart Object to adjust colors and density globally—now we need to do the burning and dodging, selective brightening and darkening of problem areas, and color correction of specific places in the image.

I go to Layer>Smart Objects>New>New Smart Object via Copy (J). This builds a new, independent Smart Object layer, complete with any Smart Filters created in the earlier steps.

In this case I'm trying to change the shadow areas to make them a little

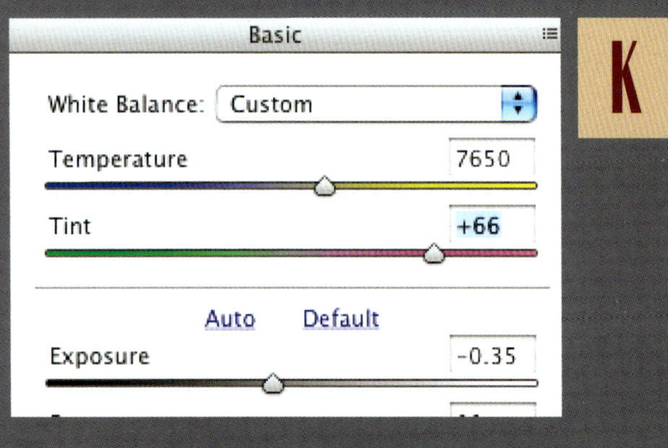

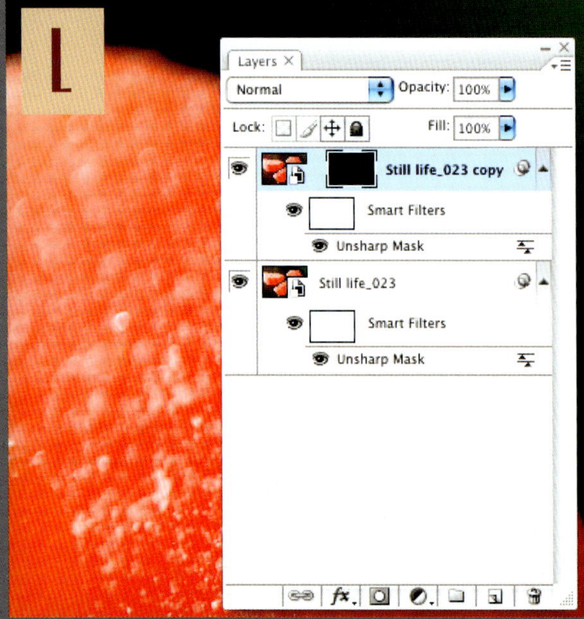

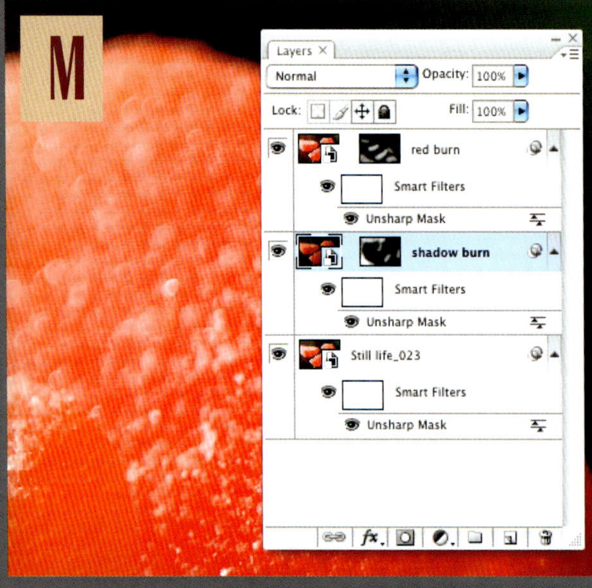

redder, less yellow. This is a spot color correction, but is the same process as burning or dodging. I make the color correction in Camera RAW (K), create a mask for the spot color corrections (L), and bring in the spot adjustments from the RAW (M).

Burning, dodging, and spot color correction in this manner actually adds data. I selectively build in more color, like a painter adding paint to a canvas. Instead of "living with" the information that you happened to bring into the shadows, midtones, or highlights and massaging it, I add exactly what I need to render the image.

Step Five: Spot Sharpening

Using the Unsharp Mask Smart Filter and applying a mask to that, (don't get confused by all those "masks" now...) I can select just the sugar on the candy and hit it hard with the sharpening effect, while leaving the rest of the image alone (N). (Layer>Smart Objects>New>New Smart Object via Copy.)

I adjust the USM (Unsharp Mask) Filter and make the selection with the mask.

There are a few things I want to check again. I want to re-check the gamut (turn on Gamut Warning again) to make sure I can print the colors I have. This also shows all the layers I have (O). The file size is huge—over 600MB—so now I'm going to drop it down to 8 bit (since I have my colors under control), to cut the files size in half (Image>Mode>8 bits per channel).

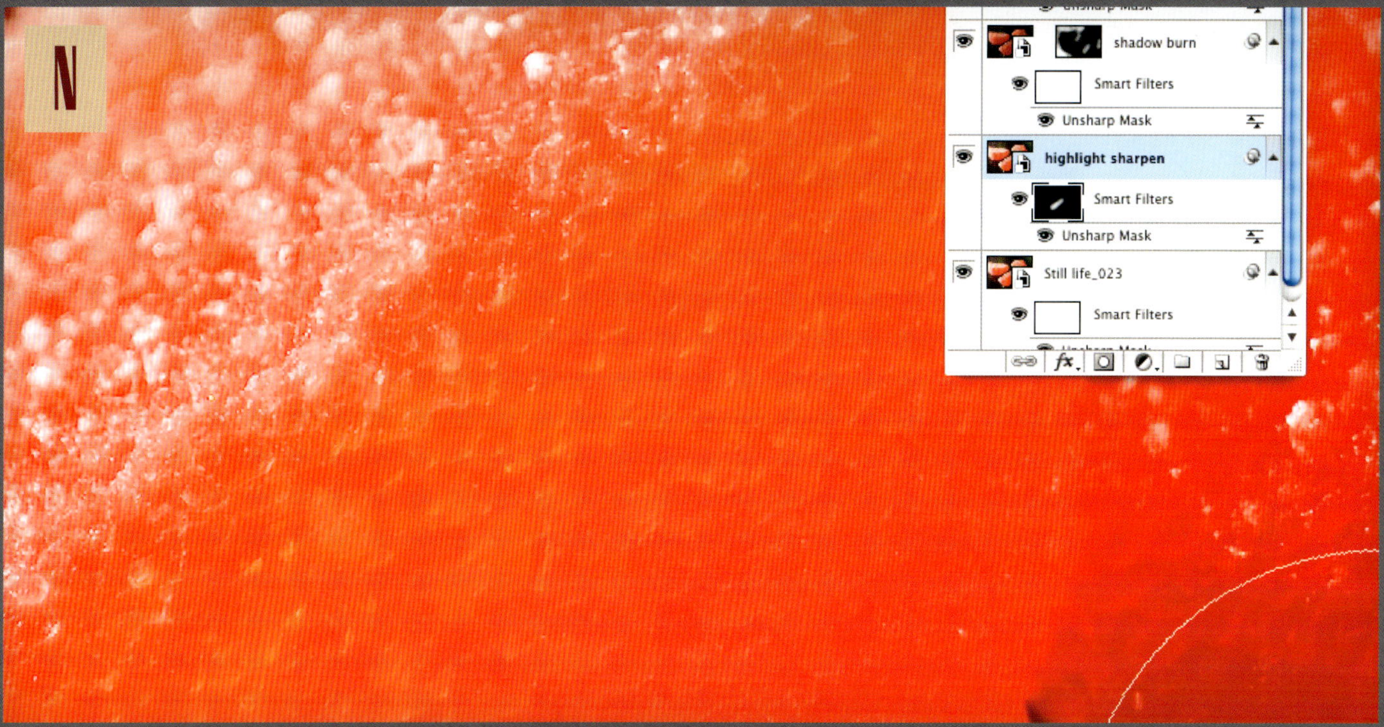

N
shadow burn
Smart Filters
Unsharp Mask
highlight sharpen
Smart Filters
Unsharp Mask
Still life_023
Smart Filters

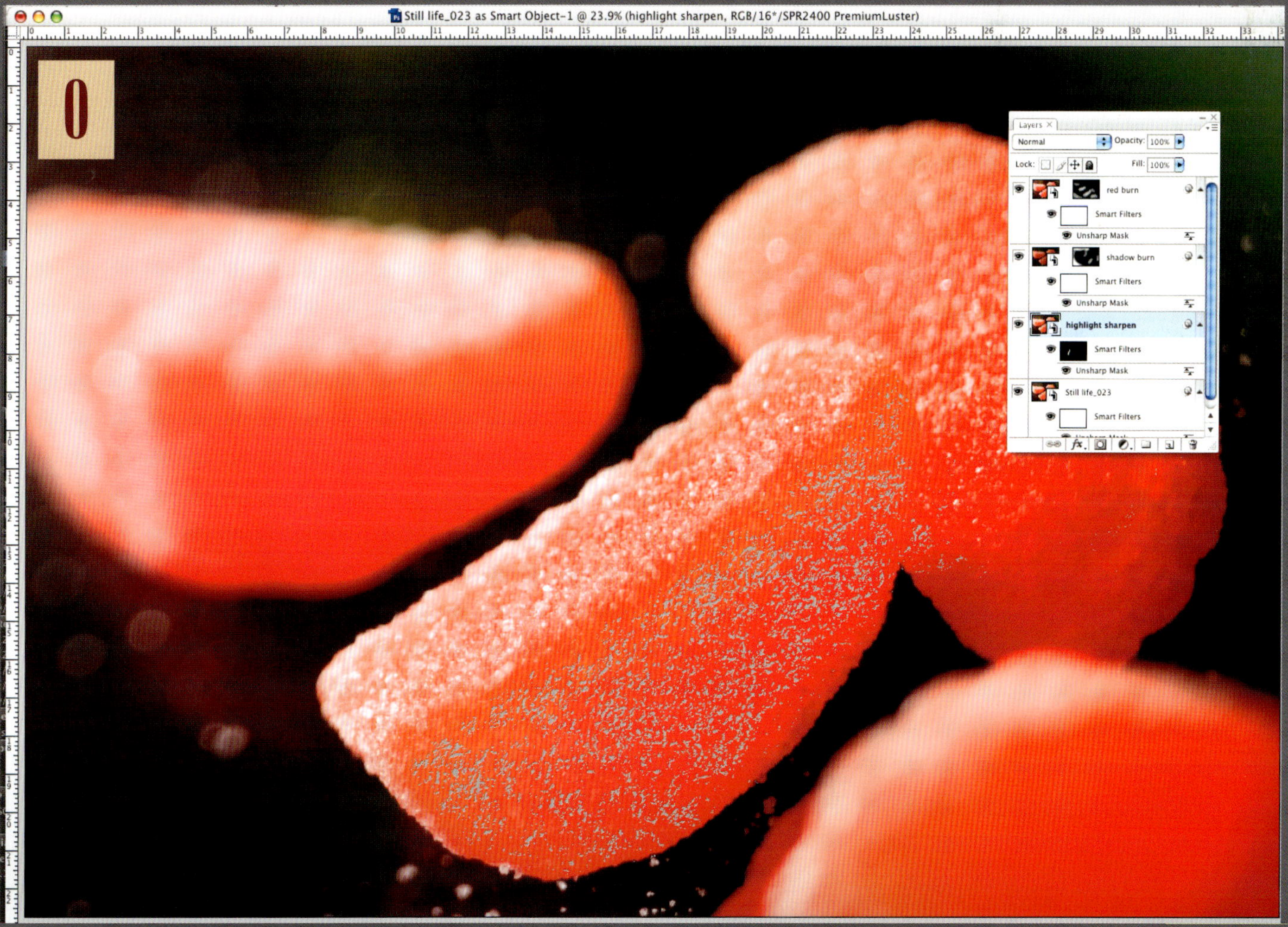

Still life_023 as Smart Object-1 @ 23.9% (highlight sharpen, RGB/16*/SPR2400 PremiumLuster)
O
Layers
Normal
Opacity: 100%
Lock:
Fill: 100%
red burn
Smart Filters
Unsharp Mask
shadow burn
Smart Filters
Unsharp Mask
highlight sharpen
Smart Filters
Unsharp Mask
Still life_023
Smart Filters

The Evolving Photographic Process

The process I describe here is built on one simple fact: the RAW file is the essential source of the image information, yet it can be endlessly reinterpreted.

Digital photography, with RAW files, Photoshop, and desktop printing has done more than simply replace the darkroom. It has produced an entirely new way to create photographs, from handling the capture to processing and controlling the final print. I am no longer concerned with evaluating my contrast range in the context of my print to dictate my original exposure. I am no longer concerned with making sure I have, on one negative, the contrast range I need and in the right places. The RAW file allows me to reprocess that "latent image," the bare, unfiltered light that comes through the lens onto the sensor. Now I look to make sure my exposure captures the tonal areas I need and that the images I capture give me the building blocks I require to fulfill my vision of the final print. It is a different way of working—a different way of seeing.

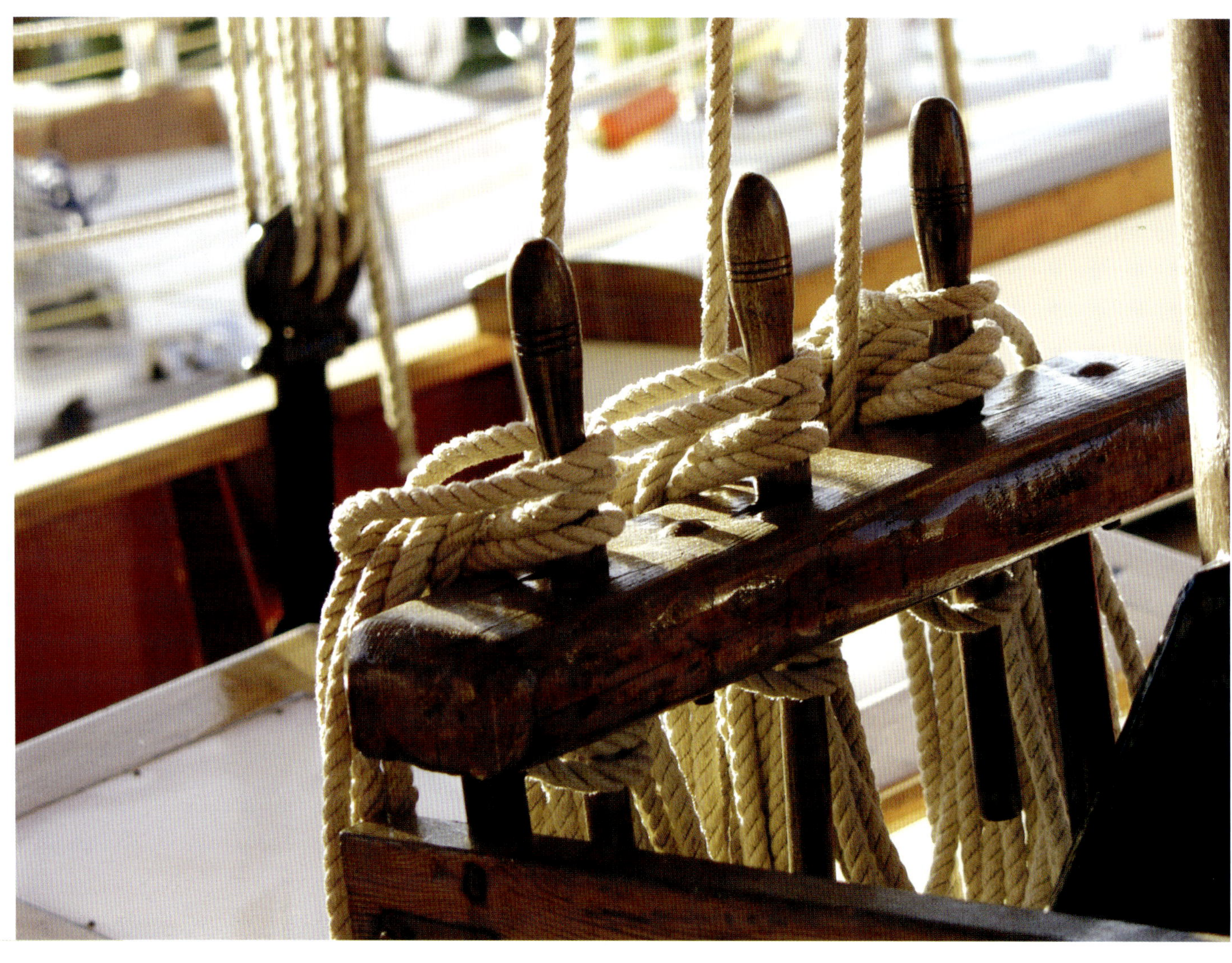

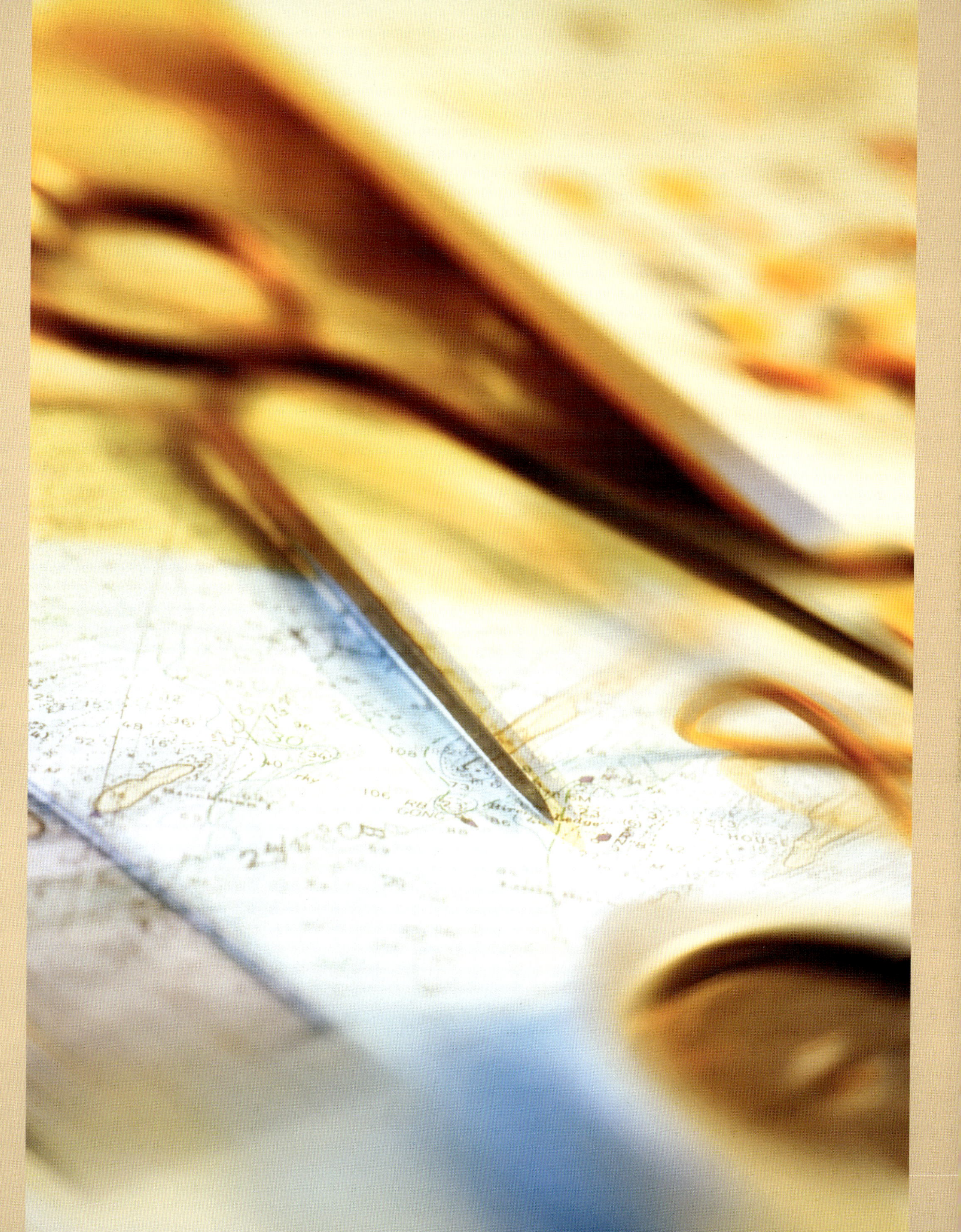

Index